Patents in Germany and Europe

Patents in Germany and Europe

Procurement, Enforcement and Defense – An International Handbook

Second Edition

Alexander Harguth
Steven Carlson

Wolters Kluwer

Published by:
Kluwer Law International B.V.
PO Box 316
2400 AH Alphen aan den Rijn
The Netherlands
Website: www.wolterskluwerlr.com

Sold and distributed in North, Central and South America by:
Wolters Kluwer Legal & Regulatory U.S.
7201 McKinney Circle
Frederick, MD 21704
United States of America
Email: customer.service@wolterskluwer.com

Sold and distributed in all other countries:
Quadrant
Rockwood House
Haywards Heath
West Sussex
RH16 3DH
United Kingdom
Email: international-customerservice@wolterkluwer.com

ISBN 978-90-411-5986-1

e-Book: ISBN 978-90-411-5994-6
web-PDF: ISBN 978-90-411-8955-4

About the Authors

Dr. Alexander Harguth is a German patent litigator. His understanding of the German system arises from 20 years litigating patent infringement actions in Germany's district and appellate courts, along with related parallel nullity and opposition proceedings, as well as German border enforcement proceedings. Mr. Harguth's experiences provide a historical depth, as well as extensive lessons for coordinating parallel U.S. litigation.

His co-author is **Steven C. Carlson**, a former clerk to the Honorable Paul R. Michel of the U.S. Court of Appeals for the Federal Circuit, and to the Honorable Roderick R. McKelvie of the U.S. District Court for the District of Delaware. Mr. Carlson litigates patents in courts throughout the U.S. through the Silicon Valley office of Kasowitz, Benson, Torres & Friedman LLP. Together, they have endeavored to present the German patent system in an understandable, practical format for counsel in the U.S. and around the world.

Table of Contents

Preface

This handbook aims to provide lawyers in the U.S. and elsewhere in the world with a practical understanding of Germany's patent system. This second edition addresses the many legal changes that have occurred since the original publication of the handbook in 2011.

This handbook is motivated by a simple reason—patent litigation is global. Many cases will inherently spread into cross-border litigation. Other disputes, which are initially confined to the U.S., could be strategically resolved by resort to the swifter, less expensive proceedings through German courts and soon through the German divisions of the Unified Patent Court. Understanding the opportunities available in Germany provides companies with a broader toolkit for enforcing their intellectual property, and defending against challenges brought by others.

Germany itself is one of the most important markets in the world. Winning a patent suit in Germany effectively provides dominance over the entire European market, and consequently gives the patent owner important leverage worldwide. Suits in Germany frequently resolve well ahead of U.S. counterpart suits, at a fraction of the cost. And because injunctive relief is generally available following a successful lawsuit, Germany offers relief that often cannot be obtained in the U.S. These factors, combined with the unique procedural structure of Germany's patent system, have made it the top jurisdiction for patent litigation in Europe, and one of the most important forums worldwide.

The present edition addresses the upcoming changes in connection with the Unitary Patent and the Unified Patent Court which will be operational in December 2017, notwithstanding Brexit. The start of the "sunrise" period for the possibility to "opt out" ordinary European patents from the Unified Patent Court is planned for early September 2017. It provides a minimum period of three months for patentees who wish to opt out their ordinary European Patents to do so before the Unified Patent Court becomes operational. The new system represents a new enforcement tool which will co-exist with the German system.

This handbook is intended to put the systems available in Germany into context for a non-German audience, and particularly for American lawyers. Proceedings in Germany are presented in relation to the U.S. system—patentability, discovery, pleadings, claim construction, trial, etc. are described in counterpart to patent litigation in the U.S. The structure provides the practitioner an informed framework for the various phases of patent procurement, enforcement and defense in Germany.

To provide this bridge between the German and U.S. systems, the authors offer their perspectives as native practitioners in their respective jurisdictions. Dr. Alexander Harguth is a German patent litigator. His understanding of the German system arises from 20 years litigating patent infringement actions in Germany's district and appellate courts, along with related parallel nullity and opposition proceedings, as well as German border enforcement proceedings. Mr. Harguth's experiences provide a historical depth, as well as extensive lessons for coordinating parallel U.S. litigation.

His co-author is Steven C. Carlson, a former clerk to the Honorable Paul R. Michel of the U.S. Court of Appeals for the Federal Circuit, and to the Honorable Roderick R. McKelvie of the U.S. District Court for the District of Delaware. Mr. Carlson litigates patents in courts throughout the U.S. through the Silicon Valley office of Kasowitz, Benson, Torres & Friedman LLP. Together, they have endeavored to present the German patent system in an understandable, practical format for counsel in the U.S. and around the world.

List of Abbreviations

ArbEG	Arbeitnehmererfindergesetz (Act on Employees' Inventions)
BeckRS	Law Journal "Beck Rechtsprechung"
BGBl	Bundesgesetzblatt (Federal Law Gazette)
BGHZ	Entscheidungen des Bundesgerichtshofs in Zivilsachen (Compilation of decisions of the Federal Supreme Court in civil matters)
BlPMZ	Blatt für Patent-, Muster- und Zeichenwesen (Gazette for intellectual property matters published by the GPTO)
BT-Drucksache	Bundestags-Drucksache (Gazette of the Federal Parliament)
CD	Community Design
EC	European Commission
ECJ	European Court of Justice
EESR	Extended European Search Report
EPC	European Patent Convention
EPO	European Patent Office
EPO-G	Decision of the EPO's Enlarged Board of Appeal
EPO-J	Decision of the EPO's Legal Board of Appeal.
EPO-T	Decision of the EPO's Technical Board of Appeal
EU	European Union
FPC	(German) Federal Patent Court
GRUR	Gewerblicher Rechtsschutz und Urheberrecht (German professional journal for intellectual property matters)
GebrMG	Gebrauchsmustergesetz (Utility Model Act)
GPTO	German Patent and Trademark Office
IIC	International Review of Intellectual Property and Competition Law published by the Max Planck Institute for Intellectual Property and Competition Law

IntPatÜG	Gesetz über internationale Patentübereinkommen (Act on International Patent Conventions)
InstGE	Entscheidungen der Instanzgerichte zum Recht des geistigen Eigentums (Compilation of decisions of Instance Courts in intellectual property matters)
ISA	International Searching Authority
ITC	International Trade Commission
Mitt	Mitteilungen der deutschen Patentanwälte (German professional journal for intellectual property matters)
NJW	Neue Juristische Wochenschrift (German professional journal for legal matters)
OJ	Official Journal of the European Patent Office
PatG	Patentgesetz (Patent Act)
PCT	Patent Cooperation Treaty
RCD	Registered Community Design
SPC	Supplementary Protection Certificate.
TRIPS	Agreement on Trade-Related Aspects of Intellectual Property Rights
UPC	Unified Patent Court
UPCA	Unified Patent Court Agreement
UP	Unitary Patent
USPTO	U.S. Patent and Trademark Office
TRIPS	Agreement on Trade-Related Aspects of Intellectual Property Rights
WIPO	World Intellectual Property Organization
WO-ISA	Written Opinion of the International Search Authority
ZPO	Zivilprozessordnung (Code of Civil Procedure)
ZGR	Zentralstelle Gewerblicher Rechtsschutz (centralized customs authority in Germany)

CHAPTER 1

Why Germany?

1. INTRODUCTION

In Europe, patent enforcement poses immediate strategic choices. Many different countries may be selected for an enforcement venue, or parallel enforcement actions may be brought in different European countries simultaneously. Typically, however, a single jurisdiction is selected in hopes of obtaining a favorable European-wide, or even worldwide, settlement. In recent years, that jurisdiction of choice has been Germany. There are multiple reasons for litigants, both patentees and potential defendants, to choose Germany as their jurisdiction of choice: the German "split system," the expertise and reputation of German infringement courts; the speed and low costs of proceedings in Germany; and the customs gatekeepers standing at the border to Europe's largest market.

2. UPCOMING CHANGES

Despite the Brexit vote in June 2016, the U.K. surprisingly announced at the end of November 2016 that it intends to ratify the Unified Patent Court Agreement (UPCA).[1] The U.K. will thus continue with the preparations to ratify the UPCA over the coming months. It is expected that the Unified Patent Court (UPC) will go into operation at the beginning of 2018. The German system will then be embedded in a new context. The new court system will be operational alongside the German system. It will provide additional tools to enforce and invalidate patents.

A major contrast with the current situation, which is mainly characterized by a country-by-country enforcement, is that the UPC will have authority to grant

1. Press release "UK signals green light to Unified Patent Court Agreement" Intellectual Property Office and Baroness Neville-Rolfe DBE CMG, Nov. 28, 2016.

injunctions and damages through a dominant number of EU states.[2] The UPC will have exclusive jurisdiction to rule on infringement and revocation of unitary patents and ordinary European patents. Unitary patents, which are an element of the so-called Patent Package,[3] will necessarily fall under the exclusive jurisdiction of the UPC, whereas a special regime will apply to ordinary European patents. For these patents, the jurisdiction of the UPC will not be exclusive during a transitional period of seven years. Instead, the UPC jurisdiction will co-exist alongside the competence of national courts. During the transitional period, actions based on ordinary European patents can thus be filed with the either the UPC or national courts. To prevent having revocation actions filed with the UPC, patentees must pro-actively "opt-out" of the UPC's jurisdiction by means of a notification to the Register as stipulated in Article 83(3) UPC Agreement. Patent applicants should not miss the opportunity to consider an opt-out notification if they particularly seek to avoid having revocation proceedings filed by third parties at the UPC. The applicant may still withdraw its opt-out notification later if it later decides to submit to UPC jurisdiction.

Until the UPC system becomes operational, patentees will need to continue enforcing patents on a country-by-country basis. At present, many difficulties may arise if the patentee wishes to enforce a patent-protected technology in several countries at the same time. Simultaneous litigation in multiple forums may result in high costs, risk of diverging decisions and lack of legal certainty. Thus, patentees generally focus on a single jurisdiction at a time, as an inevitable consequence of these difficulties, taking into account existing differences in national patent law and in procedural law, as well as differences in speed and in the level of damages awarded. The patentee will thus select the most appropriate forum for the enforcement in Europe. Subsequently, if it becomes necessary, the patentee will extend the enforcement campaign to other jurisdictions, in particular if the enforcement measures at the first court were already successful to some degree, for instance, if a German court already rendered a favorable decision. An early win in one jurisdiction can place a prevailing party in a good position to negotiate a European-wide license agreement.

3. THE GERMAN "SPLIT SYSTEM"

A defining characteristic of the German patent enforcement system is the split between infringement and invalidity rulings. Infringement and invalidity ("nullity") claims are tried in different courts, on different schedules. This split system is often advantageous to the patentee. Infringement cases frequently track ahead of counterpart invalidity proceedings, thus presenting the opportunity to have infringement resolved before

2. In order to become effective, thirteen Member States (including France, Germany and the United Kingdom) must implement national laws that reflect the Agreement. The Patent Package will take effect four months after the threshold is reached, even if other States are still in the process of ratification. The system becomes operational with the completion of the ratification process in Germany and the UK.
3. The EU Patent Package (the Patent Package) consists of two related, but independent parts: a European Patent with Unitary Effect (the Unitary Patent or UP) and a Unified Patent Court (the UPC).

invalidity is tried. While the infringement court may suspend its proceedings to allow a corresponding nullity action to resolve validity first, frequently it does not. Indeed, in one extreme case, which illustrates the unique dynamics of Germany's split system, a party won its infringement trial, and obtained a preliminary injunction, after the Federal Patent Court had already ruled the patent was invalid.[4] The structure of Germany's court system is discussed in Chapter 3. Nullity actions are presented in Chapter 7, and patent infringement trials are discussed in Chapter 8.

4. EXPERTISE AND REPUTATION OF GERMAN PATENT INFRINGEMENT COURTS

Infringement actions are filed in district courts, with the courts in Mannheim, Munich and Düsseldorf accounting for more than 80% of Germany's infringement cases introduced in first instance. Due to the large number of cases handled each year by these courts, they have significant expertise in patent matters. This expertise is recognized in Europe and throughout the world. Among European national jurisdictions, Germany leads with around 1,400 cases handled by its patent infringement courts, followed by France with around 400 cases, the U.K. with around 100 cases and the Netherlands with less than 100 cases).[5]

5. SPEED AND COSTS OF PROCEEDINGS IN GERMANY

Another advantageous characteristic is the speed of German patent litigation proceedings. In most cases, an enforceable ruling can be expected in around twelve months, or, with the District Court of Mannheim, even in seven to eight months. However, the appointment of a court expert, or a stay pending validity challenges, can markedly lengthen the proceedings. These events are discussed in Chapter 8.

Figure 1.1. Cases among European National Jurisdictions

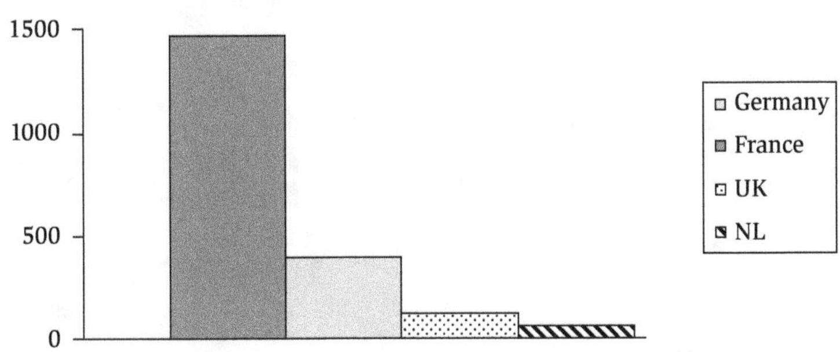

4. Appeal Court Düsseldorf, 2 W 47/07, GRUR-RR 2008, 329, Olanzapine.
5. JUVE Rechtsmarkt 04/10, 79.

German patent enforcement proceedings tend to be cost-efficient, usually ranging from Euro (EUR) 60,000 for less complex cases to EUR 240,000 for more complex cases. This is in part due to the fact that costly pre-trial discovery proceedings typical of American trials are not part of German proceedings. This is not to suggest that discovery is unavailable.[6] Chapter 11 will examine the process of evidence-taking proceedings in German courts.

Finally, there are no jury trials in patent infringement cases in Germany. Trying matters before a German judge necessarily limits time expenditure and counsel costs. The active role of the judge and the mechanics of the case are discussed in detail in Chapter 8.

6. CUSTOMS ACTIONS

Germany also allows enforcement of patents through customs proceedings, in a manner somewhat similar to the U.S. International Trade Commission. Customs proceedings are generally straightforward and cost-efficient, and tend to be particularly useful in anti-counterfeiting cases. Without having to prove infringement, the right holder can obtain a detention order, to have goods seized at the border, thus putting considerable pressure on the accused infringer. Subsequent court proceedings will decide if the goods should be released. Customs actions are discussed at length in Chapter 14.

6. September 2009, Germany enacted a new section of its Patent Act, which provides that if the patentee can show a sufficient likelihood of infringement, it can request an inspection of the accused device or the production of certain documents. See Ch. 11, "Discovery and Evidence-Taking."

CHAPTER 2

Sources of Law

1. INTRODUCTION

Germany's patent system is based on a complex interplay between international treaties, the European Patent Convention (EPC), German national codes, and (notwithstanding the civil law foundation of German law) the case law of the German courts. This chapter provides a high-level overview of these different sources of law, and provides the reader with tips on how to perform research into these various bodies of law.

2. EUROPEAN LAWS

European Laws either result from treaties concluded between countries of Europe or they represent legislation of the European Union (EU).

The EU promulgates itself directives and regulations governing intellectual property. The main difference between these two types of legislation is that a directive is not self-executing and requires Member States of the EU to achieve a particular result, without dictating the way of legally achieving that result. Directives typically afford the Member States discretion as to the rules to be adopted, often just setting minimum standards, and requiring particular legislative measures to enact the provisions of the directive into national law. An important directive in the area of intellectual property is the Enforcement Directive of April 29, 2004 setting forth common minimum standards for procedures for enforcing intellectual property among the European Member States.[1] This includes procedures for the preservation of evidence, including the physical seizure of infringing goods, and, in appropriate cases, the materials and

1. Enforcement Directive 2004/48/EC of the European Parliament and of the Council of Apr. 29, 2004 on the enforcement of intellectual property rights (the text can be found on the website: http://eur-lex.europa.eu/).

tools used in the production and/or distribution of these goods and the documents relating thereto.[2] It also addresses damages, providing that Members shall ensure that infringers must pay the patentee "damages appropriate to the actual prejudice suffered by him or her as a result of the infringement."[3] The Enforcement Directive has been implemented in almost all Member States of the EU, each with somewhat different effect, depending on the unique procedural rules of each country. Germany implemented the Directive on July 7, 2008,[4] and the particular provisions of the enactment in Germany will be discussed in Chapter 11.

On the other hand, EU regulations are self-executing and accordingly do not require any implementing measures at the national level.

Chief among the European laws governing patents in Germany is the EPC, which is the treaty among European countries that established the European Patent Office (EPO) and provides a unified system for granting (and opposing) patents in Europe. In addition, there are border control laws derived from national and European law that provide mechanisms for seizing infringing goods through the customs authorities. These will be discussed in turn.

2.1. European Patent Convention

The EPC was originally signed in Munich on October 5, 1973, and has been in force in Germany since October 7, 1977. The EPC is periodically revised, and the current version is the 16th edition of the EPC, which was published in 2016, and which contains the revised texts of the Convention from November 29, 2000 (EPC 2000).

A primary focus of the EPC is to establish and regulate the procedures for the EPO, which provides a central authority for examining patent applications. Upon grant, patents issuing from the EPO are converted into national patents for European Member States, such as Germany. The EPC is available in English and easily accessible through the EPO website at www.epo.org. A selection of the most important provisions of the EPC can be found in Chapter 17, section 1 of this book.

European patents confer on their proprietors the same rights as would be conferred by a national patent granted in each contracting country. Such rights are conferred on the date of publication in the European Patent Bulletin.[5] For example, an applicant may obtain a patent through the EPO and designate Germany as a country for which a national stage patent shall issue. Enforcement of that patent proceeds through the German national court system, as discussed in subsequent chapters.

The EPC also provides substantive laws governing patents, which include standards for patent validity and scope of protection. Many of these standards have analogs in U.S. patent law—for example, the concept of "novelty" in U.S. law is roughly the same as in Europe (see Article 54 EPC), and the U.S. concept of "non-obviousness" roughly corresponds to the concept of "inventive step" (see Article

2. Enforcement Directive, Art. 7.
3. Enforcement Directive, Art. 13.
4. Federal Law Gazette (BGBl.) I 1191, BlPMZ 08, 274.
5. Article 64(1) EPC.

56 EPC). The EPC also provides standards for patentable subject matter, including requirements for protecting computer programs, medical treatments and diagnostic methods. These matters are discussed in more detail in the following chapters.[6] The EPC comprises the texts of the Convention, its Implementing Regulations[7] and protocols[8] and the rules relating to fees.

2.2. London Agreement

On October 17, 2000 a number of Contracting States to the EPC adopted the so-called London Agreement,[9] which came into force on May 1, 2008, following lengthy ratification and accession procedures in national parliaments. This agreement is aimed at reducing costs through a post-grant translation regime for European patents. The Contracting States are Albania, Croatia, Denmark, Finland, Latvia, Lithuania, the Netherlands, France, Liechtenstein, Sweden, Slovenia, Germany, Luxembourg, Switzerland, Iceland, Ireland, Republic of Macedonia, Monaco, Norway and the United Kingdom. The Agreement distinguishes between Contracting States having an official language in common with one of the official languages of the EPO (i.e., English, French or German) and States which do not have an official language in common with one of the official EPO languages. The first group, namely those States having a national language in common with one of the official languages of the EPO have dispensed entirely with translation requirements. These States are France, Germany, Liechtenstein, Luxembourg, Monaco, Switzerland and the United Kingdom. States of the other group apply a less severe translation regime than was previously required. For instance, the Netherlands, Sweden and Denmark require that the claims of the European patent be supplied in Dutch, Swedish and Danish, respectively. In addition, these States require that the European patent specification be available or supplied in English, provided that the patent was not already published in English. Other EPC States, such as Italy, Spain, Portugal, and Greece, have not ratified the London Agreement, and thus the normal translation regime is applicable and complete translations of the patent are still required.

2.3. EU Patent Package

The EU Patent Package refers to two sets of laws that would provide for the Unitary Patent and the Unified Patent Court. These laws, which had been on track to pose a

6. *See* Ch. 5.
7. Implementing Regulations to the Convention on the Grant of European Patents of Oct. 5, 1973 as adopted by decision of the Administrative Council of the European Patent Organization of Dec. 7, 2006 and as last amended by decision of the Administrative Council of the European Patent Organization of Oct. 28, 2009.
8. Protocol on the Interpretation of Art. 69 EPC; Protocol on Jurisdiction and the Recognition of Decisions in respect of the Right to the Grant of a European Patent; Protocol on Centralization; Protocol on Privileges and Immunities of the European Patent Organization; Protocol on Staff Complement.
9. The London Agreement can be consulted on the website of the EPO: www.epo.org.

major shift to the framework of patent law in Europe, have been put on hold in light of the U.K.'s vote to leave the European Union ("Brexit"). As of publication of this book, the EU Patent Package has not yet come to fruition. The latter is expected at the beginning of 2018.

The EU Patent Package is based on two pillars: one relates to the Unitary Patent, the other on the Unified Patent Court. The Unitary Patent would be grounded in two European regulations, which would have direct effect across the participating EU Member States, and would provide for the issuance of patents that could be enforced across all those Member States. Furthermore, the EU Patent Package provides for the formation of a Unified Patent Court, based on the Agreement on the Unified Patent Court ("the Agreement"). The Agreement would establish the UPC through statute and provide a procedure for setting procedural rules.

The Patent Package would exclude non-EU States from participating in it. Thus, certain EPC[10] countries, such as Switzerland,[11] would therefore not be covered by a Unified Patent. Also, the Unified Patent Court would have no jurisdiction in those States. In addition, a few EU Member States, such as Italy, Poland and Spain have presently chosen to opt out of the system to varying degrees.[12]

The Agreement - which is the second piece of the EU patent package—requires thirteen states, necessarily including France, Germany and the United Kingdom (U.K.), to ratify it (Article 89 UPCA). At present, already eleven States have ratified the Agreement. The U.K. and Germany are stilling missing. Germany has indicated its intention to ratify it and on November 28, 2016, the U.K. Government has confirmed that it will proceed to ratify the Unified Patent Court Agreement, in spite of Britain's Brexit vote, for which reason it is to be expected that the Unified Patent Court will take up its function in 2018.

2.3.1. Regulations Relating to the Unitary Patent

On December 17, 2012, two European regulations were adopted, establishing the Unitary Patent. Accordingly, European patents may have "unitary effect" across the participating EU Member States, rather than representing a bundle of national patents, as it is the case for ordinary European Patents. Neither regulation is in force yet as of the publication date of this book. The first regulation deals with the general framework of the Unitary Patent (the UP Regulation),[13] and the second relates to the translation arrangements (the Translation Regulation).[14] Two regulations were required because

10. European Patent Convention
11. Also: Albania, Iceland, Liechtenstein, Macedonia, Monaco, Norway, Serbia, San Marino, Turkey.
12. The partial absence of these EU members limits the territorial scope of the UP and UPC. The related effects will be illustrated in detail in the following chapters.
13. Regulation (EU) No. 1257/2012 of the European Parliament and of the Council of Dec. 17, 2012 implementing enhanced cooperation in the area of the creation of unitary patent protection.
14. Regulation (EU) No. 1260/2012 of the European Parliament and of the Council Dec. 17, 2012 implementing enhanced cooperation in the area of the creation of unitary patent protection with regard to the applicable translation arrangements.

higher voting thresholds are needed for changes to translation arrangements. Regulations have direct effect in all participating EU Member State and accordingly do not require any further national implementing measures to be taken by the States.

According to Article 1(2) of the UP Regulation, the Unitary Patent shall be equivalent to "Special Agreements" under Article 142(2) EPC. This provision can be found in Part IX of the EPC, entitled "Special Agreements." They were conceived in the 1970s in connection with the Community Patent Convention, which was never ratified. The only "Special Agreement" in force was concluded between Switzerland and Liechtenstein.[15] According to the indicated remittal, the granting proceedings are largely the same for an ordinary European patent and a Unitary patent. To both the EPC is applicable.

2.3.2. *Rules of the Unified Patent Court*

The Unified Patent Court is based upon several legal instruments:

Agreement on the Unified Patent Court: The Agreement is an international treaty presently among twenty five of the twenty-eight Member States of the European Union. It is the main legal foundation of the Unified Patent Court. It was endorsed by the EU ministers in the Competitiveness Council on December 10, 2012 and by the European Parliament on December 11, 2012.[16] It was signed by the participating EU Member States on February 19, 2013. The Agreement will enter into force as soon as thirteen states, necessarily including France, Germany and the U.K., have ratified it (Article 89 UPCA). At present, already eleven states have ratified the Agreement. The U.K. and Germany have still yet to sign. *Statute of the Court:* The Statute of the Court (the Statute) is an integral part of the Agreement[17] and is included in Annex I of the Agreement. The Statute determines the institutional and financial arrangements of the UPC, including the conditions for appointing the Court's judges and electing the President of the Court of First Instance[18] and of the Court of Appeal.[19]

Rules of Procedure: The procedural framework of the UPC is laid down in a set of rules that has been adopted by the Administrative Committee of the Court.[20] The rules deal with the different stages of proceedings, general case management, proportionality and fairness (such as the right to be heard). They also contain general provisions on languages of the proceeding, parties, representation, means of evidence, experts, and define the powers of the UPC to order provisional measures (in particular preliminary injunctions) or measures to preserve evidence, e.g., *saisie-contrefaçon.*

15. Agreement of Dec. 22, 1978.
16. Document 16351/12, of Jan. 11, 2013.
17. Article 2(i) of the Agreement.
18. Article 14 of the Statute.
19. Article 13 of the Statute.
20. Article 41(2) of the Agreement.

2.4. Border Measures Regulations

Customs authorities provide powerful means for enforcing patent rights. Indeed, German border enforcement proceedings are looked upon as an analog of the United States International Trade Commission proceedings for excluding infringing goods from importation. Germany's customs system derives its authority in large part from EC Regulation 608/2013.[21] This regulation provides measures to prohibit import or export of counterfeits and infringing goods. This regulation is directly applicable in the EU Member States, such as Germany. These border control measures are discussed in detail in Chapter 14.

3. OTHER INTERNATIONAL TREATIES

Germany is a signatory to the major international treaties governing intellectual property. These treaties are not per se applicable within German territory. Rather, as in other countries, the German legislature must separately enact national laws to be in compliance with Germany's international agreements and obligations. The major patent-related treaties to which Germany is a signatory are discussed in brief below.

3.1. Paris Convention

Germany joined the Paris Convention on May 1, 1903. The convention establishes international standards for the protection of industrial property. A particularly important effect of the Paris Convention is the priority right embedded in the provisions of Article 4.[22] In particular, the Paris Convention provides that the filing of an application in one signatory country provides a right of priority, such that the applicant may later file applications in other member jurisdictions without loss of right due to activities occurring in the interval between the filings, such as publication or exploitation of the invention.[23] This period of priority is twelve months for patents and utility models.[24] The protections of the Paris Convention are codified in Article 87 of the EPC, for patents prosecuted through the EPO, and in §41 of the German Patent Act, for patents prosecuted through the German Patent and Trademark Office.

21. Regulation (EU) No. 608/2013 of the European Parliament and of the Council of Jun. 12, 2013 concerning customs enforcement of intellectual property rights and repealing Council Regulation (EC) No. 1383/2003(OJ L 181, Jun. 29, 2013, p. 15.); an excerpt of the most important provisions of the regulation can be found in Ch. 16. The complete text (in English) can be found on the website http://eur-lex.europa.eu.
22. The text of the Paris Convention can be found on www.wipo.int/.
23. *See* Paris Convention, Art. 4.
24. Six months for industrial designs and trademarks (Art. 4 of the Paris Convention for the Protection of Industrial Property).

3.2. PCT

The Patent Cooperation Treaty (PCT) was ratified by Germany in 1977,[25] and its provisions were implemented into national law the following year.[26] This treaty allows patent applicants to initiate multinational protection by filing a single international application. The treaty unifies the application proceedings and provides a prior art search, including the possibility of a non-binding, preliminary opinion on novelty and inventive step. In contrast to the EPC, the PCT does not provide unified grant proceedings.[27]

3.3. TRIPS

The Agreement on Trade-Related Aspects of Intellectual Property Rights (TRIPS) is an international treaty setting forth general guidelines for the structuring of patent systems and the enforcement of patent rights. Germany signed TRIPS in 1995.[28] Because the German legislature considered the German patent system already compatible with TRIPS, the provisions of this treaty were not directly enacted into national law.[29] The national laws of Germany must be applied in conformity with the provisions of TRIPS, and accordingly German courts must ensure that the standards provided by TRIPS are satisfied.[30]

A particularly significant application of TRIPS[31] to patent law in Germany concerns its standards for patent enforcement. Article 42 of TRIPS provides standards for procedural assertion of intellectual property rights, including patent rights. In particular, Article 43 of TRIPS provides minimum standards for evidence taking. These articles prompted German courts to expand discovery under national law, allowing patentees to gather evidence in support of their enforcement activities.

In 2002, Germany's Federal Supreme Court issued a decision-making clear that the provisions of the relevant German evidentiary laws must be construed in such a way that they satisfy the requirements of TRIPS, thereby broadening the previously limited discovery available to patentees under German law.[32] And more recently, the German legislature has enacted into national law the provisions of the European Enforcement Directive, discussed above, which further expands the availability of discovery to patentees.[33] The Enforcement Directive is viewed as providing remedies beyond the minimum requirements of TRIPS, and so is referred to as "TRIPS-plus," especially by developing countries and other entities that contend that European patent

25. Federal Law Gazette (BGBl.) II, 1978, 11.
26. Federal Law Gazette (BGBl.) II, 1978, 484.
27. The PCT can be found on www.wipo.org.
28. Federal Law Gazette (BGBl.) 1995 11, 456.
29. Gazette of the Federal Parliament (BT-Drucksache) 12/7655, 345.
30. Federal Supreme Court, GRUR 2002, 1046, IIC 2003, 331 Faxkarte.
31. The text of TRIPS can be found on www.wto.org.
32. Federal Supreme Court, GRUR 2002, 1046, IIC 2003, 331 Faxkarte, Federal Supreme Court, Aug. 1, 2006, X ZR 114/03 "Restschadstoffentfernung," IIC 2007, 97.
33. See, for instance, §140 c Patent Act in Ch. 17 s. 3.

enforcement has gone too far in terms of the seizure of goods accused of infringement, including goods in-transit to other countries.

4. GERMAN ACTS

4.1. Patent Act ("*Patentgesetz*": PATG)

The primary source of substantive patent law in Germany is the German Patent Act (Patent Act). This act deals with the grant and enforcement of German patents. The Patent Act was first enacted in Germany in 1980, and has been periodically revised. The most recent amendments to the Patent Act were enacted by the German legislature on October 19, 2013.[34] A translation of the Patent Act can be found on the World Intellectual Property Organization (WIPO) website (www.wipo.org); however, this translation does not contain the most recent amendments. Accordingly, an unofficial translation of an excerpt of the Patent Act with the latest amendments can be found at Chapter 17, section 3.

4.2. Code of Civil Procedure ("*Zivilprozessordnung*": ZPO)

While the substantive rules of patent law are provided for in the Patent Act, the procedural rules for carrying out patent enforcement in Germany are provided by the German Code of Civil Procedure.[35] This code, which governs the course of judicial proceedings, is analogous to the Federal Rules of Civil Procedure in the U.S. An English translation of the complete Code of Civil Procedure is available online.[36]

4.3. Utility Model Act ("*Gebrauchsmustergesetz*": GebrMG)

The Utility Model Act (GebrMG) is distinct from the Patent Act and provides a separate, enforceable intellectual property right known as a utility model right. A translation of that act can be found on the WIPO website, but it does not yet contain the most recent amendments of the GebrMG, at least as of the printing of this book.

An unofficial translation of an excerpt of the GebrMG with the latest amendments can be found at Chapter 17, section 4 of this book. The registration system for acquiring utility models does not provide for a substantive examination over the technology for which protection is sought. Nonetheless, the resulting utility model is an enforceable right, whereby infringement proceedings can be prosecuted and injunctions over

34. Federal Law Gazette (BGBl.) 2013 I, 3830.
35. The latest version of the Code of Civil Procedure can be found on www.gesetze-im-internet.de (website of the Federal Ministry of Justice).
36. http://www.gesetze-im-internet.de.

infringing goods can be obtained. These utility models do not have an analogous right under U.S. law, and can be very powerful tools in a patent enforcement strategy. They are discussed in the following chapters.[37]

4.4. Act on Employees' Inventions ("*Arbeitnehmererfindergesetz*": ArbEG)

Germany has enacted the Employee Invention Act, the goal of which is to solve the conflicting interests of the employed inventor and his or her employer. The Employee Invention Act was first enacted in 1957 and was most recently amended in 2009.[38] There is an English language translation of the act available in book form, although the most recent amendments are not yet reflected in it. Chapter 17, section 5 discusses the most important aspects of the Act as recently amended.

37. More details on German Utility Models *see* Ch. 4.
38. Federal Law Gazette (BGBl.) 2009 I, 2521.

CHAPTER 3

Structure of Legal System

1. INTRODUCTION

Patent disputes are resolved through a complex and evolving interplay of proceedings at both the European and German levels (in addition to the other various national court systems in Europe). European actions are well established through the European Patent Office for validity challenges of newly issuing patents. These opposition proceedings must be initiated within nine months of patent grant, after which the various national court systems take jurisdiction for validity challenges. Also at the European level, on rare occasions the Court of Justice of the EU[1] is invoked to rule on particular matters concerning the interpretation of EU law arising through the local national court systems.[2]

The German court system has been the predominant court system in Europe for resolving infringement disputes. The German system is remarkable for having a "split system," with infringement disputes resolved in the district courts and validity challenged resolved through a separate court, the Federal Patent Court. The challenges and opportunities presented by this split system are discussed in this chapter, as well as in further detail in Chapter 8.

A characteristic of the German system—as a civil law system—is that laws are codified in written principles as rules of law and not determined, as in common law, by judges. Accordingly, legislative acts are the primary source of law in Germany, and the court system is usually inquisitorial, unbound by precedent. However, German courts do carefully review previous rulings of other courts, in particular of the higher

1. The Court of Justice of the European Union is situated in Luxembourg.
2. National courts in each EU country are responsible for ensuring that EU law is correctly applied in their country. To prevent the risk that national courts in different countries interpret EU law in different ways, national courts may, and sometimes must, refer to the Court of Justice and ask it to clarify a point concerning the interpretation of EU law to ascertain that the national law complies with that law.

instances[3] and, of course, of the Federal Supreme Court. Due to the high volume of patent litigation, Germany has a well-developed body of precedent that can further lend predictability to the patent litigation process. In patent infringement cases a jury does not exist. The proceedings must follow the rules provided by the German Code of Civil Procedure.

Searching judicial precedent in Germany can be challenging. A few online databases collect German court decisions, but the decisions are usually not translated into English. A few German courts post their rulings on websites, but the lack of a central reporting agency requires the researcher to conduct a court-by-court search of opinions.[4] This is a time-consuming exercise that is fraught with the risk of missing important rulings. Accordingly, there is a premium on selecting counsel with expertise in the subject matter and extensive local litigation experience.

2. GENERAL OUTLINE OF PATENT DISPUTES

There are different ways to invalidate patents in Europe: There is a track through the patent offices, in particular the EPO, during which time the patents can be opposed. In addition, nullity actions can be filed with the Federal Patent Court in Munich.

2.1. Invalidity Challenges

2.1.1. Oppositions

Within nine months after publication of the grant of a European patent, anyone other than the patentee may file opposition proceedings with the EPO (*see* Article 99 EPC).[5] This narrow window is the only time during which the validity of a granted European Patent can be challenged with respect to all European countries in which that patent has effect. After this nine-month period, parties seeking to invalidate a patent must resort to national nullity proceedings on a country-by-country basis.

Any person except the patentee may institute an opposition proceeding.[6] A company or person who does not want to be identified in these proceedings may involve a so-called straw man that acts in its own name, but on behalf of the third party. This is a common strategy of companies that do not want to appear as a party in the proceedings, and is acceptable so long as the straw man is not used by the patentee to

3. Court Instances: District Courts, the Appeal Courts and the Federal Supreme Court are three levels or instances of the civil court system. Rulings of a court may be appealed to a higher instance. Such higher instance may either uphold or reverse the ruling from the lower instance. Patent cases typically begin at a district court level with the possibility of appeal to an Appeal court. Exceptionally, the case might be brought before a third instance, namely the Federal Supreme Court.
4. For instance: www.duesseldorfer-archiv.de/: This website contains decisions, mainly of the district and appeal courts Düsseldorf; decisions of the Federal Supreme Court can be found on the official website: www.bundesgerichtshof.de/; see also www.justizportal-bw.de.
5. Chapter 6 is devoted to the topic "Opposition Proceedings."
6. See Art. 99(1) EPC.

file an opposition against his own patents. The patentee could be tempted to do this if he believes he would be better off with a pending opposition proceeding than with a national invalidation proceeding.

Opposition proceedings are held before the EPO's Opposition Divisions, which are distinct from the Examining Divisions. Given the different compositions in personnel, opponents get a fair chance to have the patent reexamined even if the opposition is based on documents that were already considered during the examination proceedings. Furthermore, a challenger in opposition proceedings is not estopped from reasserting the same arguments later in court. Unlike *inter partes* review (IPR) and post-grant review (PGR) proceedings in the U.S., a challenger can thus have "two bites at the apple." A challenger can subsequently commence a nullity action and assert the same art that was brought before the EPO. The fact that particular arguments had been raised and lost in EPO opposition proceedings will not necessarily influence the Federal Patent Court.

Like the EPO opposition proceedings, there are analogous opposition proceedings that may be brought against a German (national) patent that was obtained through the German Patent and Trademark Office (GPTO). The window for bringing such opposition proceedings in Germany is also nine months from the publication of the German patent (§59(1) Pat Act). The proceedings are handled by the oppositions divisions of the GPTO and their decisions can be appealed at the Federal Patent Court.

2.1.2. German Nullity Actions[7]

Germany's legal structure provides for separate courts for asserting and invalidating issued patents. To invalidate a patent (separate and apart from EPO opposition proceedings), a "nullity action" may be brought. Only one court in Germany, namely the Federal Patent Court, has jurisdiction to adjudicate nullity actions aimed at invalidating a German national patent or the German part of an ordinary European patent.

The Federal Patent Court was established on July 1, 1961 and is headed by the Federal Supreme Court in Karlsruhe. Prior to the establishment of the Federal Patent Court, its functions had been fulfilled by special chambers of the GPTO. With the goal of separation of executive and judicial powers, the authority to invalidate patents was spun off into a separate tribunal, thus forming the Federal Patent Court.

In addition to its second instance jurisdiction over patent nullity actions filed with the Federal Patent Court, Germany's Federal Patent Court acts as a court for appeals against decisions of the GPTO such as decisions of an opposition division, as well as against decisions by the boards of appeal of the Federal Office of Plant Varieties concerning plant variety rights.

Nullity actions may be brought only after the opposition window has closed. Thus the earliest that nullity actions may be instituted is three months after the publication of the grant of a German patent, or nine months after the publication of the

7. Nullity actions are addressed in Ch. 7.

grant of an ordinary European patent. If an opposition against a patent is filed, a nullity action is inadmissible until the opposition proceedings are finally terminated. Nullity actions are subsidiary to opposition proceedings, in order to avoid contradictory decisions of the EPO or GPTO and the Federal Patent Court.

The Federal Patent Court has no jurisdiction over disputes concerning infringements of patents. This jurisdiction lies with the civil courts, namely the twelve district courts and twelve appeal courts, which are headed by the Federal Supreme Court.

2.1.3. Upcoming: Revocation Actions at the UPC

There are plans to establish a Unified Patent Court ("UPC"). These plans had nearly come to fruition. On November 28, 2016, the U.K. government has confirmed that it will proceed to ratify the Unified Patent Court Agreement, in spite of Britain's Brexit vote, for which reason it is to be expected that the Unified Patent Court will take up its function in 2018. Once the UPC begins operations, stand-alone revocation actions will be brought before its Central Division. The Central Division of the UPC will have jurisdiction over matters involving the validity of European patents with unitary effect. The jurisdiction will also extend to ordinary European patents as long as the patentee has not "opted out" from the competence of the UPC in compliance with Article 83 (3) of the UPCA.

Stand-alone revocation actions are directed against the patentee. Depending on the technical content of the patent in suit, a revocation action will be allocated in compliance with the classifications of the International Patent Classification of the World Intellectual Property Organization to either the seat in Paris or one of its branches in London and Munich as shown in the following chart.

Table 3.1. Distribution of Cases across the Central Division

Paris (Seat)	*London*	*Munich*
(B) performing operations, transporting; (D) textiles; paper; (E) fixed constructions; (G) physics; (H) electricity	(A) human necessities (C) chemistry, metallurgy	(F) mechanical engineering, lighting, heating, weapons, blasting

The seat of the UPC's Central Division in London will deal with chemistry, human necessities and metallurgy (Sections A and C), while the seat in Munich will deal with mechanical engineering (Section F), and Paris will handle all other technical areas. Local and Regional Divisions of the Court of First Instance of the UPC will mainly decide on infringement-related issues, whereas the Central Division has competency over validity-related issues.

2.2. Infringement Disputes

2.2.1. National Infringement Proceedings

Patent infringement proceedings are exclusively litigated through Germany's district courts. The split system between nullity proceedings and infringement proceedings is illustrated in the chart below. A particular challenge of the split system is to fairly balance the interests of the patentee to quickly enforce the patent rights with the interests of the accused infringer not to be prevented from commercial activities by an invalid patent. Of course, the proceedings are not completely disconnected from each other and there are mechanisms that guarantee a fair resolution of the conflicting interests. These mechanisms will be discussed in more detail in subsequent chapters.

Figure 3.1. Split System

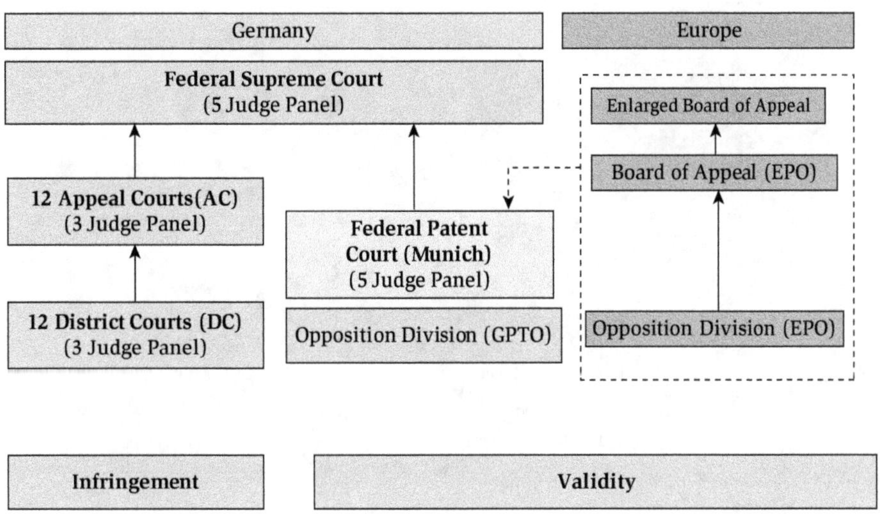

2.2.1.1. First Instance

The German government has vested twelve courts with jurisdiction over patent infringement cases. The most active German infringement court is the District Court Düsseldorf, followed by the District Court Mannheim, District Court Munich and District Court Hamburg.[8] These districts conform to one or more territories of political subdivision of the Federal Republic of Germany and are uniformly distributed across the country, as can be seen on the following map.

8. JUVE, N° 4, April 2010, 73.

Table 3.2. Patent Infringement Courts (Twelve Districts)

(1) DC Düsseldorf for *North Rhine-Westphalia*
(2) DC Berlin for *Berlin* and *Brandenburg*
(3) DC Braunschweig for *Lower Saxony*
(4) DC Erfurt for *Thuringia*
(5) DC Frankfort/Main for *Hesse* and *Rhineland-Palatinate*
(6) DC Hamburg for *Bremen, Hamburg, Mecklenburg-Western Pomerania* and *Schleswig-Holstein*
(7) DC Leipzig for *Saxony*
(8) DC Magdeburg for *Saxony-Anhalt*
(9) DC Mannheim for *Baden-Württemberg*
(10) DC Munich I for the *District of the Appeal Court Munich (Bavaria)*
(11) DC Nürnberg-Fürth for *Nürnberg* and *Bamberg (Bavaria)*
(12) DC Saarbrucken for *Saarland*

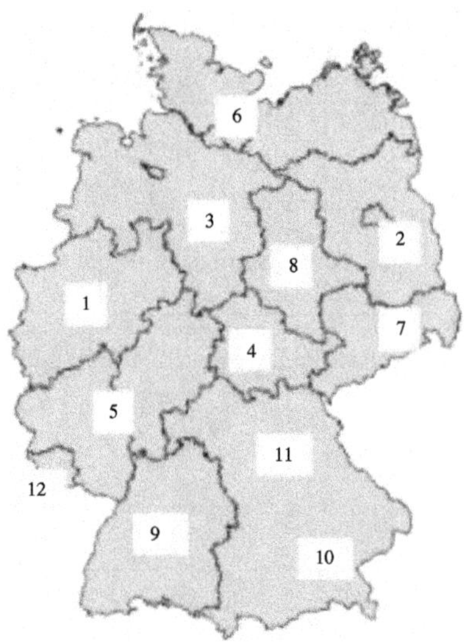

The territorial boundaries of these districts are not particularly relevant. In the German system, there is flexibility when it comes to questions of jurisdiction and venue.[9] A court has jurisdiction to hear a case if either the defendant has his residence or principal place of business within its district, or if the infringing activities were committed in the court's district. A simple offer for sale of the accused product via the defendant's website might be sufficient to establish jurisdiction in any of the twelve district courts. The selection of the court is often based on strategic considerations of the patentee. This is a main reason that patent matters are concentrated in only a few

9. Details concerning venue can be found in Ch. 8, s. 1.1.

German district courts.[10] Defendants generally cannot influence the forum selection made by the plaintiff. Even an earlier filed declaratory judgment action has no effect on that selection.[11]

The panels of the district courts are composed of three judges who are trained in patent law and have several years of practical experience with patent cases. Patent matters are assigned to dedicated chambers of the court. The district courts of Düsseldorf, Mannheim and Munich, which have especially high numbers of patent cases, each have two or three chambers dedicated to patent infringement matters.

2.2.1.2. Second Instance

Appeals from the district courts are called "second instance" proceedings, and these are heard by twelve appeal courts, with one appeals court corresponding to and taking appeals from each of the first-instance district courts. The panels of these appellate courts are also composed of three judges who are trained in patent law and have several years of practical experience with patent cases. For instance, decisions rendered by the District Court Düsseldorf are appealed before the Appeal Court Düsseldorf and decisions of the District Court Mannheim are heard before the Appeal Court Karlsruhe.

In appeals, the admission of new facts is restricted. The submission of new facts in the second instance proceeding might be rejected as belated if their consideration would lead to a delay of the proceedings. To avoid such a rejection, the late submission must be sufficiently excused. The excuse might be accepted if the newly brought facts were previously unknown to the submitting party through no fault of his own. Accordingly, it is important that all relevant and favorable facts be raised in the first instance proceedings to avoid being precluded from raising such facts at a later proceeding.

2.2.1.3. Third Instance

An appeal to the Federal Supreme Court in Karlsruhe represents a purely legal appeal in cases of general legal interest to the public, i.e., if the decision would contribute to the development of case law or if the consistency of German case law is in question. Submissions of new facts are not allowed. The facts established by the appeal courts are binding for the Federal Supreme Court, unless such findings are affected by a procedural error and this error is adequately demonstrated in the grounds for appeal. Thus, generally, no evidence is heard at the Federal Supreme Court. The panel of the Supreme Court is composed of five judges.

10. See Ch. 8, s. 1.1.
11. Details concerning the Declaratory Judgment Actions can be found in Ch. 8, s. 6.1.

Table 3.3. Basic Overview

	District Courts	*EPO/GPTO Opposition*	*Federal Patent Court*
Proceedings	Bench Trial Without Jury	*Inter Partes* Proceedings	*Inter Partes* Proceedings/Subsidiary Character vis-à-vis Opposition
Remedy	Injunction/ Rendering of Accounts/Damages	Cancellation/ Modification	Cancellation/ Modification
Duration (approx.)	One year	Two years	Two years

Presently the Federal Supreme Court has one panel handling patent cases. This panel is identified by "X," which is also reflected in the case docket number. The panel is in charge of patent infringement cases and validity cases.

The most important Federal Supreme Court decisions are contained in a compilation that is known by the abbreviation BGHZ.[12] This compilation is edited by the members of the Court, and includes those decisions that the judges believe are of basic importance. Many of these decisions can be obtained from the website of the Federal Supreme Court.[13]

2.2.2. Infringement Proceedings at the UPC

The Unified Patent Court (UPC), in the event it is finally established, is slated to have a Court of First Instance composed of Local, Regional Divisions and a Central Division. The Central Division will be based in Paris. The Court of Appeal will have its seat in Luxembourg.

12. BGHZ, Entscheidungen des Bundesgerichtshofs in Zivilsachen, Carl Heymanns Verlag.
13. www.bundesgerichtshof.de/. These decisions are published only in German. A few of these important decisions are translated and can be consulted in the legal review IIC - International Review of Intellectual Property and Competition Law, published by the Max Planck Institute for Intellectual Property, Competition and Tax Law.

Figure 3.2. Structure of the Court

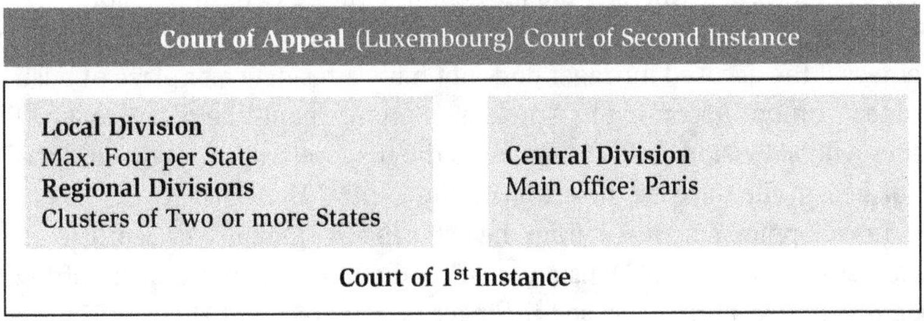

2.2.2.1. *Local and Regional Divisions (Court of First Instance)*

Local and Regional Divisions are being established in the Contracting Member States. In most countries, only one Local Division will be set up in a Contracting Member State.[14] However, States with more than 100 cases per calendar year may set up additional Local Divisions for every additional hundred cases, up to a total of no more than four Local Divisions per State.[15] Due to the quantity of patent cases handled by German courts, Germany will have four Local Divisions, to be seated in Munich, Mannheim, Düsseldorf and Hamburg. Likewise, France will have one in Paris; Belgium will have its in Brussels; Denmark will establish its Local Division in Copenhagen. Italy and the Netherlands are in the process of seating their own as well. Regional Divisions may be established on request by two or more States if they have a low number of patent cases. Sweden, Estonia, Latvia and Lithuania have established one Regional Division situated in Stockholm.

The choice of venue of filing an infringement action will be governed by the following criteria:

(1) Where the actual or threatened infringement has occurred or may occur (forum of *actus in tort*).
(2) Where the defendant or, in the case of multiple defendants,[16] where one of the defendants has its residence, or principal place of business, or in the absence of residence or principal place of business, its place of business.
(3) Furthermore, the parties may be able to agree on a venue.

Accordingly, a Local Division will have jurisdiction if the infringement occurs in the Contracting State hosting that Division (location 1) or if the residence or principle place of business of the defendant is located there (location 2). A Regional Division will have jurisdiction if the alleged infringement takes place in at least one of its Contracting

14. Article 7(3) Agreement.
15. Article 7(4) Agreement.
16. An action may be brought against multiple defendants only where the defendants have a commercial relationship and where the action relates to the same alleged infringement.

States. In a situation where the actual or threatened infringement takes place in a country that does not have a local division and does not participate in a regional cluster, the patentee may directly file his action with the Central Division.

The *actus in tort*[17] prong for the venue standard will be of particular importance for patentees if the accused infringer does not have a residence or place of business in the European Union. According to Article 33(1) Agreement, the patentee may file the case either with a division acting pursuant to the first option (i.e., at the forum of *actus in tort*) or he can file the case directly with the Central Division.

Forum shopping may result from the *actus in tort* standard for venue. A claimant can file a lawsuit at any Local Division of a Contracting State in which an infringement has been committed by the accused infringer or at a Regional Division if the alleged infringement takes place in at least one of the Contracting States which have set up the Regional Division. These are the locations where the allegedly infringing product has been produced, offered or placed on the market.[18]

2.2.2.2. Central Division (Court of First Instance)

Local and regional divisions of the UPC's Court of First Instance will mainly decide infringement-related matters, whereas the Central Division will have competency over validity-related issues, such as stand-alone revocation actions and counterclaims for revocation if referred by a local or regional division to the Central Division. Nevertheless, the Central Division may have jurisdiction over infringement-related matters if the actual or threatened infringement takes place in a Contracting State which neither hosts a local division nor participates in a regional cluster. The patentee will have then the option to file his action at the forum *actus in tort* or he may directly file his action with the Central Division. In addition, apart from cases arising through its *actus in tort* jurisdiction, Central Division may also exercise jurisdiction if the accused infringer does not have a residence or place of business in the European Union. According to Article 33(1) Agreement, the patentee may file the case either with a division in compliance with the first option, at the forum of *actus in tort,* or he can file the case directly with the Central Division.

2.2.2.3. Court of Appeal (Second Instance)

An appeal against a decision of the Court of First Instance may be brought before the Court of Appeal in Luxembourg by any party that has been unsuccessful, in whole or in part, in its submissions, within two months of the date of the notification of the decision.[19] An appeal can be based on both points of law and matters of fact.[20] Nevertheless, new facts and new evidence may, in principle, only be introduced where

17. Article 33 (1)(a) Agreement.
18. Article 25(a) Agreement.
19. Article 73(1) Agreement.
20. Article 73(3) Agreement.

the submission of them by the party concerned could not reasonably have been expected during proceedings before the Court of First Instance.

Figure 3.2. Instances of the UPC

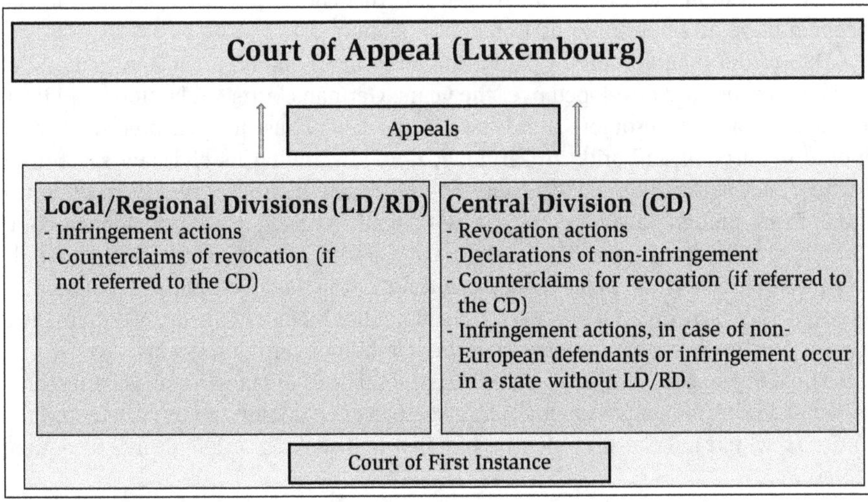

3. COURT OF JUSTICE OF THE EUROPEAN UNION

Germany's legal proceedings are influenced, directly and indirectly, by laws of the EU. Due to the European unification process, the Court of Justice of the EU situated in Luxembourg is gaining more and more importance. Under Article 267 Treaty of the functioning of the EU (TFEU),[21] German courts including the UPC may refer questions concerning the interpretation of EU law to the European Court of Justice (EUCJ). These are not appeal proceedings that can be filed by a party who is dissatisfied with the court's judgment. Instead, these proceedings are invoked pursuant to the request of a national court. This has happened with respect to the question of admissibility of the so-called transborder decisions in patent cases[22] and also frequently occurs in cases concerning supplementary protection certificates (SPC).[23] SPCs are sui generis patent extensions available for medicinal products, such as drugs, and plant protection products, to compensate for the time needed to obtain regulatory approval for putting those products on the market.[24]

21. In the past: Art. 234 of the EC Treaty.
22. In December 2002, the Appeal Court of Düsseldorf referred to the ECJ the question of whether a German court can decide a validity objection concerning a foreign patent (*GAT v. LuK*: Case C-4/03). The ECJ decided that this is not possible (but in principle infringement on foreign patents could still be decided by a German Court).
23. For instance: Case C-452/07, *Health Research Inc.*
24. See §16a Patent Act, the provision can be found in Ch. 17, s. 3.

4. ROLE OF JUDICIAL PRECEDENT

Germany is a civil law jurisdiction, and accordingly judicial precedent is less authoritative than in common law countries such as the U.S. Accordingly, the German Patent Act is the ultimate authority on substantive questions of patent law. However, many important questions are left unanswered by the code, and accordingly, judicial precedent plays an important role in patent litigation.

Due to the high volume of patent litigation in Germany, a substantial body of judicial precedent has developed over the years. German courts tend to follow judicial precedent in order to promote uniformity in the law. Thus, judicial precedent is an important source of authority in Germany, notwithstanding its civil law system. In particular, decisions of the Federal Supreme Court are rigorously respected by lower courts. Even though lower courts are not legally obliged to follow higher court opinions, this body of case law is persuasive authority, and courts are generally reluctant to break from precedent. Accordingly, the body of judicial patent law precedent may provide a further reason for potential litigants to select Germany as a patent forum, to give a greater degree of predictability over the outcome.

Thus, in practice Germany's court system functions in many respects in the same manner as in common law systems. The structure of Germany's court system and the manner in which judicial precedent is handled is discussed at length in subsequent chapters.

CHAPTER 4

Forms of Patent Protection: Background on Prosecution

Patent protection in Germany comes in different forms. Most commonly, inventors file their applications initially through the European Patent Office EPO and designate Germany among the countries in which they will pursue national stage patents ("ordinary European patents"). In addition, most likely starting from 2018 inventors may request that their European patents have "unitary effect" across the Participating Member States (unitary patents), rather than having a bundle of national patents, as is the case for ordinary European patents. Unitary patents will exclusively be litigated through the Unified Patent Court ("UPC") once that court is established. This contrasts with ordinary European patents which are subject to a complex transitional regime[1] that provides for jurisdiction in the UPC while offering the patentee the option to "opt out" to exclude it from the UPC system.

Alternatively, inventors file their applications with the German Patent and Trademark Office GPTO, resulting in national patents applicable only to Germany.

A third type of protection arises from a separate type of intellectual property called a "utility model," which functions in many respects like a patent.

This chapter aims to identify the key characteristics of each of these types of protection, so that companies may intelligently protect their inventions with the most favorable property rights, considering the often-competing considerations of speed, cost, enforceability and scope of protection. A company may elect to pursue a combination of these intellectual property rights to develop a portfolio tailored to its needs, including a combination of the following:

- Starting from 2018: Ordinary European patents, having a 20-year duration;
- German patents, also with a 20-year patent term;

1. Ch.4, s. 1.8.6.

- Utility models, which may be obtained immediately through Germany's registration system, providing 10-year protection.

What follows is a background discussion of these kinds of patent protection, with a brief discussion of how to obtain these rights. Because existing texts already explain the procedures for obtaining patents in Europe, the following sections will provide only a high-level description of the patent prosecution process. For more detailed information on European Patents refer to the regularly updated "Guidelines for Examination in the European Patent Office" published on the EPO Website (www.epo.org).

Table 4.1. Key Aspects of the Various Forms of Protection

	Ordinary European Patents	*National Patents (German Patent)*	*Utility Model*
Proceedings	Formal and substantive examination	Formal and substantive examination	Only examination of formalities
Subject Matter	Inventions	Inventions	Inventions excepting process and use claims
Grace Period	No	No	Yes (six months)
Prior Art	Every public description and public prior use	Every public description and public prior use	Every public written description, only public prior use occurring in Germany
Term	20 years	20 years	10 years
Enforceability	Publication of the mention of grant	Publication of the mention of grant	Immediately after registration (2–3 months from filing)

1. EUROPEAN PATENTS

1.1. Introduction

A dominant form of patent protection arises from a patent application initially filed with the EPO. The process of applying for a patent, which is also called granting proceedings or prosecution proceedings, begins when the inventor or his representative files an application with the EPO.[2] The application contains a request for grant of a European patent, a description of the invention including any drawings, one or more

2. The application can be filed at the EPO's offices in Munich, The Hague (Netherlands), in Berlin or if the national law permits with the central industrial property office or other authority of that state (Art. 75(1) EPC).

claims, an abstract, and is filed in writing.[3] The particularities of the upcoming unitary patent, which is a special from or a European patent, are dealt in a following chapter (1.8).

1.2 Granting Procedure

The procedures for filing applications in the EPO, whether for obtaining an ordinary European patent or a unitary patent, are governed by the EPC, and a subset of its regulations entitled the Implementing Regulations to the Convention on the Grant of European Patents.[4] The provisions of these regulations are quoted in the following as "Rules of the EPC." The contents of patent applications are governed by Part III, Chapter II of the Implementing Regulations and shall include a description of the invention (Rule 42 EPC), one or more claims (Rule 43 EPC), the drawings (Rule 46 EPC) and an abstract (Rule 47 EPC).

The filing of a European patent application can be implemented by means of a direct filing (direct EP Application) or through an application under the Patent Cooperation Treaty (so-called Euro-PCT Application). According to Article 153 EPC (Rule 159 EPC), a PCT application for which the European Patent Office is a designated or elected office, and which has been accorded an international date of filing, is equivalent to a regular European application. There are however a few procedural differences depending upon which type of application (direct EP Application or Euro-PCT Application) is under consideration.

The granting procedure for European patents can be divided into different parts. During the first part, a formalities examination and a mandatory search will be carried out (Articles 90, 92 EPC). That part is completed with the publication of the application and the search report (Article 93, Rule 68 EPC). If the search report is available in time, it will be included in the publication; otherwise it will be published separately. Then the substantive examination upon applicant's request follows (Article 94 (1) EPC).

3. The application shall be filed in one of the three official EPO languages, namely English, French or German. However, an application may be filed in any language in order to obtain a filing date. A translation into one of the EPO's official languages must be submitted within two months thereafter (Art. 14(2) EPC).
4. Implementing Regulations to the Convention on the Grant of European Patents of Oct. 5, 1973 as adopted by decision of the Administrative Council of the European Patent Organization of Dec. 7, 2006 and as last amended by decision of the Administrative Council of the European Patent Organization of Oct. 15, 2014 (see website of the EPO).

Figure 4.1. General Overview of the Granting Procedure

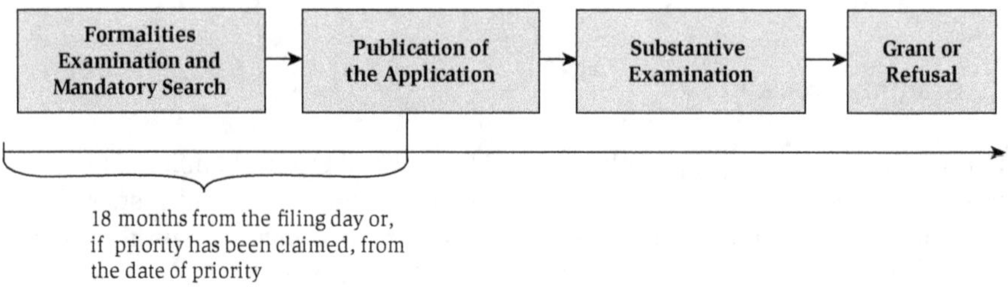

1.2.1. The EPO's Initial Formality Review and Search Report

1.2.1.1. General Remarks

Once the application is filed, the EPO checks whether the application meets the formal requirements. It also examines whether the application can be accorded a date of filing (Article 90(1) EPC, Article 80 EPC). While the formalities examination is in progress, the EPO prepares a search report that is drawn up on the basis of the claims, with due regard to the description and any drawings (Article 92 EPC).[5] The search covers patents and patent applications, but also non-patent literature. It can also cover internet sources, including online technical journals, online databases or other websites.[6] It is an essential element of the grant procedure and designed to identify prior art relevant to the application to make it possible to determine, on the basis of the documents mentioned in the search report, whether and to what extent the invention is patentable. In addition, after the search report is published the public may have a better understanding of the scope of protection that might be granted.[7] Upon the applicant's request or if the patent application is a first filing, the EPO tries to deliver the search report to the applicant in about six months from the request or filing date.[8] The EPO also draws up a non-binding opinion on patentability to accompany the search report for European applications and international applications that enter the European phase and for which a supplementary search report must be drawn up (Rule 62(1) EPC).[9]

1.2.1.2. Possible Events During the Search Phase

In the case of a European patent application filed directly at the EPO,[10] it is not possible to amend the application prior to receiving the search report (Rule 137(1) EPC). This

5. Guidelines for Examination, ed. 2014, B-IV, 1.2.
6. *See* OJ EPO 2009, 456.
7. EPO—T 1242/04.
8. The accelerated drawing up of the search report ("PACE") is set out in EPO—OJ 2010, 352.
9. Inserted by decision of the Administrative Council of Dec. 9, 2004 and entered into force on Jul. 1, 2005 (OJ EPO 2005, 5).
10. Specific rules are applicable to Euro-PCT applications.

prohibition avoids changes in the scope of the search. Nevertheless, the EPO may invite the applicant during the search phase to indicate those independent claims on the basis of which the search shall be carried out, if the application does not comply with Rule 43(2) EPC (*see* Rule 62a EPC).[11] The purpose of this invitation is to define the invention more clearly at the beginning of the search phase. According to Rule 43(2) EPC, the number of independent claims is limited to one of each category (i.e., product, process, apparatus or use). Exceptions to this rule are permitted in case of: "(a) a plurality of interrelated products," such as, transmitter-receiver, intermediate components; or "(b) different uses of a product or apparatus," or "(c) alternative solutions to a same problem, where it is inappropriate to cover these alternatives by a single claim" (*see* Rule 43(2) a), b) and c)). If the search examiner opines that an application containing multiple independent claims does not comply with this rule, he invites the applicant to indicate the claims on which the search shall be based. If the applicant does not respond to the EPO's invitation within a two-month deadline, the search is carried out on the basis of the first claim in each category.[12]

Furthermore, if the EPO considers that it is impossible to carry out a meaningful search, it may invite the applicant to indicate the subject matter to be searched (Rule 63 EPC). This invitation generally improves the quality of the search. The EPO does not search claims that are not properly drafted or that relate to unsearchable subject matter. If the applicant does not react, the EPO may draw up a partial search report or give a reasoned statement of non-search if it considers that the application is defective (e.g., missing clarity, conciseness or support).

1.2.1.3. Mandatory Reaction on Search Opinion

Receipt of the EPO's search report provides a good opportunity for reassessing the patent prosecution strategy. Along with the search report, the EPO establishes a search opinion on whether the application and the invention to which it relates seem to meet the requirements of the EPC. The search report and search opinion is aimed at streamlining the granting procedure and may encourage an early withdrawal of the application. This opinion along with the search report represents the so-called Extended European Search Report (EESR: Rule 62(1) EPC).[13]

Under Rule 70a(1) EPC, the applicant must reply to the search opinion within six months after the date on which the European Patent Bulletin mentions the publication of the European Search Report (Rule 70(1) EPC). That is, the EPO gives the applicant the opportunity to comment on the opinion, and, where appropriate, invite him to correct deficiencies, to amend the description, claims and drawings. If no objections are raised in the opinion, i.e., no invitation to remedy the defects is issued, the applicant does not need to file a reply and will be informed accordingly.

11. Inserted by decision of the Administrative Council of Mar. 25, 2009 and entered into force on Apr. 1, 2010 (OJ EPO 2009, 299).
12. Rule 62a (1) EPC.
13. Inserted by decision of the Administrative Council of Dec. 9, 2004 and entered into force on Jul. 1, 2005 (OJ EPO 2005, 5).

In the case of a Euro-PCT application where the EPO was responsible for preparing the International Search Report (ISR), the applicant is also required to respond to an ISR and a related negative written opinion (WO-ISA) within a period of six months from the date of the notification of the invitation.[14] If the EPO has also prepared the International Preliminary Examination Report (IPER), the invitation will instead relate to the IPER (Rule 161(1) EPC).

If a Supplementary European Search Report is drawn up on a Euro-PCT-application (Rule 70a(2) EPC), the applicant will likewise be invited by the EPO to respond to a search opinion within a period of six months from the notification of the invitation. A Supplementary European Search Report is established by the EPO in case of a Euro-PCT Application for which the EPO has not prepared the ISR. No such invitation will be made, however, where the search opinion is entirely positive.

1.2.2. Unity of the Invention

The EPO imposes "unity" requirements for pending claims, somewhat akin to the restriction requirements employed in the U.S., whereby PTO examiners may require an applicant to restrict the claims within a single application to a more limited set drawn to an independent and distinct invention. Likewise, under Article 82 EPC, the claims must "relate to one invention only, or to a group of inventions linked so as to form a single general inventive concept."[15] The unity requirement is typically satisfied if the invention only relates to one independent claim of each category (i.e., product, process, apparatus, or use), except in case of: "(a) a plurality of interrelated products," such as, transmitter-receiver, intermediate components; or "(b) different uses of a product or apparatus," or "(c) alternative solutions to a same problem, where it is inappropriate to cover these alternatives by a single claim".[16] If this is not the case, the search division of the EPO will usually restrict the search to the invention or the linked group of inventions first mentioned in the claims (Rule 64(1) EPC). If the search report covers additional inventions, further search fees will have to be paid.

If a "lack-of-unity" objection is raised by the searching examiner, the applicant can either pay one or more of the further search fees or simply not respond, in which case the search division assumes that the application should be prosecuted on the basis of the invention that has already been searched.[17] The applicant does not waive the unsearched subject matter by not paying the additional search fees. The unsearched subject matter can be prosecuted later through a divisional application.[18] Special rules have to be considered for international applications entering the European phase (Rule 164 EPC).

14. Decision of the Administrative Council of Oct. 26, 2010 amending the Implementing Regulations to the European Patent Convention (CA/D 12/10). The deadline is only one month in Rule 161(1) EPC, which is applicable until May 1, 2011.
15. *See also* Rule 44 EPC.
16. *See* Rule 43(2) a), b) and c) EPC.
17. *See* EPO—G 2/92, OJ 10/1993, 591.
18. *See* Ch. 4, s. 1.3. "Divisional Applications (Art. 76 EPC)."

1.2.3. *Publication of the European Patent Application*

The European patent application is published 18 months after the filing date or the earliest priority date (Article 93 EPC). The applicant may also request an earlier publication (Article 93(1) b) EPC). The publication contains the description, the claims, any drawings, all as filed and the abstract. Once the application is published, the public can inspect the files through the register and can access the information about the state of the proceedings including the application's biographic data. This can be accessed via the EPO website. If the European search report is available, it is annexed; if not, it is published separately. Amended claims filed after receiving the European search report but before completion of the technical preparations for publication will be published in addition to the claims as filed (Rule 68(4) EPC).

Even though an earlier publication of the European patent application can be requested, there are no provisions in the EPC which would permit any delaying of the publication. The public has a prevailing interest in a timely publication of the application.[19] Of course, the applicant can withdraw the application to avoid publication, if for instance he decides to keep the invention secret.[20] But the withdrawal abandons the application without the possibility of revival.[21]

A European patent application may confer provisional protection from the date of its publication. According to Article 67 EPC, it is left to the contracting states of the EPC to prescribe the content and requirements of the provisional protection for the time period between publication of the application and grant of the patent. Accordingly, there are differences from country to country. For instance, in Germany the existence of such provisional protection necessarily requires, if the application is not already published in German, that a translation of the claims be made available to the public by the GPTO or communicated to the user of the claimed invention.[22] The German provisional protection only confers a financial compensation to the applicant. Content and the special requirements of this provisional protection and the related strategic considerations are described in detail in Chapter 12, section 5.1.2 "Particularities: Published Patent Applications."

1.2.4. *Examination Proceedings*

The substantive examination and the grant decision lie in the hands of the examining divisions, which are composed of three technically qualified examiners, who may be joined, if necessary, by a legally qualified examiner.[23] Until a grant or the refusal of the application occurs, the examination is entrusted to one of the examiners, the so-called primary examiner. He or she is in charge of the communications and discussions with

19. EPO—J 2/02.
20. Rule 67 (2) EPC: *The application shall not be published if it has been finally refused or withdrawn or is deemed to be withdrawn before the termination of the technical preparations for publication.*
21. EPO—J 4/04 of Sep. 9, 2004.
22. Article II, § 1(2) InPatÜG.
23. Article 18(1) EPC.

the applicant, which are mostly held in writing, but can also be in person, or by phone.[24] If oral proceedings are requested by the applicant or (in the rare instance) initiated by the examining division, they take place before the complete examining division. The final decision, that is to say the grant or refusal of a patent, is also rendered by the full examining division.

Unless the application is directly ready for grant, communications under Article 94(3) EPC are issued by the Examining Division, inviting the applicant to file observations and, if necessary, to submit amendments to the description, claims and drawings (Rules 71(1) EPC). Even though the applicant is required to substantively respond to any objections raised in a (negative) opinion to the search report (Rules 70a(1), (2) or 161 EPC), the applicant is free to amend the application, in particular the claims (Rule 137(2) EPC) once he has received the search report and within the time limit for filing an examination request or confirming that request (i.e., in reply to the search report). This is the time period during which voluntary amendments are possible. Later, further amendments are subject to the consent of the examining division (Rule 137(3) EPC—*see* Figure 4.2).

Figure 4.2. Amending Applications During Grant Procedure

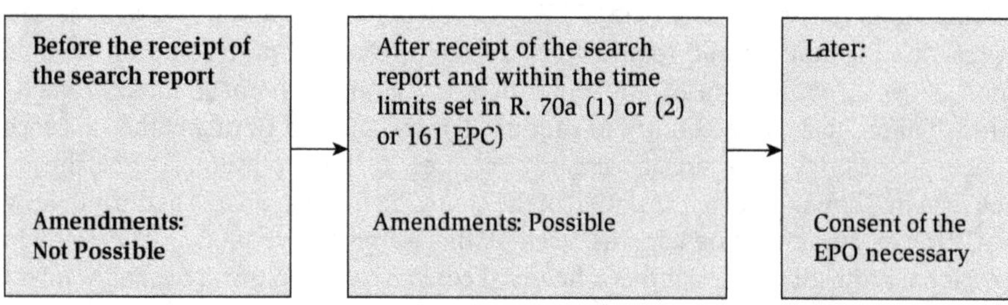

If after examining the response to the communications according to Article 94(3) EPC, the examiner considers the application not yet grantable, he will continue the examination procedure by issuing written communications or talking to the applicant in person or by phone. If the examining division is of the opinion that a patent cannot be granted, the application will be refused (Article 97(2) EPC). Otherwise, if the application meets the requirements of the EPC, the division will grant a European patent, insofar as the requisite fees have been paid in due time and a translation of the claims into the other two official languages of the EPO has been provided (Rule 71(3) EPC). The EPO then publishes the specification of the European Patent as soon as possible after the mention of its grant has been published in the European Patent Bulletin (Article 98 EPC).

24. Article 18 EPC.

1.3. Divisional Applications (Article 76 EPC)

1.3.1. Timing

Like other patent systems, the EPC allows the filing of divisional applications relating to any pending earlier European patent application ("parent application").The earlier parent application may itself be a divisional application.

A European patent application is pending until the application is granted, or more precisely until the date that the European Patent Bulletin mentions its grant.[25] An amendment of the EPC in 2010 introduced a controversial 24 months' time-limit from the Examining Division's first communication for filing divisional applications. That time restriction was removed by the European Patent Office effective April 1, 2014.[26] Accordingly, a divisional application only requires a pending parent patent application and can thus be filed until one day prior to the publication of the grant of the parent application.

When a communication is issued confirming the EPO's intention to grant a patent, the patentee should consider whether or not divisional applications are to be filed. In case of a refusal by the Examining Division the application is still pending for the purpose of filing a divisional until expiration of the time limit for filing a notice of appeal, regardless of whether an appeal is filed or not.[27] When an appeal against a refusal by the Examining Division has been filed, the divisional application can still be filed during the ongoing appeal proceedings. However, it is basically inadmissible to file a divisional application when the parent application has been finally refused, withdrawn or is deemed to be withdrawn.

1.3.2. Subject Matter and Claims

A divisional application may be filed only for subject matter that does not extend beyond the content of the original application.[28] That is, the subject matter of the divisional application must be clearly and unambiguously derivable from the parent application.[29] The divisional application is entitled to the application date of the parent application, and thereby enjoys the parent application's priority date. The divisional application shall be deemed to have been filed on the date of the earlier application (*see* Article 76(1) EPC). Hence, the term of the divisional application shall be 20 years from the date of filing of the parent application,[30] not the filing date of the divisional application.

---

25. OJ EPO 2002, 112.
26. Amended Rule 36 EPC introduced in 2010 restrictions as to when a divisional application may be filed. These restrictions have been removed with effect from Apr. 1, 2014 by decision of the Administrative Council CA/D 15/13 of Oct. 16, 2013 (OJ EPO 2013, 501).
27. EPO—G1/09.
28. EPO—T 441/92.
29. EPO—T 423/03.
30. Article 63(1) EPC: *The term of the European patent shall be 20 years from the date of filing of the application.*

To prevent "double patenting," parent and divisional application must not claim the same subject matter. The applicant has no legitimate interest in proceedings that give rise to the grant of patents with identical claims.[31] Thus, the claims of the divisional application should be confined to other subject matter that is not already claimed in the parent application. The claimed subject matter could more or less overlap.[32] Accordingly, it would be acceptable if an independent claim in the parent application includes all the features of an independent claim of the divisional application which is combined with an additional feature.[33]

1.3.3. *Strategic Use of Divisional Applications*

Divisional applications may be filed for various reasons. One reason could be that the claims of the parent application relate to more than one invention and were thus considered by the EPO to lack unity. The applicant could be interested in obtaining a first quicker protection for a preferred embodiment and pursue the general teaching in a divisional application.[34] The additional invention(s) can then be pursued by filing one or more divisional applications. Alternatively, a divisional application could form a fallback position to face the potential risk of a refusal of the parent application or possible risks of oppositions against it.

Furthermore, it must be taken into account that ordinary European patents (and national patents) may co-exist with Unitary Patents, in the event that the proposed rules governing Unified Patents and the Unified Patent Court are enacted. The jurisdiction of the UPC will govern European patents with unitary effect. Both the Unitary Patent and the UPC do not yet exist; however the potential remains that they will be in force in a few months prior to the grant of a patent application pending today. It is thus possible to strategically divide a patent portfolio in two groups: one group that shall be subject to the UPC, and a second group to be handled by national court systems. For that purpose, divisional applications could be branched off from parent applications insofar as the requirements of Article 76(1) EPC are fulfilled and it does not fall under the prohibition of "double patenting."[35]

1.4. Right of Priority (Articles 87, 88 EPC)

The right of priority is usually not checked during examination proceedings by the examining division unless prior art under Article 54(3) EPC is uncovered.[36] According to Article 87(1) EPC, a party who has filed an application to the "same invention" in

31. EPO—G 1/05 and G 1/06.
32. EPO—T 1391/07.
33. EPO—T 587/98, OJ 2000, 497.
34. EPO—G 2/10).
35. *See* Ch. 4, s. 1.3.3.
36. *See* Ch. 5, s. 2.6.

another Paris Convention jurisdiction may apply for a European patent and claim priority back to that earlier-filed application, for a period of 12 months from the first-filed application.

The priority claim may be challenged during opposition. Because of the strict requirements of Article 88 EPC, applicants should carefully consider proper drafting of their first-filed applications if they want to enjoy the benefit of the priority claim in Europe. For determining whether there is the "same invention," the EPO usually relies on the principles applicable to the "novelty-test,"[37] i.e., whether the subject matter of the subsequent application would theoretically be novel vis-à-vis the disclosure of the first filing. The priority claim can thus principally be made as to those features of the subsequent application which are directly and unambiguously disclosed in the earlier application.[38] That is, the requirement for claiming priority of "the same invention" means that priority of a previous application in respect of a claim in a European patent application is to be acknowledged only if the skilled person can derive the subject matter of the claim directly and unambiguously, using common general knowledge, from the previous application as a whole.[39]

1.5. Duty to Disclose

An important question from the outset of filing a patent application in Europe is how much prior art to disclose. Rule 42(1) b) of the Implementing Regulations provides:

The description shall:

> ...
>
> indicate the background art which, as far as is known to the applicant, can be regarded as useful to understand the invention, draw up the European search report and examine the European patent application, and, preferably, cite the documents reflecting such art;

The description of the patent application must of course disclose the invention, but—as a rule—shall also indicate the background art that can be regarded as useful to understand the invention, to draw up the European search report, and to examine the European patent application. Unlike in the U.S., in Europe there is in principle no mandatory "duty to disclose." That is, under the EPC there is no rule comparable to the 37 C.F.R. §1.56 setting a duty to disclose which challenges the applicant or patent attorney to inform the patent office whenever they become aware of any prior art that may be material to patentability. This means that a lengthy U.S.-style Information Disclosure Statement (IDS) is usually not necessary under the European rules.

37. EPO—T 18/87, OJ 1990, 250.
38. EPO—G2/98, OJ 2001, 431: *"The requirement for claiming priority of "the same invention", referred to in Article 87(1) EPC, means that priority of a previous application in respect of a claim in a European patent application in accordance with Article 88 EPC is to be acknowledged only if the skilled person can derive the subject-matter of the claim directly and unambiguously, using common general knowledge, from the previous application as a whole."*
39. EPO—T 18/87, OJ 1990, 250; T 136/95, OJ 1998, 198.

Nevertheless, according to Rule 141 (1) EPC an applicant claiming priority within the meaning of Article 87 EPC is obliged to file a copy of the search results carried out by the authority with which the previous (priority) application was filed. Other prior art that the applicant is, or becomes, aware of is not covered by this rule. It only concerns prior art that has been identified by the authority of the priority application. This search result needs to be filed in case of a Euro-PCT application on entry into the European phase, or without delay after the results have been made available to him. Where the EPO notes that this has not been done, it can invite the applicant to catch up, or at least, to ask him to state that these results are not available to him (Rule 70b(1) EPC). A failure to respond to this invitation may lead to a lapse of the application (Rule 70b(2) EPC).[40] Besides the lapse caused by a missing response to the EPO's invitation, the EPC does not provide for any other legal effects connected to an incomplete, incorrect or even missing IDS. If the applicant fails to provide search results for the authority of priority applications after they have been made available to him, and the EPO does not realize this, there is no ill effect (Rule 141 (1) EPC). Even though this could be considered a failure to comply with an EPC rule, it would not be regarded as a ground for revocation of the granted patent. The same seems to be applicable to the enforceability of the patent. This is rather a question of national law.

The literature has discussed a theory for finding patents unenforceable for failure to disclose known material art in a case where the patent has been obtained by a fraudulent misguidance of the patent office.[41] This theory refers, however, to a very exceptional situation which requires clearly false suggestions or misrepresentation. It thus does not play a role in practice. Accordingly, the question of whether the applicant has withheld information when filing the application or during the prosecution proceedings is not a litigated issue. Of course, the undisclosed prior art, to the extent it becomes available later, could be used to invalidate the patent for novelty or inventive step reasons.

1.6. Opposition, Revocation and Limitation Proceedings

After grant, ordinary European or unitary patents (if and when they become authorized) may be subject to opposition, revocation or limitation proceedings. Opposition proceedings are discussed in detail below in the Chapter "Opposition Proceedings."[42] A revocation request according to Article 105 a (1) EPC is a request which can only be filed by the proprietor and is aimed at abandoning his patent *ab initio*.

Limitation proceedings are *ex parte* proceedings used by the proprietor to narrow the scope of claims after the patent has been issued (Article 105 a–105 c EPC). The

40. *See* OJ EPO 2010, 600 on the filing of copies of search results under Rule 141(1) EPC and decisions of the EPO's President exempting applicants claiming the priority of a first filing made in Austria, Japan, UK, the USA, the Republic of Korea, Denmark or in Spain from filing a copy of the search results under Rule 141(1) EPC: OJ EPO 2011, 62; OJ EPO 2012, 540; OJ EPO 2013, 216; OJ EPO 2015, A2, OJ EPO 2016, A18). *See* also notices from the EPO, OJ EPO 2010, 410; OJ EPO 2016, A19.
41. RGZ 140, 184.
42. Chapter 6, "Opposition Proceedings."

strategic role of the EPO's centralized limitation proceedings in patent litigation may be significant, as it can be used *inter alia* to present new claims during the course of national litigation or proceedings at the UPC, whether before or after a first instance decision on infringement and validity has been rendered.[43]

1.6.1. Nature of Limitation Proceedings

Limitation proceedings may be initiated by the patent holder at any time after grant of the patent as a way to narrow the patent scope to avoid prior art. There is no time limit as to when the request for limitation can be made. However, the request may not be filed while opposition proceedings are pending (Article 105 a (2) EPC). Pending limitation proceedings will be terminated as soon as an opposition is filed against the European patent-in-suit (Rule 93 (2) EPC). These rules guarantee the principle of precedence of opposition proceedings. Proceedings initiated by the patentee for limitation of European patents fall into the jurisdiction of the examining divisions (Rule 91 EPC). Oppositions are handled by a different division within the EPO.

Limitation proceedings focus on the European patent as granted, or on the amended patent if it was previously subject to opposition or earlier limitation proceedings. Since limitations are effected by amendments of the claims, the request shall include a complete set of the amended claims (and the description and drawings if applicable). Limitation proceedings do not provide an opportunity to re-examine the whole patent. Only the amended claims are examined, namely (Rule 95(2) EPC):

- whether the amended claims constitute a limitation with respect to the claims as granted or amended;
- whether the amended claims are clear and concise according to Article 84 EPC; and
- whether the amended claims are disclosed in the originally filed application and do not contain subject matter extending beyond the application as filed according to Article 123(3) EPC.[44]

1.6.2. Strategic Use of Limitation Proceedings

Limitation proceedings could be strategically useful if a particular limitation seems to be necessary due to problematic prior art, in particular, prior art that was not subject to the grant proceedings and that anticipates an independent claim or challenges the inventiveness of the teaching as claimed. The limitation might be beneficial for a later judicial enforcement of the patent in national courts and at the UPC. Also, it could prevent competitors from filing national nullity or revocation actions at the UPC.

43. *Samsung Electronics Co Ltd v. Apple Retail UK & Apple Sales International*, [2014] EWCA Civ 250.
44. Guidelines for Examination in the EPO-Part H, IV-4.4.

Limitation proceedings have proven their usefulness on the national track. The proprietor may seek to initiate them, for example, after receiving a ruling rendered by a national court. That is, after one national court finds the claims of a national stage patent invalid or maintains them with a limited scope in view of the prior art, the patentee can invoke limitation proceedings in the EPO to obtain narrower claims. This would then have European-wide effect. For instance, if the German Federal Patent Court renders a decision maintaining the claims of the German part of a European patent with a limited scope, that decision would have no effect on other national parts of the same European patent and, accordingly, its German part would be different than the claim sets that are in force in other countries. By then instituting limitation proceedings, the patentee could adapt the claim sets of the other national parts of the European patent to the decision of the Federal Patent Court, in order to have harmonized claims in all countries.

This centralized ex-parte procedure reduces costs and contentious issues when enforcing a European patent on a European scale.

1.7. Observations by Third Parties

Upon the publication of a European patent application, any person may file observations regarding the patentability of the invention (Article 115). Although lack of novelty and/or inventive step are the most common observations, third-party observations may also be directed to clarity (Art. 84), sufficiency of disclosure (Art. 83), patentability (Art. 52(2) and (3), 53 or 57) and unallowable amendments (Art. 76(1), 123(2)).[45] The observations can be filed anonymously and are entered into the prosecution file and considered by the EPO. It is a form of public participation in the EPO proceedings. However, the filing person does not become a party to the proceedings and is thus excluded from the oral proceedings before the examining division, which are not public. This contrasts with post-grant opposition proceedings, wherein the opponent is a party to the proceedings and obtains thereby the right to be heard before any decision is taken. If someone wants to stay anonymous or if he cannot file his own opposition because the opposition period has lapsed, this party can at least file observations during pending opposition proceedings.[46]

1.8. Upcoming: Unitary Patent (UP)

Two European regulations adopted on December 17, 2012 will establish the UP. The first deals with the general framework of the UP (the UP Regulation),[47] and the second

45. Guidelines for Examination in the EPO-Part E, V-3.
46. EPO—G 9/91
47. Regulation (EU) No. 1257/2012 of the European Parliament and of the Council of Dec. 17, 2012 implementing enhanced cooperation in the area of the creation of unitary patent protection.

relates to the translation arrangements (the Translation Regulation).[48] Two regulations were necessary as higher voting thresholds are required for changes to translation arrangements. Regulations have direct effect in all Participating EU Member States and accordingly do not require any further national implementing measures to be taken by the States. Nevertheless, both regulations will only apply after the UPC Agreement (UPCA) comes into force.

1.8.1. General Remarks

Patent applicants will be able to request that their European patents have "unitary effect" across the participating EU Member States, rather than having a bundle of national patents, as is the case for ordinary European patents. The EPO will be in charge for that UP. According to Article 18 UP Regulation, UP protection may be requested for any European patent granted on or after the date of application of the Regulation. The request for unitary effect must be filed at the EPO no later than one month after the grant of the European patent.[49]

The granting proceedings through the EPC will essentially be the same for ordinary European and unitary patents (UPs). Article 1(2) and Recitals 6 and 16 of the UP Regulation classify the UP Regulation itself as a "special agreement" within the meaning of Article 142 EPC and implement the unitary patent under Part IX of the EPC. This section of the EPC contains provisions that were conceived in the 1970s in connection with the Community Patent Convention, which was however never ratified. In the past, such a "special agreement" was concluded between Switzerland and Liechtenstein.[50]

The basic idea underlying Part IX of the EPC is aimed at establishing a European patent to which unitary character is given in the post-grant stage. Nevertheless, the patent application process which precedes for a unitary patent follows the same granting rules than those applicable to for ordinary European patents. Likewise, opposition proceedings under Article 99 EPC and limitation and revocation proceedings under Article 105a *et sqq* EPC are available for unitary patents.

48. Regulation (EU) No. 1260/2012 of the European Parliament and of the Council Dec. 17, 2012 implementing enhanced cooperation in the area of the creation of unitary patent protection with regard to the applicable translation arrangements
49. Article 9(1) (g) UP Regulation
50. Patent Treaty of December 22, 1978.

Table 4.2. Comparison: Unitary Patent/Ordinary European Patent

	Unitary Patent	*Ordinary European Patent*
Pre-grant	Prosecution in compliance with the EPC	
Post-grant	Opposition proceedings in compliance with the EPC	
	Unitary protection in all Participating Member States	Protection in individually designated EPC Member States (bundle of national patents)
	Jurisdiction: UPC	Jurisdiction: During transitional period: UPC or national courts, if opted-out: Only national courts. After transitional period: UPC

1.8.2. Territorial Scope of a Unitary Patent

The proprietor of a European patent will have, within a month deadline after grant, the opportunity to file a request for unitary effect (Art 3(1) UP Regulation). He must choose whether to opt for unitary protection rather than to validate the patent on a country-by-country basis. If the formal requirements are met, the European patent then will benefit from unitary effect in those Participating Member States in which the Unified Patent Court is operating (Art 18(2) UP Regulation). These are the Participating Member States, which have ratified the UPC Agreement, when the patentee makes its request for unitary effect. For all other states, the proprietor of a European patent must validate the patent on a country-by-country basis if he wishes protection through a European Patent there. This particularly applies to EPC states which do not belong to the group of the EU states of the enhanced cooperation, such as Switzerland or Turkey and those states which are members of the enhanced cooperation but have not yet ratified the UPC Agreement, when the patent proprietor requests unitary treatment. The territorial scope of the unitary patent thus will depend on how many Participating States have ratified the UPC Agreement at the moment when the proprietor of the European patent files the request for unitary effect.

1.8.3. Ordinary European Patents versus Unitary Patents

Unitary protection is just an option. Ordinary European patent protection remains part of the system and is of importance in those states where unitary protection will not be obtainable. A main difference between both types of patents arises from the rule that UPC has exclusive jurisdiction over a unitary patent, whereas the proprietor of an ordinary European patent may sue in either a national court or the UPC during a transitional period of seven years (which may be prolonged to 14 years). During the transitional period the owner is even entitled to exclude his ordinary European patent from the jurisdiction of the UPC by "opting out" of unitary treatment (*see* Chapter "Opt-out").

1.8.4. Costs of the UP

The UP may reduce translation costs, although in many of the key countries these have already been eliminated by the London Agreement. Article 12 of the UP Regulation describes certain conditions that should be taken into account when setting the level of renewal fees, providing *inter alia*, that they should be progressive, cover the costs of the system and should take into account the situation of specific entities such as small and medium-sized entities. The "Select Committee" of the EPO's Administrative Council endorsed on June 24, 2015 the so-called True Top 4 proposal. Accordingly, the proposed fees will correspond to the sum total of the renewal fees currently paid for the four countries in which ordinary European patents are most frequently validated, namely Germany, France, UK and the Netherlands.

1.8.5. EPO Oppositions

A UP can be opposed through EPO opposition proceedings. As noted, the EPC is applicable to the UP. There is little difference to opposition proceedings based on ordinary European patents so the following rules apply.

1.8.5.1. Nine Months Window

Within nine months of publication of the grant of a UP, anyone is entitled to file opposition proceedings with the EPO.[51] After this nine-month period, parties seeking to invalidate the patent must refer to:

- the UPC in the case of a UP
- either to the UPC or national invalidation proceedings in cases of ordinary European patents. National invalidation proceedings will be available according to a transitional regime of the Agreement ("Opt-out").

Resorting to national invalidation proceedings is usually more time consuming and may lead to inconsistent results as the patent could be found valid in some countries and invalid in others. This will not be the same in revocation proceedings before the UPC, which has effect in the territories covered by the European patent.[52]

1.8.5.2. Opponent

Any person except the patentee may file opposition proceedings. A company or person who does not want to be identified in these proceedings may involve a "straw man"

51. Article 99 EPC.
52. Article 34 UPCA.

that acts in its own name but on behalf of the third party. This is a common strategy employed by companies that do not want to appear as a party in the proceedings. This is acceptable provided the straw man is not used by the patentee to file an opposition against its own patents. There is presently no reason to believe that such a strategy will not be possible with respect to the UP.

1.8.5.3. No Estoppels

Opposition proceedings are held before the EPO's Opposition Divisions, which are distinct from the Examining Divisions. Opponents therefore get a fair chance in *inter partes* proceedings to have the patent re-examined, even if the invalidation challenges are based on documents that were already considered during the examination. Furthermore, an opponent is not estopped from reasserting the same arguments later in a national court or at the UPC. The fact that particular arguments had been raised and lost in EPO opposition proceedings must not necessarily influence the judges of the UPC.

1.8.5.4. UP Court (UPC)

In contrast with the current situation of having to litigate on a country-by-country basis, the UPC will have the authority to grant EU-wide injunctions, damages and other relief. In addition, freedom to operate across the European Union will be obtainable by a single set of invalidity or non-infringement proceedings. Among certain other disputes, the UPC will have jurisdiction to decide over infringement and revocation of:

- Unitary Patents[53]
- Ordinary European patents[54]
- SPCs granted under Regulation (EC) 469/2009[55] (certificate for medicinal products) or Regulation (EC) 1610/96[56] (certificate for plant protection products).

Unitary Patents always fall under the exclusive jurisdiction of the UPC, whereas a particular regime applies to ordinary European patents (the "Opt-Out System").

53. Article 3(a) of the UPCA.
54. Article 3(c) of the UPCA.
55. Regulation (EC) No. 469/2009 of the European Parliament and of the Council of May 6, 2009 concerning the supplementary protection certificate for medicinal products, (OJEU L 152, 16.6.2009, p. 1) including any subsequent amendments.
56. Regulation (EC) No. 1610/96 of the European Parliament and of the Council of Jul. 23, 1996 concerning the creation of a supplementary certificate for plant protection products, (OJEC L 198, 8.8.1996, p. 30) including any subsequent amendments.

1.8.6. "Opt-Out"

1.8.6.1. Wait & See

For ordinary European patents a wait-and-see approach can be taken. Article 83 of the Agreement provides for a transitional period of seven years, which can be extended a further seven years by the Administrative Committee, during which time, actions as to ordinary European patents may still be brought before national courts.[57]

The competence of the UPC is not exclusive during that transitional period; instead it co-exists alongside the competence of national courts. This means that during the transitional period, actions based on ordinary European Patents can be filed either with the UPC or national courts. To ensure that revocation actions cannot be filed with the UPC, patentees must pro-actively opt-out from the UPC's competence by means of a notification to the Register as stipulated in Article 83(3) Agreement.

Opting out is not possible if an action has already been brought before the UPC. Rule 5.7 of the RoP clarifies that even if the action has already been concluded, an opt-out from the UPC jurisdiction would be impossible. Accordingly, such action creates for the lifetime of the patent or patent application an absolute bar to opt-out. The stipulation is aimed at preventing conflicting judgments of the UPC and of national courts. This opens the possibility of strategic revocation actions filed by third parties as the system goes live, with the intention of blocking the opt-out system. Conversely, patent applicants should not miss the opportunity to file an opt-out notification if revocation proceedings filed by third parties at the UPC are not wanted. The applicant may still withdraw its opt-out notification later.[58] However, according to Rule 5.9 a withdrawal of an opt-out (opt-in) is no longer possible once an action has been commenced in a national court. The withdrawal is even ineffective after the action has been concluded.

1.8.6.2. Sunrise Period

There is a sunrise period for for right holders to file opt-out notices. It shall start from a date to be announced by the European Patent Office and it will end with the coming into effect of the Agreement. During that period the European Patent Office will collect opt-out applications. The idea behind this provision is that all patent proprietors should have the possibility to opt out without being endangered of being stopped from doing so just because a third party commences a proceeding before the UPC beforehand and triggers the permanent bar for changing the jurisdiction (Art. 83(3) UPCA)

57. Article 83(1) UPCA.
58. Article 5 (8) Rules of Procedure (RoP).

1.8.6.3. Scope

A few commentators have questioned the understanding of the term "exclusive competence" in Article 83(3) Agreement. During the first seven years, the UPC does not have an "exclusive" jurisdiction over ordinary European patents. Article 83(1) Agreement instead refers to a parallel jurisdiction that co-exists alongside the jurisdiction of national courts. It has consequently been argued that the applicant may in fact opt-out from exclusivity, but not from all jurisdiction, of the UPC. The provision is therefore ambiguous. Incomplete opting-out would not comply with the intentions of the Agreement, which obviously advises that the opt-out removes all jurisdiction from the UPC in respect of ordinary European patents. This is also the opinion of the Drafting Committee.[59]

1.8.6.4. Use of Divisionals

Ordinary European patents (and national patents) will co-exist with Unitary Patents in the future. Consequently, patent applicants do not necessarily have to put their European patents under the jurisdiction of the UPC by requesting the unitary effect for their European patents. It is possible to strategically divide a patent portfolio in two groups: one group that is subject to the new court system, and a second group that is handled by national systems. For that (only) purpose, divisional applications could be branched off from parent applications.[60]

1.8.6.5. Opt-Out Fee

There will be no fee to opt out of the jurisdiction of the future UPC.[61] This was decided in a meeting of the UPC Preparatory Committee on February 24 and 25, 2016 in Brussels.

2. GERMAN PATENTS

2.1. General Remarks

German patents are granted by the GPTO. Because they are enforceable only in Germany, patents originated through prosecution proceedings at the GPTO have been

59. Note to Article 5 Rules of Procedure: "*The Drafting Committee would like to note, in response to certain written comments received, that the provisions of Article 83 of the Agreement for opting out are clear and provide for:*
  (i) a complete ousting of the jurisidiction of the UPC;
  (ii) such ouster is, subject to Rule 5.6, 5.8, for the life of the relevant patent/application including the time after the patent has expired, has lapsed or has been withdrawn; and
  (iii) covers all designations owned by the proprietor(s) in question."
60. Article 76 EPC.
61. Rules on UPC Court Fees and Recoverable Costs: Report of the 14th Preparatory Committee Meeting.

of lesser importance for international applicants than have patents obtained through the EPO. Even though the European and national patent laws are broadly harmonized, there are a few differences between proceedings at the EPO and the GPTO.

If and when the Unified Patent Court is fully authorized, German (and other national) patents may have significantly greater importance. One reason for this is that German patents will be excluded from the jurisdiction of the UPC. Thus, while potential infringers may find it advantageous to attempt to invalidate patent rights on a pan-European basis through the UPC, this option will not be available for attacking patents issued through the German Patent Office. This exclusion for German patents will be permanent, unlike the limited "transitional" period of time for patents issued from the EPO, for which an "opt out" period will be available. Ordinary European patents can be opted out from the UPC's jurisdiction during the transitional period of Article 83 UPCA.[62] At least during the transitional period the owner of an ordinary European will thus be entitled to exclude it from the jurisdiction of the UPC and would not be required to use national patents in order to be sheltered from the UPC. The situation changes as soon as the transitional period expires when an opt-out cannot be exercised anymore. At that point, ordinary European patents will fall under the jurisdiction of the UPC. It remains to be seen whether this change will increase the importance of national patents.

2.2. Procedure in General

The language of the patent prosecution proceedings through the GPTO is necessarily German. Nevertheless, a German patent application can be filed in any other language provided a translation is submitted within three months from its filing date (§35 Patent Act). This applies to subsequent and direct applications. This allows applicants to obtain a filing date that is not delayed due to the time necessary for translating the application into German.

In contrast to some other European countries, the granting proceedings at the GPTO include a substantive examination of the application. This does not apply to German utility models, which are not examined as to their substance. German utility models are discussed further below.[63]

During a first phase of the grant proceedings, the GPTO carries out an examination as to whether the application displays obvious deficiencies. In contrast to the proceedings at the EPO, the subsequent substantive examination of the application can be delayed by the applicant's filing of an examination request up to seven years after the filing date (§44(2) German Patent Act). This is an advantage particularly for small- and medium-sized companies and also an interesting option for larger companies, if it is not known how the invention will be implemented in practice. In compliance with general standards, the application is published after the expiry of 18 months from the filing date or the earliest priority date. However, interested third parties may file an

62. *See* Chapter 4, s. 1.8.6.
63. *See* Ch. 4, s. 3.

examination request on behalf of the applicant.[64] Decisions rendered by examination sections of the GPTO during the examination proceedings can be appealed to the Federal Patent Court in Munich (§73(1) German Patent Act).

2.3. Amendments

Amendments of the application are possible after filing the examination request (§38 Patent Act). As is the case with European patent applications, applicants are not permitted to add new subject matter when amending a patent application ("inadmissible extensions").[65] However, although the legal standards are the same, in practice, German case law tended to be more lenient so that it was often easier to introduce amendments in German proceedings. According to recent decisions of the Federal Supreme Court,[66] it seems however that Germany is aligning its case law with the case law of the EPO's Boards of Appeal.[67] The question of what is added subject matter depends on the content of the original disclosure. To determine the informative content of the original disclosure it is crucial to determine those statements belonging to the same technical teaching. Accordingly, it is prohibited to regroup features from different parts of the disclosure if they do not belong to the same technical concept. There must be a sufficient relationship between these features, otherwise the amendment would be considered as new subject matter that would endanger the grant of the patent and could later lead to its revocation.[68] The Federal Supreme Court[69] ruled that the original disclosure only comprises information which is "clearly and unambiguously" derivable for a person skilled in the art. Information resulting from farther reaching conclusions, which the skilled person might only draw on the basis of his technical knowledge or through modifications of the technical teaching disclosed, constitutes, by contrast, subject matter which extends beyond the original disclosure.

2.4. Divisional Applications

During all stages of the grant procedure, divisional applications may be filed (§39 German Patent Act). The only requirement is that the parent application remains pending and that the grant procedure be not yet finally concluded. The divisional application enters the same procedural stages as the related parent application, meaning that if the parent application is already examined the divisional application

64. Federal Patent Court, BPatGE 15, 134, GRUR 1974, 80: The third party must not demonstrate a reason for the application. However, the third party does not become a party to the proceedings.
65. Article 123(2) EPC: "The European patent application or European patent may not be amended in such a way that it contains subject-matter which extends beyond the content of the application as filed."
66. Federal Supreme Court, decision of Jul. 8, 2010, Xa ZR 124/07, GRUR 2010, 910, "Fälschungssicheres Dokument"; Federal Supreme Court, BGHZ 179, 168, GRUR 2009, 382, "Olanzapin."
67. Cf. EPO—T 0687/05.
68. BPatGE 3, 48, 52.
69. Federal Supreme Court, decision of Jul. 8, 2010, Xa ZR 124/07, GRUR 2010, 910, "Fälschungssicheres Dokument"; Federal Supreme Court, BGHZ 179, 168, GRUR 2009, 382, "Olanzapin."

will be considered to be in the examination phase. The divisional application is entitled to the filing date and applicable priority dates of the parent application (§39(1) German Patent Act). Hence, the expiration term of a divisional application will be calculated from the date of filing of the parent application and not from the filing date of the divisional application. Of course, it is not possible to add new subject matter to a divisional application. Similar to European divisional applications, the parent and divisional application shall not claim the same subject matter to avoid double patenting.[70] Nevertheless, it is acceptable if the independent claim in the parent application includes all the features of an independent claim of the divisional application which is combined with an additional feature.

2.5. Opposition Proceedings

Opposition proceedings against a German Patent may be filed by third parties within nine months[71] after the publication of the grant of the patent (§59 German Patent Act). After expiration of the opposition period a nullity action can be filed.[72] In comparison to opposition proceedings a nullity action is more expensive. Decisions in opposition proceedings are rendered by so-called Patent Divisions of the GPTO and can be appealed to the Federal Patent Court in Munich. As indicated, the same applies to decisions against the Examination Sections (§73(1) German Patent Act).

3. GERMAN UTILITY MODELS (*GEBRAUCHSMUSTER*)

3.1. Main Characteristics of German Utility Models

German utility models are a unique form of intellectual property protection. They function somewhat as a "baby patent," through a swift and inexpensive registration process. Like German patents, German utility models are and will be forever excluded from the future UPC jurisdiction. They confer rights similar to a patent, i.e., cease and desist claims, damage claims, claims to render account, and even destruction claims. Used in tandem with other forms of intellectual property, utility models can be a powerful part of a patent portfolio.

Utility models provide protection only for product claims, including claims that are focused on substances, such as pharmaceuticals. Utility models cannot be used to protect method or use claims (§2 N° 3 Utility Model Act), but the case law of the Federal Supreme Court seems to be rather flexible with this exception, which is detailed below.[73]

70. *Ibid.*
71. The opposition period has been extended from three to nine months by law amendment of Oct. 19, 2013 with effect from Apr. 1, 2014.
72. *See* Ch. 7, "Nullity Actions."
73. Chapter 4, s. 3.4 "Protectable Subject Matter."

The process of obtaining a German utility model is uncomplicated. The GPTO registers these rights within two to three months without examination as to novelty or inventive step. Similar to a German patent application, a utility mode can be filed in any language provided a German translation is submitted within a three month period from its filing date (§4(b) Utility Model Act).The validity of a German utility model can later be challenged by cancellation proceedings filed with the GPTO (§15 Utility Model Act). A special utility model division has jurisdiction to decide on the validity of the utility model in *inter partes* proceedings. Its decisions can be appealed to the Federal Patent Court (§18(1) Utility Model Act) and in exceptional circumstances a further appeal is possible to the Federal Supreme Court.

3.2. Different Protection Standards

A particular advantage of utility models is that the novelty standards are different compared with patents.

Of particular interest is a six-month grace period from the disclosure of the invention (§3(1) of German Utility Act), which would ordinarily preclude filing of patent applications. Publications or use within six months preceding the date relevant for the priority of the application shall not be taken into consideration if it is based on the conception of the applicant or his predecessor in title. Thus, where there has already been a barring disclosure for patent applications, an applicant may still be eligible to receive a German utility model.

Furthermore, prior public use of an invention is not a barring act for purposes of utility models if the prior public use occurred outside Germany, as provided in §3(1) of the German Utility Act. However, written publications made in and outside Germany represent relevant prior art.

Moreover, even if the invention has been the subject of European or German patents, an applicant may still receive a utility model without prohibition from double patenting rules. Thus, in some circumstances utility models may be the best, or only, option for protecting inventions in Germany.

Up until recently, the main hurdle in utility models was novelty, rather than inventiveness. This has been changed by a landmark decision of the German Federal Supreme Court, in which the court ruled that an invention protected by a utility model needed, like a regular patent, to feature an inventive step.[74]

3.3. Registration of a German Utility Model

A utility model application may be filed like any regular patent application, either without claiming a priority, or within the priority year by claiming priority of a previously filed application (§6 of the German Utility Model Act). The GPTO registers a utility model without examining its novelty or inventive step, and without

74. Federal Supreme Court, decision of Jun. 20, 2006, X ZB 27/05, “Demonstrationsschrank.”

examination of whether or not the application documents are supported by, or originally disclosed in, the parent application documents as filed.

3.4. Protectable Subject Matter

Utility model protection is possible for all product claims including claims that are directed to substances or pharmaceuticals. According to §§1(2) and 2 of the German Utility Model Act, the following subject matter is excluded from utility model protection:

- discoveries, scientific theories and mathematical methods;
- aesthetic creations;
- schemes, rules and methods for performing mental acts, games, business methods, and programs for computers;
- presentations of information;
- inventions which violate public policy or the public order;
- plant species and animal species; and
- methods.

Although no examination is carried out by the GPTO with regard to novelty and inventive step, a formal examination is indeed carried out prior to registration to make sure that no subject matter is registered that falls under the above-mentioned exclusions.

With respect to method claims that generally cannot be the subject matter of a German utility model, a few important decisions of the Federal Supreme Court illustrate that "use" or "method" elements in claims may be permissible in certain circumstances. First the Federal Supreme Court ruled that utility model protection could be sought for the use of a substance for the treatment of a disease insofar as claims would at least contain elements of a product claim, namely a drug.[75] Accordingly, the use of a known substance for a medical indication can be subject to a utility model. The Federal Supreme Court referred in its ruling to the conclusions of the German legislature when enacting the German Utility Model Act in 1986 and concluded that the legislature did not exclude from the act use claims in the context of medical indications. Furthermore, product claims containing method features may be permitted insofar as the involved method features give an indication to the skilled person whether and how structural features of a product have to be implemented according to the teaching of the invention.[76] Accordingly, product-by-process claims are not excluded from being protected by a utility model.

75. Federal Supreme Court X ZB 7/03, GRUR 2006, 135, "Arzneimittelgebrauchsmuster."
76. Federal Supreme Court, X ZR 188/01, GRUR 2005, 749, "Aufzeichnungsträger."

3.5. Reasons for Filing a Utility Model

3.5.1. *Low Fees and Prosecution Costs*

The fees for applying for a utility model are very low. Currently, the fees are as follows:

- Filing fee: EUR 40
- First renewal fee after three years: EUR 210
- Second renewal fee after six years: EUR 350
- Last renewal fee after eight years: EUR 530

Accordingly, the fees for a utility model until the end of its life are slightly above 1,000 Euros. Because the utility model is registered without examination, there are no prosecution costs. Furthermore, a utility model application provides a priority right under the Paris Convention that can be used for subsequent applications in Member States of the Paris Convention. That is, the financial investment for the prosecution of full patents in signatory countries to the Paris Convention can be postponed by means of a utility model application.

3.5.2. *Early Publication of the Invention*

In a few circumstances, the inventor may be interested to have his invention published as soon as possible so that the application documents become part of the relevant prior art under German and European standards. A German utility model is an inexpensive and fairly uncomplicated way to make the invention available to the public on the date of registration with the benefit of a priority right. This usually occurs two to three months after the filing of the application. Accordingly, the content of a utility model constitutes prior art relevant to novelty and inventive step from the date of its registration. This publication occurs earlier than the publication of a patent which is usually published eighteen months after the date of filing or, if priority has been claimed, from the date of priority.[77]

3.5.3. *Earlier Enforceability*

The utility model applicant obtains an enforceable right from the day of its registration. He can sue the accused infringer on the basis of the utility model and may achieve the goal of stopping him more quickly, even though it may still take considerable time until a parallel patent is granted. Thus, utility models can provide a powerful mechanism for blocking early entrance of infringing products into the market, while awaiting issuance of patents through the EPO or GPTO.

77. Article 93 (1)(a) EPC.

3.5.4. *Damages*

The utility model applicant can claim damages as soon as the utility model has been registered. The registration of the utility model can thus trigger the accrual of damages without having to wait for issuance of a patent or the publication of a pending application. Moreover, the damages accruing based on the registered utility model may be higher than the provisional remedies that would pertain based on publication of a pending patent application. The heightened damages based on registration of a utility model are illustrated below, as compared with the compensation that would be due based only on the publication of a pending patent application (*see* Figure 4.3 below).

Figure 4.3. Early Damage Claim Due To Utility Model Protection

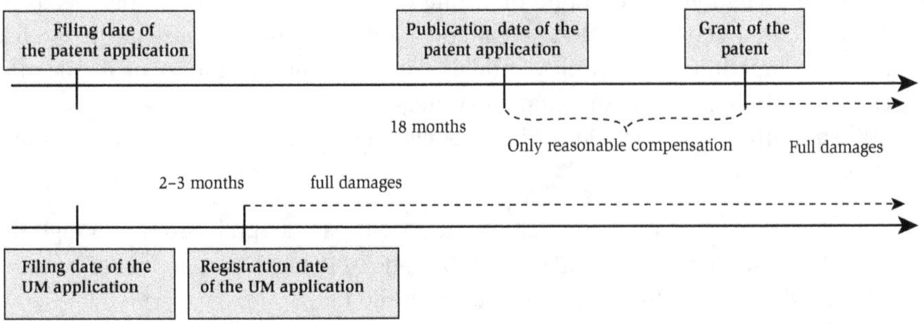

3.5.5. *Strategic "Branching Off"*

3.5.5.1. *General Remarks*

A strategic benefit of utility models is that they may be "branched off" from an earlier German, European or PCT application (§5 of the German Utility Model Act). Such branching off is admissible up to the expiration of two months from the end of the month in which processing of the patent application or any opposition procedure is terminated. Because of the shortened 10-year term of utility models, filing the "branched off" utility model must occur by the end of the tenth year from the date of filing of the earlier patent application. Normally, there must be a pending patent application to branch off a utility model because it cannot be branched off from a granted patent. An exception to this rule occurs if an opposition proceeding is commenced (under either the EPO or GPTO), at which point the patentee regains the opportunity to branch off a utility model during the pendency of the opposition.

The branched-off utility model is accorded the priority and filing date of the parent patent application insofar as the claims are supported by the earlier patent application.

3.5.5.2. Tailoring Claims in View of the Infringing Embodiment

An applicant may recognize that the claim language of an existing patent application could be improved with regard to infringing embodiments of a competitor. Utility models can be a powerful tool in this situation. By branching off a German utility model with refined claim language to more closely track a competitor's products, a patentee can continue to adapt to developments in the market.

3.5.5.3. Claim Sets for German Utility Models in Case of an Infringement

The applicant may even branch off several utility models, and assert them against a competitor. The only requirement is that the claims of these applications be somehow different when compared with each other. It might be possible to claim different aspects of an invention, or to define the same invention from different perspectives. The patentee can assert the granted patent and additionally one or more utility models against the competitor. Thus, utility models can help build a thicket of intellectual property rights to bolster an enforcement strategy

When drafting claim sets for utility models, the following considerations should be noted:

- The claims must be supported by the parent patent application, although the related standards of the GPTO and the Federal Patent Court appear to be more flexible than the formalistic approach of the EPO.
- The subject matter of the utility model claims should be novel and inventive in view of the known prior art.
- Principles of claim construction, discussed below in Chapter 10, should be taken into account.

Figure 4.4. Branching Off

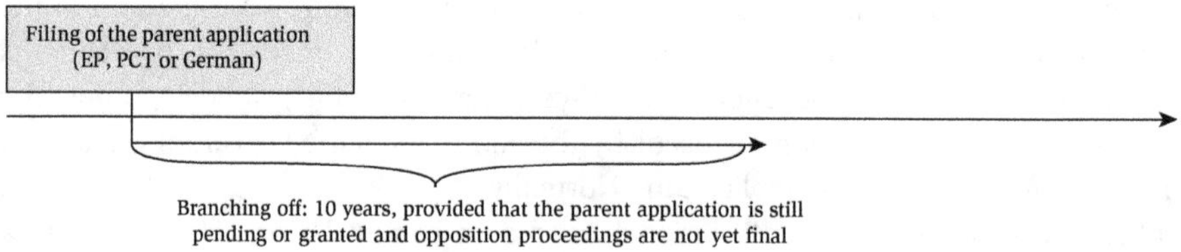

Table 4.3. Main Characteristics of Utility Models

Registration proceedings	No substantive examination. Can be branched off from PCT, EP or German patent application. Early publication and enforceability of the invention through registration.
Protectable subject matter	Product claims are possible. Use and method claims are in principle not allowed.
Prior art	Grace period of six months; public prior use only relevant if occurred within German territory.
Judicial Enforcement	Immediately after registration possible. UM gives almost the same rights as a granted patent. UM can be used to tailor claims to the accused embodiment.
Damages	Relevant calculation period begins as soon as the UM is registered.
Official fees	Very low, about 1,000 Euros for the life of the UM.

4. DESIGN PROTECTION (DESIGN PATENT)

Consumers often associate a specific design with a manufacturer and its branding, sometimes with an entire product line. An industrial design may substantially contribute to the commercial value of a product, in addition to its technical features which might be protected by technical rights. Thus, designs may additionally bolster an enforcement strategy. In particular, they represent important tools for successful customs actions.[78]

4.1. General Remarks

By means of an industrial design (design patent) the outer appearance of a two-dimensional or three-dimensional product, article or part of it may be protected. Graphical symbols or typographic fonts are also possible subjects for an industrial design. It may protect devices, consumer goods, and parts intended for assembly into a complex product. The protection could even cover the packaging in which a patented product is marketed. An industrial design is a cost-efficient intellectual property right.

There are several ways of obtaining design protection. The first is through the Office for Harmonization in the Internal Market (OHIM), which provides for a Community Design Registration (CDR). This is a design patent providing legal effect on the whole internal market of the EU. It is a full-fledged community right, which can be

78. *See* Ch. 14.

enforced through one court for the whole market of the EU. The legal framework of the Community Design is mainly contained in the Community Design Regulation adopted on December 12, 2001[79] (CD Regulation).

National design patents can be obtained through the German Patent Office. This right is based on the German Industrial Design Act.[80] It complies with the Directive 98/71/EC of the European Parliament and of the Council of October 13, 1998.[81] The Directive is intended to harmonize the main rules governing industrial designs registered in the EU Member States, and the substantive requirements for obtaining protection through the (OHIM) or the German Patent Office are mainly the same. The European Community design protection provides almost immediate protection for the whole European Market.[82] As enforceable rights they can be used in border actions to prohibit the importation of infringing products onto the European or German market.[83]

4.2. Requirements for Design Protection

To be eligible for protection, a Community or German national design must be:

- "novel", i.e., a design must not have been disclosed anywhere in the world, before the filing or priority date, and
- have an "individual character."

(§2(1) German Industrial Design Act, Article 4(1) of the CD Regulation).

A design—i.e., the appearance of the whole or a part of a product resulting from the features of, in particular, the lines, contours, colors, shape, texture or materials of the product or its ornamentation—has individual character if the overall perception it produces on the informed user is distinguished from the overall perception generated by another design which has been previously made available to the public. In other words, the public must perceive that the new design is different from prior designs.

When assessing this individual character, the degree of freedom of the designer in developing the design shall be taken into consideration (§2(3) German Industrial Design Act, Article 6(2) CD Regulation). For example, the degree of freedom of a designer of a mobile phone can be less than the degree of freedom of a designer of a fashion handbag.

Accordingly, any physical form, such as technical devices, consumer goods or packages can be subject to design protection. For component parts, only those features

79. Council Regulation (EC) 6/2002 of Dec. 12, 2001 on Community Designs, the English text of the regulation can be found on the Website of the Office for Harmonization in the Internal Market: <http://oami.europa.eu>.
80. German Act on Copyright in Industrial Designs dated Mar. 12, 2004 (BGBl. I S. 390) in its version of Feb. 24, 2014 (BGBl. I S. 122).
81. The text can be found: <http://oami.europa.eu>.
82. Articles 81, 82 and 83 of the CD Regulation.
83. *See* Ch. 14.

that are visible in "normal use" of the product into which they are incorporated are eligible for design protection. Normal use does not include maintenance or repair work (Article 4(3) CD Regulation).

Registration will also not be available for designs that are dictated by the technical function of the product (§3(1) German Industrial Design Act, Article 8 CD Regulation). Despite the unregistrability of purely technically functional features, the law does not include any specific rigorous requirement that a design, to be registrable, must have aesthetic quality.

4.3. European Community Design

Community Design protection for all countries of the European Union can be obtained at the Office for Harmonization in the Internal Market (OHIM). One important aspect of the Community Designs Regulation is that design protection can also be obtained without any registration. Such unregistered community designs are however limited monopolies lasting three years from first disclosure in Europe. The absent registration may have significant implications in enforcing the unregistered design. The designer must prove the requirements for protection and the circumstances of the disclosure to the public if he wants to assert the unregistered right against a third party.

4.3.1. Registered Community Design (RCD)

The European Community Design has a grace period of 12 months for a party's own prior use and publication before the filing date or priority date (Article 7(2) of the CD Regulation). An RCD is an exclusive right for the outward appearance of a two- or three-dimensional product or part of it, resulting from the features (in particular, the lines, contours, colors, shape, texture and/or materials) of the product itself and/or its ornamentation. An RCD is valid in the European Union as a whole and may not be limited to certain Member States. It gives an exclusive right to use the design concerned and to prevent any third party from using it anywhere within the 27 Member States of the European Union. It prevents any third party from using the RCD without the consent of the holder. It initially has a life of five years from the date of filing and can be renewed in periods of five years up to a maximum of twenty-five years (Article 12 of the CD Regulation).

The rights cover, in particular, the making, offering, marketing, importing, exporting or use of a product in which the design is incorporated or to which it is applied, or holding stock of such a product for those purposes (Article 19 of the CD Regulation).

The RCD system consists of a simple registration procedure:

- a single application (may be filed at the OHIM, or at the German Patent Office);
- a single language of filing; and
- a single administrative center.

During the examination, the applications are checked mainly for formalities. This means that no search for novelty or substantive examination takes place. It is possible to file multiple applications (i.e., to include several designs in one application, such as a whole range of similar products) and keep the design confidential for up to 30 months (Article 50 of the CD Regulation).

A European Community design can be cancelled by means of a nullity proceeding at the OHIM. The invalidity of the design can also be asserted by an accused infringer as a counterclaim in enforcement proceedings (Article 81 of the CD Regulation).

4.3.2. *Unregistered Community Design*

An unregistered community design must meet the same requirements as a registered design. The design is protected for three years from the date on which it was first disclosed to the public within the EU Market (Article 11(1) CD Regulation). That disclosure may occur through prior marketing activities or publicity. While a registered community design is protected against both deliberate copying and the independent development of a similar design, an unregistered community design is limited to protection against deliberate copying.

4.4. German Industrial Design (*Geschmacksmuster*)

A German industrial design application can be filed with the GPTO in Munich. It also provides a grace period of 12 months for the claimant's own prior use and publication before the filing date or priority date. Further, the German Industrial Design Act provides an exhibition priority for presentations at exhibitions listed by the German Ministry of Justice in the Federal Law Gazette (§15 German Industrial Design Act).

Upon request the publication of German design can be deferred by up to 30 months from the filing date or priority date.

4.5. International Design (Hague System)

The Hague Agreement Concerning the International Deposit of Industrial Designs, a treaty administered by the WIPO, offers a procedure for an international registration.[84] An applicant may file a single international deposit either with WIPO or with the national office of a country which is party to the treaty. The design will then be protected in as many member countries of the treaty as the applicant wishes. Both the European Community and Germany are members of the Hague System and Hague Agreement, respectively. Thus, the European Community and Germany can be designated by an international design under the Hague System.

84. The full text of the Agreement can be found on the website of the WIPO.

CHAPTER 5

Patentability Standards

Patentability standards across Europe are largely harmonized under the EPC. Germany and the other national Member States have adopted patentability standards into their own laws that track the requirements of the European Patent Convention EPC. At the European level, the patentability standards are codified in the EPC, specifically in Article 52, which applies to all European patents, including those with unitary effect. For national German patents, the provisions of Section 1 *et seq.* of the German Patent Act[1] are applicable. Both sets of provisions have an identical content. Even though the laws are largely harmonized, there are practical differences in the application of these laws by the various tribunals charged with their implementation, including the EPO, the German Patent and Trademark Office GPTO, and the German courts. The laws define non-patentable subject matter, and moreover require that to be patentable a claimed invention must be novel, must involve an inventive step (similar to the concept of non-obviousness under U.S. law), and must be amenable to industrial application (Article 52(1) EPC, §1(1) of the German Patent Act). Moreover, like the U.S. requirements under 35 U.S.C. § 112, European laws require that the patent specification be sufficient to enable the patented invention (although there is no "best mode" requirement). These patentability requirements are discussed in turn below.

1. PATENTABLE SUBJECT MATTER

1.1. Classes of Non-inventions

European law defines patentable subject matter in the negative, by specifying classes of technologies for which no patent may be granted. Article 52(2) of the EPC and the corresponding Section 1(3) of the German Patent Act roughly correspond to the concept of unpatentable subject matter under U.S. law, with important differences that

1. An excerpt of the German Patent Act can be found in Ch. 17, s. 3.

have emerged in the wake of the United Supreme Court's ruling in *Alice v. CLS Bank* and its progeny. European law defines classes of abstract theories, mental acts, business methods, computer programs, etc., which are basically ineligible for patent protection. Article 53 of the EPC recites classes of inventions that may not be patented for other reasons of public policy.

The classes of non-inventions specified by Article 52(2) EPC[2] are as follows:

> (2) The following in particular shall not be regarded as inventions within the meaning of paragraph 1:
> (a) discoveries, scientific theories and mathematical methods;
> (b) aesthetic creations;
> (c) schemes, rules and methods for performing mental acts, playing games or doing business, and programs for computers;
> (d) presentations of information.

This list is not exhaustive.[3] The carve-out of these subject matters from patentability is itself sharply limited, however. The next provision of Article 52(3) EPC clarifies that such non-inventions are only excluded from patentability to the extent that the patent or patent application relates to it "as such":

> (3) Paragraph 2 shall exclude the patentability of the subject matter or activities referred to therein only to the extent to which a European patent application or European patent relates to such subject matter or activities as such.[4]

Accordingly, the exclusion from patentability only applies if the claimed invention is limited to a subject matter or activity mentioned in the negative list. When the claimed invention has a technical character apart from the listed subject matters or activities, the exclusion can be surmounted, because these items are only excluded "as such."[5] Generally, an invention is considered as satisfying the requirement of a technical character[6] when it provides technical teachings based on concrete instructions with a practical usefulness which can be repeatedly realized. This European approach is more accommodating than the *Alice* standard in the U.S. which has been widely applied to invalidate patents that may have a technical character, but which may not exceed the bounds of conventional technology. In Europe, as in the U.S., defining the contours of this allowable subject matter is a task that has been left to the patent offices and the courts, to allow flexibility in adapting to new technologies.[7] Below in section 1.2.2 is a list of examples of patent claims that have either survived, or failed, this patentability test.

2. Section 1(3) of the German Patent Act contains the same list.
3. Federal Supreme Court, GRUR 1969, 672, "rote Taube."
4. Section 1(4) of the German Patent Act.
5. EPO—T 154/04, "Duns."
6. EPO—T 1173/97; Federal Supreme Court, GRUR 2000, 1007, "Sprachanalyseeinrichtung."
7. Federal Supreme Court, GRUR 1969, 672, "rote Taube."

For instance, a mathematical method is not patentable, but an electrical filter designed in compliance with such a method would not be excluded from patentability. It is therefore generally acceptable to have a mix of technical and "non-technical" features appearing in a claim.[8] As non-technical features "as such" do not provide a technical contribution to the prior art, they are principally ignored in assessing novelty and inventive step.[9]

European law imposes further limits on patentable subject matter, whose purposes are rooted in matters of public policy and morality. Article 53 and Rule 28 of the EPC (§2 GPA) recites these additional classes of invention excluded from patentability, namely *inter alia*:

(a) inventions, the commercial exploitation of which would be contrary to "ordre public" or morality; such exploitation shall not be deemed to be so contrary merely because it is prohibited by law or regulation in some or all of the Contracting States;
(b) plant or animal varieties or essentially biological processes for the production of plants or animals; this provision shall not apply to microbiological processes or the products thereof;
(c) methods for treatment of the human or animal body by surgery or therapy and diagnostic methods practiced on the human or animal body; this provision shall not apply to products, in particular substances or compositions, for use in any of these methods.

The exclusion of inventions being contrary to the "ordre public" or morality is limited to extreme cases. The patent granting system is not equipped to easily determine whether a particular exploitation is prohibited by law or regulation in some or all Member States. Article 53(a) is not aimed at preventing illegal activities. The provision rather expresses a general consideration namely that those inventions that can only be used for purposes that the legal order disapproves[10]—that specifically endanger fundamental rules of the legal order—are excluded from patentability. Accordingly, a violation of the "ordre public" requires the violation of a "fundamental provision of the legal order"[11] such as the UN-Charter or the European Convention for the Protection of Human Rights and Fundamental Freedoms.[12] Furthermore, the exclusion may also apply to violations of more general legal prohibitions, such as crimes with a minimum custodial sentence of one year according to the Penal Code. Nevertheless, the exclusion from patentability requires that all thinkable exploitation possibilities would lead to the indicated violation. One possible disapproved exploitation (for instance, weapons, toxic substances, abortion means) is not sufficient to exclude the patentability as long as there are other possibilities to exploit the invention

8. EPO—T 154/04, "Duns."
9. EPO—T 154/04, "Duns," EPO—G 0003/08.
10. Federal Supreme Court, X ZB 22/71, GRUR 1973, 585 "IUP."
11. Federal Supreme Court BlPMZ 2003, 291, Euro-Bauklötze.
12. Rome, 4.XI.1950.

in a legal manner, even if it requires a regulatory authorization. Accordingly, case law concerning the exclusion for reasons of "ordre public" is rare. The same applies to violations of morality, which are also limited to extreme cases. A violation has been affirmed by the Federal Patent Court for a coffin evacuating oxygen to avoid the awakening of an apparently dead person.[13] Such exceptional situations could also arise in the case of very dangerous, cruel or insidious weapons, as well as dangerous or medically disapproved agents. The same applies if the only purpose of the invention is a criminal offense aimed at the protection elementary rights, such as an invention concerning the construction of a letter bomb.

Further exclusions can be found in Rule 28 of the EPC (and its corresponding §2(2) Patent Act, i.e., Rule 28: (a) *cloning human beings*, Rule 28; (b) *modifying the germ line genetic identity of human beings*, Rule 28; (c) the *use of human embryos* and Rule 28; (d) *torture breeding of animals*.

1.2. Computer-Implemented Inventions

The EPC does not contain a positive definition of the term "invention." Instead it provides a list of subject matter that is not considered to qualify for an "invention." These non-inventions are listed in Article 52(2) EPC. Their subject matter do not, according to an established judicial practice of the EPO and the German Courts, have a "technical character" or, more precisely, they do not involve a "technical teaching" which instructs a skilled person to solve a particular technical problem using particular means. According to that established judicial practice, technical character is a basic criterion for an invention. Computer programs are listed among these non-inventions (52 (2) EPC),[14] as are "methods for doing business." However, Article 52 (3) EPC clarifies that this only counts to the extent that the patent claims such subject matter "as such." Accordingly, subject matter which includes a computer program is not necessarily excluded from patentability.[15]

Patent claims typically consist of a plurality of features, of which some features describe non-technical aspects and others have a technical character. The computer program might be loaded on a computer or data carrier. The storage means, or any other hardware component on which a computer program runs, may have a technical character. The assessment requires first an understanding of what is and what is not subject matter with technical character (1.2.2). The presence of only one technical feature within a feature combination might be sufficient to conclude that there is an invention. Nevertheless, the invention must additionally be amenable to industrial application, and novel and inventive. The presence of both non-technical and technical features impacts the assessment of novelty and inventive step. As described below the assessment requires a factual separation of technical and non-technical aspects in order to determine whether the invention is novel and inventive (section 1.2.2).

13. Federal Patent Court, decision of Jan. 15, 1971, 23W (pat) 248/70.
14. Section 1(3) of the German Patent Act contains the same list.
15. Federal Supreme Court, X ZB 16/00, GRUR 2002, 143 "Suche fehlerhafte Zeichenkette"; EPO—T 1173/97 (n° 5-7), "Computerprogrammprodukt I."

1.2.1. *Technical Character*

Whether the subject matter is patentable first depends upon the question whether the requirement of technicality is fulfilled—i.e., on whether the subject matter provides a technical solution to a technical problem based on technical considerations.[16] All features together are determinant of whether the claimed subject matter has a technical effect. The presence of a technical character is *sine qua non* for an invention.[17] The technical character must be determined without considering the prior art.[18] An invention in the meaning of Article 52(1) EPC simply requires "subject-matter having technical character" without regard to the prior art.[19] This determination of whether there is an invention is essentially separate from the three other requirements—novelty, inventive step and industrial application. The requirement of a "technical character" is usually fulfilled and there is an "invention" as soon as the subject matter involves a physical entity such as a computer, network, or another programmable apparatus, such as a mobile phone, or employs technical means.

Claimed subject matter which exclusively addresses a computer program is not excluded from patentability if, when executed by or loaded into a computer, it provides, or is capable of providing, a technical effect which goes beyond the normal physical interaction between software and hardware. The technical character must thus go beyond that self-evident effect—otherwise the exclusion in Article 52 for computer programs would be meaningless.[20] Nevertheless, allowable subject matter could be entirely resident within a computer. For instance, allowable subject matter would include making a computer run faster or more efficiently, to make the computer easier to use.[21] A technical effect provided by a computer program can thus be, for example, a reduced memory access time, a better control of a robotic arm or an improved reception and/or decoding of a radio signal. Hence, the technical effect does not necessarily have to be external to the computer on which the program runs;[22] reduced hard disk access time or an enhanced user interface could also be sufficient.[23] For instance, giving visual indications automatically about conditions prevailing in an apparatus or system might be sufficient as well.[24]

As indicated a concrete product or an apparatus consisting of a physical entity has per se a technical character. This applies in particular to computer-implemented inventions. They usually involve the use of a computer, computer network or other

16. Federal Supreme Court GRUR 2004, 667, "Elektronischer Zahlungsverkehr"; EPO—T 0931/95, "Steuerung eines Pensionssystems"; Federal Supreme Court Xa ZB 20/08, GRUR 2010, 613, "Dynamische Dokumentengenerierung."
17. EPO—T 641/00, "Two entities/COMVIK," OJ 7/2004, 356; Federal Supreme Court, decision of Dec. 18, 2012, X ZR 3/12, GRUR 2013, 275, n. 41, "Routenplanung"; Federal Supreme Court, decision of Jun. 30, 2015, X ZB 1/15, "Flugzeugzustand"; EPO—G 3/08.
18. EPO—T 154/04, "Duns Licensing."; EPO—T 1173/97; EPO—G 3/08.
19. EPO—T 258/03, "Hitachi."
20. EPO—T 258/03, "Hitachi."
21. EPO—T 928/03, "Konami, Video"; Federal Supreme Court GRUR 2002, 143, "Suche fehlerhafte Zeichenkette."
22. Federal Supreme Court, Xa ZB 20/08, GRUR 2010, 613, "Dynamische Dokumentengenerierung."
23. EPO—T 877/92, page 11, Reasons 4, to page 13, Reasons 5.
24. EPO—T 115/85 (OJ EPO 1990, 30), headnote 1.

programmable apparatus. If the subject matter refers, in addition, to such physical entities, usually the technical character cannot be denied. For instance, "a computer readable data storage medium" has the technical effect of being computer readable and of being capable of storing data. Also, features such as "server computer" or a "network" have a technical character. The same applies to methods and processes as long as they employ technical means explicitly set out in the claims. For instance, a method which is performed by means of a data storage system including a display would be an invention within the meaning of Article 52(1) EPC.[25] Accordingly any claimed subject matter with any explicit technical bearing is sufficient[26] to satisfy the first threshold of patentability for computer-implemented inventions. Non-inventions "as such" would typically represent purely abstract concepts devoid of any technical implications. Hence, it is even sufficient if only a partial aspect of the subject matter has a technical effect. The invention can thus also consist of a mixture of technical and non-technical features, even if the non-technical features form a dominating part of the subject matter.[27] Often at least a part of the claimed subject matter, which can even be of secondary importance, has technical character and there is consequently an invention.[28] Nevertheless, as previously indicated, the distinction of non-technical and technical aspects of an invention is particularly important for the assessment of the other technical patentability requirements (1.2.2).

1.2.2. Other Patentability Requirements

The assessment of whether the subject matter has a technical character is only the first step towards patentability. Article 52(2, 3) EPC and §1(3, 4) of the German Patent Act require that computer programs and computer-implemented inventions be susceptible of industrial application, be novel, and need to represent a non-obvious technical solution to a technical problem.[29]

As indicated in previous section 1.1, non-technical features, i.e., features from a field excluded from patentability, principally shall not be taken into account for the assessment of inventive step, unless they interact with the technical subject matter to solve a technical problem.[30] Non-technical features "as such" do not provide a technical contribution to the prior art and are thus ignored for the assessment of novelty and inventive step. In light of the negative list, it cannot be the application of the computer program itself on which the patentability is based but rather the solution

25. EPO—T 1143/06 "Data selection System."
26. Federal Supreme Court, Decision of Oct. 26, 2010, X ZR 47/07, Mitt. 2/2011, page 61, "Wiedergabe topographischer Informationen."
27. EPO—T 641/00, "Two identities/COMIVIK."
28. Federal Supreme Court, Feb. 24, 2011, X ZR 121/09, "Webseitenanzeige".
29. EPO—T 258/03.
30. Federal Supreme Court, BGHZ 159, 197, 205, "elektronischer Zahlungsverkehr"; Federal Supreme Court, X ZB 34/03, GRUR 2005, 143, 144, "Rentabilitätsermittlung"; Federal Supreme Court, X ZB 22/07, GRUR 2009, 479, "Steuerungseinrichtung für Untersuchungsmodalitäten;" Federal Supreme Court, decision of Dec. 18, 2012, X ZR 3/12, GRUR 2013, 275, n. 41, "Routenplanung"; Federal Supreme Court, decision of Jun. 30, 2015, X ZB 1/15, "Flugzeug-zustand"; EPO—G 3/08.

of a technical problem by means of a programmed computer.[31] Consequently, when assessing novelty and inventive step, the technical problem and its solution needs to be correctly identified with regard to the negative list of non-inventions.

It is often a difficult task to correctly separate the technical and non-technical aspects of the invention, in particular if they are hidden in a largely non-technical context. Even a non-technical feature may sometimes interact with technical elements and thus produce a technical effect, for instances if its application is relevant for the technical solution of a technical problem. To that extent it contributes to a technical effect and is thus not disregarded for the assessment of inventive step. In a landmark decision[32] the EPO describes the assessment as follows:

> *"An invention consisting of a mixture of technical and non-technical features and having technical character as a whole is to be assessed with respect to the requirement of inventive step by taking account of all those features which contribute to said technical character whereas features making no such contribution cannot support the presence of inventive step."*

In addition the EPO ruled in the same decision:

> *"Although the technical problem to be solved should not be formulated to contain pointers to the solution or partially anticipate it, merely because some feature appears in the claim does not automatically exclude it from appearing in the formulation of the problem. In particular where the claim refers to an aim to be achieved in a non-technical field, this aim may legitimately appear in the formulation of the problem as part of the framework of the technical problem that is to be solved, in particular as a constraint that has to be met."*

Accordingly, the assessment requires first the identification of the technical aspects of the invention in order to adequately formulate a technical problem, to apply the so called problem solution approach.[33] To allow an aim to be achieved in a non-technical field to appear in the formulation of the problem has the additional effect that non-technical aspects are consequently disregarded when assessing inventive step. Even though this approach looks simple, it often encounters the difficulty to correctly separate non-technical and technical aspects of the subject matter.

Subject matter which might be excluded from the assessment of novelty and inventive step may relate to features which are limited to abstract schemes for organizing commercial or administrative operations, business concepts, financial transactions or features which have only an aesthetic or cognitive effect.

In the following table are listed a few important cases concerning patentable or not patentable subject matter. Their full texts are available on the website of the EPO (www.epo.com). These decisions may also provide examples of technical and non-technical features. Examples of Patentable Subject Matter:

31. Federal Supreme Court, Xa ZB 20/08, 8 "Dynamische Dokumentengenerierung."
32. EPO—T 641/00, "Two identities/COMIVIK."
33. See Ch. 5, s. 4.2.

- **EPO—T 1194/97 (Philips/Data Structure Product):** Picture retrieval system comprising a record carrier on which functional data is recorded for synchronization of coded picture lines, line numbers and addresses.
- **EPO—T 1351/04 (Fujitsu/File search method):** Files search method by means of creating an index file containing management information to be used for searching a file.
- **EPO—T887/92 (HELP Facility):** User-friendly arrangement of the help facility of a computer program.
- **EPO—T 110/90**: Control items (e.g., printer control items) included in a text represented in the form of digital data which are characteristic for the text-processing systems in which they occur in that they are characteristic for the technical internal working of that system.
- **EPO—T 424/03 (Microsoft/Clipboard formats I):** Method in a computer system having a clipboard for performing data transfer of data in a clipboard format.
- **Federal Supreme Court,** decision of April 22, 2010 **(Dynamic Document Generation) Xa ZB 20/08)**: A method for dynamically generating structured documents on at least one host computer which communicates with a client.

Examples of Non-Patentable Subject Matter

- **EPO—T 258/03 (Hitachi/Auction method):** Method steps consisting of modifications to a business scheme (here: auction method) aimed at circumventing a technical problem.
- **EPO—T 154/04** (Duns Licensing Associates/Estimating sales activity): Method for estimating sales activity of a product at sales outlets.
- **EPO—T 0204/93:** Creation of concrete software written in a particular programmer language.
- **EPO—T 931/95** (PBS Partnership/Controlling pension benefits system): Methods involving economic concepts and practices of doing business even though technical means are used for that purely non-technical purpose and/or for processing purely non-technical information.
- **Federal Supreme Court,** decision of February 24, 2011, **X ZR 121/09, "Webseitenanzeige":** Method for generating a presentation for re-locating a webpage that has already been accessed, and which has been closed in the meantime.

Of course different patentability standards apply in the U.S. and thus a successful patent portfolio should account for the standards in these various jurisdictions.

1.3. Biotechnological Inventions

Biotechnology inventions represent another difficult aspect of defining patentable subject matter. According to Rule 26 EPC, these *"are inventions which concern a product consisting of or containing biological material or a process by means of which biological material is produced, processed or used."*

On July 30, 1998, the European Parliament and the Council of the EU promulgated the Biotechnology Directive on the legal protection of biotechnological inventions,[34] aimed at a consistent application of patent provisions and exclusions across the whole of the EU. On September 1, 1999, the Directive was adapted into the EPC, through Rules 26-34 EPC.[35] On January 21, 2005 the Biotechnology Directive was transposed into German law.[36] The belated transposition to German law was caused by many years of public debate in Germany. A main point of that debate concerned the absolute product protection of genes of human origin. As a result of the implementation of the Biotechnology Directive in German Law, a number of provisions of the German Patent Act have been amended or inserted. These provisions can be found in the Appendix of the present book.[37] The amendments to the existing Act are mainly aimed at making the patent provisions clearer and more specific. The wording has been largely copied directly from the Biotechnology Directive into the German Patent Act and mainly matches the provisions of the EPC.

Nevertheless, the German law on the patenting of human gene sequences or partial sequences, and the respective provisions of the EPC law are not completely identical. Whereas the EU Biotechnology Directive has been integrated into the EPC with the result that its provisions in principle allow absolute substance protection for human gene sequences, the German Patent Act limits such protection for the same subject matters. §1(a) Section 4 GPA, without counterpart in the EPC reads: (4) "if the object of the invention concerns a sequence or partial sequence of a gene, the structure of which is identical to the structure of a natural sequence or partial sequence of a human gene, its use, for which the industrial application is specifically described under subsection (3) must be included in the patent claim."[38] Thus according to §1 a (3) of the Patent Act, the industrial application of a sequence or a partial sequence of a gene must be disclosed in the patent application, together with an indication of the function performed by the sequence or a partial sequence. The quoted subsection 4 of the same provision further provides a mandatory requirement that if the subject matter of the invention is a sequence or partial sequence of a gene, the use for which the industrial application must be disclosed has to be incorporated into the patent claim. Thus, patent protection for human gene sequences needs to be limited to that particular use under German law. The EPC does not require such limitation to a particular use in the claim and may consequently provide a broader scope of protection, which seems to be more advantageous compared to the German situation.

The general allowability of biotechnology patents is provided in §1(2) German Patent Act and Rule 26(2) EPC.[39] However, an exclusion from patentability applies to "the human body at the various stages of its formation and development" (§1a (1)

34. Directive 98/44/EC, see OJ EPO 1999, 101, the text can be found on: http://eur-lex.europa.eu/.
35. www.epo.org.
36. BioPatG, Federal Gazette (BGBl. I 2005, 146).
37. See Ch. 17, ss. 2 and 3.
38. Unofficial translation.
39. The provision is contained in Ch. 17, s. 2.

German Patent Act and Rule 29 EPC). This provision of the German provision expressly includes "germ cells." On the other hand, "isolated elements" of the human body can be patented (§1a (2) German Patent Act and Rule 29(2) EPC). Furthermore, patents on human embryos, processes to clone human beings and the use of human embryos for industrial purposes are prohibited (§2 German Patent Act and Rule 28 EPC). The term "embryo" means any human ovum after fertilization, any non-fertilized human ovum into which the cell nucleus from a mature human cell has been transplanted and any non-fertilized human ovum whose division and further development have been stimulated by parthenogenesis constitute a "human embryo".[40] However stem-cell related inventions based on methods which do not destroy human embryos are not excluded from patentability under these provisions.[41] This complex body of law is beyond the scope of this book, and the reader is referred to many other excellent texts tracking this developing subject.[42]

2. NOVELTY

While the novelty requirement for patentability is common to the U.S. and Europe, important differences govern its application. Europe's "first-to-file" rules and its lack of a grace period for an inventor to seek patent protection after publicly disclosing his or her own invention are quite strict. But unlike the U.S., in Europe private disclosures, such as confidential commercial sales, do not bar patentability. The novelty requirement in Europe, set forth in Article 54(2) of the EPC, provides that the prior art for assessing novelty encompasses "everything made available to the public by means of a written or oral description, by use, or in any other way, before the date of filing of the European patent application." An identical provision is contained in the GPA, namely §3(1). Key issues relating to this requirement are discussed below.

2.1. The Absolute Novelty Rule and the First-to-File Principle

Patentability in Europe follows the "absolute novelty" rule. That is, everything that was made publicly available before the priority date of a patent application is relevant for assessing the novelty of an invention. It makes no difference where in the world the disclosure was made, or in which language. It is also irrelevant who made the disclosure. Even the applicant can destroy the novelty of his invention if he previously disclosed it to the public, in whatever form, in writing, orally, or over the Internet. This

40. European Court of Justice, decision of Oct. 18, 2011, C-34/10.
41. Federal Supreme Court, decision of Nov. 27, 2012, X ZR 58/07 "Neurale Vorläuferzellen II".
42. English literature (for example): IIC 2008, 638, Finding a "Common Morality Codex" for Biotech—A Question of Substance, Amanda Warren-Jones; IIC 2008, 511 Patenting of Pharmaceuticals—Still a Challenge?, Dieter R. Schneider; IIC 2008, 282 Biotechnological Patents in Europe—Functions of Recombinant DNA and Expressed Protein and Satisfaction of the Industrial Applicability Requirement, Rob J. Aerts; IIC 2007, 30 "The Scope of Gene Patent Protection and the TRIPS Agreement—An Exclusively Nondiscriminatory Approach? Tine Sommer; IIC 2006, 135, The Legal Protection of Plant-Biotechnological Inventions and Plant Varieties in Light of the EC Biopatent Directive, Eva Willnegger, Michael A. Kock, Susann Porzig.

rule is a frequent trap for scientists at universities who seek prompt disclosure of their discoveries to ensure scientific credit for being first. Unfortunately, such a presentation of their achievements at conferences or in scientific journals renders this information public. It becomes prior art and can be invoked by anybody against a patent application filed later by the scientist. There is generally no grace period that could help secure a patent in such a situation.

As a corollary to the absolute novelty rule, there is no exception for showing that a late applicant had nonetheless invented the subject matter before the barring disclosure. That is, Europe is a "first-to-file," not "first-to-invent," jurisdiction. In the vein of harmonizing this law, in 2013,[43] the U.S. changed their patent law from a first-to-invent to a first-to-file system

Even if the inventor had conceived an invention, and reduced it to practice, prior to the novelty-destroying disclosure, that prior work cannot save the patent. The right to a particular invention is, accordingly, with the person who first-filed the application, regardless of when the invention was made or that the invention has been made earlier by someone else. The decisive date is the filing date or the priority date of the application.

There are two exceptions to the absolute novelty rule, which may in exceptional circumstances allow a patent filing after a novelty-destroying disclosure. In these rare situations there is a grace period of six months to file the application (see the following section).

2.2. Non-prejudicial Disclosure

There are two exceptions to the general rule that there is no grace period. The first exception pertains if the disclosure has been made in one of the rare international exhibitions according to the Convention on International Exhibitions of 1928 (Article 55(1) b) EPC = §3(5) n° 2 German Patent Act). The short list of such exhibitions is publicly announced.

The second exception pertains in cases of "an evident abuse in relation to the applicant or his legal predecessor." Article 55(1) EPC or §3(5) provides that "a disclosure of the invention shall not be taken into consideration if it occurred no earlier than six months preceding the filing of the European patent application and if it was due to, or in consequence of an evident abuse in relation to the applicant or his legal predecessor." Such evident abuse concerns for instances cases in which the public obtained knowledge about the invention in violation of a legal of contractual duty vis-à-vis the inventor or his successors.[44] This is usually the case if the disclosure follows an illegal usurpation or represents a breach of contract, in particular if it occurs in violation of a Non-Disclosure Agreement (NDA), or if the disclosure is intentionally made to harm the inventor or his successor.[45]

43. The Leahy-Smith America Invents Act (AIA) signed on Sep. 16, 2011: Its central provisions went into effect on Mar. 16, 2013.
44. Report of the legal committee as to the IntPatÜG V 4 (para. 4), BlPMZ 76, 350.
45. EPO—T 0173/83, OJ 87, 465; EPO—T 0041/02.

Because there is only a six-month grace period in this circumstance, the inventor should react as soon as he becomes aware of the wrongful disclosure in order to benefit from the provision. The circumstance of the abusive disclosure must be proven by the party that relies on it, which is usually the inventor.[46] Given that the risk of wrongful disclosures is likely to increase along with the number of people with access to confidential information and the passage of time, an earlier patent application could potentially avoid this issue altogether.

In addition to these rare grace periods for seeking patent protection, the inventor may also obtain a German utility model in the event of a premature disclosure. The German Utility Model Act allows a six-month grace period for filing the utility model after the otherwise-barring disclosure (§3(1) Utility Model Act).[47] While the protection of a full patent would be unavailable, the ability to nonetheless obtain a utility model is a way to salvage some protections for an invention that was prematurely disclosed. Utility models are discussed in detail in Chapter 4.

2.3. Availability to the Public

A novelty-destroying disclosure requires "availability" to the public. It is sufficient if an unlimited group of people (not bound by confidentiality agreements) is objectively in a position to take notice of the disclosure.[48] In order to prove whether a disclosure was available to the public it is thus not necessary to prove that someone from the public actually took notice of the disclosure or the invention.

In case of a **written disclosure** with no publication date, it is necessary to show when the disclosure was made available to the public. If the publication date of a written disclosure such as a printed document, book, magazine or manual cannot be proven, it would not be considered as prior art. Accordingly, it is sufficient to show when a book or scientific journal, for example, was entered into a library database.[49] It would not be necessary to show in addition that a visitor to the library indeed took notice of the concerned book or scientific journal. As soon as a visitor would have been able to look into the book or journal the whole content of it is available to the public.[50] From a copyright or editor notice showing a date on the document is usually deduced in form of a *prima facie* proof that it was subsequently circulated and available from indicated date to the public. The *prima facie* proof can however be refuted if facts are demonstrated suggesting that there are doubts that the general assumption of such subsequent publication of the document indeed occurs.[51]

It is usually more difficult to prove the publication date of documents or any other means of disclosure, such as pictures, videos, etc., published in the Internet. The mere

46. Federal Patent Court, decision Mar. 17, 1987, Mitt. 88, 207.
47. See Ch. 17, s. 4.
48. Federal Supreme Court, X ZR 32/69, BlPMZ, 71, 230, customer prints.
49. EPO—T 0834/09.
50. EPO—T 0381/87 OJ 90, 213.
51. EPO—T 1384/05.

theoretical possibility of having access to it at a particular time was found insufficient.[52] Rather, a direct and unambiguous access to it for at least one member of the public must be shown. If the disclosure can be found by using one or more keywords related to the essence of its content by means of a search engine before the priority or filing date, it would not necessarily be sufficient to conclude that it was available to public. In addition it is necessary to show that it remained accessible at that URL for a period of time long enough for a member of the public to get access to the document.[53]

The state of the art is held to comprise everything made available to the public; this is not limited to written or oral descriptions, but also includes a public use of the invention, so-called public prior use. For instance, an invention contained in a machine which is exhibited at a trade show, becomes state of the art provided it was possible for a skilled person to recognize—or to infer on the basis of further information—the technical features and the functions of the exhibited machine to an extent which would have enabled him to reproduce the inventive teaching.[54] Commercial sales of an invention to the public will generally amount to a prior art disclosure, which will bar the patentability of that invention. However, if the invention is so hidden within the object being sold that a skilled person would not be able to recognize the invention then there may be a good argument that no barring act has occurred. But in general an object that has been made available to the public also discloses those features that are derivable from routine analytical measures without undue burden for the skilled person in the art (such as through a dismantling of a machine if the invention is hidden within a complex apparatus or by routine analytical test).[55] An incentive to carry out such tests must not be given.[56] The likelihood of analyzing such a prior sold product, and the degree of burden (i.e. the amount of work and time involved in carrying out such an analysis), is in principle irrelevant to the determination of what constitutes the state of the art. However, hidden features of a substance which might be identified through tests, but require the selection of specific test parameters, would principally not be considered public. To amount to a prior art disclosure, there must be a showing that a skilled person would be in a position to get reliable knowledge from the commercialization of the invention.

Furthermore, if an invention is a manufacturing method that could not be understood by a publicly available product, then the inventive method is not made available to the public by virtue of the product. The same may apply to computer-implemented inventions, namely where a computer program was publicly available, but it is not apparent to a skilled person how the program works by using it, assuming he has no access to the program itself and is unable to perform any reverse engineering.[57] Likewise if the invention is hidden in a complex assembly, so that the skilled

52. EPO—T 1553/06.
53. EPO—T 1553/06.
54. EPO—T 363/90.
55. EPO—G 1/92; EPO—T 2/09; Federal Supreme Court, X ZR 120/11, decision of Oct. 23, 2012, "Gelomyrtol".
56. Federal Supreme Court, X ZR 3/10, GRUR 2012, 1133, "UV-unempfindliche Druckplatte".
57. EPO—T 0461/88, OJ 93, 295; Federal Supreme Court, Xa ZR 149/07, GRUR 2011, 129, "Fentanyl-TTS"; Federal Supreme Court, X ZR 120/11, "Gelomyrtol".

person in the art would not expect the presence of it within the assembly, it is not a public disclosure. However, if the object shows interesting particularities, such as clear advantages vis-à-vis the prior art, it should be expected that a person skilled in the art would be motivated to investigate the reasons for these advantages.[58]

Of course the question of when a disclosure was made available to the public is subject to many disputes and requires an investigation of the specific circumstances. The party challenging the validity of a patent needs to prove the disclosure.

2.4. Determination of What is "Public"

To qualify as prior art, a disclosure must be made to the public. This is an important distinction from U.S. law, where confidential sales may amount to prior art disclosures. Under European law, disclosures made to a defined group of people would generally not render its content public if the group feels at least implicitly[59] engaged to keep the material secret and provided the material will not later be disseminated outside that group. Missing such implicit secrecy agreement, a technical descriptions sent to clients renders its content typically public.[60] However, a tacit obligation to maintain secrecy may result from commercial relationships or interests, such as, where business partners have common interests in keeping information confidential.[61] This applies for instance to the communication between licensee and licensor or the exchange between scientific colleagues as long as it can objectively be expected that the disclosed information will stay within that defined group (for instance in the case of a consultation). Thus, confidentiality agreements are extremely valuable in preventing an information exchange from rising to the level of a prior art disclosure. Such agreements do not require a particular form and can even be implicitly and tacitly concluded, although a formal written agreement is best.[62]

2.5. Novelty Assessment

2.5.1. Introduction

The EPO applies strict standards for the assessment of novelty. A prior art document is novelty-anticipating for a claimed feature combination only if each feature is *clearly and unambiguously disclosed* in the prior art document, and only if all the respective features are clearly and unambiguously disclosed in the claimed combination.[63] Under

58. Federal Supreme Court, X ZR 53/83, GRUR 86, 372, "Thrombozyten-Zählung"; EPO—T 0270/90 EPOR 92, 365.
59. Federal Supreme Court, decision of Jan. 15, 2013, X ZR 81/11, " Messelektronik für Coriolis-durchflussmesser."
60. Federal Supreme Court, decision of Oct. 15, 2013, X ZR 41/11, "Bildanzeigegerät."
61. EPO—T 1168/09.
62. Federal Supreme Court, I ZR 9/61, GRUR 62, 518, 521, "Blitzgerät"; Federal Supreme Court, GRUR 66, 484, 487, "Pfennigabsatz"; EPO—T 0830/90 OJ 94, 713, 722, "konkludentes Verhalten."
63. Guidelines C IV 9.2; EPO—T 0465/92 OJ 96, 32 (N° 8.4); EPO—T 701/09.

EPO rules, the skilled person shall only read the text and look at the drawings, but is not allowed to read "between the lines." A so-called implicit disclosure of a feature, i.e., a feature which is not explicitly disclosed, is only accepted if it is *directly and unambiguously* derivable from the document. But this is rarely the case. The EPO standards on implicit disclosure are thus stricter than the U.S. standards on "inherent disclosure." The EPO is rather inclined to consider this as a matter of obviousness when assessing the inventive step.[64] These standards concerning the novelty assessment are also applied by the EPO when assessing the original disclosure requirements[65] (Article 123 EPC) and when checking the validity of a priority (Article 87 EPC).

In contrast to the EPO, the German courts were more willing to read "between the lines" of the prior art to identify novelty-destroying disclosures. According to decisions of the Federal Supreme Court,[66] the prior art content of a disclosure includes not only its explicit statements, but also the self-explanatory teachings that would be recognized from the document by a person of skill.[67] Accordingly it seemed that the German approach left more leeway than the EPO when assessing the informative content of the disclosure of a document. In recent decisions however the Federal Supreme Court seems to have adopted the more restrictive case law of the EPO.[68] In these decisions the court held that the original disclosure shall only comprise information which is "clearly and unambiguously" derivable for a person skilled in the art. Information resulting from farther reaching conclusions, which the skilled person might only draw on the basis of his technical knowledge or through modifications of the technical teaching disclosed, constitutes, by contrast, subject matter which extends beyond the original disclosure.[69] Thus, at least these decisions follow a more restrictive approach, and it seems that this case law tends to close the gap between EPO and national law.

The strict interpretive approach of the EPO has advantages and disadvantages when prosecuting claims. The applicant may generally favor the EPO approach when attempting to overcome prior art references, given the stringent standard applied for finding a prior art reference to be novelty-destroying. A contrary consideration, however, is that the EPO can be quite rigid when considering an applicant's attempt to amend pending claims. This process is governed by Article 123 of the EPC which provides that: "[a] European patent application or a European patent may not be amended in such a way that it contains subject matter which extends beyond the content of the application as filed." Under a more restrictive European approach, compared to the national standards, the EPO may be unwilling to allow claims when there is not *in haec verba* support in the originally filed specification, which could be a

64. EPO—T 0071/93.
65. See Ch. 5, s. 5.
66. Federal Supreme Court, GRUR 1995, 303, 332, "Elektrische Steckverbindung."
67. Federal Supreme Court, GRUR 1995, 303, 332, "Elektrische Steckverbindung"; Federal Supreme Court, decision of Mar. 18, 2014, X ZR 77/12; GRUR 2014, 758, "Proteintrennung."
68. Federal Supreme Court, decision of Jul. 8, 2010, Xa ZR 124/07, "Fälschungssicheres Dokument"; Federal Supreme Court, decision of Dec. 16, 2009, X ZR 89/07, BGHZ 179, 168, "Olanzapine."
69. Federal Supreme Court, decision of Jul. 8, 2010, Xa ZR 124/07, "Fälschungssicheres Dokument." "Federal Supreme Court, decision of Mar. 18, 2014, X ZR 77/12; GRUR 2014, 758, "Proteintrennung."

disadvantage for the applicant. These are strategic considerations which must be discussed between the inventor and his representative on a case-by-case basis.

2.5.2. *Combination of Features*

A prior art document is only novelty-anticipating if all features of a claim are disclosed in the document combined within the same context. Accordingly, an intermingling of features of different embodiments of the specification is generally not a novelty-destroying disclosure. Features which are separately described within the same document only belong to the same disclosed subject matter if the document either explicitly states that they can be combined or if the person skilled in the art would learn such combination *directly and unambiguously* from the document.[70]

2.5.3. *Meaning of Terms*

It is a commonly accepted standard that the assessment of novelty and inventive step must be carried out from the perspective of a skilled person at the priority date. The question is which meaning the person skilled in the art would have objectively given at the priority date to a term used in the prior art document. This assessment may be performed both by reference to the particular documents being analyzed (i.e., the pending claims and the prior art of issue), and further by reference to extrinsic evidence which may give an understanding to the meaning of terms at issue. Much like in the U.S., a patentee may act as his or her own lexicographer, and provide definitions in the patent that are broader or narrower than the ordinary meaning of those terms.

2.5.4. *Incorporations by Reference*

For the novelty assessment only one document is to be considered and compared with the disclosure in the patent application in which the invention is described.[71] The disclosure of a document must generally be assessed without having regard to other documents when assessing novelty. The novelty assessment needs to be done on a document-by-document basis. The lack of novelty may not be deduced from a combination of documents. A prior art document that refers to another prior art document does not incorporate it by such reference. For assessing the novelty both documents would still be considered as separate disclosures. Only in the exceptional case of a reference to specific passages of a second document for a clearly recognizable purpose of incorporating it (such as citing a document to specify a testing method

70. EPO—T 0931/92 OJ 94 Special ed., 23, similar Federal Supreme Court, I ZR 73/52, GRUR, 54, 107, "Mehrfachschelle."
71. EPO—T 153/85.

therein) may two documents or parts of it be combined.[72] A mere statement "incorporated by reference" is thus not sufficient to extent the disclosure of a document to a second document.

2.6. So-called Article 54(3) Documents and §3(2) of the German Patent Act

The content of a European patent application or a PCT application (EP1) that has entered the EP phase may be considered prior art for purposes of assessing novelty of a second patent application (EP2), even if the application (EP1) was published after the priority or filing date of a second European patent or patent application (EP2) to be examined, if the first application (EP1) has an earlier priority or filing date. That situation is demonstrated in the illustration of Figure 5.1. Article 54(3) EPC provides "the content of European patent applications as filed, the dates of filing of which are prior to the date referred to in paragraph 2 and which were published on or after that date, shall be considered as comprised in the state of the art." The German Patent Act contains an equivalent provision namely §3(2) of the German Patent Act.[73]

Both provisions are aimed at resolving the problem of conflicting patent applications. A patent application is kept secret during the period between filing and publication. Therefore, the contents of an application before publication do not belong to the state of the art. This raises the potential for a conflict with a later application for the same or a similar application. Patent applications that fall under these provisions are considered for assessing the novelty, but not for inventive step. This is, the entire disclosure[74] of the prior application (EP1) becomes part of the art for EP2. The otherwise harsh effect of the approach to consider the whole content of the prior application is mitigated by considering it only for the novelty assessment and disregarding it in relation to inventive step. In case of European patent applications, these applications are so-called Article 54(3) Documents. That situation is demonstrated in the following illustration: The content of EP1 is prior art for EP2 (even though it is post-published) and will have to be considered when assessing novelty of EP2 (Figure 5.1).

72. Federal Supreme Court, X ZB 4/79, GRUR 80, 283, Terephtalsäure; EPO—T 0153/85, OJ 88, 1.
73. Chapter 17, s. 3.
74. So-called whole contents approach EPO—G 1/03, OJ 04, 413.

Figure 5.1. Article 54(3) Documents

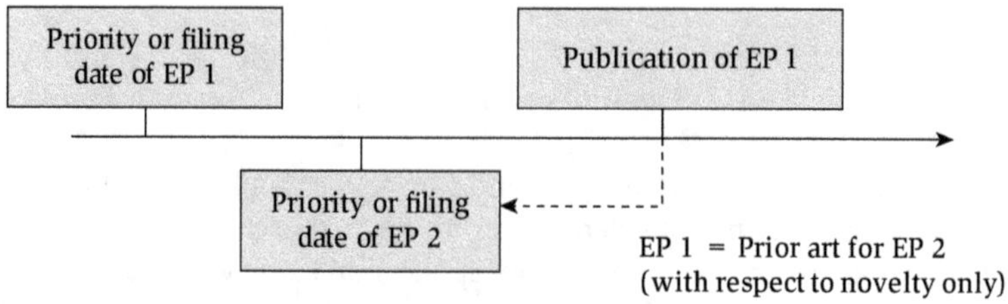

In practice, the hurdles are usually not too high for an applicant to overcome an Article 54(3) Document. As indicated the claimed subject matter must only be new and not inventive in face of such a document and the applicant may either:

- add a feature to the independent claim(s) that only irrelevantly limit the scope of protection; or
- add a "disclaimer" to the independent claim(s).

As commonly accepted, the teaching of a document is not interpreted to embrace well-known equivalents not disclosed in the document. Such equivalents are relevant only for the obviousness test. Thus, for satisfying the first method it would be sufficient to add one or more distinguishing features even though they are almost implicitly disclosed in the Article 54(3) Document. It could be a self-evident feature which is necessary for implementing the claimed invention. When adding such a feature to overcome an Article 54(3) Document, however, it is of course important to avoid adding limitations that might frustrate claims of infringement against competitors. The irrelevance of the additional feature might also be considered in light of the existing competitor products, i.e., when adding the feature care must be taken to avoid disqualifying an actual or future infringement claim.

The "disclaimer" solution is principally approved in a decision of the Enlarged Board of Appeal[75] of the EPO. In particular, limiting the scope of a claim by using a "disclaimer" to exclude a technical feature where the exclusion is not disclosed in the application as filed does not necessarily violate Article 123(2) in that case.[76] Illustrating the use of disclaimers, reference was made to claim 1 which was subject to the indicated decision of the Enlarged Board of Appeal (G 1/03)[77] which reads as follows:

75. Enlarged Board of Appeal: EPO—G 1/03, OJ 8–9, 2004.
76. See also Enlarged Board of Appeal: EPO—G 2/03, OJ 8-9/2004, 448: This case law refers to undisclosed disclaimers, i.e., disclaimers without basis in the application as filed. The question whether a disclaimer violates Art. 123 (2) EPC if its subject matter was disclosed as an embodiment of the invention in the application as filed is not yet settled and has been referred to the Enlarged Board of Appeal, where the case is pending under the docket G 2/10.
77. Decision of Technical Board of Appeal 3.3.5 dated Dec. 20, 2002, EPO—T 507/99.

1. A heat processable, metallic appearing coated article comprising:
   (a) ...
   (c) a protective layer comprising a...metal...selected from the group consisting of chromium, titanium, and nitrides and oxynitrides of silicon-metal alloys with the exception of silicon-zirconium nitride and silicon-tin nitride; with the proviso that if the metal compound film is titanium nitride the protective layer is not chromium.

The terms "with the proviso" and "not" in that claim indicate what is excluded from its scope of protection.

Note that special conditions must be respected when making an amendment that involves a disclaimer. A disclaimer represents a negative claim feature aimed at excluding specific subject matter from the scope of a claim. Nevertheless, like any other amendment, the introduction of a disclaimer may also add subject matter to the claimed teaching. This is inadmissible. Commonly, the intended disclaimer is not disclosed in the original application at all (so-called undisclosed disclaimer) or it is originally disclosed as an embodiment of the invention (so-called disclosed disclaimer). The quoted decision G1/03 of the Enlarged Board concerned the situation of a so-called undisclosed disclaimer which is exceptionally allowed in the following circumstances:

(1) to restore novelty over Article 54(3) EPC prior art;
(2) to restore novelty over an "accidental anticipation"[78] in a prior art document;
(3) to disclaim unpatentable subject matter.

In addition, as the Enlarged Board added in G 1/03, such "a disclaimer should not remove more than is necessary to restore novelty" and "the necessity for a disclaimer is not an opportunity for the applicant to reshape his claims arbitrarily". Also the disclaimer must meet the requirements of clarity and conciseness of Article 84 EPC.

The decision G1/03 must be read in the light on a further more recent decision of the Enlarged Board G2/10 of 2011 concerning the so-called disclosed disclaimer. The Enlarged Board ruled in G2/10 that also "disclosed disclaimers" are allowable in principle, however, only if the subject matter remaining in the claim is "directly and unambiguously disclosed" in the application as originally filed and that a specific "technical assessment" needs to be carried out to decide whether that requirement is met, explicitly the decision says "the case requires a technical assessment of the overall technical circumstances of the individual case under consideration, taking into account the nature and extent of the disclosure in the application as filed, the nature and extent of the disclaimed subject matter and its relationship with the subject matter remaining in the claim after the amendment". The ruling of G2/10 implies that also undisclosed disclaimer according to G1/03 must be subjected to such "technical assessment" as

78. An anticipation is considered accidental when the disclosure of the document in question is "so unrelated and remote that the person skilled in the art would never have taken it into consideration when working on the invention" (EPO—G 2/03, OJ 2004, 413).

well, in addition to the requirements outlined in G1/03. Some undisclosed disclaimers previously accepted by the EPO may now fail in view of the technical assessment requirement set out in G2/10.

In some cases, a disclaimer can be less advantageous than adding a feature. For instance if the competitor who filed the Article 54(3) Document would use the disclaimed embodiment, i.e., in the above claim example, he uses a protective layer which is made of chromium. Therefore, when drafting EP-style claims, it is recommendable to disclose all aspects and embodiments of the invention together with self-evident features. These features can be used later to distinguish from a post-published Article 54(3) Document.

In addition, it has to be taken note that national documents, such as German patent applications cannot be Article 54(3) Documents.[79] Article 54(3) EPC explicitly refers to "European patent applications" only. However, these national rights may be taken into account in national revocation proceedings, in Germany on the basis of the equivalent provision of §3(2) Patent Act.

2.7. First Medical Use/Second Medical Use

When assessing the novelty of a product claim, the structural features must be compared with the disclosure of a prior art document, while a purpose or intended use of the product mentioned in the claim is in principle irrelevant for that assessment.

However, under the provisions of Article 54(4)/(5) EPC and §3(3)/(4) German Patent Act, a substance or composition can be distinguished over the prior art by virtue of its use for a specific medical purpose, resulting in a "purpose-linked product claim." These provisions thus provide for an exception from the principle that product claims can only be obtained for (absolutely) novel products.

2.7.1. First Medical Use

Thus, although the substance or composition is already known prior art, it can be subject to a patent claim for a medical use, provided that particular medical use is new and inventive. The novelty and the non-obviousness is thus not derived from the substance or composition as such but from the claimed purpose, namely from its intended use.[80] If that substance or compound is used for the first time for a medical use, its claims may be referred to as "first medical use claims" (Article 54(4) EPC and §3(3) German Patent Act). Thus, the requirements for such purpose-linked product claim are:

- substance or composition is already known; and accordingly the substance or composition itself is not patentable anymore;

79. EPO—T 0550/88 OJ 92, 117; EPO—T 0361/06.
80. Enlarged Board of Appeal, EPO—G 2/08 of Feb. 19, 2010.

- substance or composition is intended for use in a medical method according to Article 53(c) EPC (§2a (1) German Patent Act);
- the use of the substance or composition in that method is new and inventive;

A first medical use claims may be worded "Compound A for use in the treatment ...."

2.7.2. *Second Medical Use*

There are also "second medical use claims (Article 54(5) EPC and §3(4) German Patent Act). "Second" means that the substance or compound is already known for one medical purpose, but can also be used for another purpose that was not previously known. Before the EPC 2000 entered into force, so-called Swiss-type claims were used to claim a second medical use, typically worded as: "Use of compound A for preparing a drug/medicament for treatment of disease B." Swiss-type claims were instituted by a decision of the Enlarged Board of Appeal of 1984.[81] The new provision of Article 54(5) EPC 2000, which corresponds to §3(4) of the German Patent Act, now explicitly allows claims to subsequent medical indications of a known medicament. Since the new legal framework allows for such patent protection, Swiss-type claims are no longer needed and, in fact, no longer permitted.[82] This means a simplified claim format can be used namely: "[Known substance or composition] for use in [new therapeutic application]." This has recently been confirmed by the Enlarged Board of Appeal[83] which pointed to that main change in law and stated "where the subject matter of a claim is rendered novel only by a new therapeutic use of a medicament, such claim may no longer have the format of a so-called Swiss-type claim as instituted by decision G 5/83." The Enlarged Board of Appeal[84] of the EPO also clarified that even when a medicament is already known to treat an illness, it may nevertheless be subject to a patent claim for use in a new and different treatment for the same illness. Accordingly, second medical use claims must not necessarily concern treatments for different diseases. Additionally, the Enlarged Board of Appeal clarified in the same decision that there may be novelty even if the only novel feature is the dosage regime, provided that the novel dosage gives rise to new effects.[85] A different treatment could also consist in a new administration method, such as the route of administration (e.g., orally, in a transdermal manner or by injection), the nature of the substance (solid, liquid or gaseous), the patient group or other parameters relevant as to the therapeutic effect of the substance. It could also consist in the immobilization of a patient after medication, provided that such treatment-related instructions are objectively aimed at influencing the effectiveness of

81. Enlarged Board of Appeal, EPO—G 5/83 of 1984.
82. Notice from the EPO in OJ EPO 2010, 514.
83. Enlarged Board of Appeal, EPO—G 2/08 of Feb. 19, 2010.
84. Enlarged Board of Appeal, EPO—G 2/08 of Feb. 19, 2010.
85. Similar: Federal Supreme Court, decision of Jun. 9, 2011, X ZR 68/08, GRUR 2011, 999, "Memantin."

the substance.[86] Accordingly, there must be a synergistic effect between such treatment-related instructions and the improved efficacy of the substance.

3. PATENTABILITY STANDARDS APPLICABLE TO GERMAN UTILITY MODELS[87]

In contrast to European and German patent applications, when filing a German "utility model" the inventor can benefit from a grace period of six months (§3(1) of the Utility Model Act). That is, previous publication of the invention is unobjectionable provided that the previous publications occurred within the six-month period prior to the application and were made by the applicant or his legal predecessor. Furthermore, a public prior use may not be asserted against the utility model unless it occurred within German territory (§3(1) of the Utility Model Act). The utility model thus provides inventors with patent protection in one of the biggest markets in the world despite having the traditional patent application path barred due to a disclosure of the invention to the public.

4. STANDARDS ON INVENTIVE STEP: "NON-OBVIOUSNESS"

4.1. Introduction

The European analog of the U.S. "non-obviousness" requirement is called "inventive step." The requirement to have an inventive step is provided in Article 56 EPC and the corresponding §4 of the German Patent Act, which both state that "an invention shall be considered as involving an inventive step if, having regard to the state of the art, it is not obvious to a skilled person in the art."

The determination of an inventive step first requires the definition of the skilled person of the art. For the objective assessment, the skilled person, who is a fictious person[88] with average and ordinary skills in the area of the invention, is set in the position of the inventor at the priority date of the patent application. The question is whether this person would have arrived at the invention with the knowledge of the state of the art by applying his skills.

4.2. Problem and Solution Approach

To evaluate the inventive step, reference is usually made to the so-called Problem and Solution approach, which is an analytical framework commonly employed by the EPO. It is a guideline for an objective assessment of inventive step. Subjective considerations such as the individual performance of the inventor, the story of the invention, and

86. Federal Supreme Court, decision of Feb. 24, 2014, GRUR 2014, 461 "Collagenase I;" Federal Supreme Court, decision of Feb. 25, 2014, GRUR 2014, 462 "Collagenase II."
87. Further information about the Utility Model can also be found on Ch. 4, s. 3.
88. Federal Supreme Court, X ZR 213/01, GRUR 2006, 663, "Vorausbezahlte Telefongespräche."

whether it was coincidence or the result of intensive research, are thus irrelevant. The vigorous application of that approach has proven to render the case law of the EPO relatively predicable.

The entire state of the art is relevant. In contrast to the novelty test, multiple prior art references may be combined, provided that such combination is obvious to the skilled person in the art. This basically means, combining documents with contradictory teachings[89] might not be obvious (similar to the concept of "teaching away" under U.S. law). The reference might be combined, in particular, if one document suggests the combination with another document, or at least if it does not prevent the person skilled in the art from doing so.[90] Of particular importance is that the skilled person is set in the position of the inventor at the date of the patent application to avoid an "ex post analysis" which is inadmissible, but a frequently contested mistake.[91] This is akin to the forbidden concept of "hindsight" under U.S. law.

The problem and solution approach is based on three main steps, which are illustrated in (Figure 5.2):

Figure 5.2. Problem and Solution Approach

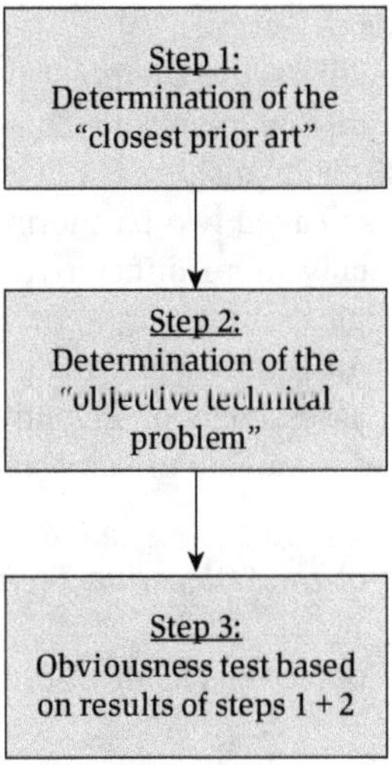

The basic question thus is: would the claimed invention, starting from the closest prior art and the objective problem, have been obvious to the skilled person?

89. EPO—T 0176/89, OJ 91 Special edn, 24.
90. EPO—T 0095/90, OJ 93 Special edn, 26.
91. Federal Supreme Court, X ZR 95/87, GRUR 89, 899, 902, "Sauerteig"; EPO—T 0229/85 OJ 87, 237.

4.2.1. Step 1: Determination of the "Closest Prior Art"

The skilled person is deemed to choose, as a starting point for his or her analysis, the springboard to achieve the technical result of the invention.[92] This "most promising starting"[93] point is the "closest prior art." The closest prior art is usually a document that is the most pertinent for challenging the inventive step. In many cases, it addresses the same technical problems as the claimed invention, discloses most of the features of a claimed feature combination, and requires the minimum of structural and functional modifications to arrive at the claimed invention. It typically belongs to the same technical field or it is at least closely connected to it. A document disclosing a laryngeal catheter, for example, is not necessarily the closest prior art for a claim directed to a vascular catheter, even if the document discloses most of the claimed feature combination. Each claim feature must be evaluated in view of its importance for carrying out the invention. The function and effect of each specific feature may also have to be considered to determine its importance in order to correctly identify which document is the closest prior art. In practice, especially in EPO opposition cases, it may be wise to concurrently point to different documents as the closest prior art. In some cases there might be several equally valid starting points for the assessment of inventive step.[94] Also it is not always predictable which line of argument will later be taken by the opposition division or the boards of Appeal.

During examination proceedings, the Examiner usually prefers that all features known from the closest prior art document are contained in the preamble of an independent claim, and that all distinguishing features appear in the characterizing portion of the claim. This is the so-called two-part form. In method claims, this is not observed so strictly as it is usually more difficult to arrange the method steps in two-part form rather than in a logical order.

The so-called closest prior art is only a starting point of the assessment. It does not mean that the subsequent assessment of inventive step is limited to a single document. It particularly helps to formulate the objective technical problem.[95]

4.2.2. Step 2: Determination of the "Objective Technical Problem"

Prior to the formulation of the "objective technical problem" two sub-steps must be carried out:

First, it is necessary to objectively determine the distinguishing features representing the difference between the closest prior art and the claimed invention. Second, it is then essential to identify the particular functions and effects achieved by these distinguishing features. As indicated in previous section 1.1, non-technical features, i.e., features from a field excluded from patentability, principally shall not be taken into account for the assessment of inventive step, unless they interact with the technical

92. EPO—T 0644/97, OJ 00, 21.
93. Guidelines for Examination in the EPO, Part C, Ch. 5, s. 4.2.
94. EPO—T 1289/09.
95. EPO—T 0939/92, OJ 96, 309 (N° 2.34).

subject matter to solve a technical problem.[96] This particularly counts for so-called non-patentable subject matter, such as pure data processing,[97] the reproduction of information,[98] economical activities such as the organization of a pension.[99]

The objective technical problem can then be formulated, precisely in view of the functions and effects derivable from the distinguishing feature(s). The claimed invention should provide a desired technical effect or function by modifying or adapting the closest prior. Principally any technical effect or function provided by the invention may be used as a basis for that reformulation so long as that effect is derivable from the application as filed. New effects submitted subsequently during the proceedings by the applicant may also be taken into account, provided that the skilled person would recognize these effects as implied by or related to the technical problem initially suggested.[100]

A common challenge when formulating the objective technical problem is that the more specifically the problem is formulated, the more obvious the solution provided by the claimed teaching might appear. Thus, it is frequently desirable for the applicant to formulate the problem as generically as possible, which may be satisfied by a simple statement such as "to improve a particular device." As a general rule, the objective problem should be formulated in view of the functions and effects achieved by the invention, and should not contain hints to the technical solution of the invention. However, features which do not, either independently or in combination with other features of the claim, contribute to the technical character of the invention cannot be weighed in that assessment. This particularly applies to subject matter that is excluded from patentability.[101]

The inventor is usually not aware of the closest prior art when drafting the original application. New prior art is often revealed later, namely during the granting, opposition or judicial proceedings. Accordingly, often a reformulation of the problem is necessary.

4.2.3. *Step 3: Obviousness Test—"Could-Would-Approach"*

Step 3 starts from the question: "Would the claimed invention, starting from the closest prior art and the objective problem, have been obvious to the skilled person?" In practice, an opponent in opposition proceedings usually tries to establish that the

96. Federal Supreme Court, BGHZ 159, 197, 205, "elektronischer Zahlungsverkehr"; Federal Supreme Court, X ZB 34/03, GRUR 2005, 143, 144, "Rentabilitätsermittlung"; Federal Supreme Court, X ZB 22/07, GRUR 2009, 479, "Steuerungseinrichtung für Untersuchungsmodalitäten;" Federal Supreme Court, decision of Dec. 18, 2012, X ZR 3/12, GRUR 2013, 275, n. 41, "Routenplanung"; Federal Supreme Court, decision of Jun. 30, 2015, X ZB 1/15, "Flugzeugzustand"; EPO—G 3/08.
97. Federal Supreme Court, decision of Dec. 18, 2012, X ZR 3/12, GRUR 2013, 275 N. 42, "Routenplanung."
98. Federal Supreme Court, decision of Oct. 26, 2010, X ZR 47/07, GRUR 2011, 125 Rn. 39—"Wiedergabe topografischer Informationen."
99. EPO—T 931/95 OJ 2001, 441.
100. EPO—T 184/82, OJ 6/1984, 261.
101. EPO—T 641/00, OJ 7/2003, 352.

distinguishing features, are disclosed in a second prior art document, and that it would have been obvious for the skilled person at the priority date to combine both teachings. It must be shown that the skilled person would have come to the claimed solution. It is not sufficient that the skilled person *could* have come to the solution. The following questions are regularly discussed when determining whether a combination of prior art documents is obvious or not:

- Does the second document belong to the same technical field? It is usually less obvious to combine documents of different technical fields. This also depends on who is the skilled person in the art.
- Does the second document give any hint as to whether the effects, on which the objective problem is based, can be achieved by the features of the characterizing portion of the claim?
- Does the closest prior art give any hint that points to the claimed solution?
- To what extent does it motivate the skilled person in the art to develop or investigate in view of the claimed solution? Are there any reasons that prevent the person skilled in the art from investigating in view of the claimed solution? Does the person skilled in the art need to overcome a technical prejudice?
- Is there an unexpected technical effect?

So-called secondary indicators may also be taken into account such as a "longfelt need" which is solved by the invention, i.e., a need that satisfies prior unsuccessful attempts to solve the objective technical problem. Commercial success will generally not be taken into consideration for the assessment of the inventive step unless this commercial success is linked to a specific technical effect or function of the claimed teaching. This is principally the same under U.S. law, where secondary indicators such as longfelt needs, unexpected results, failure of others, skepticism, commercial success, and copying may all help to overcome case of "obviousness."

4.3. German National Particularities

While in most cases the arguments for inventiveness brought forward by the parties in proceedings before the EPO or Federal Patent Court have the same weight and lead to identical results, the Federal Patent Court seems to apply slightly different and more flexible rules. This has been emphasized in a decision of the Federal Supreme Court.[102] The highest court ruled that, for assessing the inventive step, the "closest prior art" shall not necessarily represent the sole starting point. According to the Court, selecting one starting point (or several starting points) rather requires a particular justification that principally derives from the motivation of the skilled person who tries to find a better, or at least different, solution over the available prior art. This represents a deviation from the problem-solution approach used by the EPO and apparently leaves more flexibility when assessing the inventive step. The skilled person may,

102. Federal Supreme Court, Jun. 18, 2009, GRUR Int 2009, 1041, Xa ZR 138/05, "Fischbissanzeiger."

accordingly, combine documents if he is sufficiently motivated to do so. He might even combine the teachings of two distinct areas of the same technical field, if at the priority date appliances or methods were already known that crossed the boundaries between the technical areas, and if the technical problem to be solved is pertinent to both areas.[103] In addition, as can be taken from another decision recently rendered by the Federal Supreme Court,[104] the courts shall not solely rely on secondary indicia. Such secondary indicia are not suited to replace or exclusively justify the actual assessment that an invention involves an inventive step. Even though the formalistic problem-solution approach is not a guarantee for the best decision, it does however provide considerable legal security which might not be provided by a system where the assessment follows more flexible and thus less predictable ways.

5. STANDARDS ON ORIGINAL DISCLOSURE

A further important aspect of patentability is the question of whether there is any undue broadening of the original disclosure. Article 123(2) EPC provides that a European patent application, or a European patent, may not be amended in such a way that it contains subject matter which extends beyond the content of the application as filed. An applicant is thus hindered to improve his position by adding subject matter which is not disclosed in the application as originally filed. Such adding would give him an unjustified advantage endangering the legal security of the public relying on the content of the original application.[105] The amendment is not allowable if the overall change in the content of the application, through an addition, alteration or omission results in that the skilled person is faced to information which is not *directly and unambiguously* derivable from the application as originally filed.[106] Accordingly, an applicant usually cannot delete features from independent claims. Basically, claim amendments must be literally supported by a dependent claim or by the specification as originally filed, unless it is implicitly contained in it. Such "implicit disclosure," however, must represent a direct and unambiguous conclusion by the skilled person based on his common general knowledge of what is explicitly mentioned in the application as filed.[107]

For instance, a combination of two items, each taken from two lists of features, is not sufficiently disclosed unless this combination is specifically mentioned in the original disclosure.[108] It would not be sufficient to satisfy Article 123(2) EPC if the application merely conceptually comprises that combination from the two lists.)

103. Federal Supreme Court, Apr. 15, 2010, GRUR 2010, 712, Xa ZR 69/06, "Telekommunikationseinrichtung."
104. Federal Supreme Court, Jul. 30, 2009, GRUR 2010, 44 and in IIC 2010, 468, Xa ZR 22/06, "Dreinahtschlauchfolienbeutel."
105. EPO—G 1/93.
106. EPO—G 2/10
107. EPO—T 823/96.
108. EPO—T 727/00.

5.1. Removing a Feature from an Independent Claim as Originally Filed

An undue broadening may happen if non-European applicants amend the patent application during international search or during the international preliminary examination of the PCT application. They may start from an original U.S. document and it is likely that the amendment is based on U.S. rules, which are not necessarily in line with the EPC standards. When entering the regional phase, the PCT application will serve as the reference document for applying the standards of Article 123(2) EPC. It is important that applicants verify under the standards of Article 123(2) EPC that the claims are not broadened during that process beyond the scope of the original application. Removing claim limitations may be problematic, in that the applicant needs to take due account that the replacement or removal of a feature from a claim is only permissible according to the Guidelines for Examination in the EPO[109] if the "skilled person would directly and unambiguously recognize that:

(i) the feature is not essential for the invention;
(ii) the feature is not, as such, indispensable for the function of the invention in the light of the technical problem the invention serves to solve; and
(iii) the feature's replacement or removal requires no real modification of other features to compensate for the change."

These requirements are handled very strictly and formalistically by the EPO. It is generally assumed that a feature is essential for the invention if the feature is contained in an originally filed independent claim. It is thus critical to exchange or delete features from independent claims during the prosecution proceedings, even though this is desired by the applicant to get a broader or different scope of protection. From a European perspective, it is often better to draft very broad independent claims which could then be amended during prosecution by adding features from the dependent claims or from the specification.

5.2. The So-called Inescapable Trap of Article 123(2)/(3)

The so-called inescapable trap may occur due to a conflict between the requirements of Articles 123(2) and 123(3) EPC.

As previously mentioned, on the one hand, Art 123(2) EPC provides that a European patent application, or a European patent, shall not be amended in such a way that it contains subject matter which extends beyond the content of the application as originally filed, whereas, on the other hand, Article 123(3) EPC prohibits amendments to granted claims in such a way that it extends the scope of protection conferred by it. Article 123(3) EPC equally protects the interests of third parties. This is, a broadening of a claim of a granted European patent, even if there is support for such broadening in the specification, is prohibited. Accordingly, in opposition proceedings the EPO will principally revoke a European patent if the claim contains subject matter which was

109. Guidelines for Examination: Part H, Ch. V, 3.1.

not disclosed in the originally filed patent application.[110] This latter is mainly a consequence of Article 123 (2) EPC and due to Article 123 (3) EPC the applicant is not entitled to remove the added subject matter because it would broaden the scope of protection of the claim. A fundamental decision of the Enlarged Board of Appeal (G1/93) states the following:

> If a European patent as granted contains subject-matter which extends beyond the content of the application as filed within the meaning of Art. 123(2) EPC and which also limits the scope of protection conferred by the patent, such patent cannot be maintained in opposition proceedings unamended, because the ground for opposition under Art. 100(c) EPC prejudices the maintenance of the patent. Nor can it be amended by deleting such limiting subject-matter from the claims, because such amendment would extend the protection conferred, which is prohibited by Art. 123(3) EPC. Such a patent can, therefore, only be maintained if there is a basis in the application as filed for replacing such subject-matter without violating Art. 123(3) EPC.

The EPO would likewise revoke the patent if a removal of that subject matter from the claim extends the protection conferred by that claim. For example, a feature has been added to a claim or a feature has been replaced by a more generic term during prosecution proceedings. Maybe the added or replaced feature is accidentally taken from a part of the description describing a preferred embodiment which does not sufficiently disclose all other features mentioned in the independent claim. This would represent a violation of Article 123(2) EPC.

Sometimes, these kinds of mistakes may be triggered by the Examining Division. For instance, it may be that the Examining Division is of the opinion that the claimed combination is disclosed in the context of that embodiment. What is and what is not originally disclosed is sometimes not clear. The applicant needs to know that he cannot simply rely on that view and blindly follow a suggestion of the Examining Division to add or replace a feature. This can be fatal if the Opposition Division sees it differently later during opposition proceedings. Such mistakes may also occur in cases where the amendment was added prior to the entry into the regional phase of the PCT application process, leading to an inadmissibly amended claim. The result can then be a granted patent containing an independent claim with such new subject matter.

During opposition proceedings, the Opposition Division may come to the conclusion that the added or replaced feature is not allowed under Article 123(2) EPC. Unfortunately, at that stage—with the patent already granted—it is no longer possible to simply remove that feature. That removal needs to comply with Article 123(3) EPC, which bars any deletion of a feature if this broadens the scope of protection conferred by the patent.

Because the removal of a feature usually leads to a broader scope of protection, the applicant is "trapped" and the patent will be revoked. In only the very exceptional situation this could be cured, namely if the feature in question can be replaced by a feature which does not broaden the protection and for which there is support in the application as originally filed.

110. Enlarged Board of Appeal, decision G 1/93 confirmed recently by EPO—T 1180/05.

An example of the so-called Inescapable Trap can be found in a decision of the Boards of Appeal,[111] where the EPO concluded that a feature of a claim concerning a collecting bag for human body waste was not disclosed in the original filed documents. This led to a revocation of the patent. The EPO confirmed the prior case law and pointed out that a granted patent which contains subject matter which extends beyond the content of the application can only be maintained if there is a basis in the application as filed for replacing such subject matter without violating Article 123(3) EPC. It is also emphasized in that decision that a disclaimer may be permitted in order to restore novelty or to disclaim subject matter under Articles 52 to 57 EPC, but not for resolving a potential conflict between Articles 123(2) and (3) EPC.

In contrast to the EPO, the German practice is more flexible and tends to solve the dilemma by a so-called disclaimer-solution.[112] This approach has explicitly been rejected by the EPO in a decision[113] wherein it is stated: "There is no basis...for allowing a disclaimer for resolving the potential conflict between Article 123(2) and (3) EPC."

A statement such as: "feature X is not disclosed in the originally filed application and, therefore, constitutes an inadmissible extension from which the patentee cannot derive any rights" would not solve the dilemma in EPO proceedings. German courts apply a different approach: On the one hand, the claim would be limited in its scope by the non-disclosed feature, which is thus taken into account when determining the scope of protection by the claim, and, on the other hand, the patentee may not use it to distinguish the claim over the prior art. This would be sufficient for German courts.[114] In a decision, the Federal Supreme Court[115] has ruled the following:

> "A patent is not to be revoked if the insertion of a feature, which is not disclosed in the originally filed application, leads to a limitation of the claimed subject matter. In such a case, the interests of the public are sufficiently protected, if the inserted feature stays in the claim, provided it is assured...that it is not used for supporting the patentability...."[116]

According to this decision, an explicit disclaimer inserted in the patent is not even necessary for solving the dilemma as long as it is assured that the inserted and non-disclosed feature is not used to distinguish the claim over the prior art. The German approach thus allows that the inserted feature stays in the claim, without revoking the patent, provided that the insertion forms a limitation and does not exceptionally cover a new inventive aspect outside the originally filed documents ("aliud").[117] Accordingly the dilemma cannot be solved if the adding of the subject

111. EPO—T-1180/05.
112. Schulte, *Patentgesetz*, 9th edn, 2014, §21, N° 69-75.
113. EPO, decision of Feb. 2, 1994, G 1/93.
114. Federal Supreme Court, decision of Oct. 5, 2000, X ZR 184/98, GRUR 2001, 140 "Zeittelegramm."
115. Federal Supreme Court, decision of Oct. 21, 2010, X a ZB 14/09, GRUR 2011, 40, "Winkelmesseinrichtung."
116. Unofficial translation.
117. Federal Supreme Court, decision of Oct. 21, 2010, X a ZB 14/09, GRUR 2011, 40, "Winkelmesseinrichtung."

matter led to a different inventive teaching which is not disclosed in the application as previously filed.[118] The German flexible approach, which deviates from the case law of the EPO, is not only applicable to national German patents, but also to the German parts of European patents.[119] Indeed, the German approach finds a better balance between, on the one hand, the fundamental right to protection conferred by a patent and, on the other hand, the aim to avoid adverse effects for public.

Figure 5.3. Inescapable Trap of Article 123(2)/(3)

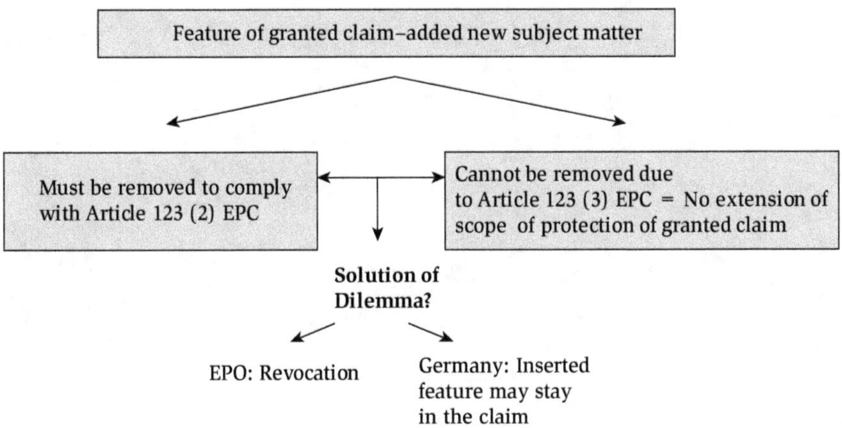

118. Federal Supreme Court, decision of Feb. 17, 2015, X ZR 161/12, "Wundbehandlungsvorrichtung."
119. Federal Supreme Court, decision of Feb. 17, 2015, X ZR 161/12, "Wundbehandlungsvorrichtung."

CHAPTER 6

Opposition Proceedings

1. INTRODUCTION

When a patent issues from either the European Patent Office EPO or the German Patent and Trademark Office GPTO, any person may challenge the patent's validity in an "opposition proceeding" at the granting agency. Opposition proceedings offer an independent *inter partes* procedure at the post-grant stage. This chapter will focus on opposition proceedings at the EPO, which are the most common. There is no need to distinguish between traditional European Patents and the upcoming European Patents with unitary effect. European Patents with unitary effect will become effective as soon as the European Patent Package is finally approved. For both types of patents the same EPC rules are applicable. Opposition proceedings in the GPTO, applicable to German national patents, as well as in the EPO must be brought within nine months after publication of the patent grant (Article 99(1) EPC, §59(1) GPA). Thus, it is important to monitor both the EPO and GPTO for the issuance of potentially problematic patents, and to recognize that there is only a very short window for bringing an opposition.

2. PATENT MONITORING PROGRAMS

Companies that may be subject to patent liability in Europe should establish programs to monitor patents issuing from the EPO and GPTO (and other national patent agencies). Particularly with respect to the EPO, an opposition proceeding represents an inexpensive opportunity to challenge the patent on a pan-European basis with *ex tunc* effect in all designated contracting states, in case of traditional European patents or for the whole territory in which European patents with unitary character have effect. Therefore, prudent companies will implement programs to monitor patents issuing from the EPO (and national level patent offices), to take advantage of the limited opportunity to bring opposition proceedings.

Monitoring programs may use the online service of the EPO (www.epoline.com). The EPO online services provides free and convenient access to the public data published during the grant procedure. Besides legal status information and search and examination reports, this database contains all the documents exchanged between the applicant and the EPO. Documents of opposition proceedings are also available, including briefs, writs and related communications. The claims are published in all three languages used by the EPO, and the proceedings are often—although not always—in English.

This monitoring can be efficiently completed with an alert service system with automatic monitoring of selected patents. As soon as a particular event (such as a communication with the EPO, a submitted brief, the grant) is entered in the register, the interested party is informed by email.

3. GROUNDS FOR OPPOSITION

Oppositions may only be filed on particular grounds mentioned in Article 100 EPC. The list of grounds for opposition as indicated in Article 100 EPC is exhaustive (*numerus clausus*). Accordingly an opposition may only be filed on the grounds that:

(a) the subject matter of the European patent is not patentable under Articles 52 to 57;
(b) the European patent does not disclose the invention in a manner sufficiently clear and complete for it to be carried out by a person skilled in the art;
(c) the subject matter of the European patent extends beyond the content of the application as filed, or, if the patent was granted on a divisional application or on a new application filed under Article 61, beyond the content of the earlier application as filed.

Other deficiencies of the patent or the granting procedure are not considered in opposition proceedings. The most important ground for an opposition is if the patent's subject matter is not patentable within the terms of Articles 52–57 EPC, in particular, because the subject matter is not novel or lacks an inventive step (Article 100(a) EPC: Missing Patentability). Ground (b) is non-enablement (Article 100(b) EPC: Insufficiency of Disclosure).[1] Finally, an opposition could also assert that the patent's subject matter extends beyond the content of the application as originally filed, which would violate Article 123(2) EPC (Article 100(c): Added Subject Matter).[2]

All available grounds should be raised when filing the notice of opposition. Introducing a new ground for opposition after the opposition period has lapsed is, in principle, not permitted. Accordingly, it is not possible to open the proceedings on the basis of a lack of patentability (Article 100(a) EPC) and later, after expiry of the nine months period, to add the new ground of added subject matter (Article 100(c) EPC).

1. Article 100 (b) refers to Art. 83 EPC: "The European patent application shall disclose the invention in a manner sufficiently clear and complete for it to be carried out by a person skilled in the art."
2. See Ch. 5, s. 5.

However, the Opposition Division can raise objections on its own motion, which might, possibly, be triggered by a belated introduction of a ground for opposition (Rule 81(1) EPC, Article 114(1) EPC). So-called ex-officio examinations may, in principal, occur in all procedures before the EPO. But, it has to be taken note that this is restricted in first—and even more in second[3]—instance opposition proceedings due to the contentious character of the proceedings between parties having opposite interests and a right to be treated in an equal and fair manner.[4] Thus, in principle, only those grounds are examined, which have been properly submitted by the opponent(s)[5]. In exceptional cases, the Opposition Division may consider other or late-filed grounds for opposition. Nevertheless, in appeal proceedings, fresh grounds for opposition may only be considered with the approval of the patentee.[6]

In weighing whether to bring an opposition proceeding, potential challengers should be aware of the issues that tend to attract heavy scrutiny by the EPO. For instance, the EPO rigidly enforces the requirements of Article 123 EPC[7] to ensure that the claims do not contain subject matter extending beyond the application as filed. If the issuing patent is not clearly and unambiguously supported by the originally filed documents, potential opponents might be inclined to file an EPO opposition, rather than waiting to bring a revocation claim with a national court which may be less insistent on enforcing this requirement.[8] On the other hand, the EPO generally seems to have a more accommodating stance than national invalidation courts in assessing inventive step.[9] Potential opponents should therefore carefully consider if a European opposition proceeding is the best strategy if the only available ground is lack of an inventive step. Of course, comparable questions will have to be answered by the patentee, which could start with enforcement measures against third parties prior to, or after, the lapse of the nine-month opposition period. A warning letter sent to an accused infringer may cause him to file an opposition. Accordingly, a patentee may choose to wait until the opposition period lapses.

4. ANY PERSON MAY OPPOSE

"Any person," with the exception of the patentee,[10] may initiate opposition proceedings. Article 99 EPC explicitly states that "any person may give notice" of opposition. The opponent need not demonstrate any legal or economic interest in the revocation

3. EPO—G 1/99: "Article 114(1) EPC, which already has a restricted application in the opposition proceedings, is to be applied in an even more restrictive manner in appeal proceedings. This was essentially because, in the Enlarged Board's view, the appeal procedure is to be considered as a judicial procedure" (see also G 9/91).
4. EPO—G 1/99.
5. EPO—G 10/91.
6. EPO—G 10/91.
7. The provision can be found in Ch. 17, s. 1.
8. See Ch. 5, s. 5 "Standards on Original Disclosure."
9. See Ch. 5, s. 4 "Standards on Inventive Step."
10. EPO—G 9/93, OJ 1994, 89: A patentee cannot oppose his own patent. Oppositions are *inter partes* procedures. Accordingly, the patentee and opponent must be different persons.

when filing the notice.[11] There is no standing requirement. This is because the opposition procedure is designed as a legal remedy in the public interest.[12]

Accordingly, it is acceptable[13] and common for interested parties to set up a "straw man" to file the notice of opposition. Indeed, competitors often prefer to stay in the background and involve a straw man for oppositions against disagreeable and uncomfortable patents of competing companies. In many of these cases it may be preferable to act anonymously through a straw man in order to avoid friction in relations with the patentee, or to be silent as to business intentions. There is no disadvantage to using a straw man even if the backer's identity incidentally becomes known during the proceedings. This tactic is prohibited only in rare cases, such as where the straw man is used to bypass a contractual promise not to challenge the validity of the patent,[14] or where the straw man is acting on behalf of the patentee.[15] Also the repeated filing of an opposition with similar focus by the same person could be objected to for lack of legitimate interest.[16]

5. MAIN STEPS OF OPPOSITIONS PROCEEDINGS

The main steps of opposition proceedings are roughly illustrated in Figure 6.1.

Figure 6.1. Steps of Opposition Proceedings (EPO)

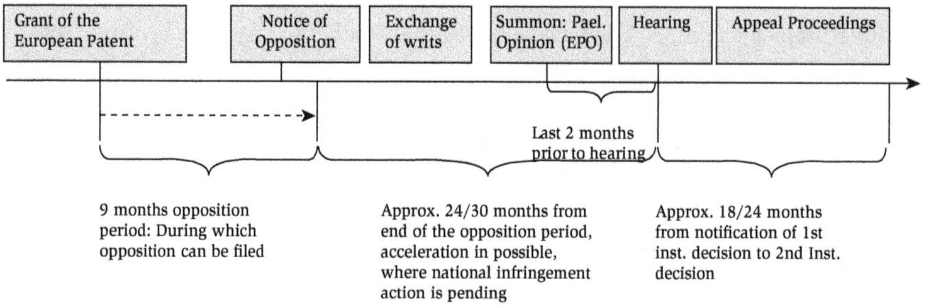

5.1. Notice of Opposition

The notice of opposition must include a reasoned statement and must be filed within the nine-month period after the grant's publication. The opposition must state at least one ground for opposition under Article 100 EPC. For the opposition to be admissible, it must fulfil the requirements of Rule 76(2)(c) EPC. Accordingly the notice of

11. EPO—T 289/91, OJ 1994, 649.
12. EPO-**G 3/97** and EPO-**G 4/97** (OJ 1999, 245, 270).
13. EPO—G 3/97, OJ 1999, 245.
14. EPO—G 03/97.
15. EPO—G 9/93, OJ 1994, 891.
16. EPO—T 9/00, OJ 2002, 275.

opposition must contain three elements: a statement of (i) the extent to which the European patent is opposed and (ii) of the grounds on which the opposition is based as well as (iii) an indication of the facts, evidence and arguments presented in support of those grounds. If a ground for opposition is alleged in the notice of opposition but not substantiated in that manner within the nine-month period for opposition, the opposition is inadmissible in that respect and the failure cannot be cured anymore.[17] Requirement (iii) is of particular importance as it is only satisfied if the contents of the notice of opposition are sufficient to be properly understood on an objective basis[18] in order that the patentee and the opposition division understand what the opponent's case is about. The criteria of "when, where and what" needs thus to be set out in detail.[19] Otherwise, the notice of opposition will be rejected. The EPO provides a form (Form 2300)[20] that sets forth all the information needed to ensure that an opposition is admissible. Notice of opposition may be filed either electronically using the EPO opposition filing software, by fax or by mail.

The notice of opposition shall be complete and contain all available evidentiary support that might be used against the patent and possible attempts of the patentee to get a patent in an amended form. The reason for this is that evidence and facts submitted after the expiration of the opposition period may potentially be rejected as late-filed. This evidentiary support should include prior art references, witness declarations, test reports, etc., which may be used to argue against the patentability of claims.

A notice of opposition is not deemed to have been filed until the opposition fee (presently: EUR 785) has been paid.[21] The payment must occur within the nine-month opposition period. [22] The failure to pay it within that period leads to the rejection of the opposition.[23]

5.2. Amendments During the Proceedings

Shortly after expiration of the opposition period or the period provided for remedying deficiencies or presenting evidence, the patentee is invited to file observations and, where appropriate, amendments, within a period specified by the EPO (usually four months). Opposition proceedings do not represent a continuation of the examination proceedings. In that stage the patentee is thus limited in amending his patent. The amendments must be occasioned by a ground for opposition even if that ground has not been raised by an opponent (Rule 80 EPC). For instance, the patentee is allowed to remove inadmissibly added subject matter in opposition proceedings opened by an opponent on the ground of patentability. However, the patentee is normally not

17. EPO-T 182/89 (OJ 1991, 391).
18. EPO-T 222/85 (OJ 1988, 128).
19. T 522/94, OJ 1998, 421.
20. The form can be downloaded from the EPO website and used as checklist for the information which is necessary for the notice: www.epo.org/.
21. Schedule of fees and expenses of the EPO, applicable as from Apr. 1, 2016.
22. Article 99(1) EPC.
23. EPO-T 152/85 (OJ 1987, 191).

allowed to amend dependent claims or to correct errors in the description. It would be an abuse of opposition if the patentee were allowed merely to improve the disclosure by amendments not specifically necessitated by the grounds advanced for the opposition.[24]

The patentee may request that the patent be maintained in its granted or amended form and he may file a main request and one or more auxiliary requests. The main request is typically aimed at a confirmation of the claims of the patent as granted or in a slightly amended, more narrow form, whereas auxiliary requests typically relate to sets of claims which are filed as fallback positions with a further narrowed scope of protection than the main request. Auxiliary requests are made in case the Division does not allow the main request. They will be considered in the sequence chosen by the patentee.

It is a general principle of the EPC that opposition proceedings are held in the interest of the public and not for the benefit of the patentee. Therefore, it is inadmissible to amend the patent in any way other than to overcome a ground of opposition. Thus, the patentee is not allowed to introduce amendments meant solely to clarify the claims, to amend dependent claims or to correct errors in the description unless these amendments are directly triggered by amendments to the independent claims.

If an amendment responds to an attack, then combining granted claims is an appropriate reply to an opposition, even if this generates two independent claims in the same category.[25] The requirement of unity must not be met in opposition proceedings. The patentee may also base amendments on the patent specification, provided they are clearly and unambiguously supported therein. Dependent claims should represent the primary source for amendments in opposition proceedings. If the request represents a simple combination of granted claims, the risk of unity and clarity objections is lower and the Opposition Division is also more indulgent if the request is late filed.

During the proceedings, the Opposition Division invites, within fixed time periods, the parties to file observations on their own or other parties' communications by the Opposition Division. Upon receipt of such a communication, the patentee may amend the description or claims and drawings to respond to the grounds raised by the opposition(s). Of particular importance is the deadline which is typically set in the summons for filing written submissions or amendments in preparation for the oral proceedings (see next Chapters). New facts and evidence presented after that date will most likely not be considered by the Opposition Division, except that there are good reasons for such late submission. The division has discretion to consider such amendments, whereby the common standard is that any amendment must be made in the most expedient manner, taking into due account the interests of all parties. Also undesirable delays should be avoided.[26]

24. EPO—T 127/85.
25. EPO—T 263/05, OJ 2008, 329: Pursuant to Rule 43(2) EPC, a plurality of independent claims in the same claim category are allowable in only exceptional circumstances, which are listed in Rule 43(2)(a), (b) and (c). The Boards of Appeal of the EPO held that Rule 43(2) was not applicable in opposition proceedings, but such amendment must be occasioned by a necessary and meaningful reaction on a ground of opposition.
26. EPO-**T 648/96.**

5.3. Summons

Oral proceedings take place either upon the order of the Opposition Division if it considers this to be expedient or on request by a party to the proceedings (Article 116(1) EPC). Typically, oral proceedings are requested by the parties. Summonses are issued by the Division, normally about three to six months, but at least two months, before the date of the final hearing.[27] The oral proceedings will take place at a specified date, time, and place (Munich, The Hague or Berlin).

In a note annexed to the summons, the Opposition Division usually lists and explains the points that it believes need to be discussed. This note normally also includes the Division's non-binding provisional opinion on the positions adopted by the parties, and specifically on amendments to the patent filed by the patentee. This opinion is called the "Preliminary Opinion." Even though this opinion is not binding, it challenges the parties to carefully review its points and objections in order to better focus their arguments.

At the same time, the Opposition Division fixes a final date, which is generally one or two months before the hearing, for filing written submissions or amendments in preparation for the oral proceedings.

5.4. Late-Filed Requests by the Patentee

Any request to amend the claims filed after the deadline set in the summons is considered untimely and may be rejected on that basis (Rule 116(1) EPC). Normally, the EPO sets the final deadline for submissions one month before the date of the oral hearing. This deadline is not extendable. Untimely filed amendments must be based on good reasons.[28] This is the case if they represent a reaction on a change of the proceeding, which might be caused by the submission of a relevant new prior art document. In general, the Board of Appeal admits amendments filed in response to comments and objections made by the EPO or the other party.[29] An untimely request is more likely to be accepted if it proposes a combination of granted claims submitted in order to overcome objections raised by an opponent during the proceedings.[30] Accordingly, opponents should be prepared for requests possibly being filed during the oral proceedings.

Late-filed requests should also contain prima facie allowable subject matter.[31] That is, they must be manifestly clear, they should not contain subject matter that extends beyond the content of the application as filed (Article 123(2) EPC),[32] and must

27. Rule 115(1) EPC.
28. EPO—T 382/97.
29. EPO—T 648/96.
30. EPO—T 648/96.
31. EPO—T 382/97.
32. See Ch. 5, s. 5 "Standards on Original Disclosure."

be responsive to the objections raised up to then. Any doubts as to those issues may result in the request being rejected. The Boards of Appeal are much more restrictive than the Opposition Divisions with regard to late evidence, submissions or requests. In that respect, the Rules of Procedure of the Boards of Appeal clearly provide a legal framework under which such late submissions or requests might be refused, as relevance is no longer the sole criterion.

5.5. Late-Filed Facts or Evidence by the Challenger

The EPO may disregard late-filed facts or evidence according to Article 114(2) EPC. Their filing could be considered as being belated if a careful preparation would have given rise to an earlier submission.[33] This is the reason why the opponent is principally required to submit all facts and evidence during the nine-month opposition period.[34] Belated filings may, in exceptional circumstances, be accepted, provided that they are manifestly relevant to the matter, particularly if the evidence or facts are more relevant than what is already on file.[35] A belated document might also be accepted if it is filed in response to another party's submission[36] or if it is an appropriate and immediate reaction to developments in the previous proceedings.[37] Usually the division disregards late-filed evidence, and/or states that the newly submitted evidence is cumulative.[38] Accordingly, late-filed evidence, documents and other matter could be rejected on the ground of their irrelevance, i.e., on the basis that they were no more "weighty"[39] than documents which were already on file. Of course, as soon as a submission is considered as being abusive it shall not be permitted.[40]

5.6. The Hearing

The chairman of the Division identifies the issues to be investigated and their order of treatment. Each party is then invited to present its case in the order of the issues as determined by the chairman. The opponent usually begins, and then the patentee has an opportunity to reply. Each party is given a second or further opportunity to speak on the same issue in question. Once a decision on a given issue has been reached and then announced by the chairman, the issue is considered to be settled and cannot be subject to further discussions.

33. EPO—T 156/84.
34. EPO—T 117/89, OJ 1989, 401.
35. EPO—T 1557/05.
36. EPO—T 951/97.
37. EPO—T 855/96.
38. EPO—T 237/03.
39. EPO—T 611/90, OJ 1993, 50.
40. EPO—T 273/84, OJ 1986, 346.

5.7. Decision of the Opposition Division

It takes an average of two to three years from the end of the nine-month opposition period before a hearing takes place and a first instance decision is then rendered by the Opposition Division.

The proceedings can be accelerated if a party to the proceedings files a request containing legitimate interests for acceleration. This is, in cases where an infringement action in respect of the European patent is pending before a national court, a party may request an accelerated processing of the opposition.[41] The EPO will then endeavor to issue the next procedural action (for instance: summons to the oral proceedings) within three months from the receipt of the request, or where the request is filed within the opposition period, within three months after the patentee's response to the notice of opposition.[42]

The decision is usually announced at the end of the hearing. A written decision follows several weeks later. The Opposition Division may reject the opposition and affirm the patent, may revoke the patent completely, or as a middle ground may maintain the patent in an amended form.

Table 6.1. Possible Result of Opposition Proceedings

Revocation	*Limitation by Amendment of the Claims*	*Maintenance of the Patent as Granted*
- **Scope of Decision**: It applies in all Contracting States in respect of which it has been granted. - **Costs**: Each party to the opposition proceedings shall bear the costs it has incurred, unless the Opposition Division, for reasons of equity, orders, a different apportionment of costs.		

5.8. Appeal of Decisions of the Opposition Division

Decisions of the Opposition Division can be appealed to the Board of Appeals (Article 106 EPC).[43] Note that according to Article 111 EPC the Board of Appeal may itself exercise any power within the competence of the opposition division (such as revocation, maintenance or limitation of the patent), or it may remit the case to the opposition division. A remittal may result from new facts or evidence (not rejected as belated) introduced for the first time in the appeal proceedings.

41. See Notice of the EPO dated Mar. 17, 2008, OJ EPO 2008, 221.
42. See Notice of the EPO dated Mar. 17, 2008, OJ EPO 2008, 221.
43. The provisions governing the appeal procedure are set out in Art. 106 EPC to Art. 111 EPC and R. 99 EPC to R. 103 EPC and in the Rules of Procedure of the Boards of Appeal (OJ EPO 2007, 536).

A notice of appeal shall be filed within two months of the notification of the decision of the Opposition Division, along with payment of the fee for appeal. The appellant has four months from the notification of the decision to make the statement setting forth the grounds for appeal (Article 108 EPC).

Any opponents then have four months from notification of the grounds for filing a written reply to it.[44]

The Board of Appeal principally acts as the final instance in opposition procedures before the EPO. Only on exceptional grounds (Article 112(a) EPC) such as in a case of the "fundamental violation of Article 113," which guarantees the right to be heard, can a further appeal for review of a decision rendered by the Board of Appeals be filed with the Enlarged Board of Appeal. Accordingly, the EPO Opposition proceedings end with the decision of the Boards of Appeal in the vast majority of cases.

If the decision represents a full revocation of the patent, it is binding on the national courts, and the patentee will lose the patent forever. The situation is different if an amended patent emerges after the end of opposition proceedings. The patent might then be subject to national invalidation proceedings, which are limited to national territorial boundaries and the respective national part of the European Patent.

6. WITHDRAWAL OF OPPOSITION

Opposition proceedings may be continued by the EPO on its own motion if the opposition is withdrawn (Rule 84(2) EPC). The opposition division has discretion to continue the proceedings after a withdrawal. For instance, the proceedings may be continued if the proceedings are in an advanced stage and it is likely that they result in a limitation or revocation of the patent.[45] The situation is different if the withdrawal of the opposition occurs during appeal proceedings. If the opponent is the sole appellant his withdrawal would immediately and automatically terminate the appeal proceedings, irrespective of the patentee's consent.[46] Thus, the Board of Appeal cannot continue the appeal proceedings on its own motion. If, however, the opponent is the respondent, withdrawal of the opposition does not affect the appeal proceedings.[47]

7. INTERVENTION AFTER THE NINE-MONTH OPPOSITION PERIOD

After the nine-month opposition period has passed, a party may intervene in an on-going opposition proceeding if it has been sued for patent infringement. (Article 105 EPC). Likewise, a party may intervene in an opposition if the party has received a request from the patentee to cease infringement of the patent, and the party has

44. See Art. 12 of the Rules of Procedure of the Boards of Appeal: An extension of this time limit may exceptionally be allowed at the board's discretion following receipt of a written and reasoned request. Reasons lying entirely within the control of the party, such as holiday related absences, would however not be considered as exceptional.
45. EPO—T 197/88, OJ 1989, 412.
46. EPO—G 8/93, OJ 1994, 887.
47. EPO—T 340/05.

instituted proceedings for a court ruling of non-infringement. The accused infringer may intervene in the opposition proceedings within three months of the date on which infringement proceedings were instituted against the party, or on which the party instituted proceedings for a court ruling of non-infringement. Intervention is permissible as long as opposition or appeal proceedings are pending.

8. STATISTICS

Approximately 6% of all granted European patents are subject to opposition proceedings.[48] Of those, about one-third are revoked, one-third are maintained in an amended form, which generally means that the scope of protection is reduced, and one-third are maintained as granted. This is a rough estimation and there are significant differences among the various technical sectors.

9. INTERACTION OF EPO OPPOSITION AND NATIONAL COURT

EPO opposition proceedings may lead to the revocation of the entire patent, its maintenance with the originally granted scope, or the allowance of a more limited scope.

In several European jurisdictions, opposition proceedings at the EPO and national revocation actions cannot be implemented simultaneously. For example, in Germany the admissibility of a national revocation action requires that no opposition proceedings against the patent be pending and that the time period for filing an opposition against the patent have passed.[49] This requirement is mainly aimed at avoiding contradictory decisions. A German nullity action against the German part of a traditional European patent can also be filed by any person,[50] including the previous opponents from the opposition proceedings and independent upon the fact that an opposition has been previously conducted.

One is not stopped in Europe from re-litigating arguments that failed in opposition proceedings, unlike the U.S. This is an important difference from proceedings in the U.S. through the Patent Trial and Appeal Board ("PTAB"), from which a losing challenger would be estopped from making the same invalidity arguments in district court (including arguments that could reasonably have been raised). Thus, challengers in Europe may get "two bites at the apple" in attempting to invalidate a patent first through opposition proceedings, and then through a nullity action in the national courts.

Decisions rendered by the EPO are not binding on the Germany's Federal Patent Court and Supreme Court.[51] However, as such, a European patent that has been finally

48. www.epo.org.
49. Federal Supreme Court, decision of Apr. 19, 2011, X 124/10, "Mautberechnung"; Section 81(2) German Patent Act.
50. See Ch. 7, s. 3.2.
51. Federal Patent Court, decision of Oct. 8, 1992, 3 Ni 50/91.

revoked by the EPO (for instance, after Appeal) cannot be "revived" by national courts. In addition, as soon as a European Patent gets a particular (limited) scope of protection through EPO opposition proceedings, national courts are prevented from reinstating a previously applied broader scope of protection.

CHAPTER 7

Nullity Actions

1. SPLIT SYSTEM

Germany is one of the few countries in the world where infringement proceedings are tried separately from validity challenges. Patent validity must be attacked through "nullity" proceedings in the Federal Patent Court, after the limited time window for challenging patents in opposition proceedings has closed. This split system, with infringement tried in the District Courts of general jurisdiction, and nullity proceedings tried in the Federal Patent Court, is a defining characteristic of German patent litigation.

The separation of infringement and nullity proceedings continues even to the Federal Supreme Court, where both sets of proceedings could be ultimately litigated. An infringement case started with one of the District Courts will not be heard together with a parallel invalidation case filed with the Federal Patent Court. Even in the last instance, these cases are heard as independent cases and are un-coordinated with regard to timing.

Most commonly, nullity actions trail behind the associated infringement proceedings. This results from the fact that the first phase in a patent dispute is frequently the filing of an infringement complaint, and also from the fact that infringement proceedings are typically faster than nullity actions (at least when the infringement court does not appoint experts or stay the case pending the nullity action). The "head start" of infringement cases over the corresponding nullity action, and the District Court's presumption that patents are valid, can put enormous pressure on the accused infringer. Frequently the District Court will impose injunctive relief before a nullity challenge can be heard.

Figure 7.1 illustrates the split system. Nullity proceedings in the Federal Patent Court are described in the left side of the table. Infringement proceedings (the focus of Chapter 8), which are tried in the District Courts of general jurisdiction, are shown on the right.

Figure 7.1. Split System

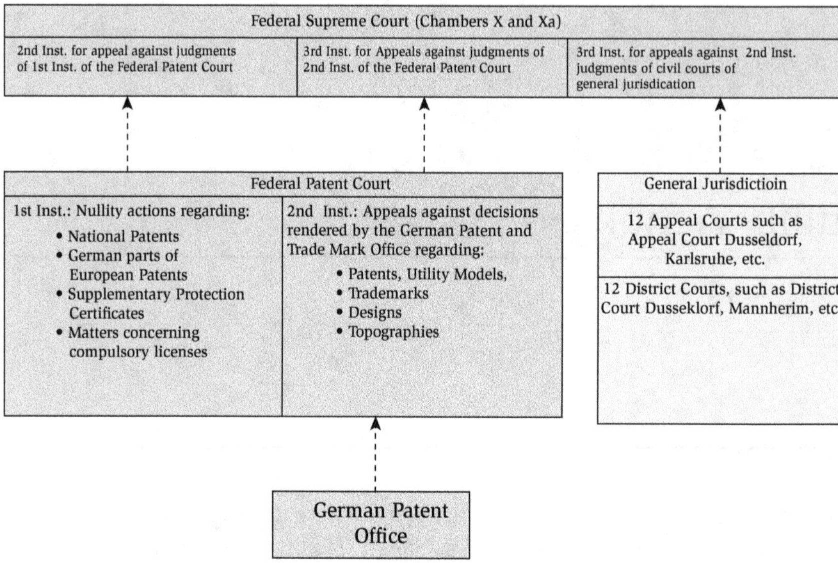

2. COURT STRUCTURE

The Federal Patent Court in Munich was established on July 1, 1961. Until that date, the main tasks of today's Federal Patent Court were handled by the German Patent and Trademark Office. Because this was considered to represent a conflict with the constitutional principal of separation of powers,[1] the tasks had to be handed over to a judicial authority that was independent of the German Patent and Trademark Office. This is today the Federal Patent Court, with its independent judges appointed by the Federal President of Germany.

2.1. Federal Patent Court

The Federal Patent Court is a Court of First Instance for nullity actions (shown in the left box of the table "Split System"). The Federal Patent Court also has second instance (i.e., appellate) jurisdiction over decisions rendered by the examining sections and patent departments of the German Patent Office (middle box of Figure 7.1). An appeal to the Federal Supreme Court may be lodged based on questions of law, without further review of facts. The same applies to judgments rendered in utility model matters (cancellation proceedings according to §§17, 18(4) Utility Model Act).

1. Federal Administrative Tribunal, decision of Jun. 13, 1959, NJW 1959, 1507 or BVerwGE 8, 350.

In contrast to the courts of general jurisdiction, the composition of the Federal Patent Court is not limited to legal judges. This court includes technically trained judges, who have the same duties as legally trained judges, and whose role is not limited to assisting the legally trained judges. These technical judges are appointed by the Federal President of Germany[2] only after they have typically worked for many years in a technical profession and have completed a degree in one of the natural or technical sciences at a German university. Many of the technically trained judges previously served as examiners at the Patent Office.

2.2. Federal Supreme Court

The court of last resort is the Federal Supreme Court in Karlsruhe. Until October 2009, appeals on judgments rendered by the Federal Patent Court on nullity actions could be focused on a review of points of law and on facts. Thus, the Federal Supreme Court had to take evidence and appointed a court expert in almost all cases. Since the enactment of the Patent Law Modernization Act on October 1, 2009 the role of the Federal Supreme Court has been significantly changed. According to §111(1) of the German Patent Act, the Supreme Court's role is now principally limited to a review of questions of law. The intention of the legislature was aimed at concentrating the burden of the factual assessment, including the related evidence taking, on the first instance proceedings.[3] Accordingly, the assessment of the factual aspects of the case is on the shoulders of the Federal Patent Court.

The Federal Supreme Court has one chamber dealing with nullity actions in second-instance proceedings, namely Chamber X. The chamber is composed of five judges. Even though these judges do not have a technical background, and tend to fall within the category of traditional judges, they are highly qualified and well regarded in the area of patent law. Many of them were previously either judges at the Federal Patent Court or were promoted from prominent infringement courts such as the District Court Düsseldorf. Chamber X is presided over by Justice Meier-Beck, who previously presided over Chamber 4 of the District Court Düsseldorf.

3. MAIN PROCEDURAL ASPECTS OF NULLITY ACTIONS

3.1. Priority of Opposition Proceedings over Nullity Actions

Opposition proceedings and nullity actions must follow in chronological order. They may not be implemented simultaneously.[4] Section 81(2) of the Patent Act sets a timeline for the filing of a nullity action. A nullity action requires that no opposition proceedings against the patent be pending and that the time period for filing an opposition against the patent has passed. If a nullity action is filed too early, the Federal

2. Section 65(3) of the Patent Act.
3. BlPMZ 2009, 307.
4. Federal Supreme Court, X ZR 29/05, GRUR 2005, 967, "Strahlungssteuerung."

Patent Court would dismiss it on that basis. This rule is applicable to oppositions at the German Patent Office and the EPO. This requirement is aimed at avoiding contradictory decisions (Figure 7.2).[5]

Even if the Board of Appeals of the EPO remands the case for further prosecution to the Opposition Division (Article 111(2) EPC), a nullity action is not permissible as long as the opposition proceedings have not been closed. A third party which cannot file an opposition due to the lapsed opposition period may join pending opposition proceedings provided that an infringement lawsuit has been filed against this party (§59(2) Patent Act, Article 105 EPC).[6] A nullity action is even inadmissible with regard to a opposition pending with the European Patent Office even if it is exclusively based on a national patent application with better prior-right effect under Article 139(2) EPC which can only be alleged in national revocation proceedings.[7]

After the opposition window has closed, a nullity action may be filed at any time. Nullity actions may even be brought after patent expiration, in the limited case where the challenger can show a special legal interest in the invalidation of the patent, such as where the patentee has sought damages for infringement that arose during the life of the patent.

3.2. Parties to the Nullity Action

Nullity actions may be filed by any person or legal entity.[8] When filing a lawsuit against a patent with the Federal Patent Court, the plaintiff is not required to demonstrate a particular interest. He or she can file the nullity action without being sued or otherwise threatened by the patentee. A party who filed an unsuccessful opposition proceeding is not precluded from bringing a second attack against the same patent through a subsequently introduced nullity action (*i.e.*, two bites at the apple are permitted). The nullity action can even be based on the same arguments used in the opposition proceedings.[9] Furthermore, a final and non-appealable decision rendered in a previous nullity action does not hinder a subsequent nullity action. The filing of a subsequent nullity action is however impermissible if the same party files it based on the same ground for revocation, even if this action is based on new facts and evidence.[10] It is however acceptable if the same plaintiff subsequently files a nullity action based on a different ground for revocation. Thus, it would be possible for the same party to file a first nullity action based on the ground of missing patentability and a second based on lack of enabling disclosure.

5. Federal Supreme Court, X ZR 29/05, GRUR 2005, 967, "Strahlungssteuerung."
6. *See* Ch. 6, s. 7.
7. Federal Supreme Court, decision of Apr. 19, 2011 – X ZR 124/10, GRUR 2011, 848, point 8 et seq. = IIC 2012, 475 "Mautberechnung."
8. Federal Supreme Court, decision of Jan. 1, 1963, Ia ZR 174/63, GRUR 63, 253, "Bürovorsteher."
9. Federal Supreme Court, GRUR 1996, 753, Zahnkranzfäser.
10. Federal Supreme Court, Ia ZR 64/63, GRUR 1964, 18, "Konditionierungseinrichtung."

Figure 7.2. Priority of Opposition over Nullity

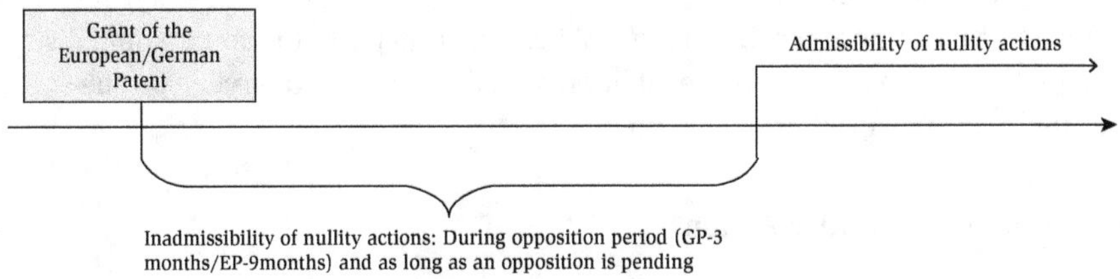

Even a "straw man," i.e., someone who acts in his own name, without interest in the proceedings, but on behalf of an anonymous party, may file such an action. This is in fact a common method of staying anonymous.[11] Often competitors prefer to stay in the background and involve a "straw man" to take measures against disagreeable and uncomfortable patents of competing companies. In many of these cases, they prefer to take the anonymous route in order to avoid problems in their relationship with the patentee, or they simply do not want to raise awareness of their business intentions. There are, however, limits to the straw man action, in particular if the party which stands behind the straw man is contractually obligated not to challenge the patent, as may be the case in a license agreement.[12] Using a straw man is also impermissible for a party who has already lost a nullity action, and is seeking to retry it on the same ground for revocation.[13] But the burden falls upon the patentee to prove an objection to a nullity proceeding on the basis of prohibited party, and this can be a difficult burden to meet.

Figure 7.3. Simplified Chronology of Invalidation Proceedings

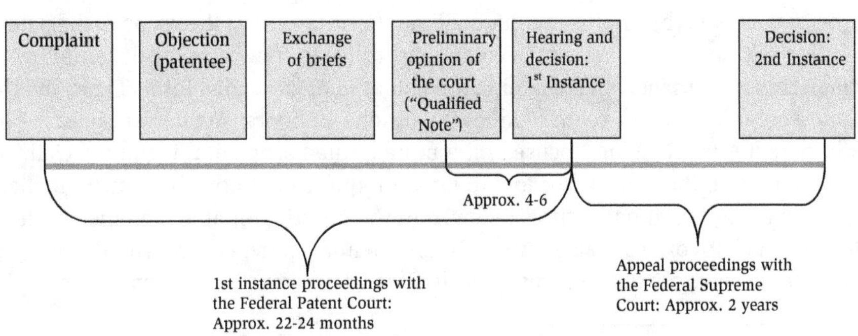

The nullity action shall be directed against the person or legal entity registered as the patentee in the patent register (§81(1) Patent Act). This provision applies regardless

11. Federal Patent Court, decision of Nov. 13, 2008—10 Ni 30/07.
12. Federal Patent Court, decision of Mar. 30, 2004—1 Ni 28/02.
13. Federal Patent Court, decision of Nov. 13, 2008—10 Ni 30/07.

of whether or not that person or entity actually owns the patent. Only the party registered as the patentee is the right addressee of the complaint. This is also applicable if the actual owner differs from the registered one. The patentee must appear in the register at the latest by at the day of the oral hearing, otherwise the court would dismiss the action.[14] Third parties with a legal interest in the suit may intervene on the side of either the nullity plaintiff or defendant.

3.3. Timing of a Nullity Action

Nullity actions are decided in the first instance by the Federal Patent Court, usually within 22 to 24 months from the filing date of the complaint. The appeal proceedings usually last roughly an additional two years. Thus, the total length of nullity actions through two instances generally amounts to approximately four years.

3.3.1. Chronology of First Instance (Federal Patent Court)

Complaint. The complaint contains the grounds for revoking the patent.[15] According to §82 of the Patent Act, as soon as the nullity complaint is filed the court serves the complaint on the named defendant. This should be the person or entity named as patentee in the register of the Patent Office,[16] even if the patent has been assigned to a third party and no longer belongs to the person or entity named in the register.[17]

Reply. The court invites the defendant to reply to the complaint within one month. If the patentee fails to object to the revocation in due time, a decision complying with the plaintiff's request may be rendered without a hearing (§82(2) Patent Act). In this default situation, the factual allegations of the plaintiff are regarded as proven by the court, and if plaintiff's requests are coherent, the court will grant them.

Self-limitations. The patentee may choose to strengthen his position by narrowing the patent—i.e., by offering additional limitations to restrict the scope of the patent (so-called self-limitations). It is thus common practice to file an appropriate number of auxiliary requests in view of sustaining the patent in an amended form. Typically, the patentee submits a main request followed by one or more auxiliary requests. The auxiliary requests which are focused on a more limited scope of the granted claim(s) are made in case the court considers the main request not allowable. Such auxiliary requests may be based on features taken from the description and combined with an independent claim or, if suitable, by combining an independent claim with the features of one or more dependent claims. The limited claim must itself comply with the

14. Federal Supreme Court, Ia ZR 261/63, GRUR 1966, 107, "Patentrolleneintragung."
15. *See* Ch. 7, s. 3.5.
16. The register is available online: https://dpinfo.dpma.de/: It contains information about name/address of the patentee, name/address of the representative, if there is any, as well as the status of the patent i.e., whether it is in force or not. It also contains some information about the history of the patent, in particular, whether nullity actions have been filed against the patent. If this is the case, the register provides the docket number by which means a files inspection can be made at the Federal Patent Court.
17. Federal Patent Court, decision of Apr. 16, 2015, 2 Ni 8/13.

patentability requirements. In that respect, it is essential that the feature combination in the limited claim be sufficiently disclosed in the application as originally filed.[18]

Qualified note: After having given the parties the opportunity to present their arguments in writing, the Federal Patent Court typically issues an order highlighting the aspects of particular importance, and setting forth a deadline for the parties to submit additional pleadings (§83(1) and (2) Patent Act). At present, such notes are issued approximately four to six months prior to the hearing. In particular, for defendants of infringement proceedings it would be desirable that the qualified note is issued earlier. They typically have an interest in that nullity and infringement proceedings are synchronized. Indeed, a note questioning the validity of the claims as asserted in the parallel infringement proceedings renders a stay of the proceedings more likely.

With the note, the court directs the parties to the facts that it considers of particular importance for the decision. Also, the court typically provides a preliminary opinion on the legal situation. The qualified note is of particular importance for the parties because it sets forth the panel's understanding of the state of the art being applied for an assessment of novelty and inventive step (non-obviousness). It thus enables the parties to adequately react on the position of the court and to focus their previous submissions though new facts and arguments.[19] Accordingly, the court may ask the parties to file further pertinent pleadings concerning issues of particular importance, and to complete their pleadings within a deadline. Typically, the court sets in the note a deadline of one month for the additional pleadings. To this deadline one further month is added in order that each party may respond to the pleadings of the adversary party. Submissions, such as new facts and new requests,[20] filed after these deadlines may be rejected as being late-filed if the delay is not sufficiently excused (§83(1), (2) and (4) of the Patent Act). Prior to the deadline set in the qualified note a submission of new facts can principally not be rejected as being late filed.[21]

Hearing. The hearing takes place approximately two years after filing the complaint.[22] At the beginning of the oral hearing the presiding judge may ask the parties if they are interested in settling the matter in an amicable way without a court decision. If unsuccessful, the court then proceeds with substantive issues of the case. Witnesses are only heard in exceptional cases. The discussion of the facts follows after the presiding judge has given an introduction on the decisive facts of the case and relevant questions of law. He reports on the essential content of the files. Following the presiding judge's introduction, the court gives the parties the opportunity to argue on the matter (§90(2) Patent Act). This discussion takes, in average cases, one day. In more complicated cases this can extend to two or more days. If the matter—in the view of the court—is sufficiently discussed, normally at the end of the hearing day, the presiding judge declares the hearing closed. In contrast to the infringement courts, which do not announce an oral judgment the same day, the Federal Patent Court

18. Federal Supreme Court, GRUR 2002, 49 "Drehmomentübertragungseinrichtung"; Federal Supreme Court, GRUR 2015, 249, Schleifprodukt.
19. Federal Supreme Court, GRUR 2012, 1236, "Fahrzeugwechselstromgenerator."
20. Federal Patent Court, decision of Jul. 31, 2014—6 Ni 3/14.
21. Federal Patent Court, decision of May 28, 2013—3 Ni 6/12.
22. BPatG Annual Report 2015 Business Report.

usually renders and announces a judgment. This judgment is announced orally in front of the parties after deliberation. The judges' deliberations (non-public of course) take place at the end of the hearing, usually last no longer than an hour, and the parties await the judges' return. In exceptional cases the parties are sent away and the decision is rendered at a later, separate session.

3.3.2. Appeal to the Federal Supreme Court

Notice of Appeal: According to §110 Patent Act, the notice of appeal must be filed within one month of the service of the written judgment of first instance. The one-month deadline for the notice of appeal is not extendable. The written judgment is usually provided four to six weeks after the rendering of the oral judgment. The one-month deadline starts to run on the date of the receipt of the full text of the judgment. However, in the rare instances when a written decision is not provided in a timely manner, the appeal must be filed at latest five months after the announcement of the oral judgment (§110(3) Patent Act).

Reasons for Appeal: The appellant must also give reasons for the appeal. These reasons may be contained in the notice (see above) or in a subsequent brief, which must be filed within a term of three months after a timely reception of the written judgment (§112(2) Patent Act). However, upon request of the appellant this term may be extended by the Chairman of the Chamber at the Federal Supreme Court in charge of nullity appeal proceedings (presently Chamber *X*) if the opposing party consents to it. The Chairman of the Chamber may extend this deadline even without the consent of the opposing party if the appellant demonstrates considerable reasons for the extension, or if the proceedings would not be delayed by the request (§112(2) Patent Act).

Before the Patent Law Modernization Act[23] came into force, the Federal Supreme Court usually appointed court experts. These experts were selected from the specific technical field in question (in many cases professors at universities). They mostly helped to provide the appropriate understanding of the terminology used in the disclosure of the originally filed documents and to illustrate the knowledge of the person skilled in the art at the priority date.

A court does not rely on court experts for assessing inventive step. The question of whether or not an inventive step is involved in a particular case was and still is regarded as a question of law which falls within the competence of the court. In other words, the court must take its own decision on inventive step. Under the present law, the Federal Supreme Court will not take evidence and appoint court experts to the extent it did in the past. Nevertheless, if the facts gathered in first instance are not sufficient to determine whether there is an inventive step it is likely that the Federal Supreme Court will remand the case back to the first instance court (§119 of the Patent Act).

According to §118(1) Patent Act, the decision of the Federal Supreme Court is rendered on the basis of an oral hearing. If a party duly summoned to the proceedings

23. Federal Gazette BGBl. 2009 (Patent Law Modernization Act came into force on Oct. 1, 2009).

does not attend the oral hearing, a decision can nevertheless proceed (§118(4) Patent Act). In the oral hearing the parties submit their requests and the Chairman of the Chamber of the Federal Supreme Court introduces the factual and legal issues. The parties are then given an opportunity to present their conclusive arguments. Finally, usually at the end of the hearing day, the Federal Supreme Court sets a date for the rendering and announcement of the decision.

Since the decision of the Federal Supreme Court is a final decision—i.e., no legal remedy is provided against a decision of the Federal Supreme Court—it takes effect upon its announcement.

3.4. Object of Nullity Actions

A nullity action may be initiated against:

- German patents; or
- German parts of European patents;
- Supplementary protection certificates issued for patents covering medical or plant protection products. According to §16a of the Patent Act, supplementary protection certificates form a separate category of intellectual property rights. However, their main purpose is to extend the term of a basic patent, which is in force when filing the application covering products that required an administrative authorization for their commercialization according to Regulations of the European Economic Community (EEC), such as the EEC directive concerning medical products[24] or plant protection products.[25] Supplementary protection certificates are particularly aimed at alleviating the consequences resulting from lengthy administrative authorization proceedings during which a commercialization of the product is not possible.

It is the object of nullity actions to determine whether or not the challenged patent is to be revoked in total, revoked in part or maintained as granted. The requests of the plaintiff in the complaint are binding for the scope of the nullity action.[26] If plaintiff's requests are limited to particular claims, the court will not render a decision on the remaining claims not covered by the request.[27]

3.5. Grounds for Revocation

The grounds that may be raised to challenge a patent in nullity proceedings are limited to those listed in §§22, 21(1) of the Patent Act (for German national patents) or in

24. Council Regulation (EEC) 1768/92 of Jun. 18, 1992 concerning the creation of a supplementary protection certificate for medicinal products (OJ L 182, Jul. 2, 1992, 1).
25. Regulation (EC) 1610/96 of the European Parliament and of the Council of Jul. 23, 1996 concerning the creation of a supplementary protection certificate for plant protection products (OJ L 198, Aug. 8, 1996, 30).
26. Federal Supreme Court, I ZR 49/53, GRUR 1954, 317, "Entwicklungsgerät."
27. Federal Patent Court, BPatGE 24, 36; Federal Patent Court BlPMZ 04, 58.

Article II §6 IntPatÜG (for German parts of European Patents). This listing is exhaustive and contains in total five grounds of revocation. These grounds do not exactly match the grounds for opposition in EPO proceeding. In particular N° 3 "Usurpation" is unknown on the European level (see Chapter 6, section 3). Section 22, 21 of the Patent Act is applicable to German Patents, however Article II §6(1) IntPatÜG in connection with Article 138 EPC aligns the situation for European Patents. Therefore, there is no reason to differentiate between German parts of European Patents and national German patents.

N°1—Lack of patentability (§§22, 21(1) N°1 Patent Act): This refers to the lack of a patentable invention, which might be a lack of novelty, inventive step and/or industrial applicability. Also statutorily barred subject matter, such as schemes, rules and methods of doing business as such, aesthetic creations as such, and computer programs as such[28] fall under this category.

N° 2—Lack of an enabling disclosure (§§22, 21(1) N° 2 Patent Act): This ground refers to the patentability requirement that the claimed subject matter shall be disclosed in a manner sufficiently clear and concise as to enable a person skilled in the art to carry out the invention. The relevant skilled person in the art must, with the aid of his general skills, be in a position to implement the invention with the information he takes from the patent's disclosure. In general, lack of an enabling disclosure is a minor issue in most nullity proceedings, but may be of greater significance particularly for patents covering biotechnological inventions.

N° 3—Usurpation (§§21, 22 (1) N° 3 Patent Act): If the injured party was in possession of an invention which was unlawfully taken away from him (usurpation) and then filed—without his consent—as a patent application, this is ground for revocation of the patent.[29] If the court finds that there was indeed usurpation, a revocation of the patent will result. In the alternative, an action can be filed seeking an assignment of the patent right according to §8 of the Patent Act. An action filed on the basis of §8 Patent Act is usually the better option for the injured party, because it results in the assignment of the patent, whereas a nullity action based on the ground N° 3 of §21(1) Patent Act "Usurpation" would lead to a revocation of the patent.

N° 4—Inadmissible extensions (§§21(1) N° 4 Patent Act): A further ground for revocation exists where the subject matter of the patent extends beyond the content of the application, such as when extensions incorporated into the application during the course of the proceedings reach beyond the application as originally filed. This ground for revocation requires a comparison of the subject matter of the patent with the content of the application as filed. Where the subject matter exceeds the application as filed, there is an inadmissible extension. The subject matter of the patent is defined by the patent claims, specifically their scope of protection, which can be determined according to the general rules of claim construction.[30] The comparison requires a determination of the content of the application as originally filed, from the standpoint

28. *See* Ch. 5, s. 1 "Patentable Subject Matter."
29. If the German part of a European Patent is subject to a German nullity action, reference should be made to Art. 138(1)(e) EPC, Art. II §6 N°. 5 IntPatÜG.
30. Federal Supreme Court, X ZR 184/98, GRUR 2001, 140, "Zeittelegramm."

of what a skilled person may deduce in total from the claims, descriptions and figures. If the skilled person may directly and unambiguously deduce the subject matter of the patent, i.e., its claims, from the content of the original application, then the extension would be admissible.[31]

N° 5 — Extension of the scope of protection (§22 (1) Patent Act (second alternative): The grant of the patent limits the right of the patentee to amend the claims in subsequent proceedings such as opposition, limitation or nullity proceedings. The scope of the patent, defined by the subject matter of the claims as granted, is the reference for assessing the admissibility of amendments. Inadmissible amendments limit the patentee's options with regard to claim amendment during nullity proceedings. Whereas amendments enlarging the scope of protection are not admissible, amendments which limit the scope of the patent are admissible, provided the combination of features is disclosed in the application underlying the patent as originally filed and is also comprised in the patent as granted. It is also admissible to introduce new features into a claim as long as the combination of features of the amended claim does not extend beyond the disclosure of the patent application underlying the challenged patent as originally filed.[32]

Almost all grounds of revocation find their analogs in the provisions applicable to European Opposition proceedings. The plaintiff of a nullity action may base the action on the same grounds as he did in antecedent opposition proceedings. He is not barred in that respect.

3.6. Special Procedural Aspects

3.6.1. Scope of Nullity Actions

Nullity proceedings are adversarial. They are not initiated ex officio and depend on the requests of the plaintiff (§99(1) Patent Act in combination with §308 Code of Civil Procedure). Accordingly, if the plaintiff requests the invalidation of particular claims, the court would not review the validity of claims that are not covered by that request. The court's review is also limited to the asserted grounds of revocation. For instance, lack of enabling disclosure (§§22, 21(1) N°2) is not contained in the court's review if it is not explicitly asserted.[33] Furthermore, the patentee is entitled to either fully object to the defendant's requests or to pursue a limited defense in view of a limited maintenance of the patent. He can request the complete or partial dismissal of the action. A partial dismissal of the request may be sought if only a limited scope of protection is reasonably defendable due to newly discovered prior art.

Even though the proceedings are adversarial in nature, the court considers the legal questions of the case and evaluates the facts on its own motion (ex officio) once the lawsuit has been initiated. According to §87(1) of the Patent Act the court investigates ex officio the facts of the case. The court is not bound by the parties'

31. *See* Ch. 5, s. 5 "Standards on Original Disclosure."
32. *See* in detail Ch. 5, s. 5 "Standards of Original Disclosure."
33. Federal Patent Court, decision of Jul. 9, 1980, 3 Ni 31/79.

statements or their offers of proof. The court can even search for prior art on its own initiative if this is considered to be reasonable. However, in the context of an alleged public prior use, the court may request the alleging party to substantiate the alleged public prior use in detail, namely as to what was used, by whom, when and where. Due to the concept of ex officio proceedings, it is less problematic to submit newly discovered prior art during the proceedings provided that such submission is not considered abusive. However, if the court has set a deadline for submitting suitable requests or completing the pleadings, the need is even greater for submitting new prior art. Such a deadline could be set in a court order issued early in the proceedings in compliance with §83(1) of the Patent Act. In such an order the court will point to the aspects of the case that are presumably important to the decision and to which the parties are asked to adequately respond. If this order contains a deadline, the parties should do their best to sufficiently respond within the set time frame because further attacks, including the submission of prior art, might be considered belated and would only be admitted if sufficiently excused (see §83(4) Patent Act).

3.6.2. Withdrawal of Nullity Actions

The nullity proceedings can be terminated by means of a withdrawal. The plaintiff can file such a withdrawal at any time until the final termination of the nullity proceedings, even without the consent of the defendant.[34] The court would then not decide on the validity of the patent.[35] In contrast to opposition proceedings, the court cannot continue the proceedings on its own motion.

An already-issued negative preliminary opinion of the court expressing concerns as to the validity of the patent becomes legally ineffective if the nullity action is withdrawn. No further legal effects would result from that negative preliminary opinion. It nevertheless has an unfavorable effect for the patentee in that it is a public file which could be discovered by any third party through a file inspection[36] and used in support of subsequent nullity proceedings. Even if the parties agree on it, there is no way to render the preliminary opinion confidential.

Even a first instance decision invalidating the patent would become ineffective if the withdrawal occurs prior to the rendering of the second instance decision of the Federal Supreme Court.[37] Withdrawals of nullity actions are usually caused by settlements reached during the proceedings. Of course, the first instance decision of the Federal Patent Court is discoverable for everybody through a file inspection. Even though the ineffective decision might challenge competitors to attack the patent with the same arguments in subsequent proceedings, the decision has no legal effect on the validity of the patent and does not represent a legal obstacle to enforce the patent.

34. Federal Supreme Court, GRUR 2014, 911, "Sitzgelenk"
35. Federal Supreme Court, BlPMZ 1953, 382, 386, "Konservendose," Federal Supreme Court, decision of Sep. 30, 2010, Xa ZR 57/08, BeckRS 2010, 28218.
36. *See* Ch. 7, s. 4 "Inspection of Files."
37. Federal Supreme Court, I a ZR 64/63, GRUR 1964, 18, "Konditioniereinrichtung"; Federal Supreme Court, X ZR 25/86, GRUR 1993, 895, "Hartschaumplatten"; Federal Patent Court, decision from May 14, 2014, 5 Ni 50/12.

However, it must be anticipated that a third party would refer to the negative decision and argue that it could successfully challenge the decision by means of a new nullity action. The strength of such argument depends on the particular situation and the extent to which the patentee can demonstrate that the first instance decision was wrong.

3.6.3. Amendment of the Nullity Actions During the Proceedings

Even though the principle of ex officio proceedings is applicable once the proceedings have been started,[38] the subject matter of the proceedings lays basically in the hands of the parties. It is mainly determined by the submissions of the plaintiff in the complaint brief. The admissibility of later amendments to the action is determined by §263 Code of Civil Procedure. This provision requires either that the defendant agrees to it or that the court finds the amendment pertinent.[39] If the plaintiff for instance failed in the complaint brief to attack an independent claim of the granted patent, the court may include that omitted independent claim in the proceedings, if the defendant agrees (which he likely would not) or if the court considers it pertinent. The same applies if the plaintiff raises a new ground of revocation[40] that is not yet included in the filed nullity complaint brief.[41] The court is bound to the grounds of nullity as raised by the plaintiff and is not entitled to consider new grounds that were not raised.[42] An amendment to the action is difficult if it is requested after the lapse of the deadline set by the court in the order in compliance with §83(2) of Patent Act. This is the court order issued early in the proceedings wherein the court points to those aspects that are presumably important for the decision and to which the parties are asked to respond. If this order contains a deadline, the parties should do their best to sufficiently respond within the set time frame as further procedural changes requested by the parties after the lapse of the term might be considered belated and would only be excusable in exceptional cases (see §83(4) Patent Act).

Therefore, unless there are strategic reasons for limiting the attack on the patent, the plaintiff should include all of the granted claims into the nullity action and preferably base his attack on all possible grounds of nullity to avoid a possible inadmissibility of a later amendment of the action.

3.6.4. Admissibility of Claim Amendments filed During the Proceedings

The patentee may usually amend the claims of the patent during the course of validity proceedings, provided that the amendment does not exceed the scope of the original

38. *See* Ch. 7, s. 3.6.1.
39. Federal Patent Court, decision from Sep. 9, 2015, 5 Ni 30/13 (EP).
40. *See* Ch. 7, s. 3.5.
41. Federal Supreme Court, decision of Jun. 24, 1997, X ZR 13/94, Vorrichtung zum Auspressen; Federal Supreme Court, decision of May 11, 2010, X ZR 51/06, "Polymerisierbare Zementmischung" GRUR-Prax 2010, 366.
42. Federal Patent Court, BlPMZ 2004, 58.

disclosure and/or the scope of protection of the patent as granted. Accordingly, the patentee may defend his patent with a main request and a set of auxiliary requests that generally represent suitable fallback positions. The court may set deadlines to file such requests (§83(2) Patent Act). An auxiliary request may combine features of an independent claim with features of dependent claims and/or features disclosed in the description.[43]

4. INSPECTION OF THE FILES

In contrast to opposition proceedings at the EPO,[44] the files of the Federal Patent Court cannot be investigated through an online service. They can be inspected—in the form of photocopies or disks—by either party, or by third parties on request (§99(3) Patent Act). The third party need not provide any reason or justification for inspecting the files, or reveal for whom the inspection is carried out.[45]

Objections by the patentee to grants of inspection requests usually fail. In exceptional cases, provided that he can demonstrate a *protectable interest* (§99(3) Patent Act), the Court may exclude parts of the file from inspection. Such protectable interests may concern trade and commercial secrets or internal company data.[46] Information that has been introduced under violation of a protective order from U.S.-pretrial discovery proceedings may likewise be excluded from inspection.[47] Even statements concerning the scope of protection of the patent with respect to an infringing device have been excluded from inspection.[48]

However, usually the interests of the public in reviewing the files are considered more important. In particular the patentee will not be protected against the discovery of facts, such as expert opinions,[49] or prior art contained in the file that may be problematic for the validity of the patent. The patentee is also not protected against a file inspection if the nullity action has been withdrawn after a settlement.[50]

If the request is accepted, the files are rendered available to the claimant usually by means of copies taken from files or provided on compact discs.

43. The combination of features contained in auxiliary request must be sufficiently disclosed and shall not extend beyond the disclosure of the patent application underlying the challenged patent as originally filed: *See* details in Ch. 5, s. 5.
44. *See* www.epoline.org.
45. Federal Supreme Court, X ZR 4/00, GRUR 2001, 143, "Akteneinsicht XV"; Federal Supreme Court, X ZR 84/11, decision of Dec. 7, 2011.
46. Federal Supreme Court, X ZA 1/71 GRUR 1972, 195, "Akteneinsicht VIII."
47. Federal Patent Court, BPatGE 34, 83.
48. Federal Supreme Court, X ZR 133/05, GRUR 2007, 133, "Akteneinsicht XVII"; Federal Supreme Court, decision of Jan. 30, 2008, X ZR 1/07, GRUR 2008, 633, "Akteneinsicht XIX."
49. Federal Patent Court, BPatGE 22, 66, 68.
50. Federal Patent Court, BPatGE 34, 9.

5. INTERPLAY WITH INFRINGEMENT PROCEEDINGS

5.1. Stays of Infringement Proceedings Pending the Resolution of Validity

An important aspect of the split system is §148 of Code of Civil Procedure, which allows the infringement court to stay the proceedings if the invalidation attempts in parallel nullity proceedings significantly endanger the right holder's position. The threshold questions that need to be addressed by the court before it can stay the infringement proceedings are illustrated in a separate chapter.[51]

5.2. Effects of the Nullity Decisions

Once the patent has been finally revoked in part or in total—i.e., by a decision that cannot be appealed—the revocation of the patent is effective *ab initio* and has effect for everybody. In other words, it is as if the patent and application had never existed (§21(3) Patent Act).

The revocation of a patent also has important implications for pending infringement proceedings. The infringement proceedings will be closed to the extent the patent was revoked. In situations where a patent has been nullified after termination of the infringement proceedings, and the proceedings have already been closed by an executable final decision (favorable to the patentee), the adversary party, i.e., the former accused infringer, must begin a separate new trial if he seeks to correct an inconsistency between the nullity and infringement proceedings.[52] This action is called an action for restitution. It would be directed against the final infringement judgment and is aimed at obtaining a reopening of the infringement proceedings so that the action for infringement can be lifted. This remedy can also be applied in case of only a partial nullification of the patent, for instance where the use of a feature additionally incorporated in the patent claim by the revocation decision was not considered in the previous infringement proceedings and is not used in the alleged infringement.[53] The filing of an action for restitution is subject to a time limit of one month from the date on which the party concerned becomes aware of the cause for restitution.[54] In addition, the action for restitution can only be filed during a time of five years after the infringement judgement became final. This even applies if the cause of restitution, such as the revocation of the patent, occurs after the five-year time period. That time limit shall provide legal peace even though it may have a detrimental effect on the accused "infringer" in such an exceptional case of late patent revocation.

Limitations of the claim imposed in nullity proceedings by the Federal Patent Court result in a retroactive legal change to the wording of the claim. An added feature must then be considered when construing the claim. Such a change should be

51. *See* Ch. 8, s. 3.6.2 "Suspension of the Proceedings."
52. Section 580 N° 6 Code of Civil Procedure (action for restitution).
53. Federal Supreme Court, decision of Apr. 17, 2012 - X ZR 55/09, GRUR 2012, 753 = IIC 2012, 855, "*Tintenpatrone III*".
54. Section 586(1) and (2) ZPO.

anticipated by the plaintiff in the infringement proceedings and if possible the factual submissions should cover features of the accused embodiment that are also reproduced by a presumably limited scope of protection.

The relevant grounds of the decision dealing with the change to the wording of the claim are deemed to replace or stand alongside the patent description and have to be considered for the claim construction, even though these parts of the grounds have no binding effect on the infringement courts.[55] Accordingly, if a European patent is maintained in limited form, the reasons for the decision can be used, like a part of the description, to interpret the claims, but only insofar as they concern the amendment,[56] and only if the description is not also amended.

Also the grounds rejecting an action for nullity do not bind the trial judge but may give an indication as to how the skilled person would interpret the claim.

Moreover, licenses become invalid to the extent the license is based on a revoked patent or on revoked parts of the patent from the time of revocation of the patent. The revocation, however, has generally no impact on the validity of the license in general, and for the payment of royalties in particular, for the past.[57] This is, royalties paid for the past must not be reimbursed even if the patent is later revoked. This case law has recently by confirmed by a decision of the European Court of Justice.[58] It ruled that competition law does not prevent royalties being paid for technology protected by revoked patents.

5.3. Inconsistent Statements

Statements made during the prosecution are basically without relevance for the interpretation of the patent claim so long as such statements are not explicitly taken from the patent specification.[59] Thus problematic statements made by the patentee during prosecution concerning the understanding of the patent claim are irrelevant for the claim construction.[60] They may however represent an indication of how the relevant skilled person in the art would understand the patent.[61] Even statements made by the patentee during nullity proceedings are principally irrelevant for the claim construction.[62] There is however an exception to this rule,[63] namely where the patentee

55. Federal Supreme Court, GRUR 2007, 778 – "Ziehmaschinenzugeinheit I"; decision of Apr. 15, 2010 – Xa ZB 10/09, GRUR 2010, 950 = IIC 2011, 363– "*Walzenformgebungsmaschine*".
56. Federal Supreme Court, decision of May 12, 1998 –X ZR 115/96, GRUR 1999, 145 = IIC 1999, 805– "Stoßwellen-Lithotripter"; decision of Apr. 17, 2007 – X ZR 72/05, GRUR 2007, 778 = IIC 2008, 223 – "Zugmaschinenzugeinheit".
57. Federal Supreme Court, GRUR 1957, 595 – "Verwandlungstisch"; GRUR 2002, 787 – "Abstreiferleiste"; GRUR, 2005, 935 – "Vergleichsempfehlung II m.w.N."
58. ECJ C-567/14.
59. Federal Supreme Court, X ZR 43/01, GRUR 2002, 511, 513, "Kunststoffrohrteil."
60. Federal Supreme Court, X ZR 73/95, NJW-RR 1998, 184, "Weichvorrichtung II."
61. Federal Supreme Court, X ZR 57/96, GRUR 1998, 895, "Regenbecken."
62. Federal Supreme Court, X ZR 6/91, GRUR 1993, 886, "Weichvorrichtung I"; Federal Supreme Court, X ZR 73/95, NJW-RR 1998, 184, "Weichvorrichtung II."
63. Federal Supreme Court, X ZR 6/91, GRUR 1993, 886, "Weichvorrichtung I"; Federal Supreme Court, X ZR 73/95, NJW-RR 1998, 184, "Weichvorrichtung II."

declares during nullity proceedings that she or he does not claim patent protection for particular embodiments. The accused infringer may refer to that statement or declaration provided that he was involved in those proceedings. He is thus allowed to argue in the parallel infringement proceedings that a narrower understanding of the claim must be applied. The accused infringer can rely on these statements made by the proprietor, provided the statements were made in parallel nullity proceedings between the same parties.[64] This is taken from the general prohibition of a *venire contra factum proprium* which prohibits the same party from taking inconsistent positions and acting contradictorily vis-à-vis the other party in the two proceedings. This is an exception to the rule that statements made by the applicant in grant proceedings, or by the patentee in nullity proceedings, are irrelevant for the claim construction in infringement proceedings. Because this prohibition against contradictory behavior also applies to the accused infringer, his submissions should be uniform in both proceedings as well.

6. FINANCIAL ASPECTS OF NULLITY ACTION

Court fees along with attorney fees need to be considered when budgeting the case.[65] When filing the nullity action the plaintiff has to advance the court fees for the first instance proceeding. At the end of the proceedings these costs have to be paid by the party who lost the case. If there is no fully prevailing party then the costs are shared among the parties. A further financial aspect concerns the question of whether a security for the defendant's costs of the proceedings must be provided (see: section 6.2).

6.1. Court Fees

The court fees depend on the litigation value. At the beginning of the proceedings the plaintiff provides a preliminary estimate, which is indicated in the complaint brief. The litigation value should correspond to plaintiff's objective economic interests of the claims as requested in the complaint. It is often difficult to determine the litigation value. If the defendant does not object to plaintiff's estimation, usually the court renders a decision based on the preliminary fixed litigation value. However, a litigation value that is applied in parallel infringement proceedings is usually decisive for the nullity proceedings. Due to the public nature of nullity proceedings the value of the infringement proceedings is even increased by 25 %.[66] The court fees of both instances can be taken from the charts below, which start from a rather low litigation value (EUR 0.5 million) to the maximum cap value (EUR 30 million).

64. Federal Supreme Court, Weichvorrichtung I/II, X ZR 6/91 and X ZR 73/95.
65. *See* Ch. 15 concerning fees and costs.
66. Federal Supreme Court, GRUR 2011, 757, "Nichtigkeitsstreitwert".

6.1.1. *Court Fees: First Instance (Federal Patent Court)*

Litigation Value (EUR)	*Court Fees (EUR)*
500,000	15,912
1,000,000	24,012
2,000,000	40,212
5,000,000	88,812
10,000,000	169,812
30,000,000	493,812

6.1.2. *Court Fees: Second Instance (Federal Supreme Court)*

Litigation Value (EUR)	*Court Fees (EUR)*
500,000	21,216
1,000,000	32,016
2,000,000	53,616
5,000,000	118,416
10,000,000	226,416
30,000,000	658,416

6.1.3. *Costs for Court Expert*

The law has recently been modified in a way that may lead to fewer appointments of court experts in future cases. As of this writing it is expected that the Federal Supreme Court will no longer appoint court experts. In the authors' experience the costs of court experts range from EUR 10,000 to EUR 20,000, depending on the complexity of the case.

6.2. Security for Defendant's Costs of the Proceedings

Upon request of the defendant, the plaintiff must furnish security for the costs of the proceedings, provided its general residence lies outside the European Community, (§81(6) Patent Act). Some countries—e.g., Japan, the Russian Federation, and Switzerland—have concluded bilateral agreements with Germany exempting their residents from this duty. However, residents of the United States of America, China, Canada and Korea are currently not exempted from the duty to furnish security of costs. These costs are determined by the Court and have to be paid within a time limit set by the Court. Instead of payment of the security costs a bank warranty of an accredited German Bank may be furnished as a security.

7. UPCOMING: REVOCATION PROCEEDINGS AT THE UPC

7.1. Venue of Revocation Actions

According to Articles 32(1)(d) and 33(4) of the UPCA, (standalone) revocation actions will be have to be brought in principle before the Central Division. These actions are directed against the patentee. Depending on the technical content of the patent in suit, these actions will be allocated to the seat in Paris or the branches in London and Munich.

7.2. Competence

Within nine months of publication of the grant of a UP, anyone is entitled to file opposition proceedings with the EPO.[67] After this nine-month period, parties seeking to invalidate the patent must refer to:

- The UPC in the case of a Unitary Patent
- Either to the UPC or national invalidation proceedings in cases of ordinary European patents. National invalidation proceedings will be available according to a transitional regime of the UPCA ("Opt-out System").

Revocation proceedings before the UPC will have effect in the territories covered by the European patent.[68]

7.3. Parties

For EPO opposition proceedings, Article 99 EPC states explicitly that "any person may give notice" of opposition. Accordingly, the opponent does not need to demonstrate any legal or economic interest in the revocation of the patent when filing the notice and it is acceptable for interested parties to use a "straw man" to file the notice of opposition. Competitors often prefer to stay in the background and involve a straw man for oppositions against disagreeable and uncomfortable patents of competing companies. The same principles apply to German nullity proceedings filed with the Federal Patent Court.

It remains to be seen whether or not the same flexible approach will apply in revocation proceedings before the UPC. According to Article 47(6) UPCA, "*any other natural or legal person, or anybody entitled to bring actions in accordance with its national law, who is concerned by a patent, may bring actions in accordance with the Rules of Procedure.*" On one hand, the term "who is concerned by a patent" could be understood to mean that not "any" claimant is entitled to file a revocation action. This could be understood as meaning that at least some showing of an individual concern or interest is necessary to establish the admissibility of the action. Rule 44 of the RoP,

67. Article 99 EPC.
68. Article 34 UPCA.

however, does not indicate specifically that the statement for revocation must contain a statement of interest. The general public interest in reducing the number of invalid patents favors the indicated flexible approach of the EPO. Frivolous actions might not occur because the claimant has to pay a fee when filing the action.

7.4. Grounds of Revocation

The UPC may revoke a patent, either entirely or partly, only on the grounds referred to in Articles 138(1)[69] and 139(2)[70] of the EPC.[71] The most important ground is if the patent's subject matter is not patentable within the terms of Articles 52–57 EPC, in particular, because the subject matter is not novel or lacks an inventive step (missing patentability). Another ground is non-enablement (insufficiency of disclosure), when the patent does not disclose the invention in a manner sufficiently clear and complete for it to be carried out by a person skilled in the art. It could also be asserted that the patent's subject matter extends beyond the content of the application as originally filed, which would violate Article 123(2) EPC (added subject matter). It may also be revoked if the proprietor of the European patent is not entitled under Article 60 (1) EPC. All available grounds should be contained in the written statement for revocation.[72] If the grounds for revocation affect the patent only in part, the patent will be limited by a corresponding amendment of the claims and revoked in part.

As the grounds for revocation depend mainly on the provisions of the EPC, the pre-existing case law of the EPO will thus have a decisive factor for the UPC even though the UPC is not legally bound by EPO case law.

69. *Article 138 Revocation of European patents*
(1) Subject to Article 139, a European patent may be revoked with effect for a Contracting State only on the grounds that
(a) The subject matter of the European patent is not patentable under Articles 52 to 57
(b) The European patent does not disclose the invention in a manner sufficiently clear and complete for it to be carried out by a person skilled in the art
(c) The subject matter of the European patent extends beyond the content of the application as filed or, if the patent was granted on a divisional application or on a new application filed under Article 61, beyond the content of the earlier application as filed
(d) The protection conferred by the European patent has been extended
(e) The proprietor of the European patent is not entitled under Article 60, paragraph 1.

70. *Article 139 EPC Prior rights and rights arising on the same date*
(1) ...
(2) A national patent application and a national patent in a Contracting State shall have with regard to a European patent designating that Contracting State the same prior right effect as if the European patent were a national patent.
(3) ...

71. Article 65(2) UPCA.
72. Rule 44(1)(e) Rules of Procedure.

CHAPTER 8

Pre-suit Considerations and Infringement Trial

Patent infringement suits in Germany are fundamentally different in structure than those in the U.S. First, there is no jury. Because there is no jury, there is no need for a separate "Markman" hearing—i.e., there is no dedicated hearing or briefing for the purposes of claim construction, which leaves fundamental issues of claim scope unresolved until the overall merits of a case are tried. Second, due to the unique judicial structure in Germany, challenges to the validity of the patent are tried separately, in "nullity" proceedings, in a different court—the Federal Patent Court—which greatly streamlines the infringement proceeding, often to the advantage of the patentee. Third, there is no "summary judgment" phase in a case. These proceedings tend to be rapid, with a first-instance ruling typically occurring within a year of commencement (insofar as various delaying events, such as appointment of a court expert, or stays pending validity challenges, do not arise). In view of all these factors, the costs to try a case in Germany are a fraction of the costs in the U.S.

This chapter provides an overview of patent infringement cases in Germany, starting with pre-suit considerations, followed by the complaint, and the subsequent court filings and events through the first-instance ruling. Of course, every case is different, and the following serves only as a model of how cases typically play out.

1. INTERNATIONAL ASPECTS

1.1. National and International Jurisdiction

According to §143 of the German Patent Act, for all patent infringement actions, the civil chambers of the District Courts have exclusive jurisdiction without regard to the litigation value in dispute. This exclusive jurisdiction is conferred upon twelve District Courts, which are divided geographically throughout Germany. These courts are namely: District Court Berlin, District Court Braunschweig, District Court Düsseldorf,

District Court Erfurt, District Court Frankfort, District Court Hamburg, District Court Leipzig, District Court Magdeburg, District Court Mannheim, District Court München, District Court Nürnberg-Fürth, and District Court Saarbrucken. The District Courts of Düsseldorf, Mannheim and Munich adjudicate the vast majority of patent infringement cases.

The selection of one of these courts depends in part upon the question of "local competence." It is permissible to file a complaint with the court where the defendant is located or has its seat (§12 Code of Civil Procedure), but more important is the forum of *actus in tort* (§32 Code of Civil Procedure).

Accordingly, the plaintiff can file the lawsuit within a district wherein the infringement has been committed. These are the places where the accused product has been produced, has been offered, or brought onto the market. In cases of an offer the infringing acts are not only committed where the offer has been made, but also where the offer is received or can be perceived by potential interested parties.[1] This basically also applies to an offer published through a webpage that can be perceived by an Internet user in Germany. Accordingly, when there has been an Internet offer of the accused product, a lawsuit could be filed in any of the twelve District Courts and the choice of the court would only depend upon plaintiff's strategic considerations. The language of the offer does not change the forum determination. Thus, the webpage of interest need not be written in German to confer jurisdiction.

It is well-established case law that a webpage in English is sufficient to confer jurisdiction on a German court. A foreign company, even without any affiliates in Germany and without having shipped any products in the past to Germany, which presents its products on its website, could unknowingly infringe a German patent, provided that the webpage is objectively addressed to the German public.[2] This is usually the case as long as German Internet users might have the impression that the webpage is addressed to them. A diligent company could avoid these consequences by means of a disclaimer posted on its website clearly indicating that the concerned products are not available for sale in Germany. However, the disclaimer would not be effective if the accused products are nevertheless shipped to the German market, even if the transaction was triggered by a test purchase prior to litigation, for instance by a straw man tied to the patentee.[3]

Indeed, patentees will commonly secure jurisdiction in Germany by ordering a product through a straw man, particularly in cases where there is no clear offer on the Internet to sell into Germany. Even the shipment of accused products to a company situated outside German territory might be considered as an infringement of a German patent as soon as it is known that these products are supposed to be commercialized on the German market.[4] Accordingly, it may be sufficient to establish jurisdiction in Germany by showing that a shipment was made to a company which the accused

1. Appeal Court Düsseldorf, decision of Feb. 23, 2012, I-2 U 134/10, "Run-Flat-Vorrichtung."
2. Court of Justice of the European Union, decision of Jan. 22, 2015; C 441/13 "Hejduk."
3. Appeal Court Düsseldorf, decision of Jan. 28, 2010, GRUR-RR 2010, 368, I-2 U 131/08, "Testkauf patentverletzender DVDs."
4. District Court Düsseldorf, 4b O 199/06, "Elektrisches Steckergehäuse."

infringer knows would subsequently sell the products on the German market.[5] The first offer or presentation of a product at a tradeshow in Germany may be sufficient to establish jurisdiction in Germany.[6] Even an international tradeshow taking place outside Germany could potentially provide a basis for exercising jurisdiction in Germany if German visitors attend such fairs. The plaintiff must aver sufficient facts to show that the offer made by the accused infringer on such an international tradeshow has an impact on German territory. It would thus not be sufficient to only refer to the attendance of German visitors at such a tradeshow and that by experience of life the offer will be conveyed by them onto the German territory. However, it could be sufficient if the plaintiff names at least one German fair visitor who took along advertisement material, which is used later in discussions with colleagues or superiors in Germany.[7] Accordingly, a company presenting products on an international tradeshow outside Germany is not completely immune from jurisdiction of German courts.

German courts need to satisfy additional jurisdictional requirements if a foreign party is sued. German courts must address the established rules concerning international jurisdiction over any such foreign defendant, in addition to the aforementioned rules of jurisdiction from the German Civil Code. In particular, the European Convention on Jurisdiction and the Enforcement of Judgements (Reg. 1215/2012) has to be taken into account. The general rule, which complies with the national rule of §12 Code of Civil Procedure, is contained in Article 4 of the Regulation, according to which *"persons domiciled in a Member State shall, whatever their nationality is, be sued in the courts of that Member State."* Furthermore, almost identical to the German national provision of §32 Code of Civil Procedure it is possible to select the forum of the "*actus in tort.*" Article 7 (2) of Reg. 1215/2012 stipulates *"in matters relating to tort, delict or quasi-delict,"* one may also be sued *"in the courts for the place where the harmful event occurred or may occur."* Beyond the application of EuGVVO, in particular, with respect to U.S. or Japanese Companies, it is generally accepted that the international jurisdiction will follow from the local rules.[8] Thus, once local jurisdiction is established by satisfying the "*actus in tort*" requirement, for example, German courts would affirm also the international jurisdiction.

In light of the above considerations, choosing among Germany's courts involves far fewer jurisdictional considerations than in the U.S. For the vast majority of patent infringement cases, each of Germany's District Courts will have jurisdiction to hear the suit. Accordingly, much of the wrangling over forum choice that is typical in the U.S. is inapplicable in Germany.

5. District Court Düsseldorf, InstGE 1, 154, "Rohrverzweigung"; District Court Düsseldorf, 4a O 212/08, "Schneeketten."
6. District Court Düsseldorf, 4a O 113/06, "GPRS-Mobiltelephone," Appeal Court Düsseldorf, decision of Feb. 23, 2012, I-2 U 134/10, "Run-Flat-Vorrichtung;" Appeal Court Düsseldorf, decision of Mar. 27, 2014, 15 U 19/14, "Sterilcontrainer II."
7. Appeal Court Düsseldorf, decision of Feb. 23, 2012, I-2 U 134/10, "Run-Flat-Vorrichtung."
8. Federal Supreme Court, GRUR 2015, 467, "Audiosignalkodierung"

1.2. Trans-Border Jurisdiction

An important jurisdictional issue is whether national courts within the EU can decide on patent infringement that does not occur within the national territory. The general answer is no. In the past, a few European courts, in particular in the Netherlands[9] and Germany, were open to granting injunctions with an effect outside the national territory. Such trans-border decisions were based on a generous interpretation of the so-called Brussels Regime, which regulates which courts have jurisdiction in legal disputes of a civil or commercial nature between individuals resident in different Member States of the EU and the European Free Trade Association. This open-minded trans-border jurisdiction case law was later restricted by two decisions of European Court of Justice.[10] Their rulings have been transposed into the Regulation 1215/2012, applicable since January 10, 2015.[11]

According to the Regulation, *"(...) persons domiciled in a Member State shall, whatever their nationality be sued in the courts of that Member State"* (Article 4(1) of the Regulation 2015/2012). Accordingly, a patent infringement suit can be brought at the location where the accused infringer lives or—in case of a company—its corporate seat. However, this does not mean that the patentee is free to file a lawsuit at the seat of the infringer asserting the infringement of foreign patents based on infringing activities occurring outside the German territory. Such action is restricted by Article 24(1) of Regulation 1215/2012.[12] This provision stipulates that courts of a Member State have exclusive jurisdiction over cases challenging the validity of patents issuing from that Member State (including EPO patents designating that Member State). Accordingly, validity proceedings can only be filed in the country where the patent has been granted or in which a European patent has been designated. The provision also interferes with infringement proceedings wherein foreign patents have been asserted. For example, if a non-German patent were to be asserted in a German court, as soon as the validity of the foreign patent is challenged in such proceedings either by means of a plea for invalidity or in a request to stay the infringement proceedings in reaction to a validity challenge pending with a foreign court, the German court would be unable to proceed with the infringement action based on that foreign patent. Upon the filing by the defendant of a plea of invalidity of a foreign patent, an infringement case in Germany

9. *Expandable Grafts v. Boston Scientific* (Gerechtshof Den Haag, Apr. 23, 1998).
10. *Primus v. Roche* (C-539/03); GAT/LUK C-4/03.
11. Regulation (EU) No 1215/2012 of the European Parliament and of the Council of 12 December 2012 on jurisdiction and the recognition and enforcement of judgments in civil and commercial matters (recast).
12. "[...] shall have exclusive jurisdiction, regardless of the domicile of the parties in proceedings concerned with the registration or validity of patents, [...] irrespective of whether the issue is raised by way of an action or as a defence, the courts of the Member State in which the deposit or registration has been applied for, has taken place or is under the terms of an instrument of the Union or an international convention deemed to have taken place. Without prejudice to the jurisdiction of the European Patent Office under the Convention on the Grant of European Patents, signed at Munich on 5 October 1973, the courts of each Member State shall have exclusive jurisdiction in proceedings concerned with the registration or validity of any European patent granted for that Member State."

as to that foreign patent would have even to be dismissed.[13] For instance, if a patent holder asserts infringement of both the German part and the French part of a European patent (due to infringing activities in Germany and France) in Germany, the accused infringer would have the ability to stop the proceedings with respect to the French part of the European patent. Typically, it is thus not recommended to add a foreign patent to the case.

Regulation 1215/2012 is not literally applicable to a lawsuit filed in Germany by a U.S. company asserting the infringement of a U.S. patent against a company seated in Germany. The court would have to apply the general international rules applicable to civil procedures. These rules do not provide a clear answer to the question as to how the assertion of U.S. patents are handled in front of German courts. There is a strong likelihood that German courts would draw parallels to Regulation 1215/2012. Initially, it would not be prohibited to file a lawsuit on the basis of a U.S. patent against an accused infringer in Germany. However, a German court would likely dismiss an action focused on that U.S. patent as soon as a plea of its invalidity has been raised in the German proceedings.

1.3. "Torpedo"

The so-called Torpedo refers to a tactic which is aimed at pre-empting the exercise of jurisdiction by a national court by commencing proceedings before another court in a different country which usually, though not always, lacks jurisdiction. Typically, such a "Torpedo" action is filed in a country with a notoriously slow docket—hence the "Italian Torpedo," for example. Torpedo actions were often pursued by seeking a declaratory judgment in a slow docket jurisdiction, which had the effect of preventing proceedings on the merits by the patentee before a court of its choosing. This tactic relied on Article 29 of Regulation 1215/2012 which provides:

> *1. [...] where proceedings involving the same cause of action and between the same parties are brought in the courts of different Member States, any court other than the court first seized shall of its own motion stay its proceedings until such time as the jurisdiction of the court first seized is established.*
> *2. [...]*
> *3. Where the jurisdiction of the court first seized is established, any court other than the court first seized shall decline jurisdiction in favor of that court.*

For instance, Company A sends a warning letter to Company B due to infringement of the German part of a European patent. Company B reacts and files a declaratory judgment action seeking a declaration of non-infringement of the German patent in an Italian court, just prior to any lawsuit filed by Company A in Germany.

What happens if Company A later files a regular infringement lawsuit in Germany? A "negative" action seeking a declaration judgment on non-infringement

13. Advocate General Philippe Léger (C-539/03) and L.A. Geelhoed (C-4/03).

filed in Italy by the accused infringer and its "positive" counterpart, i.e., an action on the merits filed by the right holder in Germany represent the *same cause* according to Article 29 of Regulation 1215/2012.[14] The German court would thus stay the proceedings, at least, until the jurisdiction of the court first seized is established. Thus, the action in Germany is "torpedoed" and blocked for a considerable period of time.

For some time Italian courts were known for their slow proceedings. Most of the torpedoes were thus fired in Italy. However, Italian courts became speedier and some of them have curtailed the effects of the torpedo.[15] This development has removed some explosiveness of the torpedo tactic. It needs to be evaluated case by case if it represents a useful strategy for the accused infringer. The evaluation needs to take into account that a torpedo can also be filed in other European jurisdictions than Italy. Each may have its own approach to deal with such tactical measure.

Some German courts, in particular the District Court Düsseldorf,[16] however render the application of the torpedo tactic more difficult. They allow an objection based on an abuse of rights, namely if the jurisdiction of the first seized court is obviously unfounded and if the accused infringer abusively delays the proceedings at the first seized court. This does not completely eliminate the effects of a torpedo because the objection requires that at least some time has passed to demonstrate a delay of the proceedings at the foreign court. The tactic is thus still a strategic aspect which needs to be considered before warning the accused infringer. A complete description of the various strategic options for an accused infringer to block German proceedings goes beyond this presentation.

2. CONTACTING THE ACCUSED INFRINGER

Before contacting the alleged infringer, the right holder (patentee) should exhaust his basic investigative options, and collect and analyze information the alleged infringer produced in proceedings in other jurisdictions, including new prior art. Test purchases may be useful means to gather information on the accused product. In particular, they are useful and permissible means to prove that the accused product is sold on the German territory.[17] Information and evidence produced in U.S. discovery proceedings, for example, may be used in German infringement proceedings (subject to applicable constraints from U.S. protective orders). Failure to perform due diligence at this investigatory stage could cause problems later (see "unjustified warning letters" below).

14. Appeal Court Düsseldorf, GRUR-RR, 2009, 401 "Italian Torpedo."
15. Court of Milan, decision of Jan. 27, 2014, Judgment No. 1143/2014; in favor of a more generous application of the torpedo standards: Italian Supreme Court, decision of Jun. 10, 2013 (judgement 14508/2013, "*The General Hospital Corporation and others v. Asclepion Laser Technologies*").
16. District Court Düsseldorf, InstGE 3, 8, "Cholesterin-Test."
17. Federal Supreme Court, GRUR 1999, 1017, "Kontrollnummernbeseitigung"; Appeal Court Düsseldorf, decision of Jan. 28, 2010, I-2 U 124/08.

Once these preliminary investigations are complete the question becomes whether and how to contact the accused infringer. Contacting the alleged infringer prior to commencing court proceedings is not legally required. Indeed, filing a lawsuit without advance warning might be advisable in some situations. But there are potential penalties involved with suing without forewarning. This is, an accused infringer that had not been previously and sufficiently warned by the right holder may, as soon as the complaint is served, admit the claims asserted, in which case the court would render a decision pursuant to this admission (§307 Code of Civil Procedure). This refers to the rare situation where the accused infringer immediately gives up and discontinues the accused activities. In this situation, the right holder would indeed win the case immediately, but the costs of the proceedings might be imposed on him, including the accused infringer's "statutory costs." This follows from §93 Code of Civil Procedure which provides that *"if the defendant did not induce the bringing of a suit by his conduct, the costs of the proceedings shall be paid by the plaintiff if the defendant immediately admits.*"[18] Thus, the right holder may avoid the imposition of these costs if he gives the accused infringer a sufficient opportunity to comply with a warning letter.

There are of course situations where a prior warning is not recommended. The prior warning might be superfluous if it is expected that the accused infringer would refuse the right holder's requests. A lawsuit without prior warning could also reduce the risk of the so-called Torpedo[19] which might be fired off by the warned infringer to create a temporary obstacle for a lawsuit in Germany. These strategic considerations must be carefully weighed when approaching the accused infringer. Of course, there might be good reasons to contact the accused infringer prior to the lawsuit:

- The contact could result in a settlement without judicial proceedings. A lawsuit is not a regular element of a company's business. It absorbs man-power, it may create unexpected effects on the financial situation of a company. As the speed of German proceedings does not leave much time to find acceptable design arounds and solutions for the company's customers, the possible result of a lawsuit could have dramatic consequences for the business of a company. This situation gives leverage for settlements and makes it worthwhile to use the extrajudicial discussion to negotiate solutions acceptable to both sides.
- The contact may result in discussions through which the accused infringer furnishes information with respect to the accused embodiment which was previously unknown to the right holder. The accused infringer may also provide strategically valuable information with regard to previously undis-closed prior art.

There are two usual methods used for extrajudicially approaching the accused infringer: the "warning letter" and the "inquiry letter."

18. Unofficial translation.
19. *See* Ch. 8, s. 1.3.

2.1. Warning Letter (*Abmahnung*)

A warning letter immediately puts the alleged infringer on notice that he is infringing and demands that he cease and desist. If the alleged infringer ignores the warning letter, the patentee may then file a lawsuit, without being exposed to the risk that the costs of the proceedings might be imposed on him after an immediate acknowledgement of the asserted claims by the accused infringer. One of the main reasons of a previous warning of accused infringer consists in avoiding the imposition of these costs.

2.1.1. Content of Warning Letter

A sample of a warning letter can be found in Chapter 16, section 1. It should contain information on the identity of the right holder and the enforceability of the asserted right. As evidence, it is sufficient to reference the patent register. A copy of the excerpt of the register and the asserted patent or utility model should be enclosed. The status of the right should also be described. Thus, if there are pending invalidity actions or opposition proceedings, they shall be mentioned in the letter as well.

Furthermore, the warning letter must contain sufficiently concrete information about the accused infringing activities. The accused infringer must be able to verify whether the warning letter is justified.[20] A vague allegation is not sufficient. If there are particular infringing products, these should be identified, and photos may be helpful in this regard to avoid confusion. Once the identification and description is complete the letter should contain a clear demand that the accused infringer cease and desist from the infringing activities described.

The warning letter should include a draft of an undertaking. The undertaking identifies the different claims asserted by the right holder, such as the right to prevent the use of the patent which obliges the accused infringer to cease and desist with the accused activity. It also covers the other claims resulting from the patent, namely the rendering of accounts, and states that the accused infringer has to pay damages to be calculated on the basis of the figures furnished by the accused infringer when rendering the accounts.

Finally, the letter should set forth a deadline for the accused infringer to return a signed copy of the undertaking. The deadline should leave sufficient time to the accused infringer to verify the allegations. Normally, three weeks are reasonable. If the deadline is too short, the warning letter does not become ineffective, but a reasonable deadline starts to run and replaces the unreasonably short deadline.[21]

There might be situations where a shorter deadline is permitted, such as in a tradeshow situation where a quick intervention is required. In that case, it might be sufficient if only a few days or even one day are left to the accused infringer.[22]

20. Appeal Court Düsseldorf, decision of Nov. 11, 2011, I-20 W 132/11.
21. Federal Supreme Court, I ZR 63/88, GRUR 1990, 381, 382, "Antwortpflicht des Abgemahnten."
22. Appeal Court Düsseldorf, InstGE 4, 159, "INTERPACK."

Finally, the warning letter needs to contain a threat that in case of non-compliance with the right holder's demand, a lawsuit might be filed.[23]

2.1.2. *Unjustified Warning Letter*

Before sending out a warning letter the right holder must perform an adequate investigation to warrant a warning letter. The investigation shall reasonably allow the conclusion that the patent is indeed infringed (which requires sufficient knowledge of the accused embodiment) and that the underlying patent right is valid.[24] An unjustified warning letter may trigger a claim for damages. The damages typically consist at least of the costs incurred by the lawyer involved by the warned party as a consequence of the warning letter.[25] Damages may also result from the termination of the production and/or commercialization of the accused product unless these measures were taken imprudently and too hastily.[26]

A sufficient factual investigation should thus precede the warning letter. In addition, the accused infringer shall be well informed through the warning letter about the factual circumstances, in particular about the status of the asserted patent and the scope of the assertion. The accused activities must be well specified and should not overreach the scope of protection of the asserted patent.[27] The right holder may assume the validity of the issued patent by relying on the granting decision of the patent office, unless that validity has been questioned by means of unexamined prior art submitted in pending invalidation proceedings.[28] The situation is different for a patent where new prior art has been identified which has not been considered by the patent office. The patentee must diligently review such new prior art, and this examination should be reflected in the warning letter. Decisions rendered by the EPO, the German Patent and Trademark Office or German courts such as decisions of the Federal Patent Court in relation to the asserted patent shall not be omitted to be mentioned.[29]

The need for due diligence is even more important in case of unexamined rights such as Utility Models. These rights require that the right holder has made a proper search and has sufficiently considered the resulting prior art before sending the warning letter.[30] If that due diligence has sufficiently resolved any doubts, he may proceed with a low risk of a claim for damages due to an unjustified warning letter.

23. Federal Supreme Court, GRUR 2011, 995, "Besonderer Mechanismus."
24. Federal Supreme Court, GRZR 2005, 882, "Unberechtigte Schutzrechtsverwarnung."
25. Appeal Court Düsseldorf, decision of Jan. 31, 2013, 1-2 U 54/11.
26. Federal Supreme Court, GRZR 2005, 882, "Unberechtigte Schutzrechtsverwarnung."
27. District Court Düsseldorf, InstGE 3, 86, "Hochdruckreiniger."
28. Federal Supreme Court, I ZR 98/02, GRUR 2006, 432, "Verwarnung aus Kennzeichenrecht II."
29. Appeal Court Düsseldorf, InstGE 9, 123, "Multifeed."
30. Federal Supreme Court, I ZR 59/50, GRUR 1951,452, "Mülltonne"; Federal Supreme Court, GSZ 1/04, decision of Jul. 15, 2005, "Unberechtigte Schutzrechtsverwarnung."

2.2. Inquiry Letter (*Berechtigungsanfrage*)

The soft warning, which we call the "inquiry letter," invites the accused infringer to a discussion about validity and infringement. It is an exchange of views and does not contain a demand to cease and desist or a threat to take judicial measures. The letter accordingly contains the simple demand to only indicate why the other party believes he is entitled to use the protected invention.

Table 8.1. Differences: Warning Letter versus Inquiry Letter

Characteristics	*Warning Letter*	*Inquiry Letter*
Content	Demand to cease and desist including threat to start litigation in case of incompliance.	Invitation to exchange views on validity and infringement.
Liability?	Only if warning is unjustified.	No
Cause for Declaratory Judgment Action?	Yes	No
Avoids imposition of legal costs if defendant admits at the beginning of lawsuit	Yes	No

A sample of an inquiry letter may be found in Chapter 16, section 2. Such a letter would not trigger the effects of unjustified warning[31] and would not create sufficient cause for a declaratory judgment action.[32] A prudent right holder could first send such a letter and, depending upon the outcome, follow-up with a warning letter.

3. LAWSUIT ON THE MERITS (FIRST INSTANCE)

3.1. Overall Timeline

A key difference between patent litigation in the U.S. and Germany is the overall timeline for a typical case. Germany has a far more streamlined process, with the main hearing on the merits taking place within about a year. Although the District Court may determine that further expert proceedings are necessary, or that the proceedings should be stayed pending resolution of opposition or nullity proceedings, it is quite possible the court will take up the merits of the case, and perhaps award relief, within about a

31. District Court Mannheim, decision of Feb. 23, 2007, 7 O 276/06, BeckRS 2007, 03873 "Abgrenzung von Verwarnung und Berechtigungsanfrage."
32. *See* Ch. 8, s. 6.1 "Declaratory Judgment Action."

year.[33] Figure 8.1 is a brief overview of the primary events in a typical patent infringement case, with each of these events discussed in greater detail below.

Differences between the different German courts are not reflected in the following figure. For instance, the District Court Munich follows its special rules called "Munich procedure" aimed at finishing first-instance proceedings within eight to twelve months.[34] Accordingly, a first oral session takes place within approximately three to six months followed by the complaint and the submission of defendant's statement of defense. The Court usually provides in that oral session first indications as to the claim construction as well as a first non-binding view on the question of infringement of the patent-in-suit. In this first oral session, also deadlines for further written submissions as well as a date for the main hearing are set. Other questions, such as the question of staying the proceedings, are left to the main hearing. The deadlines for the submissions are about two months and the Court only grants extensions in exceptional cases for short terms not exceeding one week. In addition, the Munich Court requires compliance with certain well defined formalities, such as the submission of a short summary limited to ten pages prior to the main hearing.

A different approach is taken by the District Courts Mannheim and Düsseldorf. At the District Court Düsseldorf, a first early session, if it takes place, does usually not result in any substantive discussion, rather it serves to set the deadlines for the different submissions to be exchanged until the main hearing, which takes place approximately 12 to 14 months after service of the complaint. Any indications as to the claim construction or the question of infringement of the patent-in-suit will thus not be provided in that first oral session. This discussion is postponed to the main hearing. At the District Court Mannheim, all is concentrated on one main hearing without any meetings of the parties and the court occurring prior to the main hearing which typically takes place eight to nine months after service of the complaint.

Figure 8.1. Timeline of Patent Infringement Proceedings

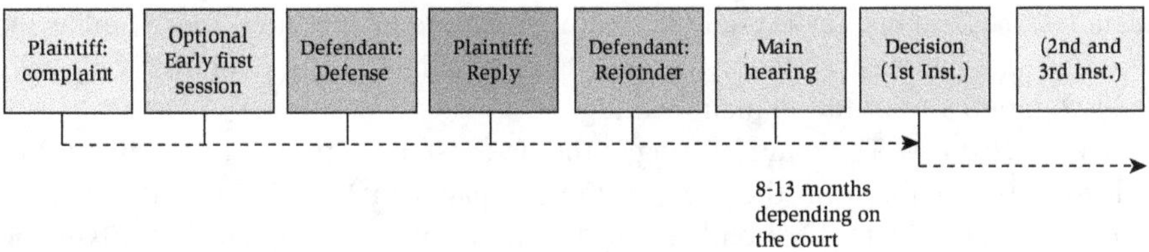

Complaint: As in the U.S., a patent infringement case starts with a complaint (*Klageschrift*). Complaints in Germany are more detailed than in the U.S. Whereas complaints in the U.S. are governed by the "notice pleading" standard, which permits patentees to file rather bare-bones complaints that merely give the defendant "notice"

33. The District Court Mannheim is even quicker and renders decisions within approximately eight months.
34. https://www.justiz.bayern.de: Hinweise zum Münchner Verfahren in Patentstreitsachen (Dec. 2016).

of the claim, Germany requires that plaintiffs set forth in their complaints a prima facie showing of entitlement to relief. As soon as the plaintiff has filed the complaint and has paid the court fee, the court will serve the complaint on the defendant(s).

Case Management Conference or Order: After service of the complaint, the court will set a schedule for the case. This may be done at an in-person hearing (as is typical in District Court Düsseldorf), or the schedule may be provided in a written order. The case management proceedings do not address the substance of the merits of the case, but may identify procedural insufficiencies in the complaint, such as inaccurately formulated requests[35] or incomplete submissions. Normally these insufficiencies can be corrected during the hearing or later by means of the exchanged briefs.

The court's schedule typically contains the following deadlines: a deadline which is set for the defendant's defense to the complaint brief; a deadline for the plaintiff to reply to the defendant's defense; a deadline for the defendant's final briefing; and the date of the main hearing. Often the plaintiff will additionally file a brief in the days before the hearing, although this is not expressly allowed by the rules.

Defendant's Defense: Germany's analog to a U.S. "answer" is called a "defense" (*Klageerwiderung*). This defense is typically filed two to three months after service of the complaint. And like the complaint, the defense is a much more detailed pleading than a U.S. answer.

Plaintiffs' Reply: The plaintiff's reply (*Replik*) is usually the plaintiffs' ultimate written submission on the merits. The reply will typically contain additional arguments and refinements of position beyond what was provided in the complaint. With the defendant having set out its positions in its defense, the reply is the opportunity for the plaintiff to crystallize its case and more fully present its entitlement to relief. These briefs are styled more like "trial briefs," addressing all issues across the merits of the case. The plaintiffs' reply is typically filed—including deadline extensions—four to six months after service of the defense.

Defendants' Rejoinder: The defendants' final written submission before the main hearing is called its rejoinder (*Duplik*). Because there is no analog of "summary judgment" in Germany, these rejoinders address the overall merits of a case (unlike the more rifle-shot nature of summary judgment briefs in the U.S.). A rejoinder is typically filed two months prior to the main hearing.

Main Hearing: The main hearing is the first-instance "trial." It typically occurs eight to nine months from the filing of the complaint in Mannheim (District Court Mannheim), and 12 to 13 months from the filing of the complaint in Düsseldorf (District Court Düsseldorf), which are the two jurisdictions where most patent infringement suits are brought. The main hearing is typically the court's first substantive involvement addressing the merits of the case. These main hearings are bench trials (i.e., no jury), and are remarkably fast in comparison to U.S.-style trials. They typically last on the order of two hours and there are usually no live witnesses.

In this main hearing, the District Court takes up not only the ultimate issues of infringement, but also the more basic issues that would tend to be resolved in the U.S.

35. *See* Ch. 8, s. 3.2.1 as to typical requests in a complaint brief.

on motions to dismiss, or for summary judgment. This main hearing is not just the court's first substantive hearing in a case, it is also frequently the last. Accordingly, threshold issues are resolved at the same time as the ultimate merits, unlike the U.S. where a defendant would frequently have several "outs" from litigation prior to trial, such as through motions to dismiss, or *Markman* proceedings, or summary judgment.

Decision: Following the main hearing, the court will determine if further proceedings will be necessary, such as by appointing an expert to resolve questions of claim construction and infringement, or if the matter should be stayed pending opposition or nullity proceedings. In those instances, the otherwise fast-track German patent litigation may get delayed. Involving a court-appointed expert tends to add six to twelve months to the typical schedule. And a stay pending opposition or nullity actions may add a similar time, or longer, to the proceedings. The court will typically issue a formal written ruling within a few weeks after the hearing, and this normally marks the end of the first-instance proceeding, from which the second instance and third-instance appeals are taken. If favorable to the patentee, this decision will likely contain an injunction prohibiting the infringer from using the patented invention.

Monetary Damages: If the patentee wins in the first instance, and demonstrates an entitlement to monetary damages, the amount of damages owed is subsequently determined in a separate proceeding.

The following sections address in further detail each of these phases in a case.

3.2. Contents of the Complaint

Patent infringement proceedings begin by filing a complaint. The contents of the complaint are governed by §253 of the Code of Civil Procedure, which is the set of rules that is analogous to the Federal Rules of Civil Procedure in the U.S. A complaint in Germany needs to fulfill particular requirements. First, the complaint brief shall indicate the names and addresses of the parties and the selected court to which the complaint brief is addressed. In addition, the plaintiff needs to state a litigation value (which may be subject to an accounting in an ancillary proceeding, as discussed below).[36] A sample complaint is provided in Chapter 16, section 3. Second, the plaintiff must make a precise statement of the subject matter and the grounds of the asserted rights, as well as a specific request for relief. Unlike the "notice pleading" standard of the U.S., Germany requires a substantiated complaint. That is, the complaint must provide enough factual basis and legal framework to justify relief in the event of a default judgment. This includes the different asserted rights, such as the particular patent claims that are infringed, and the particular accused devices, complete with an explanation of why they infringe (including, where applicable, claim construction reasoning). All the above must be factually substantiated to a sufficient degree to justify relief.

36. Concerning the litigation value: see Ch. 8, s. 7.1.

3.2.1. Rights and Requests

The complaint must specify all relief that the complainant seeks in the case. Under the rule of *ne ultra petita*, specified in §308(1) of the Code of Civil Procedure, the court is bound by the plaintiff's requests and is not allowed to award relief beyond what is demanded in the complaint. The formulation of the requests is therefore an important task, to which due attention must be given.

3.2.1.1. Right to Prevent the Use of the Patent

Requirements: According to §139(1) of the Patent Act, any person who uses an invention without authorization may be sued by the injured party to enjoin such use. The plaintiff must be an injured party, usually the patentee or the exclusive licensee. The claim for relief is focused on the future and accordingly requires that the injured party demonstrates a "danger of recidivism" or that future infringements are imminent. To show a danger of recidivism, it is normally sufficient to demonstrate past infringement. The accused infringer may avert the alleged recidivism by agreeing to cease and desist, so long as such an agreement contains a binding promise, coupled with penalties for failure, to refrain from future infringing acts.[37] The accused infringer may send such a written undertaking to the injured party prior to any lawsuit. Usually, such undertakings follow a warning letter sent to the accused infringer during the pre-litigation phase.[38] In case of a sufficient undertaking to cease and desist, the injured party would be barred from filing any action with respect to claims covered by the undertaking. The accused infringer could also issue such undertaking during pending litigation, in which case the plaintiff would have to declare that the lawsuit has been settled, which finishes the proceedings and the court would only decide on the costs (§91 a of the Code of Civil proceedings). Nevertheless, an abandonment of infringing acts or a simple declaration to refrain from using the patent in the future may not be sufficient to remove the grounds of the action.

A request aimed at preventing the accused infringer from using the invention must indicate the different acts that are forbidden to the defendant. These acts are enumerated in §9 of the Patent Act.[39]

Product Claims: If a product claim is asserted, the prayer for relief may be directed against the manufacture and commercialization of accused embodiments (§9 Patent Act: "manufacturing, offering, putting on the market or using or possessing for the aforementioned purposes" the accused embodiment). The prayer for relief addresses the acts that the defendant shall be prohibited from performing. The prayer should not reach beyond the provable "risk of recidivism." If infringing acts have been committed, it is typically assumed that there is a risk that infringing acts would also occur in the future. The risk of recidivism can be proven by means previously occurred infringing acts. If manufacturing activities can be detected on the German territory it can be

37. Federal Supreme Court, I ZR 212/93, GRUR 1996, 290, 292, "Wegfall der Wiederholungsgefahr."
38. As to the particular form for such undertaking: *See* Ch. 8, s. 2.1.1 and Ch. 16, s. 1.
39. A translation of §9 Patent Act is contained in Ch. 17, s. 3.

assumed from these activities that the produced products will subsequently be sold. The request could thus address all acts defined in § 9 Patent Act, namely "*manufacturing, offering, putting on the market or using or possessing*" of the accused products. However, in case of a company which commercializes but does not manufacture the accused products in Germany, the request should not refer to acts of manufacturing -- otherwise the request would be too broad and thus partially incorrect.

A typical request in case of an asserted product claim may have the following language:

> *It is requested in the name and on behalf of the plaintiff,*
>
> *I. to find defendant liable*
>
> *1. in order to avoid a penalty to be set by the court for each case of violation of up to € 250,000.00, as an alternative confinement, or confinement of up to 6 months, in case of repeated violations a confinement of up to a total of 2 years, to refrain from manufacturing, offering, putting on the market or using or possessing for the aforementioned purposes a product comprising...*
> [Description of the accused embodiment]

In addition, the request must contain a description of the accused product or process. The request, if granted by the court, shall form a proper basis for the enforcement of the judgment. It shall specify the features of the accused product in relation to the features of the asserted claims. In case of literal infringement of the claim, lower courts usually accept the use of the features of the asserted claim to describe the accused embodiment.

However, mere reproduction of the wording of the claim for the description of the accused embodiment may not be sufficient if the alleged infringement does not literally make use of features of the asserted patent claim and represents an infringement of the patent claim outside its literal wording.[40] For instance, if the infringement is based on the doctrine of equivalents[41] and thus the accused embodiment makes use of equivalent features, the request shall specify those feature(s) that are replaced and are different from the asserted claim. According to the Federal Supreme Court,[42] the courts shall ensure that the patentee's infringement allegations are identified in the request so specifically that a wording of the judgment in accordance with the petition can form a proper basis for a later enforcement.

In situations where the defendant is himself manufacturing the product within German territory the request should also be directed against the manufacture of the product. If the defendant is an importing company or a reseller of the accused products without own production, the term "manufacturing" would have to be removed from the request.

---

40. Federal Supreme Court, decision of Mar. 30, 2005, X ZR 126/01, IIC 2006, 83, "Blasfolienherstellung."
41. The doctrine of equivalents is described in Ch. 10, s. 4.2.
42. Federal Supreme Court, decision of Mar. 30, 2005, X ZR 126/01, IIC 2006, 83, "Blasfolienherstellung."

Method Claim: Where the request refers to a method claim various strategies may be deployed.

First, according to §9 N° 2 of the Patent Act, the request can be aimed at preventing the defendant *"from using a method."* The accused method must be described in the same way, and with sufficient particularity, as with product claims (see above).

Second, if the accuser can demonstrate that the infringer knew, or should have known from the circumstances, that the use of the process is prohibited without the consent of the patentee, he can request the accused infringer to refrain *"from offering the process for use within German territory."* This also applies to the situation where the accused infringer not only uses the claimed method, but also offers and sells a machine or device that implements the patented method.

Third, under the assumption that a product can be directly obtained from the method, the request may furthermore be aimed at excluding the accused infringer *"from offering, putting on the market, using or importing or stocking for such purposes the product obtained directly by a claimed process"*[43] (see §9 N° 3 Patent Act). Thus, the patentee may not only prohibit the implementation and commercialization of the process, but moreover he can foreclose offers and sales of products which have been directly obtained with the patented process. Physical products, as well as non-physical products such as video data, may fall under the provision.[44]

The claim according to §9 N° 3 Patent Act is particularly useful if the claimed method is actually not used within the German territory. That is, even for products produced outside Germany by a method that would otherwise infringe, §9 N° 3 Patent Act nevertheless applies, as long as the accused product is subsequently commercialized on the German market.[45] Accordingly, a method claim can be infringed by a product which has been (maybe legally) produced outside Germany but later sold within Germany.[46]

Contributory infringement: Contributory infringement consists in supplying, or offering to supply, an infringing *"means relating to an essential element of the claimed invention"*[47] (see §10(1) of the Patent Act). It protects the patentee in advance of a threat, without requiring an established direct infringement. On the other hand, it does not confer an absolute prohibition on supplying such means. It thus requires additionally that the supply occurs in view of an exploitation of the invention within German territory. This involves a certain level of knowledge on the part of the contributory infringer.[48] This contributory aspect[49] must be reflected in the prayer for relief. When formulating the prayer, care should be taken to avoid attempting to prohibit those activities that do not represent an infringement of the patent. This is of particular

43. Unofficial translation.
44. Federal Supreme Court, judgment of Aug. 21, 2012, X ZR 33/10, "MPEG-2 Videosignalcodierung."
45. Schulte, Patentgesetz, Kühnen §9 Rn. 81.
46. Details concerning the infringement of method and process claims can be found in Ch. 10, s. 5.
47. Unofficial translation.
48. Details concerning the concept of contributory infringements can be found in Ch. 10, s. 5.2.
49. Federal Supreme Court, X ZR 79/04, GRUR 2006, 570, "extracoronales Geschiebe."

importance where the offered or supplied means can also be used in a non-infringing manner. The request is thus aimed at preventing the activities of the contributory infringer that would result in patent infringement. The manner of drafting these requests differs from court to court. A typical way is to seek to impose on the contributory infringer an obligation to include in future offers and sales a warning notice stipulating that a particular use of the means would fall within the scope of a patent in dispute. Another method consists of attempting to impose on the contributory infringer an obligation to pursue a contractual stipulation with customers to use the means only in a non-infringing manner, and with non-compliance triggering the payment of a penalty.[50] Such a request may have the following language:

> *It is requested in the name and on behalf of the plaintiff,*
>
> *I. to find defendant liable*
>
> *1. in order to avoid a penalty to be set by the court for each case of violation of up to € 250,000.00, as an alternative confinement, or confinement of up to 6 months, in case of repeated violations a confinement of up to a total of 2 years, to refrain from offering and/or supplying within the German territory a means with the following features:*
>
> [Description of the accused means]
>
> *for a product with the following features:*
>
> [Description of the product according to the patented invention]
>
> *without*
>
> *a) in case of an offer, explicitly and visibly indicating that the means...*[indication of the accused means] *cannot be used without the authorization of the plaintiff as owner of the German Patent* [indication of the Patent N°]...*for a product*...[indication of the product according to the patented invention];
>
> *b) in case of a delivery, imposing on customers the written obligation not to use the...*[indication of the accused means] *for...*[indication of the product according to the patented invention] *without the authorization of the patentee whereby each non-compliance with this obligation by the customer is subject to a penalty of the amount...to be paid to the plaintiff.*

For a more detailed description of contributory infringement in Germany, please see Chapter 10, section 5.2.

3.2.1.2. Right to Claim Damages

According to §139(2) Patent Act, the injured party also has the right to claim damages. In contrast to the right to enjoin the accused infringer from using the invention, this right requires that the infringement has been negligently or intentionally committed. However, it is generally presumed that the accused infringer acted at least

50. Federal Supreme Court, X ZR 153/03, GRUR 2006, 839, "Deckenheizung."

negligently.[51] It is commonly accepted that anybody who participates in a commercial environment is required to sufficiently investigate and analyze opposing rights of third parties (e.g., through the publicly accessible patent registers). For that investigation only a one-month period is given to the market participants. This is a commonly accepted standard. If the accused infringer fails to sufficiently investigate and analyze his exposure within the one-month time period, he is deemed to have failed to exercise reasonable care, and thus acts negligently (§276 of the German Civil Code). This presumption is undisputed in most cases. This means that, in contrast to the U.S., a marking of the product with the label "patented" is not required to ensure the patentee's right to damages and the failure to mark a patented product does not limit the time period by which one can recover damages. It is rather presumed that the accused infringer knew about the patent or should have known that it exists. This is a sufficient trigger for a damages claim.

Only in exceptional instances can this presumption be refuted, for example if the accused infringer's acts are limited to transporting or storing the accused products. Such a party would not be held liable, at least until he becomes aware of the patent rights concerned, for instance through a warning letter.[52]

The scope of the damages claim is usually unknown when starting the proceedings. Due to the missing information, the injured party is not yet in a position to request a specific amount of money. The Code of Civil Procedure provides an opportunity to file a declaratory action (§256 of the Code of Civil Procedure) requesting the court find that a damage claim exists for infringing acts committed by the defendant since the date of publication of the mention of the patent grant.[53] Such request could have the following language:

> *It is requested in the name and on behalf of the plaintiff,*
>
> ...
>
> *II. to find, that the defendant is obliged to compensate plaintiff for all damages invoked on plaintiff by the acts indicated under I.1, committed since...* [date of the mention of the grant plus one month[54]] *and which will be invoked in future;*

The assessment of the amount of damages is separate from the infringement proceedings on the merits. This assessment depends on the plaintiff's discovery of relevant information from the accused infringer through a rendering of accounts, which is discussed in the following chapter.

51. Federal Supreme Court, X ZR 79/90, GRUR 1993, 460, "Wandabstreifer."
52. District Court Düsseldorf, decision of Dec. 14, 2006, InstGE 7, 172; Federal Supreme Court, GRUR 2009, 1142, decision of Sep. 17, 2009, "MP3-Player-Import."
53. Federal Supreme Court, I ZR 189/99, GRUR 2001, 1177, "Feststellungsinteresse II."
54. The damage claims are calculated starting one month from the publication of the grant of the patent. The one-month period is considered to be sufficient for identifying the patent.

3.2.1.3. *Right to be Informed and Rendering of Accounts*

The injured party has the right be informed about the scope of the infringing acts in order to assess the amount of damages. Such right is commonly accepted and its legal basis is taken from customary law.[55] In addition, rights of information shall help to identify the origin and distribution channels (§140 b of the German Patent Act). It shall also give information to calculate the reasonable compensation for use of the claimed invention after publication of the patent application (§33 of the German Patent Act).[56] Thus, the injured party usually files a request aimed at a so-called rendering of accounts.[57] It specifies what the defendant will have to do. The request typically contains the following language:

> *It is requested in the name and on behalf of the plaintiff,*
>
> *I. to find defendant liable*
>
> *1....*[See Chapter 8, section 3.2.1.1]
>
> *2. to render plaintiff account as to the extent to which defendant committed the acts defined under number I.1. since...*[date of the publication of the patent application plus one month] *namely by indicating:*
>
> *a) production amount and production time;*
>
> *b) amount of received and ordered products, names and addresses of the manufactures, supplier and other pre-possessors, including the paid price;*
>
> *c) the individual deliveries, broken down by amounts, times and prices of delivery and type names as well as names and addresses of the commercial recipients and the selling points, for which the deliveries were supposed;*
>
> *d) the individual offers, broken down by amounts, times, and prices of offer as well as the names and addresses of the commercial recipients of offers;*
>
> *e) the advertisement conducted, broken down by advertisement media, their number of edition, period and area of distribution;*
>
> *and for time the from...*[date of the mention of the grant plus one month]
>
> *f) the overall costs and the profits made, broken down by the individual cost factors;*
>
> *- whereby the names and addresses of non-commercial recipients and addressees of offers shall not be disclosed to the plaintiff, but to a certified auditor domiciled in Germany and bound to confidentiality vis-à-vis the plaintiff, which shall be named by the defendant, provided the defendant bears the costs of the auditor and instructs and authorizes him to respond to concrete questions of plaintiff whether a particular recipient or addressee of an offer is named in the report.*
>
> *- whereby the indications as to b) and c) shall be supported by the provision of sales documents (invoices or bill of delivery) wherein confidential information which is irrelevant for the rending of account may be redacted.*

---

55. Federal Supreme Court, X ZR 72/94, GRUR 1997, 116, "Prospekthalter."
56. *See* Ch. 12, s. 5.1.2.
57. *See* example in the Undertaking N° IV in Ch. 16, s. 1.2.

If this request is granted by the court (in the first-instance decision), the injured party can then enforce the corresponding operating part of the judgment to get the necessary information for a proper assessment and determination of the amount of damages and reasonable compensation. That is, during the first-instance proceedings no discussions concerning the amount of damages and the relevant basis for calculating them takes place. Rather, the assessment and determination is allocated to subsequent proceedings, which are discussed in more detail in the following chapters.[58]

3.2.1.4. Other Rights

Besides the aforementioned rights, there are other rights which might be judicially asserted. For example, according to §140 a of the Patent Act, the injured party may require the destruction of the products that are the subject matter of the patent, including materials and equipment that have served overwhelmingly for the manufacture of such products, provided that the enforcement is not disproportionate in the individual case. The accused infringer can also be required by the plaintiff to recall the products or to remove them definitively from the distribution channels (§140a (3) Patent Act). In addition, the plaintiff may assert reasonable compensation for the use of the claimed invention during the time from the publication of the patent application (§33 Patent Act).[59]

Table 8.2. Typically Asserted Rights

Right to prevent the use of the patent	**§139(1) Patent Act:** • Requires "danger of recidivism" which can be deduced from already committed infringing acts or requires at least a danger of imminent infringements.
Right to claim damages	**§139(2) Patent Act:** • Dependant on fault: Acts must be committed intentionally or negligently, (usually presumed). • Assessment/calculation of the amount of damages is separated from proceedings on the merits: Only declaratory judgment as to the existence of the claim, but no decision on the amount.

58. *See* Ch. 8, s. 5.4; details concerning the calculation of damages can be found in Ch. 12.
59. *See* Ch. 12, s. 5.1.2.

Right to be informed/rendering of accounts	**Customary law, §140b Patent Act:** • To enable injured party to determine amount of damage claim and to identify other infringers.
Destruction	**§140a (1) Patent Act:** • Destruction must be proportionate
Recall of accused products and/or removal from distribution channels	**§140a (3) Patent Act:** • Recall or removal must be proportionate
Reasonable compensation	**§33 Patent Act:** (in addition to damage claim) • Meant to compensate use of the patented invention during the time between publication of the application and the grant.

3.2.2. Information about the Subject Matter of the Case

A further purpose of the complaint brief is to sufficiently inform the court about the subject matter of the case. The complaint brief should be well prepared and begin with the factual information that was gathered prior to the proceedings, followed by the requests for relief described in the previous chapters.

This first, factual part of the complaint brief is typically subdivided into two main sub-chapters. The first sub-chapter basically describes the subject matter of the patent-in-suit with respect to the asserted claims of the patent. The description should provide additional illustrative background information. The invention should be described in the context of the prior art cited in the patent document. This information is aimed at facilitating understanding of the technical field and the invention for the court, which is presumably composed of judges who do not have the level of knowledge of the skilled person to whom the patent description is addressed. Thus for the sake of comprehensibility it is also helpful to provide illustrative material demonstrating the working of embodiments of the prior art and of the invention. Particular emphasis needs to be put on prior art that is decisive in understanding the claimed invention and is thus relevant to the interpretation of the asserted claims and the underlying claim construction. Because the language of the proceedings is German, German translations of these prior art documents must be provided.

This part of the complaint brief ends with the formulation of the technical problem solved by the invention. This technical problem must have been objectively determined, without hindsight, in light of the prior art. If the technical problem was inaccurately formulated in the patent, the complaint may clarify it. The complaint is the appropriate place to correct existing inaccuracies.[60]

60. Significance of the formulated problem for the claim construction: *See* Ch. 10.

After the technical problem is properly determined, the teaching of the claimed invention needs to be described. This description of the invention should be presented with an eye to claim construction, in order to facilitate a favorable claim scope determination from the court. The asserted claims, in particular the independent claims, are broken down in a logical and comprehensive outline of features, which is called the feature chart. The feature chart is aimed at facilitating the court's reading and understanding of the claims. Care should be given to breaking down the elements of the claims in a manner that promotes a favorable claim construction. In many cases the feature chart, which is decisive for the infringement test, is subject to discussions between the parties later during the proceedings.

A very simple example of such a feature chart is provided below. Here the patent concerns an invention relating to a sports shoe, particularly a running shoe that features a rigid cover covering the upper on the exterior surfaces thereof, in the region of the ball of the foot and extending from the sole. The features of claim 1 could be subdivided in the following manner:

A sport shoe comprising

1) *a sole;*

2) *an upper portion attached to the sole and*

3) *a rigid cover*

- *made of resisting material;*

- *angular in cross-section and*

- *defining a securing band and a protective shield;*

4) *the securing band is affixed between said sole and said upper portion,*

5) *the securing band extends from said sole, upwardly over the exterior of the upper portion in the area of the ball of the shoe.*

The complaint must then describe the accused technology. The feature chart is used to show, feature by feature, that the accused embodiment or method uses the asserted claim. This requires each feature to be mapped onto the accused embodiment. For this feature mapping the plaintiff should refer to evidence that has been collected prior to the introduction of the proceedings. It may be—if available and feasible—the accused product itself, photos of it, literature describing the accused embodiment, advertisements, or tests which have been previously carried out by the plaintiff. In the example above, it would be useful to have a photo of the shoe, which might be taken for instance from the advertisement collected at a tradeshow, in which the references of the claim features are incorporated.

This demonstration is more complicated if the claim contains features referring to characteristics of a product which need to be detected through tests or analysis, for instance if the product claim refers to a particular composition of a chemical substance. The available product literature of the accused infringer might be sufficient for demonstrating the infringing quality of the product. Nevertheless, it may be worth-while to carry out independent tests and analysis, especially where the publicly available information on the accused product is insufficient or cannot be relied upon because it contains errors or could be misinterpreted. If the accused product is a chemical substance, these tests and analysis can be carried out by laboratories and attached, either as a report or in the form of a private expert opinion, to the complaint brief.

Unlike in U.S. litigation, general discovery proceedings do not take place under German law. However, there may be situations where some form of limited discovery is necessary and available. Discovery and evidence taking is discussed in detail in Chapter 11.

An outline of a complaint brief with its usual subparts can be found in Chapter 16, section 3.

3.3. Defendant's Defense

After the complaint brief is filed and served on the defendant, the defendant will have to respond to the complaint. Depending on the deadlines set in the court's schedule this will have to be done approximately two to three months after the filing of the complaint. Counterarguments can be directed against the plaintiff's presentation of facts, including the proposed claim construction. Furthermore, legal and procedural objections can be raised by the defendant at this stage.

3.3.1. Factual Submissions

The defendant's defense must carefully identify those facts that are admitted or denied. Anything not expressly denied shall be deemed as admitted, unless the denial is obvious from other statements of the party (§138(3) Code of Civil Procedure). It is thus crucial to emphasize and clearly point to those facts in the complaint that are denied. A simple denial (e.g., "*the plaintiff's allegation is incorrect*") without giving any further explanatory reasons for the denial is *not* sufficient and would be disregarded. According to §138(1) Code of Civil Procedure, statements made by the parties concerning factual circumstances must be "complete and truthful." This duty is independent of which party carries the burden of proof. In order to comply with this duty the denial must be substantiated, and thus contain a complete and truthful explanation. The duty requires that the denying party have knowledge of the factual circumstances or could reasonably obtain access to it.[61] This is usually the case if the concerned factual circumstances are within the knowledge of the denying party. Thus, the assertion of the plaintiff that a chemical substance is composed of A, B and C, requires a substantiated denial. This means the accused infringer cannot offer only a bare denial that his or her product does not contain these components. He must at least state that the product is composed of different components (specifying components A, B, C' (which is different to C, etc.). An unexplained bare denial would not be accepted by the court and could lead to a shift in the burden of proof. However, an assertion of lack of

61. Federal Supreme Court, BGHZ 100, 190, 196.

knowledge is permissible, and must be considered by the court, if it concerns facts that are outside the knowledge of the denying party (§138(4) Code of Civil Procedure).

This procedural interplay between substantiated submissions and substantiated denials serves to crystallize triable questions of fact and facilitates the court's understanding of the patent and claim construction.

3.3.2. *Legal and Procedural Defenses*

Beyond admitting or denying the facts of the complaint, and submitting the defendant's own characterization of the patent, there are several defenses which may be available depending on the particular case. These defenses might have a legal nature, i.e., they result from the substantive law, or they may be procedural. Procedural defenses raised by the defendant are mainly directed against the venue and jurisdiction of the court,[62] or the defendant claims a missing security for the procedural costs.[63] The main defenses resulting from the substantive law are as follows:

(1) *Right based on prior use*: According to §12 of the Patent Act, a patent has no effect against a person who, at the time of filing the application[64], possessed the inventive teaching in Germany. That is, he had already begun to use the invention, or at least has made serious arrangements for doing so. The prior user may use the invention for the needs of his own business in his own plant or the plants of others. If the defendant proves the circumstances of such prior use—provided that the use does not go beyond the indicated scope—the action is to be dismissed. The right requires that the user (the accused infringer) have had possession of the invention at the priority date of the asserted patent. Such possession is deemed to exist if the claimed teaching is objectively completed and if it is subjectively recognized that the actual implementation of the invention is possible.[65] That is, the user must have recognized the inventive teaching as described in the asserted patent and was therefore in a position to methodically realize and repeat the inventive result.[66] The prior user need not have understood the physical or chemical reactions that are responsible for the effects according to the teaching of the patent.[67] Likewise, it is irrelevant whether he had realized the particular advantages of the inventive teaching or not.[68] Such right based on prior use is to be denied, however, if the patented subject matter was only unknowingly and coincidentally used, which would not have enabled the user to

62. *See* Ch. 8, s. 1.1.
63. *See* Ch. 8, s. 7.3.
64. I.e., prior to the filing date or priority date of the application underlying the asserted patent.
65. Federal Supreme Court, decision of Jun. 12, 2012, X ZR 131/09, "Desmopressin."
66. Federal Supreme Court, I ZR 114/58, GRUR 1960, 546, "Bierhahn"; Federal Supreme Court, Ia ZR 224/63, GRUR 1964, 496, "Formsand II."
67. Appeal Court Düsseldorf, InstGE 11, 198, "Desmopressin."
68. Federal Supreme Court, decision of Jun. 12, 2012, X ZR 131/09, "Desmopressin;" Appeal Court Düsseldorf, InstGE 11, 198, "Desmopressin."

methodically realize and repeat the inventive result.[69] It would not be sufficient if the realization is merely achieved by chance in only some instances.[70] In addition, the possession of the invention must be confirmed—i.e., the user must at least have implemented bona fide arrangements to manufacture or commercialize it.[71] The right based on prior use is limited in scope to acts that were already committed or intended at the priority date of the patent.[72] It does not extend to inventive features of preferred embodiments of the asserted patent that are outside of what the user effectively recognized at the priority date. Nevertheless, it covers not only the prior user, but also subsequent trade levels,[73] such as customers who have bought a product covered by the prior use.

(2) *Contractual licenses*: The defendant may be entitled to rely on an existing license agreement, under which the infringement claim is barred. This requires that the agreement has actually been concluded and that the activities of the defendant are within its scope. Such agreement could be limited both to particular activities and geographic regions (§15(2) Patent Act). Licenses granted by a previous right holder are not affected by a later assignment, and can be asserted against a new owner (§15(3) Patent Act).

(3) *Exhaustion of patent rights*: This defense refers to a situation where the product was previously put on the EU/EEC market with the permission of the patentee or of someone who was duly authorized by the patentee. The details of the exhaustion of patent rights are described in Chapter 10, section 6.

(4) *Defense arising from antitrust law*: This defense may arise when a market-dominating position follows from the assertion of the patent. The details of this defense are described in the following Chapter 6.2.

(5) *Usurpation*: The defendant may argue that he is the rightful owner and has been illegally dispossessed of the invention (usurpation). In such a situation, plaintiff's requests would not be made in good faith and thus violate a fundamental requirement of the civil law (§242 of the Civil Code). However, this can also arise in situations where the plaintiff did not acquire ownership of the asserted patent (often unknowingly) due to incorrect application of the rules concerning employees' inventions. These rules are important formalities, and have, historically, posed problems for infringement plaintiffs. Under the previous Employees' Invention Act, employers frequently claimed their employees' inventions incorrectly, and therefore did not acquire ownership of the inventions, despite filing and obtaining patents. The employers' failure to comply with the complex laws on employee inventions usually only came to

69. Federal Supreme Court, I ZR 114/58, GRUR 60, 546, "Bierhahn"; Federal Supreme Court, Ia ZR 224/63, GRUR 64, 496, "Formsand II."
70. Federal Supreme Court, decision of Jun. 12, 2012, X ZR 131/09, "Desmopressin."
71. Federal Supreme Court, I ZR 114/58, GRUR 60, 546, "Bierhahn"; Federal Supreme Court, Ia ZR 224/63, GRUR 64, 496, "Formsand II.
72. Federal Supreme Court, X ZR 32/99, GRUR 2002, 231, "Biegevorrichtung."
73. Federal Supreme Court, decision of Jun. 12, 2012, X ZR 131/09, "Desmopressin; "Appeal Court Düsseldorf, InstGE 11, 198, "Desmopressin."

light after patent enforcement had begun—much to the plaintiffs' surprise and annoyance undoubtedly. These rules can be exploited by a defendant, who, if he acquires the patent from the employee, can succeed with a usurpation defense.[74]

(6) *Statute of limitation*: According to §141 of the Patent Act, rights resulting from the infringement of a patent shall become time-barred in compliance with the provisions of the 5th Chapter of the 1st book of the Civil Code. These provisions are applicable to European and German patents:
   (a) For all rights the *standard limitation of three years* is principally applicable, which commences at the end of the year in which the right arose and in which the right holder obtained or could have obtained knowledge of the accused infringement (§§195, 199 of the German Civil Code).
   (b) If the standard limitation is not applicable, the rights principally become statute-barred 10 years after they arose, provided the right holder did not know the circumstances giving rise to the right, or if it cannot be proven that he at least negligently ignored these circumstances (§199(3) N° 1 Civil Code).[75]
   (c) However, it has to be taken into account that the right to prevent the use of the patent arises continuously with each act of infringement. Therefore, a defense based on the statute of limitations does not usually lead to a dismissal of the action. It may reduce the scope of plaintiff's infringement assertion for the time prior to the standard limitation of three years. But even if the short standard limitation is applicable and accordingly a damage claim (§139(2) Patent Act) could not be asserted for infringing acts committed prior to the three year limitation, the accused infringer will not be released from any financial payments for that time, as he is obliged to provide restitution for all the benefit he obtained without legal grounds at the expense of the right holder (claim to return of unjust enrichment according to §812 of Civil Code). That is, even if the damages claim is time-barred, a restitution claim under the provisions for the return of unjust enrichment would be applicable, calculated analogously to a reasonable license.[76] This claim would be time-barred 10 years after it arises, or, irrespective of the date on which it arises, 30 years after the date on which the act causing the injury was committed.[77]

(7) *Forfeiture*: The defense of forfeiture arises in the exceptional situation where the right holder has knowingly tolerated, for a considerable time period, the infringing activities, such that the accused infringer may objectively presume

74. The Employees' Inventions Act is discussed in Ch. 13.
75. For the sake of completeness, it has to be noted that a thirty year limitation may exceptionally be applicable if the moment of the infringing act and the occurrence of the injury diverge in time (§199 (3) N° 2 Civil Code). In that particular case the right becomes statue barred latest thirty years from the infringing act.
76. *See* Ch. 12, s. 2.
77. Federal Supreme Court, X ZR 81/72, GRUR 1977, 250, "Kunststoffhohlprofil"; Federal Supreme Court, X ZR 7/80, GRUR 1982, 301, "Kunststoffhohlprofil II."

from the circumstances that the right holder would never assert the patent in question. The defense of forfeiture includes: first, a time aspect—the toleration of the infringing acts must have lasted for a considerable time period;[78] second, there must be particular circumstances which objectively create an impression in the accused infringer that his use of the patented invention may continue into the future; and, third, he must, from such use, have thus acquired economic value. The concept of forfeiture results from a fundamental principal, according to which a right holder has a duty to proceed in good faith when asserting a claim (§242 of the Civil Code). The Federal Supreme Court sets very high thresholds for this defense.[79] The forfeiture statute term starts to run from each infringing act.[80]

3.3.3. *Requests of the Defendant*

Usually the defendant requests the dismissal of the complaint and, as a precautionary or additional request, the suspension of the proceedings.[81] Requesting the suspension of the infringement proceedings requires that opposition or nullity proceedings against the asserted patent be already pending, regardless of whether the proceedings were instituted by the defendant or a third party.

The interplay of invalidation and infringement proceedings could have an impact on the claim construction proposed by the defendant since his or her interests might be different in both proceedings. It might be more favorable for challenging validity to have a broad understanding of the asserted claims, whereas it is easier to argue non-infringement on the basis of narrow claim understanding. The interplay between claim construction in infringement and nullity proceedings is discussed in Chapter 10, sections 3.2.3.2 and 3.2.3.3.

3.4. Further Briefs until the Main Hearing

When drafting the complaint, the plaintiff cannot anticipate all the arguments of the accused infringer. Thus it is necessary for the plaintiff to reply to the various defenses in a subsequent brief (reply brief, *"Replik"*), and, in particular, to any new elements raised by the defendant.

A patentee's complaint typically assumes the validity of a granted patent and usually does not contain a critical discussion as to the validity of the patent. But a discussion of validity will likely be warranted upon responding to the defendant's defense. If the defense contains a request for suspending the proceedings it must also

78. Federal Supreme Court, X ZR 150/98, GRUR 2001, 323, "Temperaturwächter": Subject to this case was a situation where the patentee waited more than ten years, before he started to assert his rights against the accused infringer.
79. Federal Supreme Court, X ZR 150/98, GRUR 2001, 323, "Temperaturwächter."
80. Federal Supreme Court, NJW-RR 2006, 235.
81. *See* Ch. 8, s. 3.6.2.

contain a discussion of the merits of the request. This discussion, which is aimed at convincing the court to suspend the proceedings, might be built up on prosecuted prior art or previously unknown prior art documents.[82] The plaintiff will have to respond to these aspects of the defense in the third brief of the proceedings.

Thereafter, in response to the plaintiff's reply, the defendant is afforded a second opportunity to submit additional arguments and facts with relevance to plaintiff's response. Accordingly, at least four briefs, including their exhibits, are on file on the day of the hearing. In contrast to the typical volume of materials familiar in U.S. litigations, the records in German litigations are typically quite thin, sometimes numbering less than 100 pages.

3.5. Hearing

The chambers of the District Courts are composed of three judges. One judge, usually the most experienced judge, presides over the chamber. He or she has the predominant role of directing the hearing. Due to the quantity of patent cases, the District Courts of Mannheim and Munich each have two chambers, the District Court Düsseldorf has even three chambers for trial of such cases.

Besides the setting of deadlines and the grant of time extensions, the court does not substantially involve itself in the course of the proceedings until the day of the hearing. Of course, the court internally prepares the case by means of the submitted briefs. But until the day of the hearing, which takes place approximately eight months after the filing of the complaint (in some courts later), the parties will not know which claim construction will be applied. The various disputes analogous to "motions to dismiss," which a U.S. court would have resolved on a Rule 12(b) motion (such as for lack of standing, lack of jurisdiction, lack of controversy, etc.), are all handled at the main hearing, along with the overall merits of a case. As a general rule, the court does not issue any preliminary opinions on the claim construction or any other decisive aspect of the case prior to the hearing.

The hearing is introduced by the presiding judge. This introduction is the result of an internal deliberation among the judges of the chamber, which takes place after they have studied the exchanged briefs and shortly prior to the day of the hearing. One of the three judges, the so-called reporting judge, is responsible for drafting a preliminary opinion for the purpose of the preliminary internal deliberation.

This introduction usually contains an outline of a preliminary opinion containing the main aspects that the court expects to be of particular importance for the decision. The presiding judge's introduction is aimed at concentrating the subject matter under discussion during the hearing, focusing only on the critical aspects of the case. This is one reason why the hearings tend to be of short duration. The introductory remarks of the court may also contain statements as to a particular favored claim construction. Typically, this preliminary opinion disfavors one of the parties, but that party will most probably get the first opportunity to argue his case, preferably with an emphasis on

82. Details concerning the suspension of the proceedings can be found in Ch. 8, s. 3.6.2.

those aspects which have been highlighted in the introduction of the presiding judge. These pleadings are followed by the arguments of the other side, which might be short if no persuasive new elements or arguments have been brought up, and if the judges seem to follow the preliminary opinion. Of course, the judges pose questions during the course of the hearing, or comment in response to statements of counsel.

Once the parties have sufficiently exchanged their arguments—this usually takes one to two hours, longer in more complex cases—the presiding judge closes the hearing and indicates a day for the announcement of the decision. This usually takes places four to six weeks after the hearing. In contrast to the Federal Patent Court, the trial court does not deliver a decision at the end of the hearing. Because the hearing is dominated by the preliminary opinion contained in the presiding judge's introduction, it is often possible to deduce from the hearing which party will likely win the case. Accordingly, the written portion of the proceedings is very important, and well-prepared submissions represent a key element for success.

3.6. Outcome of the First Instance Proceedings

The decision may take different forms. Most likely, the court either grants the requests of the complaint or either completely or partially dismisses the complaint. Due to rather high standards, it is less likely that the court suspends the proceedings. This may, however, happen if highly pertinent prior art is discovered which was not considered during the prosecution proceedings.[83] Usually there is no evidence taking and the court makes a decision based on the evidence and facts submitted by the parties. In exceptional situations, such as if the relevant facts are still in dispute or not sufficiently proven by the evidence submitted by the parties, the court will appoint an expert. It is rather unlikely that witnesses will be heard in patent infringement proceedings, but it may occur for instance in cases where the accused infringer asserts a right based on prior use (§12 of the Patent Act).[84] Accordingly, in patent infringement proceedings, the most important means of taking evidence are court experts, rather than witnesses.

The most frequent forms of decision taken after the hearing are illustrated in Figure 8.2.

3.6.1. Grant of the Action or Complete/Partial Dismissal (Decision on the Merits)

A decision granting the requests follows basically the same structure as the complaint. It starts with an operating part containing plaintiff's requests and a decision imposing the costs of the proceedings on the defendant. According to §91 of the Code of Civil

83. *See* Ch. 8, s. 3.6.2.
84. *See* Ch. 8, s. 3.3.2.

Procedure, the losing party bears the statutory costs[85] of the proceedings. The operating part forms the basis for the enforcement of the judgment.[86]

Figure 8.2. Possible First Instance Decisions

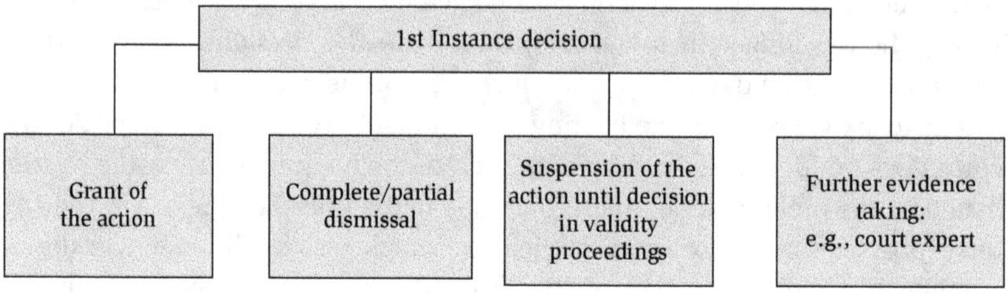

In case of partial dismissal, the court grants the requests with a reduced scope and dismisses the rest of the action. The costs are then proportionally divided (§91 of the Code of Civil Procedure). For instance, where the plaintiff succeeds to a large extent with his claims, the court may impose one quarter of the costs on the plaintiff and three quarters of the costs on the defendant. In case of a complete dismissal, all statutory costs of the proceedings are born by the plaintiff.

In all these cases, the decision will contain extensive reasoning highlighting why the court has decided in a particular way. This reasoning typically refers to the case law established through the decisions of higher courts. A particular emphasis is put on the most pertinent decisions of the Federal Supreme Court which are decisive for the subject matter of the case. Accordingly, besides other important elements, the court's claim construction is part of the decision. Samples of first court decisions translated into English can be found in the International Review of Intellectual Property and Competition Law published by the Max Planck Institute for Intellectual Property, Competition and Tax Law, in Munich, Germany.

3.6.2. Suspension of the Proceedings

The District Courts may order suspension of the proceedings in anticipation of another action (§148 Code of Civil Procedure). Requesting the suspension of the infringement proceedings requires that opposition or nullity proceedings against the asserted patent be already pending by the time of the suspension request, regardless of whether the proceedings were instituted by the defendant or a third party. The defendant thus does not need to be a party to these parallel opposition or nullity proceedings. According to §148 Code of Civil Procedure there are two aspects that are decisive to the District Court's decision to suspend. The first aspect requires a dependency between both proceedings, namely that a decision of the infringement court depends on the decision to be expected in the parallel invalidation proceedings. Typically, such dependency

85. Details concerning costs and fees can be found in Ch. 15.
86. Details concerning the enforcement of the decision can be found in Ch. 8, s. 5.

could be denied if the court concludes that the asserted patent is not infringed. In that case, the court would simply dismiss the action. Nevertheless, as the indicated dependency between both proceedings has an abstract meaning, it is not a compelling requirement that the court—prior to a decision on the suspension—first concludes that there is infringement. In particular, in complex cases where such decision on the infringement cannot easily be answered and would require substantial evidence taking, it may be appropriate to first determine whether the case should be stayed.[87]

Second, the court has discretionary power to suspend the proceedings, pursuant to §148 Code of Civil Procedure. Based on the submitted record,[88] the court makes its determination as to whether there is a predominant probability (or high likelihood) that the asserted claim will be invalidated in parallel invalidation proceedings.[89] The court's usual reasoning is roughly summarized in Figure 8.3.

Figure 8.3. Court's Reasoning as to the Question of Suspension

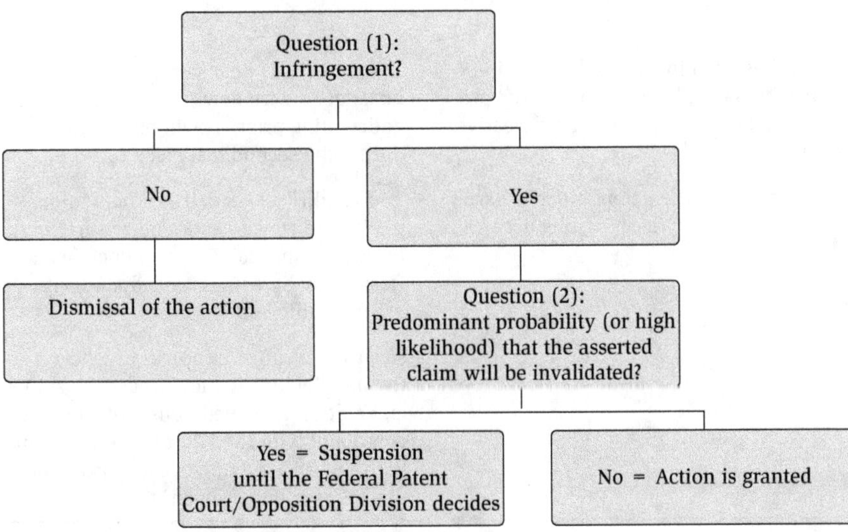

When approaching this decision, the court will weigh the interests of the parties. On the one hand, there is the depreciation in the value of the patent, as the enforcement would be delayed until a decision is taken in parallel invalidation proceedings. On the other hand, there is the interest in avoiding an infringement ruling when the patent may be invalid. Also, the behavior of the parties during the proceedings with regard to timing may be influential. An invalidation attack made very late in the proceedings lowers the chances of a suspension.[90] Since there is no evidence taking in respect to the question of suspension, the court makes a summary assessment based on the material

87. *See* Kühnen, Schulte, 9th ed., §139, N° 281.
88. District Court Düsseldorf, 4b O 8/09, GRUR-RR 2010, 369.
89. Federal Supreme Court, X ZR 56/85, GRUR 1987, 284, "Transportfahrzeug."
90. District Court Düsseldorf, InstGE 3, 54, "Sportschuhsohle."

submitted by the parties. The parties submit the briefs and the prior art documents that have been filed in the parallel invalidation proceedings. Because the district court's determination on the stay request is based on the probable outcome of the parallel invalidation proceedings, the district court's ruling is concerned only with the prior art that is the subject of these parallel proceedings.

Table 8.3. Considerations in the Suspension Decision

Pro	Contra
- Prior art, which was not considered during prosecution proceedings and is novelty anticipating;[91]	- Simple doubts on the validity of the patent, doubts referring to inventive step;[92]
- The inventive step has become so questionable in view of the prior art presented by the infringer that there is no reasonable argument in favor of validity left;[93]	- The nullity action only contains validity attacks (prior art) which were already considered by the patent office;[94]
- Patent has been invalidated in first instance by the Federal Patent Court[95] provided that this is not based on a clearly wrong decision;[96]	- The patent has been confirmed in first instance, unless new, unknown, novelty-anticipating prior art will be identified during the second instance;[97]
- The decision of the patent office is based on a clear and obviously wrong decision;[98]	- The validity attack is based on a prior public use which cannot be consistently proven by means of written documents (testimony by witnesses and affidavits are not sufficient);[99]
	- Accused infringer unnecessarily delays the parallel invalidation proceedings; this is, he does not expeditiously file a nullity complaint with the FPC or an opposition with the EPO after he became aware of the accused infringement;[100]

The likelihood of a suspension is typically very low if defendant's request is exclusively based on prior art documents which were already considered by the patent office during the granting or opposition proceedings. The chances for obtaining a stay

91. Federal Supreme Court, X ZR 56/85, GRUR 1987, 284, "Transportfahrzeug."
92. Schulte §139, N° 273.
93. Court of Appeals Düsseldorf InstGE 7, 139, 146, GRUR-RR 2007, 259, "Thermocycler."
94. Federal Supreme Court, I ZR 93/57, GRUR 1959, 320, "Moped-Kupplung."
95. Appeal Court Munich, InstGE 3, 62, "Aussetzung bei Nichtigkeitsurteil II."
96. Court of Appeals Düsseldorf decision of May 29, 2008, Az. 2 W 47/07, GRUR 2008, 1077, "Olanzapin."
97. Federal Supreme Court, I ZR 93/57, GRUR 1959, 320, "Moped-Kupplung."
98. Schulte §139, N° 273.
99. Appeal Court Düsseldorf, 2 U 129/78, GRUR 79, 636, "Ventilanbohrungsvorrichtung."
100. District Court Düsseldorf, InstGE 3, 54, "Sportschuhsohle."

are higher if the request is based on previously undisclosed, novelty-destroying prior art. It is commonly understood that there is a high threshold to achieve a stay of infringement proceedings. Statistical information on the success of stay requests is not available, but based on our experience litigating many patent disputes in Germany, suspensions or the appointment of court experts (see next section) generally occur in less than a third of the cases.

The Federal Supreme Court since recently seems[101] to have loosened the strict standards for suspending infringement proceedings toward a greater protection of the accused infringer. This trend is reflected in the following statements of the Federal Supreme Court[102] emphasizing the importance of due process rights for the accused infringer which has mounted a credible challenge to the patent's validity:

> *"A provisionally enforceable judgement on the defendant [...] to cease and desist, to provide information, to render accounts, and to destroy products in accordance with a patent is generally not justified if it may be expected with reasonable certainty that the basis underlying such a judgement will be eliminated by the revocation of the patent-in-suit. The right to due process that derives from a rule-of-law principle (Art. 20 Para. 3 of the Constitutional Law) in combination with fundamental rights, which is therefore constitutionally guaranteed (see e.g. BVerfGE 88, 118, 123), demands that the party accused of infringement be permitted to an effective legal recourse if it wishes to defend itself against a challenge arising from the patent in suit by means of a counterattack against the legal validity of this patent. This requires not only an effective recourse to conduct this attack via a nullity action, but also adequate consideration of the fact that this attack is also a means of defense—possibly the only one—against the claim arising from the patent. Due to the statutory provision, which requires only a valid patent for the revindications in accordance with Sec. 139 ff. of the Patent Act, and which offers nullity action, lying exclusively within the jurisdiction of the Patent Court, as the only tool to undo this legal standing, the attack on the patent in suit cannot be conducted as an objection in the infringement proceedings or by filing a countersuit for nullity, as would be the case in other legal systems. However, the resulting effect cannot be that such an attack has no impact on the infringement proceedings. Rather, the suspension of the infringement proceedings is fundamentally appropriate if it can be expected with sufficient certainty that the patent in suit will not survive the challenge of the action for nullity.*[103]

If the court finds that there is a sufficient likelihood that the patent will be invalidated in the parallel proceedings, it stays its own proceedings until a decision as to invalidity is rendered, resuming only if the patent validity has been upheld. But if the patent is held valid, the infringement proceedings may be resumed regardless of any appeal proceedings. There have also been cases where an infringement proceeding was suspended when new prior art was identified for the first time on appeal of a first-instance nullity action.[104] Some courts apply a more defendant-friendly approach in case a patent assertion company or so-called non-practicing company is asserting the patent. Indeed, the strategy of a non-practicing company is typically aimed at a

101. Federal Supreme Court, X ZR 61/13, "Kurznachrichten I," Federal Supreme Court, X ZR 68/13, "Kurznachrichten II."
102. Federal Supreme Court, X ZR 61/13, "Kurznachrichten I."
103. Unofficial translation of the authors.
104. Federal Supreme Court, I ZR 93/57, GRUR 1959, 320, "Moped-Kupplung."

pecuniary result by forcing the conclusion of a licensing agreement. The stakes are not the same for an original patent holder. He might be locked in commercial competition. He may thus refer to a legitimate interests in getting swifter relief than a company exclusively pursing a pecuniary interest. The following simplified situation presents the typical suspension scenario (see Figure 8.4).

Figure 8.4. Typical Suspension Scenario

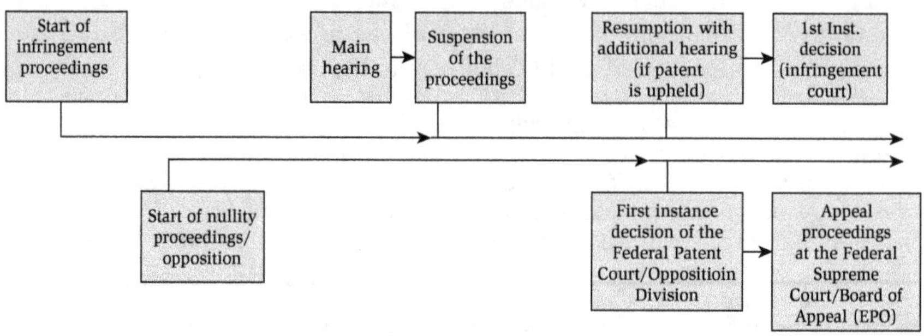

If the validity of the patent is reasonably doubtful, the patentee may consider asserting a narrower claim to better differentiate over the prior art. Of course, this new limited claim still needs to be infringed by the accused embodiment. Such a claim could be construed by features of the independent claim and features of one or several dependent claims, or the combination could be based on features taken from the description that are incorporated in the independent claim. Of course this requires a sufficient disclosure of the new combination in the patent description[105]—in particular, if features are taken from the description and then combined with an independent claim, resulting in a "new claim." Plaintiff will need to unconditionally limit the request on the new combination. This is a risky strategy but some courts, such as the District Court Düsseldorf, tend to accept it, whereas other courts are more conservative and would rather suspend the proceedings. It is a last resort strategy to deal with problematic prior art and to avoid a stay of the proceedings. In fact, the assertion of a claim with a narrower scope of protection as granted through the inclusion of additional feature(s) in the granted claims could be understood as an admission that the scope of protection as granted is not valid, impairing the value of the underlying patent office's granting decision.[106] The granting decision may not serve anymore as sufficient proof for the validity of the asserted claim. In addition, the amended claim may give rise to formal challenges such as the question of whether the amended claim is sufficiently disclosed.[107] Such formal challenges are typically not heard by the infringement courts in case of granted claims. These aspects should be taken into account before filing a lawsuit on the basis of a limited patent claim.

105. *See* Ch. 5, s. 5.
106. Benkard, 11th ed., Grabinski/Zülch on Sec. 139 PatG, marginal no. 107.
107. Federal Supreme Court, Xa ZR 70/08, "Maschinensatz."

If the court does order a suspension, the plaintiff may file within two weeks an immediate request for relief (§577 of the Code of Civil procedure). The Appeal court is, however, only entitled to review whether the infringement court has properly exercised its discretion. That is, the immediate request is only successful if the first-instance court is found to have abused its discretion in granting the suspension.

3.6.3. *Further Evidence Taking: Appointment of a Court Expert*

The court may conclude that the technical expertise of an expert is necessary. The appointment of a court expert is the most frequently used form of judicial investigation. According to the Supreme Court,[108] even an experienced court must order an expert opinion if the skilled person's understanding of the technical expressions in the patent claim is in doubt. Whether and to what an extent an expert opinion is necessary depends on the circumstances of the case.

On the other hand, fact witnesses are rather rare in patent infringement cases. Their appearance might be important, for instance, if the defendant raises the defense of prior use according to §12 of the Patent Act.

In most cases, the court renders a decision without appointing an expert. The probability of the involvement of a court expert differs from court to court. It also depends on the subject matter of the case. Precise estimations are difficult, but based on our experience litigating many patent disputes in Germany, the appointment of a court expert generally occurs in less than a quarter of the cases. In most cases, the court bases its decision on its own assessment of the technology, as understood through the material submitted by the parties.[109] The following approximation concerning three major infringement courts might additionally be taken into consideration when selecting the court (Table 8.4).[110]

The likelihood of the court appointing an expert also depends on the technical field of the concerned subject matter, which might be differently distributed among German infringement courts. That is, certain courts have built up technical expertise over the years by nature of the cases over which they have previously presided. Because the court files are not public, the patentee must necessarily rely on the expertise of his German counsel, who must continuously acquire this knowledge through a multitude of sources, such as discussions with colleagues, articles written by colleagues, and published and unpublished decisions to which he might have access through involvement in a case. Patentees will typically want to avoid the court appointing an expert, which may significantly lengthen the proceedings, sometimes by more than one year.

108. Federal Supreme Court, decision of Oct. 28, 2003, X ZR 76/00, GRUR 2004, 413, "Geflügelkörperhalterung."
109. Federal Supreme Court, X ZR 121/88, GRUR 1991, 436, Befestigungsvorrichtung II; Federal Supreme Court, X ZR 41/89, GRUR 1991, 744, "Trockenlegungsverfahren."
110. Magazine, JUVE Rechtsmarkt 04/10.

Table 8.4. Tendency to Appoint an Expert per Court

District Court Düsseldorf	Lower tendency
District Court Mannheim	Middle
District Court Munich	Higher tendency

A judicial investigation by means of a court expert might be necessary to illuminate the knowledge of the "skilled person" in the art, and to facilitate an understanding of the patent. Likewise, an expert may be appointed if the configuration of the accused embodiment remains disputed with respect to details that cannot be readily assessed by the court.[111] Usually, university professors within the relevant technical field, selected from lists proposed by the parties, are appointed. Unlike in the U.S. system, these experts are not experts retained by a particular party. They are neutral experts appointed by the court. Accordingly, the parties must avoid any contact with the expert prior to and after the appointment. Parties may successfully object to proposed experts if they can establish that there is a past or actual relationship between the expert and the opposing party giving sufficient reason to believe that there is a risk of bias.

The parties should have no direct contact with the expert during the proceedings. The correspondence with the expert is established through the court. The expert's working guidelines are contained within the court's order. This order contains a set of questions to be answered by the expert, as well as explanatory instructions to limit the expert's inquiry to particular matters within the expert's competence (and to avoid straying beyond that competence). The expert is tasked with explaining to the court the knowledge and experience of the skilled person in the art in question, as well as his working method and how he deals with technical problems. Whether the patent's solution was obvious is a question for the judge and not the expert.[112] Statements of the expert are therefore reviewed and placed in a legal context by the judge. For instance if the expert defines a term used in the patent claim in compliance with the concerned specialized field, it does not release the judge from the duty to make use of the description in order to clarify the meaning of this term in the context of the patent claim.[113] The interpretation of the patent falls within the responsibility of the court.[114]

The expert prepares a written report. This may take time and is the primary reason for the prolongation of the proceedings. As soon as the written expert opinion

111. Kühnen in Schulte §139, N° 292.
112. Federal Supreme Court, decision of Nov. 25, 2003, X ZR 162/00, GRUR 2004, 411, "Diabehältnis."
113. Federal Supreme Court, decision of Feb. 13, 2007, X ZR 74/05, GRUR 2007, 410, "Kettenradanordnung," an English translation of this decision can be found in IIC 2007, 726.
114. Federal Supreme Court, X ZR 76/04, GRUR 2006, 131, "Seitenspiegel," an English translation of this decision can be found in IIC 2007, 743.

is ready, it will be submitted to the parties, which then have an opportunity to make statements in response. Following this exchange of briefs, a further hearing will take place. The Court may also order the appearance of the expert, and is in fact obliged to do this upon request of any party. These further proceedings will prolong a decision on the merits far beyond the usual one-year timeline. It may be two years from the filing of the complaint to receive a first-instance decision if an expert is appointed (Figure 8.5).

Figure 8.5. Usual Course of Infringement Proceedings with Appointed Expert

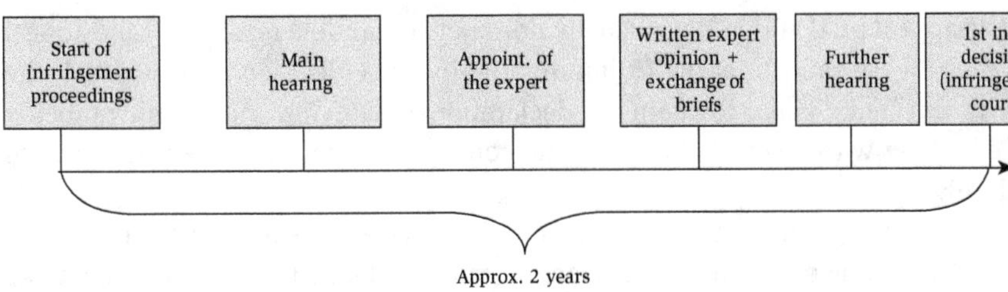

In view of the delay that appointing an expert may cause, it is incumbent on the plaintiff to attempt to streamline the issues and thoroughly digest the technology to simplify the issues for the court. Well-prepared arguments and submissions naturally help frame the issues for the court, and there is an increasing trend for parties to submit their own expert statements. These expert statements are often submitted along with the briefing papers of the parties. Whether or not to submit such a statement is a case-by-case determination, and should be discussed depending on the strategic goals of the case.

4. RELIEF

4.1. Appeal of First Instance Decisions

An appeal may be taken against first-instance decisions granting either completely or partially plaintiff's requests or dismissing the action (§511 Code of Civil Procedure). The period for filing the appeal is one month (§517 Code of Civil Procedure). This term begins upon service of the first-instance decision.[115] It is not extendable.

115. The term ends latest upon the expiration of five months after the pronouncement of the decision, assuming a written decision has not been served in time.

Figure 8.6. Usual Course of Appeal Proceedings

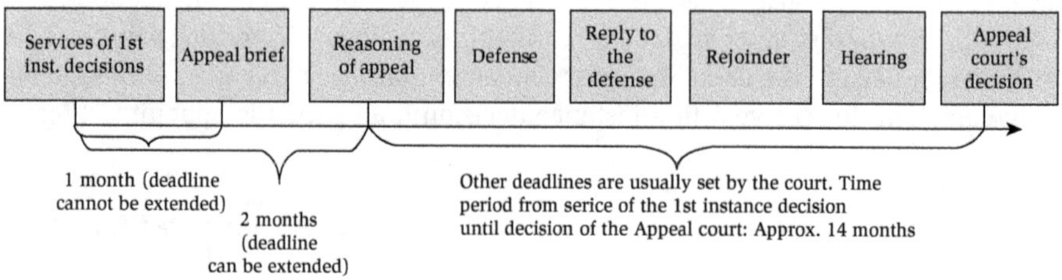

The appeal brief at this stage usually does not contain the reasons for the appeal and is thus a very short brief indicating the first-instance decision against which the appeal is directed. It also contains a declaration identifying the judgment being appealed, along with a certified copy of the contested judgment (§519 Code of Civil Procedure).

The appellant then has two months from the service of the first-instance decision to file his "reasoning of appeal." This deadline can be extended by the presiding judge upon request, provided the opposing party consents to the extension, or, without that consent, if the court determines that the proceedings will not be delayed and the appellant presents material grounds justifying the deadline extension (§520(2) Code of Civil Procedure).

The reasoning of appeal contains a declaration stating to what extent the first-instance decision is contested and what modifications are requested. The reasoning may allege a legal mistake—that a provision of law was incorrectly applied by the first-instance court—or that the submitted facts justify a different judgment (§513 Code of Civil Procedure). When drafting the reasoning of appeal the general rule is that parties may not submit new facts. There are exceptions, namely if there are concrete indications that the facts as established by the first-instance court are incorrect or incomplete (§529(1) N° 1 Code of Civil Procedure). In addition, according to §529(1) N° 2 Code of Civil Procedure, the submission of new facts will be allowed if they were unknown during the first instance, or at least if their omission was excusable. According to §531 of the Code of Civil Procedure, new attacks and defenses are only allowed if:

- they concern aspects of the case which have obviously been ignored by the first-instance court, or could not be asserted in first instance due to a procedural mistake; or
- the missing submission is not caused by carelessness.

The parties are accordingly well advised not to hold back facts, evidence, possible claims or defenses that could be brought forward in the first-instance proceedings. The risks are too high that such evidence may be deemed belated in the second instance.

4.2. Appeal of Appellate Decisions: Federal Supreme Court

Only a few cases may be appealed to the Federal Supreme Court, which reviews cases in the third instance. The threshold to bring a case to the Federal Supreme Court is very high. An appeal to the Federal Supreme Court requires leave of the second instance appellate court. If such leave is denied, the appellant may petition directly to the Federal Supreme Court, which may then grant the appeal right directly. To be successful, particular grounds of admissibility (§543 Code of Civil Procedure) must be given, namely that:

- the case is of fundamental importance; or
- a decision of the Federal Supreme Court is necessary for the development of law or to unify the case law.

Most cases do not meet these standards. In most cases, the appeal court of second instance will not allow the appeal to the Federal Supreme Court, or the petition of the denial will be rejected by the Supreme Court. In the rare cases where the appellant manages to surmount these thresholds, the proceedings will usually be limited to violations of law and legal provisions (§§546, 547 Code of Civil Procedure).

5. ENFORCEMENT PROCEEDINGS

5.1. Provision of Security

Even though an appeal has no suspending effect, a first-instance decision is not automatically enforceable. As long as the decision is not final, the prevailing party needs to provide a security for the enforcement. Thus, a first-instance decision usually contains the additional sentence: "The decision is provisionally enforceable against a security of an amount of … . " This sentence may be more precise in that it requires that the security shall be provided by a guarantee of a bank with a seat in Germany. It must be a bank that is officially accredited to operate and provide financial services within Germany territory. It does not necessarily need to be a German bank, but it must be a financial institution with sufficient capital to answer for the amount of the guarantee.

The right to an injunction and the claim to render account can only be enforced—prior to a final decision—by means of such security. The purpose of the security is to cover eventual damages which could arise from an unjustified enforcement of the decision, namely if an appeal is successful in the second or third-instance proceedings. If the right holder intends to enforce only a part of the claim (for instance, a rendering of accounts), he should accordingly request a particular attribution of the litigation value to the different requested claims.

The amount of the guarantee must comply with the form set forth in §108(1) Code of Civil Procedure. The security shall be provided by a written instrument, be irrevocable, unlimited in time, absolute, unconditional and directly bank guaranteed. If it is too difficult or time consuming to find a suitable bank, the enforcing party may also deposit the amount with a special office of the Court, namely the deposit agency where the money is deposited in a trust account. However, this requires the availability and transfer of the full amount. A sample of such bank guaranteed can be found in Chapter 16, section 7.

5.2. Motion for Temporary Suspension of Enforcement

Permanent injunctive relief primarily depends on whether there is infringement. In contrast to the U.S.,[116] German courts do not apply equity principles when considering whether to award permanent injunctive relief to the prevailing party. Whether the patentee or right holder uses or intends to use the patent is not relevant to the permanent injunction analysis. German infringement courts do not consider, during regular proceedings on the merits, whether the patent or right holder is a practicing or non-practicing company. In contrast, U.S. courts would apply a four-factor test, which requires a plaintiff to demonstrate: (1) that it has suffered an irreparable injury; (2) that remedies available at law are inadequate to compensate for that injury; (3) that considering the balance of hardships between the plaintiff and defendant, a remedy in equity is warranted; and (4) that the public interest would not be disserved by a permanent injunction. The decision to grant or deny such relief is an act of equitable discretion by a U.S. court.

German courts do not apply equity principles for granting the injunction. However, in enforcement proceeding equity considerations may play a role. This is, the judgment debtor, faced with enforcement of the judgment, may file a motion for a temporary suspension (§§719(1), 707 Code of Civil Procedure), which the court may grant at its discretion. In contrast to regular proceedings on the merits until grant, in such enforcement-related proceedings the court may weigh the conflicting interests of the creditor and the debtor. When weighing these interests, precedence is usually given to the judgment creditor, i.e., the patentee who wants to enforce the decision against accused infringer. The duration of the patent and thus the conveyed cease and desist order are restricted with regard to time, and each delay in the enforcement would lead to a diminishing of the injunctive relief. Therefore, it is generally assumed that the judgment debtor (or accused infringer) is sufficiently protected by the security that has been posted by the creditor when starting the enforcement.[117] A suspension of the enforcement is only exceptionally possible[118], but could occur if the enforced judgement is obviously wrong[119]. More frequent situations justifying a stay of the enforcement proceedings are given if the patent on which the enforced judgement is based was later nullified in parallel invalidation proceedings.[120] If the patent was only partially invalidated, it is additionally required to justify that the limited claim is clearly not infringed by the accused product(s). Also, prior art which was identified too late for

116. *eBay v. MercExchange*, 126 S. Ct. 1837 (2006).
117. Appeal Court Karlsruhe, 6 U 38/09, GRUR-RR 2010, "Patentverwertungsgesellschaft."
118. Appeal Court Düsseldorf, I-15 U 132/14, decision of Dec. 21, 2015; Appeal Court Düsseldorf, I-2 U 24/15 decision of Oct. 27, 2015; Appeal Court Karlsruhe GRUR-RR 2015, 326—Mobiltelefone; Appeal Court Düsseldorf GRUR-RR 2010, 122—"prepaid telephone calls."
119. Appeal Court Düsseldorf, I-15 U 65/15, decision of Jan. 13, 2016.
120. Federal Supreme Court, GRUR 2014, 1273, "Kurznachrichten."

being considered in the decision making process of the instance, could be exceptionally sufficient, provided that the newly identified prior art would have justified a suspension of the proceedings on the merits.[121]

A motion to stay the enforcement proceedings may also be given if the enforcement reasonably endangers the existence of the debtor, or at least poses a threat of significant and unexpected damages. Due to the high threshold, motions for temporary suspension of injunction enforcement are rarely successful, even if the patentee is a non-practicing company. The fact that the patentee is a non-practicing company may however have the effect to tip the scale. In a decision rendered in 2009,[122] the Appeal Court Karlsruhe had to address the enforcement of an injunction granted by the District Court Mannheim initiated by a non-practicing company. The Court weighed the conflicting interests of both parties and finally concluded that the interests of the non-practicing company were of lower importance. When weighing these conflicting interests the court took into account the unsettled validity of the patent, as evidenced by the pending parallel invalidation proceedings. The court also determined that the non-practicing company was interested in a license agreement, based on earlier negotiations where the defendant had made a reasonable offer (in the court's view) that was rejected. The significance of the damages to the defendant (85% of his annual sales) was also considered. Although this case may appear at first blush to disfavor injunction enforcement by non-practicing companies, the conclusion of the court was rather based on a combination of plurality of factors.

5.3. Compliance with Injunctive Relief

When injunctive relief is awarded, non-compliance with the court's cease and desist order is punishable by a fine of up to EUR 250,000, or imprisonment. The fine can be imposed several times if the violations of the judgment are repeated. The amount of the fine depends on the seriousness of the continued infringement.[123]

In the case of a provisionally enforceable decision, the compliance obligations only become effective if the winner has posted a security bond—that is, the decision is not automatically enforceable. As soon as the requirements of enforceability are fulfilled, the debtor needs to take reasonable measures to avoid any non-compliance with the judgment. In bigger entities this requires that employees, sales people, sales agents—in particular people who were involved in sales activities related to the accused products—are sufficiently informed. The remainder of infringing merchandise stock must be taken out of circulation. Sufficient protective measures must be undertaken to avoid future unintended non-compliance with the injunctive relief by subsidiaries and associates.

The accused infringer might have meanwhile changed the accused embodiment. Whether the modified embodiment still falls under the judgment depends on its scope.

121. Appeal Court Düsseldorf, decision of Aug. 10, 2010, I-2 U 19/10.
122. Appeal Court Karlsruhe 6 U 38/09, GRUR-RR 2010, "Patentverwertungsgesellschaft."
123. Federal Supreme Court, I ZR 323/98, GRUR 2001, 758, "Mehrfachverstoß gegen Unterlassungsverpflichtung."

The determination of the scope of the judgment requires a careful analysis of the judgment. Principally, the cease and desist order is not limited to those acts to which the decision explicitly refers, but also applies to acts that fall within the "kernel of the infringement."[124] Minor and insignificant modifications of the accused embodiment, such as changing its color, are usually not sufficient to escape the scope of the judgment.

5.4. Rendering of Accounts and Lawsuit Concerning the Amount of Damages

A favorable decision requires the accused infringer to render an account on which the calculation of the amount of damages can be later based. Assuming the right holder has fulfilled the requirement to enforce the decision—he has posted a bond or deposited a security—he may then demand the accused infringer to render an accounting, usually by means of a letter written by his counsel wherein he sets a deadline for provision of the report. Because the creation of the report usually takes some time, the deadline should give sufficient flexibility to fulfill the duty. Usually three-to-four weeks should be allotted to the accused infringer. He must then provide a report containing all items as required by the ruling. Usually, the following information with respect to a particular time frame must be provided:

(a) the production amount and production time;
(b) the amount of received and ordered products as well as the names and addresses of the producers, suppliers and previous possessors of the products;
(c) the individual deliveries, broken down by amounts, times and prices of delivery as well as names and addresses of the commercial purchasers;
(d) the individual offers, broken down by amounts, times, and prices of offer as well as the names and addresses of the commercial recipients of offers;
(e) the advertisement conducted, broken down by advertisement media, their number of edition, period and area of distribution; and
(f) the overall cost and the profits made, broken down by the individual cost factors.

The report containing the rendering of accounts of the infringer should enable the right holder to decide on which calculation mode he intends to use for calculating the damages.[125] The figures should be sufficiently clear to calculate the amount of damages[126] by means of the selected calculation mode. Furthermore, the report shall give relevant information as to the distribution channels and origins of the accused products. The report shall enable the patentee to eventually identify still unknown infringers.

124. Federal Supreme Court, I ZR 15/92, NJW 1994, 2820.
125. Details concerning the calculation of damages can be found in Ch. 12.
126. Federal Supreme Court, X ZR 54/81, GRUR 1982, 723, "Dampffrisierstab I."

The patentee can refuse a partial or incomplete rendering of account. If the infringer does not comply in time with his duty, the judgment creditor may request the imposition of fines until a sufficient and complete report is provided.

If it turns out, or if there are reasons to believe, that the report is wrong, the creditor should additionally force the accused infringer to make a sworn declaration. The sworn declaration, made before a competent court, should state for the record that he has rendered the accounts to the best of his knowledge and as completely as he is able (§259(2) of the Civil Code). This applies to situations where there is reason to assume that the information contained in the account has not been provided with the requisite care. A false declaration made by the accused infringer would represent a criminal offense (§156 of the Penal Code).

Once a sufficient report is provided by the accused infringer, the patentee should be in a position to decide how to calculate the amount of damages. He would most likely select the calculation mode that appears most favorable.[127] Accordingly, he should be in a position to derive an amount from the figures in the report, and demand the accused infringer pay the derivated amount.

The parties may also negotiate a damages amount. If however they cannot reach an agreement on an amount, it may be necessary for the right holder to file an additional lawsuit seeking a court determination of the proper damages figure (so-called *Höheverfahren*). These proceedings would only concern the correct amount, and would not cover other issues such as the question of infringement or validity of the patent. This lawsuit is based on the findings of the first-instance decision wherein it is ordered "that the defendant is obliged to compensate plaintiff for all damages invoked on plaintiff by the acts indicated under...committed since...[date of the mention of the grant plus one month] and which will be invoked in future." In these separate proceedings, the court would thus apply the principles as described in Chapter 12 and use the information submitted by the party, in particular, the result of the rendering of accounts, to determine the right amount of damages. Frequently, a separate court determination is not necessary because the parties extrajudicially reach agreements on the amount.

5.5. Reimbursement of Costs

It is a characteristic of German patent infringement proceedings that the losing party has to reimburse the costs of the proceedings. The costs of the proceedings are the court fees and the statutory fees of the winning party.[128] Depending upon the litigation value these fees can be derived precisely from tables which are predetermined by the legislature.[129] If the plaintiff does not completely prevail, the court then accordingly apportions the costs among the parties. The allocated reimbursement claim can then be

127. Chapter 12.
128. The overall financial aspects of infringement proceedings are described in Ch. 15.
129. Court fees can be found in the table of Ch. 8, s. 7.

enforced against the other party through special cost fixing proceedings pursuant to which the court will issue an order containing the exact amount that has to be paid by the debtor.

6. PARTICULAR ISSUES

6.1. Declaratory Judgment Action

A declaratory judgment action is defensive in character and is aimed at preventing the patentee from asserting rights against an alleged infringer. A declaratory judgment action for a finding of no infringement would not address the validity of the underlying patent, because this is an issue on which only the invalidation authorities (Federal Patent Court, Patent Offices) may render a decision. The declaratory judgment action usually comes as a response by the accused infringer to a warning letter by the right holder.

The admissibility requirements of a lawsuit on the merits, in particular as to jurisdiction and venue,[130] are mirrored in a declaratory judgment action. However, the declaratory judgment action additionally requires a legitimate interest of the plaintiff (the accused infringer) in the declaration sought from the court (§256 Code of Civil Procedure).[131] Such legitimate interest is usually given if a warning letter has been sent to the accused infringer.[132] A simple inquiry letter[133] of the right holder asking the party why he believes that he is entitled to use the claimed teaching is not sufficient to create such legitimate interest in the judicial declaration.[134] Accordingly, the legal system leaves some margin to the right holder to approach the accused infringer without risking a declaratory judgment action. But the inquiry should be carefully formulated.

A declaratory judgment action does not hinder the patentee's ability to file a positive action on the merits. Accordingly, the accused infringer cannot take advantage of an earlier filing of a declaratory judgment action. Irrespective of a pending declaratory judgment action, the patentee is still free to select any court of his choice, according to the general rules. He is not bound by the choice taken by the plaintiff in the declaratory action. The legitimate interest required for a declaratory judgment action ceases to exist when a later positive action on the merits is later filed in a different court.[135] This is a consequence of the principle of subsidiarity of declaratory judgment actions when weighed against the positive action on the merits filed by the patentee.

---

130. *See* Ch. 8, s. 1.1.
131. Section 256 Code of Civil Procedure: *"An action may be brought for the determination of the existence or non-existence of a legal relation..., if the plaintiff has legitimate interest that the legal relation...is judicially determined"* (unofficial translation).
132. Federal Supreme Court, I ZR 85/93, GRUR 1995, 697, "Funny Paper."
133. Form and content of an inquiry letter are described in Ch. 8, s. 2.2.
134. Appeal Court Munich, decision of Mar. 6, 1997, 6 U 4793/96, Mitt. 1998, 117.
135. Federal Supreme Court, GRUR 2006, 217, X ZR 17/03, "Detektionseinrichtung I." The legitimate interest ceases to exist as soon as the subsequently filed positive action cannot be withdrawn anymore. This is typically the case if a hearing has taken place and/or in case the plaintiff of the positive action has waived the right to withdraw his action.

Take for example a situation where a declaratory judgment action has first been filed with the District Court Munich, and the patentee later files an action on the merits with the District Court Düsseldorf, bringing a mirror-image set of claims for infringement. It will have the effect that the case pending at the District Court Munich will have to be discontinued without a decision on the merits and the action at the District Court Düsseldorf will take its normal course.

6.2. Defense resulting from Antitrust Law: FRAND

Patented inventions may refer to subject matter that is covered by technical standards. A conflict may arise if technical standards, which have been defined either individually by an enterprise or jointly by a group of firms (so-called club-standards) or collectively by industry-wide operating standard-setting organizations, cannot be applied without using a patented invention (so-called essential inventions). The telecommunication sector, for example, is heavily penetrated by standards, including USB, 3G, 4G, USTM and many others. Standards make it possible for telecommunication devices, such as smart phones, to work almost anywhere in the world and run applications from a plurality of software developers. If a standard cannot be applied without using a patent, the industry terms such a patent a "standard-essential patent." Such patents may conflict with the need for market participants or entrants to have access to standards. This situation is particularly critical in areas where standards have obtained market- or industry-wide recognition and where products that do not provide "standard compliance" may therefore be unsalable. This is an important issue, particularly given the ongoing patent wars relating to smart phones and tablets taking place in the German courts and elsewhere. Conflicts between the exclusionary effects of patent protection, in particular in cases where the standard has obtained market or industry-wide recognition and the need and desire to have access to standards, are inherent. A patentee of a standard-essential invention might be tempted to exploit these effects by requesting, on the basis of his exclusivity, the acceptance of unreasonable licenses.

The legal framework of the defense under antitrust law, in particular in connection with standard essential-patents (SEP) was under extensive discussion over the last years. It led to a decision of the European Court of Justice (ECJ) rendered in summer 2015, in which general principles have been determined. Meanwhile, these principles have been refined by the national courts.

6.2.1. Situation Prior to the Decision of the ECJ

The Federal Supreme Court[136] was faced with such a conflict for the first time in 2004 when an Italian manufacturer of barrels for chemical liquids, who had been sued for damages, objected to the claim with an antitrust defense. The accused infringer argued that the patentee's refusal to grant him a license constituted an abuse of the patentee's market-dominating position by discriminating against him in comparison to other

136. German Federal Supreme Court, Jul. 13, 2004, 36 IIC 2005, 741, Standard Tight-Head Drum.

manufacturers of the patented product to whom licenses had been granted. The Federal Supreme Court concluded that in case of an industry standard (or standard-like general conditions) that forces entrants to a downstream market to adhere to the technical specifications of a patent, a market-dominating patent proprietor can be in breach of the anti-discrimination provisions when he exploits this situation to restrict access to the market by applying criteria for granting licenses that contradict the purpose of the freedom of competition. The German Federal Supreme Court thus recognized a duty to license a patent in that standardization situation, which could be raised as a defense by an accused infringer.

In a second important decision, in May 2009, which is called the "Orange Book Standard" decision,[137] the Court maintained its general position that the defendant can raise an antitrust defense in patent litigation when a market-dominating position results from the assertion of a patent (Article 102 TFEU).[138] The Orange Book Standard case refers to joint innovation efforts mainly made by Philips and Sony, which have been internationally accepted under the IPR declaration and licensing policies of the European Computer Manufacturers Association (ECMA), and internationally recognized by ISO/IEC. The parties in that case were not competitors within the product market—rather, the patentee was essentially in the business of selling licenses offered publicly on the Internet at standard terms. The defendant, who found these terms to be commercially unacceptable, mainly sought to obtain more favorable conditions. When he continued to use the patented invention by adhering to the technical standard, the plaintiff brought an infringement action seeking injunctive relief. The defendants claimed that they were entitled to a license under Fair, Reasonable and Non-Discriminatory (FRAND) terms. This was refused by the patent owners and, according to the defendant, should therefore have barred them from asserting claims for patent infringement.

The Federal Supreme Court concluded that such defense was admissible and could be applied against a request for an injunction, provided that the defendant had behaved like a "hypothetical licensee." Accordingly, a successful defense requires that:

(1) the patentee has a market-dominating position;
(2) the hypothetical licensee

137. Federal Supreme Court, decision of May 6, 2009, KZR 39/06, Orange Book Standard.

138. Article 102 *(previously Article 82 TEC)*: *Any abuse by one or more undertakings of a dominant position within the internal market or in a substantial part of it shall be prohibited as incompatible with the internal market in so far as it may affect trade between Member States. Such abuse may, in particular, consist in:*

(a) directly or indirectly imposing unfair purchase or selling prices or other unfair trading conditions;

(b) limiting production, markets or technical development to the prejudice of consumers;

(c) applying dissimilar conditions to equivalent transactions with other trading parties, thereby placing them at a competitive disadvantage;

(d) making the conclusion of contracts subject to acceptance by the other parties of supplementary obligations which, by their nature or according to commercial usage, have no connection with the subject of such contracts.

(a) has made an unconditional offer to license under fair, reasonable, and non-discriminatory terms which could not be rejected by the proprietor without violating the prohibition of discrimination and obstructive practices;
(b) behaves like licensee and renders account; and
(c) pays a reasonable royalty (or deposits the amount into a trust account) for the time he uses, or has used, the technology covered by the patent.

The Federal Supreme Court admitted that the hypothetical licensee may have difficulties determining the proper royalty rate. The hypothetical licensee may solve this problem by leaving the specification of the amount of the royalty to the patentee at his reasonably exercised discretion. It would not be binding on the defendant to the contract if such an amount is evidently inequitable. The specification is made in this case by judicial decision (see §319 of the German Civil Code).

In a decision rendered on March 21, 2013, the DC Düsseldorf[139] raised concerns as to the *Orange Book Standard*- case law. The DC Düsseldorf also referred to a view of the EC expressed in a press release dated December 12, 2012: Therein the EC indicated, *"where a commitment to license SEPs on FRAND terms has been given by* ... [i.e. the patentee], *and where a potential licensee, ..., has shown itself to be willing to negotiate a FRAND licence for the SEPs, then recourse to injunctions harms competition."*

In the light of these concerns, the DC Düsseldorf asked the CJEU to consider a set of questions concerning the understanding of how patent monopolies and standard-essential proprietary technologies can be incorporated in European Union's rules on competition and antitrust. A translation of these questions can be found here:

> *"1. Does the owner of a SEP, who has declared to a standardisation body that he is willing to grant any third party a licence on FRAND terms, abuse his dominant market position if he files an action for an injunction against an infringer although the infringer has declared that he is willing to negotiate concerning such a licence,*
>
> *or*
>
> *is an abuse of the dominant market position only given if the infringer has made to the owner of a SEP an acceptable, unconditional offer to conclude a license agreement which the owner cannot refuse without unfairly impeding the infringer or breaching the prohibition of discrimination, and the infringer fulfils—in anticipation of the licence agreement to be conclude—his contractual obligations for acts of use already committed?*
>
> *2. If abuse of a dominant market position is already to be presumed as a consequence of the infringer's willingness to negotiate:*
>
> *Does Article 102 TFEU lay down particular qualitative and/or time requirements in relation to the willingness to negotiate? In particular, can such willingness to negotiate be presumed if the patent infringer has merely stated (orally) in a general way that he is prepared to enter into negotiations, or must the infringer already have entered into negotiations by, for example, submitting specific conditions upon which he is prepared to conclude a licensing agreement?*

139. District Court of Düsseldorf, Huawei v. ZTE, Mar. 21, 2013, 4b 104/12.

3. If the submission of an acceptable, unconditional offer to conclude a license agreement is a prerequisite for an abuse of a dominant market position:

Does Article 102 TFEU lay down particular qualitative and/or time requirements in relation to that offer? Must the offer contain all the provisions which are normally included in licensing agreements in the field of technology in question? In particular, may the offer be made subject to the condition that the SEP is actually used and/or is shown to be valid?

4. If the fulfilment of the infringer's obligations resulting from the licence agreement to be concluded is a prerequisite for an abuse of a dominant market position:
Does Article 102 TFEU lay down particular requirements as to those acts of fulfilment? Is the infringer particularly required to render account for acts of use committed in the past and/or to pay royalties? May the payment of the royalties fulfilled by the provision of security?

5. Do the conditions under which an abuse of a dominant position is committed by the owner of the SEP apply also other claims resulting from a patent infringement (rendering of accounts, recall of products, damages)?"

On November 20, 2014, the Advocate General published his opinion[140] about the conditions of the commitment to grant licenses to third parties on FRAND-terms and it seemed that the (patentee-friendly) approach taken by German courts following the Orange book decision of the German Federal Supreme Court could not be maintained.

6.2.2. Decision of the ECJ

The Court of Justice of the European Union (ECJ) confirmed in its judgement of July 16, 2015 that the owner of a standard-essential patent (SEP) subject to a fair, reasonable, and non-discriminatory (FRAND) commitment may seek an injunction against an alleged infringer that fails to negotiate towards a license in good faith without infringing Article 102 of the Treaty on the Functioning of the EU (TFEU). The ECJ notes the need to *"strike a balance between maintaining free competition ... and safeguard-[ing] that proprietor's intellectual-property rights and its right to effective judicial protection."* In an effort to strike that balance, the ECJ describes the conditions in which the owner of a SEP subject to a FRAND commitment may pursue an injunction without the risk of violating Article 102 TFEU:

- It is not abusive for the owner of a SEP subject to a FRAND commitment to seek an injunction if he has, first, alerted the alleged infringer by designating the patent in question and specifying the way in which it has been infringed, and second, the alleged infringer has failed to signal his willingness to conclude a license under FRAND terms.
- Where the alleged infringer has expressed his willingness to conclude a license on FRAND terms, the SEP owner may pursue an injunction if he has, first,

140. Opinion WATHELET, Nov. 20, 2014, Case C-170/13, *Huawei Technologies Co. Ltd v. ZTE.*

provided a written offer, specifying the royalty and the way in which it is to be calculated, and, second, the alleged infringer has failed to respond to the written offer in good faith.

Accordingly, Article 102 TFEU limits a SEP owner's ability to seek an injunction where the alleged infringer acts in good faith to negotiate a license after receiving a written offer. This stands under the proviso that a market dominant position is conferred by the SEP to its owner. A patent, even a standard-essential patent must not compellingly have such a quality.[141] This is, the existence of a market dominant position needs to be assessed case by case. It is typically given if the patent bars or at least significantly impedes the market access for the accused infringer in downstream markets.[142]

Good faith of the alleged infringer is to be determined according to objective factors which may include whether the alleged infringer has promptly provided the SEP owner with a specific FRAND counteroffer, has not employed delay tactics, and has otherwise acted "*in accordance with recognized commercial practices.*" The patentee is however not prohibited from filing an action for infringement against the infringer seeking the rendering of accounts in relation to past acts of use of that patent or an award of damages in respect of those acts of use. The FRAND defense represent a defense against the injunction, i.e., the cease and desist claim, the destruction claim and recall claim. That is, while negotiating with the accused infringer, the patent owner can file an infringement action asserting claims for accounting and for a finding of liability for (past) damages.[143] Such lawsuit could later be extended by bringing claims for injunctive relief if the negotiations fail because of non-diligent behavior of the infringer.

Where the alleged infringer makes a counteroffer but the parties cannot reach an agreement, he must demonstrate continued good faith from the time its counteroffer is rejected by providing the SEP owner with appropriate security (bank guarantee or deposit) for ongoing use of the patent according to recognized commercial practices.

An alleged infringer does not, however, demonstrate bad faith by merely challenging infringement or validity while negotiating the terms of a license.

Where the alleged infringer does not evidence good faith by reference to objective criteria, Article 102 TFEU does not bar the SEP owner from pursuing an injunction after it has provided notice and a written offer to license on FRAND terms. The Court also held that the owner of a SEP subject to a FRAND commitment may seek damages or a rendering of accounts without restriction.

141. Opinion WATHELET, Nov. 20, 2014, Case C-170/13, *Huawei Technologies Co. Ltd v. ZTE.* Appeal Court Düsseldorf, Decision of Jan. 13, 2016, I-15 U 65/15.
142. Appeal Court Düsseldorf, Decision of Jan. 13, 2016, I-15 U 65/15.
143. Appeal Court Düsseldorf, Decision of Jan. 13, 2016, I-15 U 65/15.

6.2.3. *Application of the Decision of the ECJ by German Courts*

The decision of the ECJ fundamentally deviates from the patentee-friendly "Orange Book Standard" decision.[144] Standard users received more flexibility under the ECJ approach. Nevertheless, German courts tend to apply the principles of the ECJ decision in a patentee-friendly manner. At present, the FRAND defense requires following the following steps:

Step I Notification: The patentee must inform the accused infringer about the infringed patent. This notification requirement shall occur prior to the filing of the complaint.
Step II Declaration of Willingness: The accused infringer swiftly[145] declares its willingness to take a license.
Step III FRAND Offer: The patentee must provide a specific written offer to license the SEP on FRAND conditions.
Step IV Counter-FRAND Offer: The accused infringer must react in good faith and without delay. If the accused infringer does not accept the FRAND offer, he must make a counteroffer in reasonable time on FRAND conditions. The obligation of the alleged infringer to respond diligently by providing a FRAND counteroffer will be triggered provided the patentee previously comply with Step III.[146] Thus, the court has a duty to assess and determine whether the license offer of the SEP owner complies with FRAND terms. This also requires that the SEP owner has explained "*the way in which that royalty is to be calculated.*" He must thus indicate why be believes that the proposed royalty rate is non-discriminatory and non-abusive under the conditions prevailing on the relevant market. The latter could be done for instance by submitting comparable licenses concluded in the past.[147] Unless those agreements have been concluded under the pressure of an injunction, such previously concluded license agreements based on the SEP provide a strong indication for those terms being reasonable.
Step V Rendering of Account and Provision of Security: If the patentee does not accept the counteroffer, the accused infringer must—also for the past—render account and provide security for the royalties. The latter represents a minimal requirement. It needs to be fulfilled independently upon the specific details of the offer and the counteroffer. In addition, the rendering of account and the provision of the bond has to be done swiftly[148] after the rejection of the counteroffer.

144. Federal Supreme Court, decision of May 6, 2009, KZR 39/06, Orange Book Standard.
145. Five month is clearly to long: District Court Düsseldorf, 4a O 73/14.
146. Appeal Court Karlsruhe, Decision of May 31, 2016, 6 U 55/16; Appeal Court Düsseldorf, Decision of Nov. 3, 2015, 4a 4a O 144/14.
147. District Court Düsseldorf, 4a O 73/14.
148. Within one month: Appeal Court Düsseldorf Decision, Nov. 3, 2015, Cases 4a O 93/14 and 4a O 144/14.

Step VI Third-Party Determination: In case of deadlock *"where no agreement is reached on the details of the FRAND terms following the counter-offer by the alleged infringer"*—the parties *"may, by common agreement, request that the amount of the royalty be determined by an independent third party, by decision without delay."* If offer and counteroffer complies with FRAND and the parties may still not agree, the determination of the royalty amount may, even must[149] be deferred to a third party.

It is crucial for both sides to deal with these requirements thoroughly, during any already-pending patent infringement proceedings and, preferably, well in advance of a potential litigation. Swift and diligent fulfillment of these requirements is particularly advantageous for the accused infringer, which may resort to this FRAND defense to avoid an injunction.

7. FINANCIAL ASPECTS OF INFRINGEMENT PROCEEDINGS

When filing a lawsuit, the plaintiff must advance the court fees for the first-instance proceedings. Even though the losing party is liable for these costs, one party, namely the plaintiff, must pay these fees in advance. Of course, the plaintiff may later, if he wins the case, claim reimbursement of the advanced court fees from the loser, along with other costs such as the fees paid to his lawyer.

If the plaintiff is a non-European company, he must additionally provide a security for the potential cost reimbursement claim of defendant in case the complaint is dismissed. Both the security and court fees are calculated on the basis of an estimated litigation value. As soon as the litigation value is determined, the exact fee can be taken from a table.

7.1. Litigation Value

The litigation value is set at the free discretion of the court, taking into account the objective economic interest of the plaintiff. However, at the beginning of the proceedings the plaintiff gives a rough and preliminary estimation of the litigation value, and indicates this amount in the complaint.[150] If the defendant does not object to plaintiff's estimation, usually the court renders a decision based on the preliminary fixed litigation value. In most cases, the litigation value is not in dispute between the parties. Accordingly, the preliminary estimation of the plaintiff at the beginning of the proceedings is decisive for the calculation of the overall costs of the proceedings, including the financial risk assessment. However, if the patentee negligently or intentionally indicates a lower litigation value in order to "save" court fees in

149. T: Kühne, Handbuch der Patentverletzung, 8th ed., 2016, p. 537- 538, E. 304.
150. A sample of a complaint is contained in Ch. 16, s. 3.

consideration of an uncertain outcome of the litigation, it could have severe consequences in case it is later revealed to the court. The indication of lower litigation value could be considered to be an act to the detriment of the state which accordingly receives lower court fees than it would otherwise be entitled.[151] Prior of filing a lawsuit, the facts underlying the litigation value should be well discussed with the legal representatives. They should be able to base the litigation value on reasonable argument.

The litigation value should correspond to plaintiff's objective economic interests. It is represented by the value of the claims as requested in the complaint. In case of a regular infringement lawsuit this is the value of the right to prevent the use of the patent. This value depends on the expected lifetime of the patent, but also on the market share and market position of the parties, and more precisely the turnover related to the accused embodiment. Furthermore, the amount of the expected damages has to be added to the litigation value. As a rule of thumb, the request founded on the potential injunction value usually corresponds to approximately 80% of the litigation value, whereas the other claims asserted in the complaint (such as expected damages, rendering of accounts) amounts to 20% of the litigation value. This means that if the sales figures would expectedly result in a damage claim of EUR 1 million, a litigation value of EUR 5 million would typically be reasonable, assuming that the patent still has an average expected lifetime. For a soon-to-expire patent, the litigation value would be limited to objectively expected damages. The calculation of the litigation value is based on an approximation whereby the court has a considerable margin of discretion.

Typically, litigation values range in patent cases between EUR 1 and EUR 5 million. EUR 30 million is a maximum value and is a ceiling for the fees.

7.2. Court Fees

As soon as the litigation value is fixed, the plaintiff may take the corresponding court fee from a cost table which can be found in the Court Fees Act.[152] The following cost table is taken form this Act. The Act is more detailed and contains a more precise breakdown of litigation values starting from values of EUR 10 to EUR 30 million, which represents the highest value and is a ceiling for the fees.

7.2.1. Court Fees for the First Instance

Table categorizes the values from very low, which are below average to values which are definitely above average.

151. Appeal Court Düsseldorf, decision of Apr. 15, 2010, I-2 W 10/10; InstGE 12, 107 "Du sollst nicht lügen!"
152. GKG Gerichtskostengesetz.

Litigation Value (EUR)	*Court Fees (EUR)*
250,000 (= very low)	6.312
500,000 (= low value)	10,608
1,000,000 (= moderate)	16,008
2,000,000 (= average)	26,808
5,000,000 (= above average)	59,208
10,000,000 (= high value)	113,208
30,000,000 (= maximum)	329,208

7.2.2. *Court Fees for the Second Instance*

Average court fees for the second instance proceedings are slightly higher than for the first instance:

Litigation Value (EUR)	*Court Fees (EUR)*
1,000,000	21,344
2,000,000	35,744
5,000,000	78,944

7.2.3. *Costs for the Third Instance*

Third-instance proceedings are extremely rare. The court fees are increased by about 30% relative to the second instance.

7.3. Provision of a Security for Defendant's Legal Costs

7.3.1. *Principle*

Plaintiffs without residence or principal place of business, respectively, in a Member State of the European Community must, upon request of the defendant, provide security for the potential cost reimbursement, which is due if defendant finally prevails and the complaint is dismissed. This also applies to companies with headquarters in the U.S. The following table considers cases with only one involved defendant and indicates the security to be provided according to the litigations value. The indicated amount is slightly higher if more than one defendant is sued.

7.3.2. *Amount of the Security*

The amount of the security depends upon the litigation value. The higher the litigation value, the higher the corresponding statutory fees covered by the foreign plaintiff. In compliance with §108 (1) Code of Civil Procedure, the security can be provided by means of a bond issued by a bank officially accredited to operate in Germany. Sometimes it is difficult for foreigners to find a bank which meets these criteria. In that case, the foreign plaintiff may also deposit the money in a trust account at the deposit agency of the court.

Litigation Value (EUR)	*Security (EUR)*
250,000	53,500
500,000	75,000
1,000,000	107,500
2,000,000	172,500
5,000,000	367,000
10,000,000	692,000

8. UPCOMING: INFRINGEMENT PROCEEDINGS WITH THE UPC

8.1. Venue

8.1.1. Introduction

Where the parties do not agree on the venue, the action can be filed at one of two locations:

1. Where the actual or threatened infringement has occurred or may occur.
2. Where the defendant or, in the case of multiple defendants,[153] where one of the defendants has its residence, or principal place of business, or in the absence of residence or principal place of business, its place of business.

Accordingly, a Local Division has jurisdiction if the infringement occurs in the Contracting State hosting that Division (location 1) or if the residence or principle place of business of the defendant is located there (location 2). A Regional Division will have jurisdiction if the alleged infringement takes place in at least one of its Contracting States. In a situation where the actual or threatened infringement takes (also) place in a country not hosting a local division nor participating in a regional cluster, the patentee may directly file his action with the Central Division.

153. An action may be brought against multiple defendants only where the defendants have a commercial relationship and where the action relates to the same alleged infringement.

8.1.2. *Non-European Parties*

Location 1, the forum of *actus in tort*[154] will be of particular importance for patentees if the accused infringer does not have a residence or place of business in the European Union, given that such a patentee could not rely on the option of location 2. According to Article 33(1) Agreement, the patentee may file the case either with a division in compliance with the first option, at the forum of *actus in tort,* or he can file the case directly with the Central Division.

8.1.3. *Forum Shopping*

The first option may allow forum shopping. A claimant can file at the forum of *actus in tort*. These are the locations where the allegedly infringing product has been produced, offered, or placed on the market.[155] In the case of an offer, the infringing act might not only be the place where the offer has been made, but also where the offer is received or can be perceived by potential customers. This typically applies to an offer published through a webpage that can be perceived by an internet user in a Contracting State. Accordingly, when there has been an internet offer of an allegedly infringing product, a case could (most likely) be filed in any Division. The choice would depend upon the claimant's strategic considerations. As a result, for the vast majority of patent infringement cases, each Division of the UPC will have jurisdiction to hear the case.

8.2. Bifurcation or Unification

8.2.1. *General Remarks*

Where a patentee has brought infringement proceedings in a Local or Regional Division under Article 33(1), the alleged infringer may lodge a counterclaim for revocation of the patent concerned. This is typically the case in most patent infringement proceedings. The Local or Regional Division may then choose a course of actions from a number of options:[156]

- Proceed in a unified manner, namely with both the infringement action and the counterclaim for revocation; or
- Bifurcate by referring the counterclaim for decision to the Central Division; and
  (a) Suspend; or
  (b) Proceed with the infringement proceedings.

154. Article 33 (1)(a) UPCA.
155. Article 25(a) UPCA.
156. Article 33(3) UPCA.

If the revocation action is already pending when filing an infringement action, the local or regional division may, similarly, continue with the infringement proceedings, stay the infringement proceedings or, if the parties agree, refer the infringement action for decision to the Central Division.[157]

Most of the Member States currently follow a unified approach of handling patent litigation. A defining characteristic of the current German patent enforcement system, however, is the bifurcation between infringement and invalidity determinations, *i.e.*, infringement and invalidity ("nullity") claims are tried in different courts, on different schedules. The bifurcated system is generally advantageous for the patentee. Infringement cases frequently move ahead of counterpart invalidity proceedings, thus presenting the opportunity to have infringements resolved before invalidity is tried. While the infringement court may suspend its proceedings to allow a corresponding nullity action to resolve validity first, it does so only rarely.

The bifurcated approach leads to an outsourcing of the in-depth discussion on the validity of the asserted patent and reduces the work load at the Local/Regional Division. At the same time, it has a positive effect on the speed of the proceedings. Article 33 (3) UPCA leaves it to the discretion of the Division hearing the infringement case to decide whether to proceed with both the infringement and counterclaim for revocation or whether to refer the counterclaim to the central division. In the latter case, it is also left to the discretion of the seized division whether to proceed with the infringement action or whether to stay the proceedings until the central division has decided on the counterclaim for revocation. As the concerned division will have to weigh all relevant circumstances of the case, including fairness, it is expected that a bifurcation might be the exception.

8.2.2. Stay When Bifurcated

Rule 37(4) Rules of Procedure refers specifically to the question of when the Local or Regional Division stays the proceedings in cases where they follow the bifurcated approach and refer the revocation claim to the Central Division. The rule states:

> *Where the panel decides to proceed in accordance with Article 33(3)(b) of the Agreement, the panel may stay the infringement proceedings pending a final decision in the revocation procedure and shall stay the infringement proceedings where there is a* ***high likelihood*** [authors' emphasis] *that the relevant claims of the patent (or patents) will be held to be invalid on any ground by the final decision in the revocation procedure.*

A particular challenge of bifurcating the proceedings is the need to balance fairly the interests of the patentee (who is often interested in quickly enforcing the patent rights) with the interests of the accused infringer (who should not be prevented from commercial activities by an invalid patent). The Division will make a summary assessment based on the material submitted by the parties. If it concludes that a high

157. Article 33(5) UPCA.

likelihood of invalidation of the relevant claims is given, the Division will have to suspend the proceedings, whereas a simple likelihood of revocation leaves that decision to the Division's discretion.

The scope of this discretion is still unknown. However, existing German case law could provide a reference for defining this standard for staying cases. Accordingly, the likelihood of stay is low if the motion to stay is based exclusively on prior art that was already considered by the EPO during the granting or opposition proceedings. The chances for obtaining a stay might be higher if the request is based on previously unknown, in particular, novelty-destroying prior art.

8.2.3. Interplay: Opposition and Revocation

In several European jurisdictions, opposition proceedings at the EPO and national revocation actions cannot be implemented simultaneously. For example, in Germany the admissibility of a national revocation action requires that no opposition proceedings against the patent be pending and that the time period for filing an opposition against the patent has passed.[158] This requirement is mainly aimed at avoiding contradictory decisions. A third party that cannot file an opposition owing to the lapsed opposition period may join pending opposition proceedings provided that an infringement lawsuit has been filed against that party.[159]

The Agreement does not prioritize opposition proceedings over revocations actions. Articles 33(8) and (10) Agreement indicate that both proceedings could be pending in parallel. Article 33(8) Agreement stipulates that the claimant in revocation proceedings at the UPC is not required to file a notice of opposition with the EPO. Accordingly, the claimant can directly file a revocation action or do both.

According to Article 33(10) Agreement, the claimant is, however, required to "inform the Court of any pending revocation, limitation or opposition proceedings before the European Patent Office." Furthermore, the provision stipulates that "the Court may stay its proceedings when a rapid decision may be expected from the European Patent Office."

The UPC may—but not necessarily—stay proceedings in cases relating to a patent that is also the subject of opposition proceedings or limitation proceedings (including subsequent appeal proceedings) before the EPO.[160] The interplay between parallel EPO opposition proceedings and revocation proceedings at the UPC is not detailed further in the Agreement or the RoP. The establishment of standards for such stays is left to the UPC.

Of course, the UPC will only be entitled to take decisions within the boundaries determined by the EPO. As such, a UP that has been finally revoked by the EPO (for instance, after Appeal) cannot be "revived" by the UPC. In addition, as soon as a UP

158. Section 81(2) German Patent Act.
159. Article 105 EPC.
160. see also Rule 295 RoP.

obtains a particular (limited) scope of protection in EPO opposition proceedings, the UPC will be prevented from reinstating a previously applied broader scope of protection. This procedural framework will have to be taken into account when establishing the standards for staying proceedings at the UPC. UPC case law will have also to be motivated to avoid contradictory decisions of the EPO and the UPC and to reduce the duplication of work at the EPO and the UPC.

8.3. Non-Infringement Actions

Declaratory actions for non-infringement will be filed with the Central Division. If, however, an action for infringement between the same parties relating to the same patent has been brought before a Local or a Regional Division, both actions may only be dealt before the same Local or Regional Division. Accordingly, declaratory actions for non-infringement do not prevent the patentee from filing his own infringement action at the forum of *actus in tort* or at the seat of the accused infringer. A declaratory action for non-infringement could not be used by the accused infringer to predetermine the venue of the Central Division.

8.4. Linguistic Issues

8.4.1. Translating the Unitary Patent

In the case of asserting the UP owing to an alleged infringement, the patentee will have to provide, at the discretionary request of the alleged infringer, a full translation of the UP into the language of the State in which the alleged infringement took place or the alleged infringer is domiciled.[161] During legal proceedings, the proprietor of the UP will have to provide a full translation of the patent into the language of the proceedings at the request of the UPC.[162]

Examples

A company situated in France is sued in the United Kingdom on the basis of a UP that has been granted in English and translated into German. Even though the infringement takes place in the United Kingdom, the French company may still request a translation of the patent into French.

The situation can be even more burdensome if, for example, a Greek company is sued in Germany. Under the assumption that the patent has been published in English and translated into a further language that is not German, the German Division may ask for a translation of the patent into German and the Greek company could ask for a translation into Greek.

161. Article 4(2) Translation Regulation.
162. Article 4(2) Translation Regulation.

8.4.2. *Language of the Proceedings of the Court*

8.4.2.1. *First Instance*

Basic Rule

The basic rule is that the language of proceedings before:

- Local Divisions is typically the official language (or one of the official languages)[163] of the Contracting Member State hosting the relevant Division;
- Regional Divisions is one of the official languages of the Contracting Member States hosting the relevant Division, or the official language(s) designated by the Contracting Member States sharing a Regional Division.
- the Central Division is the language in which the patent concerned was granted, i.e., English, French or German.

Exceptions

The Agreement leaves some margin for the Contracting States to deviate from the basic rule. They may designate one or more of the official languages of the EPO (English, French or German) as the language of proceedings of their Local or Regional Division.[164] The parties may also—if approved by the Division—agree on the use of the language in which the patent was granted.[165] Exceptionally, at the request of only one party, the UPC may, on grounds of fairness, approve the use of the language in which the patent is granted.[166]

Predominant Languages at the Central Division

As more than 50% of all European patent applications are prosecuted in English, it is foreseeable that English will be the predominant language at the Central Division in Paris. German will take second place with 39%. Only 9% of European patent applications are prosecuted in French. As a result, even though the main seat of the Central Division will be in Paris, English and German are likely to dominate the proceedings.

Example

The language for proceedings introduced in front of a Division located in Germany will be German. If the defendant makes a counterclaim for revocation of the patent, it is possible that the Local Division refers the counterclaim for decision to the Central Division. If the patent was not prosecuted in German, the language at the Central Division will be either French or English.

---

163. I.e., if the Contracting Member State has more than one official language.
164. Article 49(2) UPCA.
165. Articles 49(3) and (4) UPCA.
166. Article 49(5) UPCA.

Translation of Documents

Briefs, statements of claim and defenses will have to be submitted in the language of the proceedings.[167] Some flexibility is given to the panels of the UPC, which may dispense with translation requirements for documents being used by the parties during the proceedings, i.e., whenever it is "deemed to be appropriate."[168] This flexibility is appreciated; it would not be appropriate to require translations of each submitted document into the language of the proceedings.

8.4.2.2. Second Instance

The basic rule is that the language used during the first instance will also be spoken at the Court of Appeal in Luxembourg.[169] The parties may agree on the use of the language in which the patent was granted. In exceptional cases, and to the extent deemed appropriate, the Court of Appeal may decide on another official language of a Contracting Member State as the language of proceedings for the whole or part of the proceedings, subject to agreement by the parties.

8.5. Conduct of a Case

The Rules of Procedure form the framework of the case. The RoP are influenced significantly by existing Continental European laws. This means the proceedings will largely be in writing. It is expected that hearings will seldom last longer than a single day.[170] A first-instance decision will be handed down within one year of the filing of the complaint, whilst recognizing that complex cases may require more time.[171] There will be a right of appeal which should typically add an additional year to the proceedings.

Witnesses may be summoned to appear at the hearing and expert evidence may be provided either by the parties or by an expert appointed by the Court. In compliance with Continental European legal concepts there will be no discovery as it is known in the U.S. Disclosure of specific evidence under the control of another party may, however, be ordered by the Court.

To summarize, the main characteristics of the conduct of the case are:

- A written procedure will take place during which the written pleadings will be exchanged.[172]
- There will be an interim procedure, which may include an interim conference with the parties.

167. Rule 14 RoP.
168. Article 51(1) UPCA.
169. Article 50(1) UPCA, Rule 277 RoP.
170. Rule 113 RoP.
171. Preamble to the UPCA.
172. Rule 12 RoP.

- There will be an oral procedure, which will include an oral hearing of the parties, lasting approximately one day.

Proceedings before a Division will have a duration of no longer than one year.

8.5.1. Written Procedure

The written procedure is mainly dominated by the exchange of briefs. These briefs are:

- The statement of claim, made by the claimant "complaint brief."[173]
- The statement of defense, made by the defendant.[174]
  There is also the option to include:
- The reply to the statement of defense, made by the claimant.[175]
- A rejoinder to the reply, made by the defendant.[176]

The statement of defense may include a counterclaim for revocation, to which the claimant may respond. If necessary, the *judge-rapporteur*[177] may allow the exchange of further written pleadings.

8.5.2. Case Management

During the written procedure and the interim procedure, a *judge-rapporteur* will be responsible for the case management.[178] He will make all necessary preparations for the oral hearing, such as ordering the parties to provide further clarification on specific points, answering specific questions, producing evidence and lodging specific documents. For the same purpose, he may hold (possibly by telephone or video) an interim conference with the parties, during which he shall also explore with them the possibility of settling the dispute or to making use of the Patent Mediation and Arbitration Centre.

The presiding judge will be responsible for the case management of the oral procedure. The main element of the oral procedure is the hearing, which will be held before the panel and directed by the presiding judge.[179] The presiding judge will endeavor to complete the oral hearing within one day.

173. Rule 13 RoP.
174. Rules 23 and 24 RoP.
175. Rule 29 RoP.
176. Rule 29 RoP.
177. The presiding judge of the panel to which the case has been assigned will designate one legal judge of the panel as *judge-rapporteur.*
178. Rule 101 RoP.
179. Rule 112 RoP.

8.5.3. *Substantiation and Burden of Proof*

The burden of proof rests principally with the claimant.[180] The patentee's duty to gather information (fact presentation) prior to commencing the lawsuit is in parallel with his burden of proof: he must prove each element of the asserted claims of action in order to prevail, and must substantiate each and every element of the claim. Rule 171 RoP stipulates that "a party making a statement of fact that is contested or likely to be contested by the other party shall indicate the means of evidence to prove it."

Rule 171 RoP also states that "if a statement of fact is not specifically contested by any party, it shall be held to be true." It does not appear that a bare denial or unreasoned contestation of a statement is sufficient to avoid the application of Rule 171 RoP. According to Rule 24 RoP, the defendant has to indicate in his defense "*the reasons why the action shall fail, arguments of law including any assertion that the patent (or patents) concerned is [are] invalid and [...] where appropriate any challenge to the claimant's proposed claim interpretation.*"

Accordingly, if the claimant substantiates his claim sufficiently by means of facts in the complaint, it seems that a duty of presentation would then shift to the defendant. The defendant must then substantiate and give reasons in his defense brief why he believes that a particular factual assertion of the patentee is not true, incorrect or incomplete.

This means that, unlike in the U.S., a bare denial would be insufficient. There should, of course, be an exception, if the facts concerned were not subject to the party's own activities or personal perception and, can still be denied without giving particular reasons. Furthermore, facts must be truthfully and completely disclosed in response to particular allegations raised by the other party.

The burden of proof stays principally with the claimant. Nevertheless, if the defendant does not sufficiently comply with his duty of presentation in response to the claimant's factual statement, these submissions could then be deemed as true. Through this method of allegation and response, the UPC would attempt to spur efficient and effective fact disclosure, without applying the measures to produce and preserve evidence.

8.5.4. *Evidence*

The legal framework of evidence is outlined in Rules 170 to 202 of the RoP. The taking of evidence resembles the procedural frameworks of the Continental European legal systems rather than U.S. discovery procedures. This implies that the patentee must first independently investigate and gather the relevant facts and evidence from openly available sources prior to commencing a court action.

The allegedly infringing product is often freely available on the market and can be dismantled, reverse engineered and then analyzed. In addition, the patentee may hire a private investigator or a private expert who could help to identify further factual

180. Article 54 UPCA.

material. A private expert might be used to carry out testing, or to analyze the infringing quality of the product, such as the composition of a chemical substance. In most cases, the investigation carried out by the patentee on his own initiative is sufficient to set out the relevant facts in the written pleadings during the proceedings.

It should also be taken into account that other elements commonly found in U.S. litigation, such as the doctrine of inequitable conduct, will not exist under the UP system. Consequently, evidence taking on those issues will not be necessary. The patentee may use the various means at his disposal to conduct this investigation and analysis.

Rule 170 RoP distinguishes between "means of evidence," which includes pre-existing material that can be presented in form of written documents, expert reports, physical objects, electrical files or audio or, video recording, and "means of obtaining evidence," which enable the production of evidence either prior or during the proceedings, for instance through the appointment, hearing and interrogation of court experts,[181] private experts or witnesses,[182] inspections and measures to preserve evidence.

8.5.5. *Experts*

The Court may conclude that the technical knowledge of an expert is necessary.[183] The Court expert will be appointed by way of an order after the parties have had the chance to make suggestions regarding his or her identity, and technical background and the questions to be put to him or her.[184] The Court experts will guarantee independence and impartiality and will therefore have a different evidentiary status than the parties' own experts,[185] who are inclined to comply with the view of one party.

8.6. Costs

8.6.1. *Losing Party Pays*

The system is based on the concept that "reasonable and proportionate legal costs and other expenses" shall, as a general rule, be borne by the losing party.[186] This means that the successful party will be entitled to recover his costs and expenses.

The Preparatory Committee agreed on February 26, 2016 on a Draft document Rules on Court Fees and Recoverable Costs for the UPC. It is a proposal which will have to be enacted by the Administrative Committee. A ceiling is put on the recoverable costs:

---

181. Rules 175–181 RoP.
182. Rules 185–188 RoP.
183. Article 57 UPCA.
184. Rule 185 RoP.
185. Rule 181 RoP.
186. Article 69 (1) UPCA.

Value of the proceeding (EUR)	*Ceiling for recoverable costs (EUR)*
Up to and including 1,000,000	Up to 112,000
Up to and including 2,000,000	Up to 200,000
Up to and including 4,000,000	Up to 400,000
Up to and including 8,000,000	Up to 600,000
Up to and including 16,000,000	Up to 800,000
Up to and including 30,000,000	Up to 1,200,000
Up to and including 50,000,000	Up to 1,500,000
More than 50,000,000	Up to 2,000,000

Exceptionally (for instance, in case of particular complexity of the case), the ceiling may be raised by the UPC of up to 50% if the value of the case is below EUR 1 million, up to 25% if the value ranges between EUR 1 and EUR 50 million, or up to EUR 5 million in cases the value is higher than EUR 50 million. Upon request of a party, the UPC can also lower the ceiling if the economic existence of that party is endangered.

In case of partial success or in exceptional circumstances, the UPC may order the parties to bear their own costs, or apply a different apportionment of the costs, based on equity (Article 69 (2) UPCA).

8.6.2. Court Fees

The UPC will be self-financed, primarily through court fees, which have to be paid by the parties to the proceedings and are to be advanced by the plaintiff. The amount of the court fees will finally be determined by the Administrative Committee. The Preparatory Committee agreed on February 26, 2016 on draft Rules on Court fees and recoverable costs for the UPC. Accordingly, Court fees will be due for infringement or revocation actions. The statement of claim will not deemed to have been lodged until the fee for the action has been paid.[187] If later during the proceedings the defendant launches a counterclaim for revocation of the patent, he will also be obliged to pay a court fee.[188]

These fees are composed of a fixed fee and a value based fee.[189] For actions relating to infringement the fixed fee shall be EUR 11,000. If, in addition, the determination of damages is requested, the fixed fee for that determination shall be EUR 3,000. For actions with a value of more than EUR 500,000 a value based fee will be added ranging from EUR 2,500 (for actions with a value between EUR 500,000 and EUR 750,000) up to EUR 325,000 (for actions with a value of more than EUR 50,000,000).

187. Rule 15.2. RoP.
188. Rule 26, 53 RoP.
189. Rule 370 RoP.

For stand-alone revocation actions, a fixed court fee of EUR 20,000 will be due. The same applies to counterclaims for revocation. For provisional measures, a fixed fee of EUR 11,000 will have to be paid.

Small enterprises and micro-enterprises[190] may benefit from a reduction of 60% of the fixed and value based fees.[191] However, the UPC can on its own motion order payment of the remaining 40%, if the 60% reduction is manifestly disproportionate and unreasonable with respect to the financial capacity of the applicant. The UPC can also order payment of the remainder of the regular fee plus an additional 50% if the affirmation given by the applicant is found to be wholly or partially incorrect. These security mechanisms have been introduced to avoid abuse by so-called patent trolls.

The court fees for the appeal proceedings shall in principle be the same as those due in first instance.

8.6.3. Security

At the request of the defendant, the Court may order the applicant to provide adequate security for the legal costs and other expenses incurred by the defendant which the applicant may be liable to bear.

190. Defined in Title I of the Annex of the Recommendation of the European Commission n° 2003/361 of 6 May 2003.
191. Rule 370.8 RoP.

CHAPTER 9
Preliminary Injunction Proceedings

1. INTRODUCTION

The German judicial system allows patentees to seek preliminary injunctive relief on expedited proceedings. Such preliminary relief may be particularly appropriate when patent infringing goods are being exhibited at a trade show, for example. These expedited proceedings allow for swift injunctive relief, and do not allow for damages and accountings. A claim for destruction may also be secured through an order to surrender the accused goods to a bailiff who stores them until a decision on the merits is taken on the destruction claim. In addition, the proceedings may yield discovery into the nature of distribution channels of the accused products, and to eventually determine the identities of previously unknown infringers (§140 b (7) Patent Act).[1] However, in most instances, preliminary injunction proceedings are used for getting quick injunctive relief.

A request for a preliminary injunction is usually filed prior to the introduction of a regular lawsuit. A preliminary injunction may be granted in an *inter partes* proceeding. In very urgent cases, the grant of injunctions in ex parte proceedings is possible. German courts are generally reluctant to grant preliminary injunctions,[2] but some German courts apply more generous preliminary injunction rules than others. The differences are bigger between the courts in Germany because preliminary injunctions are not appealable to the Federal Supreme Court (§542(2) Code of Civil Procedure). Missing the harmonizing effect of the Federal Supreme Court and prevailing local differences, it is thus crucial to select the most appropriate court for preliminary injunction proceedings.

As sample request for a preliminary injunction is provided in Chapter 16, section 5.

1. An unofficial translation of §140 b Patent Act can be found in Ch. 17, s. 3.
2. District Court Düsseldorf, 4 O 286/79, GRUR 1980, 989, "Sulfaveridin"

2. PROPER COURT

A request for preliminary relief must be filed with a competent court of proper jurisdiction. The selection of the court follows the same standards that are applicable to regular lawsuits (see Chapter 8). Accordingly, patentees have considerable leeway in selecting a favorable forum within Germany, to maximize the chances of obtaining preliminary relief. In case of a Germany-wide commercialization, which can be demonstrated sufficiently by, for example, a single offer made through a webpage, all twelve District Courts have jurisdiction.

3. BASIS FOR A PRELIMINARY INJUNCTION

A request for injunctive relief must provide a sufficient basis to justify entitlement to this extraordinary remedy. In that respect, in addition to satisfying the requirements for a complaint in regular proceedings, the applicant must additionally substantiate the urgency needed to justify preliminary relief.

In the U.S., courts apply a four-factor test to govern the award of preliminary injunctive relief. That is, U.S. courts consider: (1) the likelihood of the patentee's success on the merits; (2) whether the patentee will suffer irreparable harm if the injunction is denied; (3) the balance of hardships between the parties; and (4) the public interest.[3]

In Germany, comparable aspects are considered when deciding on a request for a preliminary injunction but the courts apply a different methodology. The requirements basically rely on two main criteria: first, the claim on which the preliminary injunction shall be based (*Verfügungsanspruch*), and second, a well-founded reason to grant this claim in preliminary injunction proceedings (*Verfügungsgrund*). Both the foundation of the claim as well as the well-founded reason for extraordinary remedy must be sufficiently substantiated and supported by prima facie evidence. Regular evidence taking proceedings will not take place and the court has to decide within a tight time framework.[4]

3.1. Claim on which the Injunction is Based (*Verfügungsanspruch*)

The injunction is typically based on the right to prevent the use of the patent according to §139(1) Patent Act (see Chapter 8, section 3.2.1.1). Thus, the patentee must sufficiently substantiate and prove on the basis of prima facie evidentiary means that the asserted patent is infringed.

First, he must demonstrate in the written documents underlying the request that the asserted patent is in force and that he is entitled to assert rights resulting from the patent-in-suit. Both can typically be demonstrated by means of an excerpt from the

3. For example, *Abbott Laboratories v. Andrx Pharmaceuticals, Inc.*, 473 F.3d 1196, 1200–1201 (Fed. Cir. 2007).
4. District Court Düsseldorf, 4 O 286/79, GRUR 1980, 989, "Sulfaveridin."

register of the Patent Office, which is available online (https://dpinfo.dpma.de/). The indication "patent is in force" contained in the excerpt, and the name of the owner of the patent mentioned in it, is sufficient for that demonstration so long as the applicant corresponds to the registered owner.[5] The patentee's licensee may also bring the request for preliminary relief, insofar as the licensee's status can be substantiated. Specifically, he needs to submit a copy of the license agreement including an affidavit demonstrating that the agreement is still valid (and not terminated). If the applicant is not an exclusive licensee, but a simple licensee, he needs to submit an authorization (in addition to the copy of the agreement and affidavit) granted by the patentee, permitting the suit.

Second, the patentee needs to demonstrate that the patent is infringed by the accused infringer. Similar to a complaint filed in regular proceedings,[6] the request must describe the prior art to which the patent-in-suit specifically refers, and explain the invention and proposed claim construction. An appropriate claim chart, mapping feature-by-feature the claim to the accused embodiment, is usually contained in the request as well.

It is necessary to base all factual statements made in the request on evidence, but this evidentiary demonstration is simplified and can be carried out on a prima facie basis. It is sufficient to render the allegation credible (§294 of Code of Civil Procedure). Regular evidence taking will not occur in preliminary injunction proceedings. The patentee needs to rely on all present means of evidence to render the allegation credible, such as the submission of:

- samples of the accused product, provided a submission is feasible;
- copies of documents, such as promotional documents, manuals describing the application of the accused product;
- photos of the accused embodiment; and
- affidavits.

To help substantiate the underlying facts, one possible form for such an Affidavit would be as follows:

Affidavit

My name is...I am living in..., and I am head of the IP department of company..., situated in....I hereby confirm for presentation before a court, being aware of the criminal liability for bearing false witness, the following:

I am familiar with the product which is called...That product is shown in the following figures and has the following characteristics:

...

Signature, Date

---

5. The entry in the register at the patent office is **not** necessarily a reliable proof that the registered entity has indeed the right to sue: Federal Supreme Court, decision of May 2, 2013, X ZR 69/11, "Fräsverfahren"
6. Chapter 8 deals with regular infringement proceedings.

3.2. Particular Reasons for a Preliminary Injunction (*Verfügungsgrund*)

3.2.1. Urgency

Beyond establishing a likelihood of success on the merits, the patentee (or licensee as the case may be) also needs to substantiate the urgency of the case. This does not mean that the patentee has a duty to observe the market to identify suspect products—a defense alleging that the right holder could have identified the accused products earlier would, as a matter of principle, not be successful.[7] The right holder must at least become aware of tangible indications that the patent is infringed. As soon as he has such knowledge, a swift handling of the matter is recommended. This is, if the right holder learns of suspect products by which infringement cannot be readily determined, he should swiftly analyze them, carry out necessary tests, and make possible further investigations in order to confirm whether the patent is infringed or not. Unnecessary and inexcusable delay with such investigations may endanger the success of the request.[8] The time period conferred to the right holder depends on the complexity of that investigation. The right holder shall have sufficient time for determining the infringing quality of the suspect product. A longer time period is granted to the right holder if complex and sophisticated tests are necessary to clarify the technical particularities of the suspect product.[9] It is shorter in simple cases. As soon as the right holder has sufficient knowledge of the infringing quality of the accused product, he needs to file the request as soon as possible.[10] He should not wait longer than one month.[11] Even though this is not a fixed deadline, the right holder needs to pursue the proceedings without delay. A diligent representative would urge him to file the request as soon as this is possible.

It is a critical to assume that negotiations with the accused infringer may prolong the time before filing, to the patentee's detriment.[12] The right holder should take into account that the accused infringer may tactically use ongoing negotiations to "burn the clock" and make it more difficult for the right holder to obtain a preliminary injunction.

Some important courts[13] will generally not grant preliminary injunction requests unless the validity of the patent was previously confirmed by a first instance decision in invalidation proceedings, either through an European Patent Office (EPO) opposition or nullity proceedings. A request based on a recently granted patent which did not undergo invalidation proceedings might thus be considered too weak for successful enforcement in a preliminary injunction proceeding, because a reasonable prior search could not yet have been implemented by the accused infringer. As long as the court is not thoroughly convinced that the patent will survive invalidation proceedings, the

7. Appeal Court Cologne, GRUR-RR 2014, 127.
8. Appeal Court Düsseldorf, Decision of Jul. 5, 2012, I - 2 U 12/21.
9. Appeal Court Hamburg, 3 U 83/87, GRUR 1987, 899, "Verbandsmaterial."
10. Appeal Court Hamburg, MDR 2011, 557.
11. Appeal Court Munich, WPR 2008, 972; decision of Jun. 28, 2012, 29-U-539/12.
12. Appeal Court Munich, InstGE 3, 301, "Fälschungsverdacht II."
13. Appeal Court Düsseldorf, InstGE 12, 114, "Harnkatheterset;" Appeal Court Karlsruhe, decision of Sep. 23, 2015, 6 U 52/15.

request will likely not be successful.[14] If there are already pending invalidity proceedings, the right holder may be allowed to wait for the outcome of those invalidation proceedings to file for preliminary relief.[15]

3.2.2. Other Interests Weighed

Preliminary injunctions are aimed at a provisional protection of the right holder. This consequently leads to a lower degree of judicial analysis of the critical subject matter of the case. On the other hand, preventing someone from commercializing particular products by means of an injunction may decisively affect, even endanger, his business. The law requires weighing these conflicting interests to find an equitable solution. Favorable and unfavorable arguments taken from the case law are set forth in Table 9.1.

14. District Court Mannheim, InstGE 11, 159, VA-LCD Fernseher II; Appeal Court Düsseldorf, InstGE 12, 114, "Harnkatheterset"; the District Court Munich I, decision of Nov. 16, 2015, 21 O 20498/15 seems to apply a more patentee-friendly approach.
15. District Court Düsseldorf, decision of Apr. 22, 2014 – case 4c O 3/14, BeckRS 2014, 19176.

Table 9.1. Pros and Cons for Granting a Preliminary Injunction

Favorable	*Unfavorable*
- Teaching of the patent is simple and understandable and infringement can easily be assessed;[16] - Patent is literally infringed;[17] - Patentee has already successfully asserted the patent in Court proceedings against other infringers and the validity of the patent has not been sufficiently questioned;[18] - The validity of the patent is sufficiently secured. This is in principle only the case if the patent successfully survived opposition proceedings at the EPO or first instance nullity proceedings with the Federal Patent Court in Munich;[19] - The accused infringer was already involved in granting proceedings and was able to make objections; - Competitors have acknowledged the validity of the patent, for instance through license agreements; - Credible concerns against the validity of the patent could not be brought up. This can even exceptionally be the case if the patent has been revoked in first instance nullity proceedings with the Federal Patent Court provided that this decision is evidentially wrong and that significant interests of the right holder are at stake;[20]	- Delay by the patentee in asserting rights;[21] - If the validity of the patentee is doubtful to a degree which would justify a suspension of regular lawsuit.[22] In particular, in case of pending parallel nullity or opposition proceedings containing critical fresh prior art; at the District Court Mannheim and Düsseldorf the request will—in principal—not be granted.[23] - The accused infringer could credibly demonstrate that the patent will be in validated in parallel opposition proceedings;[24] - Technical subject matter is complex and complicated; - Infringement is questionable, infringement is based on the doctrine of equivalents;[25] - High risks of significant economic disadvantages for the accused infringer's market position in case of interruption of activities due to an injunction; - Patentee does not practice the inventive technology (unless he shows that he has particular interests in the injunction such as to protect his licensee's interests);[26] - Private prior use could be credibly demonstrated;[27]

16. Appeal Court Karlsruhe, decision of Jul. 26, 1989, Mitt. 1990, 120.
17. Appeal Court Frankfurt, 6 U 83/81, GRUR 1981, 905, "Schleifwerkzeug."
18. District Court Düsseldorf, decision of May 26, 1994, Mitt 1995, 190.
19. Appeal Court Düsseldorf, InstGE 12, 114, "Harnkatheterset;" Appeal Court Karlsruhe, decision of Sep. 23, 2015, 6 U 52/15.
20. Appeal Court Düsseldorf, decision of May 29, 2008, Az. 2 W 47/07, "Olanzapine."
21. Appeal Court Frankfurt, 6 W 58/84, GRUR 1984, 693, "Messe-Abmahnung."
22. Appeal Court Düsseldorf, Mitt 1996, 87, "Captopril."
23. District Court Mannheim, InstGE 11, 159, VA-LCD Fernseher II; Appeal Court Düsseldorf, InstGE 12, 114, "Harnkatheterset"; the District Court Munich I, decision of Nov. 16, 2015, 21 O 20498/15 seems to apply a more patentee-friendly approach.
24. Appeal Court Frankfurt, 6 U 83/81, GRUR 1981, 905, "Schleifwerkzeug."
25. Appeal Court Frankfurt, 6 U 83/81, GRUR 1981, 905, "Schleifwerkzeug."
26. District Court Düsseldorf, 4 O 187/99, GRUR 2000, 692, "NMR—Kontrastmittel."
27. District Court Mannheim, InstGE 6, 194, "Etikettieraggregat."

Favorable	*Unfavorable*
- Expiration of the patent is close. The accused infringer should not benefit from the normal length of regular proceedings which would typically not allow the grant of an injunction until the expiration of the patent; - Risk of significant economic disadvantages for the patentee's market position in case of ongoing activities of the accused infringer; - Accused infringer is a foreign company and exhibits infringing products at a tradeshow.	- Preliminary injunction shall not be granted if the patent has been revoked in first instance opposition or nullity proceedings except for the very exceptional case that the appealed decision nullifying the patent is evidently wrong and that the patentee would suffer serious disadvantages if the injunction is not granted.[28] - Patentee is exploiting the patent exclusively though licenses.

Patent validity is key to the preliminary injunction calculus. If a patent has successfully survived first instance opposition or nullity proceedings then there is de facto sufficient certainty that the asserted patent is valid and thus suitable to be enforced through preliminary injunction proceedings. The patentee can wait for such a favorable first instance decision rendered in validation proceedings before starting preliminary injunction proceedings. But of course the patentee should not wait until the end of validation proceedings if that would be unreasonable due to a particular market situation.[29]

4. PARTICULAR SITUATION: TRADE SHOWS

Preliminary injunctions are particularly useful in trade show situations. Germany hosts a large number of high-profile trade shows in a wide variety of industries. For many companies trade shows are their most important sales points and critical to their business. Right holders are therefore understandably interested in disabling the alleged infringer's ability to display infringing products at trade shows. Furthermore, as soon as the trade show is over and the accused infringer has left German territory, the application of judicial measures are, due to lengthy international service proceedings and the necessary involvement of foreign authorities, more difficult, more expensive, and less effective. The particular situation is taken into account when weighing the conflicting interests as illustrated in the previous sections. Since trade shows usually take place over the span of a few days, there is consequently a compressed time period to investigate and file a preliminary injunction, if appropriate. Accordingly, the retention of counsel sufficiently prior to any German trade show where infringing products are likely to be shown is imperative. In some instances, the measures can be accompanied by customs action proceedings.[30]

28. Appeal Court Düsseldorf decision of May 29, 2008, Az. 2 W 47/07, "Olanzapine."
29. District Court Düsseldorf, Nov. 26, 2009, 4b O 155/09, "Fluvastatin."
30. cf. Chapter 14.

5. NORMAL COURSE OF PRELIMINARY INJUNCTION PROCEEDINGS

The process starts with the right holder's investigation and the preparation of a writ requesting the grant of a preliminary injunction. As previously mentioned, counsel should be retained at the earliest possible stage. While normal evidentiary proceedings do not take place, facts must be consistently and coherently demonstrated based on prima facie evidence. The early involvement of appropriate counsel is crucial to identify and fill remaining gaps in the storyline and to efficiently gather any missing information, documents and, in particular, to prepare sufficient affidavits. The result of the investigation will be incorporated in the writ. Due to the tight time frame, which is given to the court to assess the matter, the quality of the writ decisively contributes to the success of the request. Decisions on preliminary injunctions may be appealed to the Appeal Court, but a further appeal to the Federal Supreme Court is not permitted (§542(2) Code of Civil Procedure). Accordingly, because Federal Supreme Court review does not apply, a diverse body of procedural rules has developed within the twelve jurisdictions.

5.1. Ex Parte Proceedings

The right holder may try to obtain the preliminary injunction in ex parte proceedings (§937(2) Code of Civil Procedure). Nevertheless, ex parte preliminary injunctions, without having an oral hearing or notifying the accused infringer, are the exception. Given that an ex parte proceeding interferes with a fundamental right, namely the right to be heard, a successful applicant must demonstrate why a few days' delay to summon the accused infringer for a hearing would cause irreparable harm.

Such situations might occur where foreign companies present infringing products at trade shows. *Inter partes* proceedings would not sufficiently protect the interest of the right holder. There is not enough time until the end of the trade show for *inter partes* proceedings and the measure would be pointless if the parties are summonsed for a hearing that takes place after the end of the trade show.

In such an exceptional case, it is likely that an injunction can be obtained in less than 24 hours. The speed of the proceedings significantly depends on the interaction between the right holder and the court. An efficient handling of the case and counsel's knowledge of the particularities of the selected court is critical.

Although ex parte proceedings are, in theory, the exception, some German courts nevertheless follow a rather flexible approach and grant ex parte injunctions even outside the context of trade shows.[31] Accordingly, any company that is about to bring an important product to market should evaluate the risk of an ex parte injunction and take adequate preparatory measures. Indeed, a cautious company, under the right circumstances, might consider the preparation and filing of a protective brief that can be filed in anticipation of an eventual request for a preliminary injunction.[32]

31. District Court Munich I, decision of Nov. 16, 2015, 21 O 20498/15.
32. See Ch. 9, s. 6.1 "Protective Brief of the Presumably Accused Infringer."

An ex parte injunction is granted in the form of a court order. The applicant's task is to serve the order on the accused infringer. This is a necessary and therefore important element of the enforcement. Service is only effective if done within one month from the notification of the order (§929 Code of Civil Procedure). Thus, if a month has expired since the date on which the right holder was notified of the grant of the order and it has not been properly served on the infringer, it becomes unenforceable. If the injunction is confirmed—i.e., after an objection of the accused infringer, or by the Appeal court—this decision must be served on the accused infringer as well, even though the court serves the decision on its own.[33]

The right holder certainly can, and in certain strategic situations should, withhold the granted order from the accused infringer, for instance while waiting for a positive reaction from the accused infringer to a warning letter, or otherwise to see how negotiations with him progress. If negotiations appear to be unsuccessful, the right holder may then serve the order, so long as it is within the indicated term.

In the trade show situation, the right holder is presumably interested in quickly implementing the service proceedings, usually as soon as a certified and enforceable copy of the order is available. Typically, counsel does not wait until the court notifies him of the order by mail. Rather, he personally obtains the order at the courthouse and brings it to the locally competent bailiff who serves the order on the tradeshow at the accused infringer's booth.[34] The injunction then becomes effective vis-à-vis the accused infringer.[35]

The accused infringer then needs to stop the commercialization of the accused embodiment. Otherwise, he risks harsh fines, imposed through enforcement proceedings. Counsel may additionally include in the request further duties that must be fulfilled by the accused infringer, such as providing the accused embodiments to the bailiff who will keep them then in custody.[36]

If the court is unwilling to grant the injunction, which might be ascertainable from the first reaction of the court to the request (phone call, indications by the court in writing, etc.), the applicant can withdraw the request. If the request is directed on an ex parte injunction, the presiding judge may inform the applicant by phone that the court intends not to grant the injunction without a hearing. A right holder who is only interested in ex parte proceedings may choose at this point to withdraw the request, in which case the opposing party would not be informed about the intentions of the right holder, the application or the withdrawal. The normal course of ex parte preliminary injunction proceedings is illustrated in Figure 9.1.

33. Appeal Court Düsseldorf, decision of Apr. 21, 2015, I-20 U 181/14; Appeal Court Munich, MDR 2013, 422.
34. The service can be effectuated at any place of business of the accused infringer, the momentary booth of the accused infringer on the trade show is sufficient (Zöllner, §178 ZPO, N° 15).
35. The addressee of the service is the accused infringer, but if a representative (legal counsel) has officially taken over the representation, the order has necessarily to be served to the representative.
36. District Court Düsseldorf, decision of May 11, 2004, 4a O 195/04.

Figure 9.1. Normal Course of Ex Parte Preliminary Injunction (PI) Proceedings

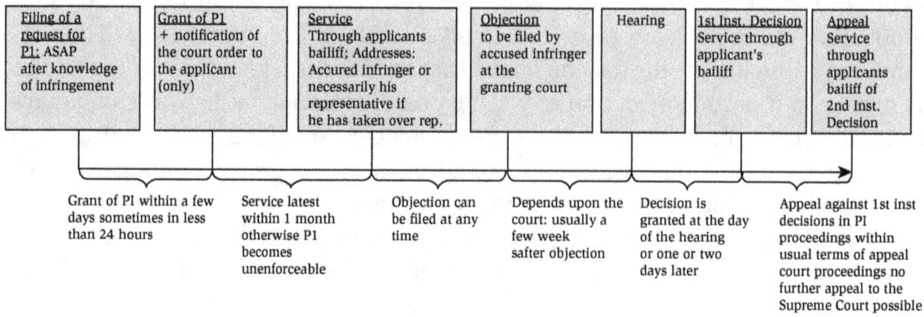

5.2. Inter Partes Proceedings

In case of *inter partes* proceedings, the parties are summoned for a hearing. An *inter partes* hearing is mandatory for any right holder who desires that the injunction also be enforceable outside German territory. Enforcement abroad requires that the German court order be first recognized by the foreign authorities, who require that the accused infringer has been heard by the court prior to the grant of the injunction. Article 34 of the Council Regulation 44/2001[37] provides regarding any EC Member State that a judgment shall not be recognized, "where it was given in default of appearance, if the defendant was not served with the document which instituted the proceedings or with an equivalent document in sufficient time and in such a way as to enable him to arrange for his defense." This requirement would obviously not be fulfilled in case of an ex parte order.

The hearing takes place generally a few weeks after the right holder's request has been filed. The accused infringer gets an opportunity to raise the usual defenses directed against validity. In addition, he may show that there are no reasons for an injunction. In particular, he might be in a position to demonstrate that the requirement of urgency is not met. Usually, this is done in a defense brief filed prior to the hearing.

37. Council Regulation (EC) 44/2001 of Dec. 22, 2000 on jurisdiction and the recognition and enforcement of judgments in civil and commercial matters.

Figure 9.2. Normal Course of Inter Partes Preliminary Injunction Proceedings

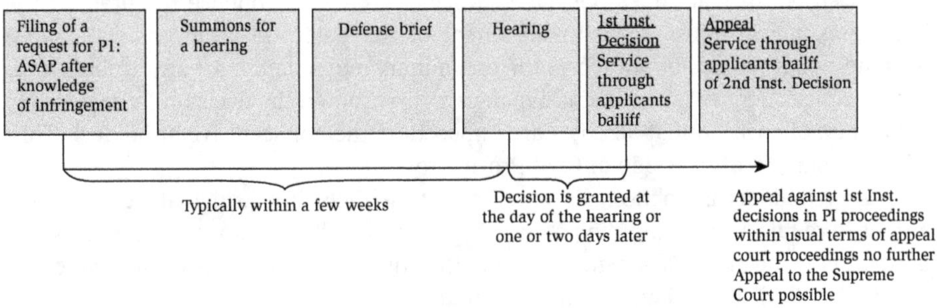

6. POSSIBLE REACTIONS OF THE ACCUSED INFRINGER

6.1. Protective Brief

A cautious party seeking to avoid a preliminary injunction may file a so-called protective brief with courts in which a preliminary injunction request is likely to be filed. This is appropriate where a party that believes it will be accused of infringement and has sufficient knowledge to name both the right holder and the particular product that will likely be the subject of judicial action. As sample request for a protective brief is provided in Chapter 16, section 6.

For instance, the presumably accused infringer intends to introduce a new product on the German market and knows that there is a patent that could be asserted against it. The urgent need for a protective order could occur in other scenarios besides a new product launch. Even products that have been available for sale for some time could potentially be subject to a preliminary injunction. The urgency could arise on the day of the grant of the patent, i.e., the day when the patent becomes enforceable, or if a decision (in opposition or invalidation proceedings) confirming the validity of the patent is rendered.

The protective brief is thus filed under the presumption that the right holder will file a request for a preliminary injunction. The protective brief contains all arguments that could be raised against the claim of the injunction (in particular all non-infringement arguments) and its reasons, namely that there is no urgency, and/or that the patent is invalid. Unless these arguments are obviously without merit, the protective brief would at least cause the court to not issue an ex parte decision. Instead, the court would set a date for a hearing.

The "protective brief" is usually filed with each of the twelve competent patent infringement courts.[38] Assuming, a preliminary injunction request is then filed with one of these courts, the judge first checks with the clerk whether a protective brief has been deposited. They are usually kept with the court for timeframe of six months.

38. See Ch. 3, s. 2.2.1.

6.2. Acceptance and Final Warning Notice

If the accused infringer does not have sufficient grounds to oppose the preliminary injunction, for instance if the infringement of the patent is clear and validity is uncontested, he could simply accept the preliminary injunction. If a warning letter was not previously sent to him, he could make an objection on the decision limited to the imposition of costs so that all costs are imposed on the applicant (right holder). This follows from §93 of the Code of Civil Procedure.

A preliminary injunction has a preliminary character and principally covers only a right to refrain from using the patent. Typically, so-called final warning notices are used to settle the matter also with respect to the other claims (damage claim, rendering of account, etc.). It contains a draft of an undertaking.

If the accused infringer accepts the undertaking the situation is settled between the parties and no regular proceedings are necessary anymore. Without such final settlement through a "final warning notice," either party (§926 Code of Civil Procedure) may request in addition to the remedies available in preliminary injunction proceedings (see Figures 9.1 and 9.2)[39] the implementation of regular proceedings on the merits to affirm or lift the preliminary injunction measures.

7. UPCOMING: PRELIMINARY INJUNCTIONS AT THE UPC

The UPC will have authority to grant preliminary injunctions to prevent imminent and ongoing infringement of a European Patent. The Court is granted discretion to weigh up the interests of the parties and, in particular, to take into account the potential harm to either of the parties resulting from the granting or the refusal of the injunction. This will also depend on the reasonable evidence provided by the applicant in order to satisfy itself, with a sufficient degree of certainty, that the applicant is the right holder and that the applicant's right is being infringed, or that such infringement is imminent.

The Court may also order the seizure or delivery up of the products suspected of infringing a patent so as to prevent their entry into, or movement, within the channels of commerce. If the applicant demonstrates circumstances likely to endanger the recovery of damages, the Court may even order the precautionary seizure of the movable and immovable property of the alleged infringer, including the blocking of bank accounts and of other assets.

39. The accused infringer may file an objection against a preliminary injunction order rendered in ex parte proceedings (§924(1) Code of Civil Procedure). The preliminary injunction will then be either confirmed or lifted after a hearing in a court decision which can be appealed (see Figure 9.1). In *inter partes* proceedings, the preliminary injunction is rendered after a hearing in a decision which can be directly appealed (Figure 9.2).

CHAPTER 10
Claim Construction and Infringement

1. APPLICABLE CASE LAW

Construction of German patents[1] and utility models[2] proceeds under identical rules as construction of European patents (issued from the EPO).[3] Nevertheless, this does not provide an answer to the question whether different standards of claim construction are applicable depending upon the type of intellectual property right.

German patents and utility models are basically not affected by the new European patent system. Such intellectual property rights are safe from the competence of the UPC. On the basis of national law they may only be litigated in German courts. The situation of these intellectual property rights remained unchanged and will stay untouched also in the future. It therefore can basically be concluded, that the body of previously established case law is and will be applicable without restriction.

However, different considerations will apply for European patents with or without unitary effect. During the transitional phase, traditional European patents may either be litigated in national courts or at the UPC, whereas for European patents with unitary effect, the UPC has exclusive competence.[4] The overall aim of harmonization of the patent law through the UPC would not succeed if established case law of individual Member States would have "binding character." References to national law through the provisions of the UPCA and the Regulation may not imply that established case law of individual jurisdictions is binding. Rather, the rules of claim construction for the UPC will emerge from the case laws of the various Member States. The national case law thus only serves as a source of inspiration without binding character. This counts not only for European Patents with unitary effect. The goal of harmonization required by European law thus renders subordinate the established national case law, including

1. §14 Patent Act.
2. §12 a Utility Model Act.
3. Article 69 EPC.
4. See Ch. 8, s.8.

for traditional European patents. The view of the authors is that this approach must even be applied to opted-out traditional European patents (Article 83 UPCA). There are sound reasons that Article 83 UPCA only opens a choice of forum.[5] An opt-out declaration should not trigger application of a different body of substantive law; rather, the laws applicable to a traditional European patent should be the same whether an opt-out has been declared or not.[6] In other words, the opt-out does not change the legal framework of the traditional European patent. Consequently, it is expected that German courts will have to apply the same body of law used by the UPC.

It can be anticipated that the body of law from the UPC for European patents will also have a harmonizing influence on the case law generated by German courts in the context of German patents and utility models. There is no compelling reason that a separate body of divergent case law will be developed for these titles.

The German case law described in the following sections remains highly influential for decisions of the UPC. Germany is the country with most of the decisions in the context of the scope of protection of patents. However, the case law will have to be integrated in the European context and some of the standards of the German case law described in the following chapters might be differently approached by the UPC which will likely start to operate at the beginning 2018.

2. CLAIM CONSTRUCTION PROCEDURE

There is no "Markman" hearing in German Courts. Because there is no jury in patent infringement trials, the concerns addressed by the U.S. Supreme Court's *Markman* ruling,[7] such as asking a lay jury to interpret the scope of legal documents, are inapplicable. It is the role of the court to interpret patent claims, and this duty is carried out in the context of the court's other decision-making tasks. Thus, in contrast to the U.S. system, which commonly provides for a dedicated claim construction hearing, with specialized briefing (and a vast body of case law focused solely on claim construction), the German system simply includes claim construction as part of the other proceedings.

The infringement proceedings start with the filing of a complaint. Beyond merely setting out the claims of the plaintiff to put the defendant on notice of the basis of the lawsuit (as is typical under the U.S.-style notice pleading rules), a complaint in German commonly serves as an opening claim construction brief. The plaintiff provides a description of the patent and its claims in a way that provides a *prima facie* basis for the court to find infringement by the defendant's accused products. After the court serves this complaint on the defendant and announces the schedule and deadlines[8] of the case, the defendant files its defense, which will typically provide a contrary view of claim construction, to support its non-infringement position.

5. Tilmann, The Transitional Period of the UPCA, Mitt 2/2014.
6. Preparatory Committee: Cf. Note of the Preparatory Committee of Jan. 29, 2014.
7. *Markman v. Westview Instruments* 517 U.S. 370 (1996).
8. *See* Ch. 8.

3. CLAIM CONSTRUCTION

3.1. Aim of the Claim Construction

The claim language, of course, is the basis for determining the scope of protection. This is codified in Article 69 of the EPC (or §14 Patent Act), which provides as follows:

> (1) The extent of the protection conferred by a European patent or a European patent application shall be determined by the claims. Nevertheless, the description and drawings shall be used to interpret the claims.

The description and drawings are accordingly used only to facilitate the interpretation of the claims. Subject matter that is not specifically claimed may not be asserted even though it is disclosed in the description or drawings.[9] A Protocol[10] on the Interpretation of Article 69 EPC, which is an integral part of the EPC, further describes the often-difficult task of interpreting the claim language in view of the teachings of the specification as follows:[11]

> **Article 1**
> General principles
>
> Article 69 should not be interpreted as meaning that the extent of the protection conferred by a European patent is to be understood as that defined by the strict, literal meaning of the wording used in the claims, the description and drawings being employed only for the purpose of resolving an ambiguity found in the claims. Nor should it be taken to mean that the claims serve only as a guideline and that the actual protection conferred may extend to what, from a consideration of the description and drawings by a person skilled in the art, the patent proprietor has contemplated. On the contrary, it is to be interpreted as defining a position between these extremes which combines a fair protection for the patent proprietor with a reasonable degree of legal certainty for third parties.

This Protocol thus frames the same challenges faced by U.S. courts in cases such as the *Philips v. AWH* opinion from the U.S. Court of Appeals for the Federal Circuit.[12] The Protocol recognizes that there is a tension between interpreting the claims solely on the basis of claim language versus relying on the teachings of the patent description and drawings to help interpret the claims. The Protocol acknowledges that there is no bright line in terms of how to interpret claims in light of the specification. The ultimate aim of the interpretation consists in finding a balance between a "fair protection" for the patentee and a "reasonable degree of certainty" for third parties. In other words, the patentee must be compensated for the disclosure of his invention, but third parties must be reasonably informed about the scope of protection through the patent claims.

9. Federal Supreme Court, X ZR 20/86, GRUR 1987, 626, "Rundfunkübertragungssystem."
10. Protocol on the Interpretation of Art. 69 EPC of Oct. 5, 1973 as revised by the Act revising the EPC of Nov. 29, 2000.
11. The Protocol is applicable not only on European Patents, but also on German Patents: Federal Supreme Court, Mitt. 2002, 216, 218, "Schneidmesser."
12. *Phillips v. AWH Corp.*, 415 F.3d 1303 (Fed. Cir. 2005 (en banc)).

3.2. Significance of the Claims

According to Article 69(1) EPC and the corresponding provision §14 of the Patent Act, the terms of the claims govern the scope of protection. Descriptions and drawings have an auxiliary function for the claim construction. They are just means of interpreting the content of the claims.

*3.2.1. Semantic Content (*Sinngehalt*)*

The claims of the patent are construed in view of the overall teachings of the patent, to arrive at the "semantic content" of the claims.[13] That is, the patent claims are not limited to the strict literal meaning of the claim language. Rather, terms of the claim are interpreted to sufficiently cover the technical teaching as disclosed in the description. Terms can thus be given the broadest possible technical understanding under the disclosed teaching. For the determination of the scope of protection, claim terms shall be construed in the context of the solution the patent specification objectively discloses.[14] The skilled person needs to read the specification in a reasonable way to identify the understanding of the terms in the context of the claimed teaching in a manner that harmonizes the language of the claims and the technical description of the invention.[15] In particular, the patent claim should be read in a way to cover the preferred embodiments illustrated in the description in the context of the claimed teaching, insofar as the claim language accommodates that reading.[16] In making the determination of the semantic content of a claim, the meanings of the claim terms are to be analyzed step by step, in order to assess the overall meaning of the claim as a unit.[17] It is thus necessary to determine the semantic content of the claim in its entirety as well as the contribution of the individual features to the overall performance of the teaching.[18] Principally, the latter determination requires a previous identification of the problem to be solved by the claimed teaching. This is, the problem to be solved by the claimed teaching shall comply with the interpretation result.[19]

German courts often name this a "function oriented interpretation" of patent claims: Terms of the claim are construed in the context of the solution that the patent application objectively discloses.[20] In other words, the skilled person needs to read the specification in a reasonable way to identify the particular function(s) of the terms by which they provide for the inventive solution. The understanding of a term is thus

13. Federal Supreme Court, X ZR 74/05, IIC 2007, 726 (in English), "Kettenradanordnung"; Federal Supreme Court, X ZR 82/03, GRUR 2004, 845, "Drehzahlermittlung."
14. Federal Supreme Court, decision of Nov. 7, 2000, X ZR145/98, GRUR 2001, 232, "Brieflocher."
15. Federal Supreme Court, X ZR 16/09, Decision of May 10, 2011, "Occluder," see also s. 2.2.2. and footnote 17.
16. Federal Supreme Court, X ZR 16/09, Decision of May 10, 2011, "Occluder."
17. Federal Supreme Court, X ZR 82/03, GRUR 2004, 845, "Drehzahlermittlung."
18. Federal Supreme Court, X ZR 117/11, Decision of Jul. 17, 2012 BGHZ 194, 107 = GRUR 2012, 1124 Rn. 27 - Polymerschaum I); Federal Supreme Court; X ZR 29/15, Decision of Jun. 14, 2016, "Pemetrexed."
19. Federal Supreme Court; X ZR 29/15, Decision of Jun. 14, 2016, "Pemetrexed."
20. Federal Supreme Court, decision of Nov. 7, 2000, X ZR145/98, GRUR 2001, 232, "Brieflocher."

primarily influenced by the function it fulfills within the claimed teaching. The function-oriented interpretation finds its limits where terms used in the claim have a clear spatial or physical defined configuration. The unambiguousness of such terms could not be circumvented by means of a function-oriented interpretation. For instance, a "nail," which is explicitly required in the claim, could not be converted into a simple mere fixing means, which would involve screws even if a merely functional approach allows it.

3.2.2. Main Sources for the Claim Construction

Descriptions and drawings shall be used to construe and clarify the patent claims and the terms used in the patent specification (Article 69(1) EPC, §14 of the Patent Act). As noted above, the descriptions and drawings serve as a source for interpreting the claim language, but they do not themselves provide for the scope of claim protection. That is, the description and drawing cannot extend the scope of protection conferred by the claims, beyond what the claim terms themselves may permit. Thus, no protection can be provided for subject matter that is not included in the patent claims, even though it is explicitly contained in the description and drawings.[21] Thus, like in the U.S., it is essential to identify a "hook" in the claim language to justify interpreting that claim language in light of the teachings of the patent specification.

3.2.2.1. Definitions in the Description

Court decisions often state that the patent specification forms its "own dictionary"[22] (similar to the rule in the U.S. that a patentee may be his or her own lexicographer). The definition for a term found in the description will govern the claim construction, even if this definition differs substantially from the usual technical meaning of the term. Terms of the patent claim may thus have a broader or narrower meaning than definitions taken from the common technical literature or belonging to a common use in the relevant technical field.[23] Nevertheless, this does not mean that recourse to the habitual language use of technical terms is excluded. The patent description does not provide a definition for all terms and it is usually assumed that the patent is written in the typical and common language of the concerned technical field. However, the interpreter of the patent shall always check whether a diverging understanding is applicable.[24] For instance, if the person skilled in the art concludes, in the light of the description and drawings, that a possible interpretation of the claim needs to be excluded, then that claim can be restricted to a narrower teaching even where the literal understanding of the claim term suggests a broader construction. This rule

21. Federal Supreme Court, X ZR 9/89, GRUR 1992, 305, "Heliumeinspeisung," Federal Supreme Court, X ZR 16/09, Decision of May 10, 2011, "Occluder."
22. Federal Supreme Court, X ZR 85/96, IIC 1999, 932 (in English), "Spannschraube."
23. Federal Supreme Court, X ZR 85/96, IIC 1999, 932 (in English), "Spannschraube."
24. Federal Supreme Court, X ZR 74/05, GRUR 2007, 410, "Kettenradanordnung."

comes from the landmark Federal Supreme Court "*Spannschraube*" (Tension Screw)[25] decision. Nevertheless, the fact that a patent claim may be written so broadly as to cover the prior art is not itself a basis for interpreting the claim more narrowly than its strict literal meaning.[26]

3.2.2.2. *Examples and Preferred Embodiments*

Preferred embodiments and examples disclosed in the description do not—as a general rule—limit the scope of protection of a claim describing the invention in more generic terms.[27] This rule of claim construction is similar to the approach taken in the U.S. Preferred embodiments are supposed to explain the claimed invention in an exemplary manner, but not exhaustively.[28] Likewise, numbered references pointing to the drawings that have been left in the patent claim do not restrict the scope of protection either.[29] Drawings only serve to explain the principle of the claimed teaching and thus do not disclose particular dimensions.[30]

3.2.2.3. *Dependent Claims*

A main claim determines the protected teaching in the most general form within the same claim hierarchy. Dependent claims that refer back to the main claim by definition contain more specific embodiments of the invention, but never go beyond the scope of protection in the main claim. Such dependent claims usually protect preferred embodiments, whereas the main claim aims at protecting a more generic form of the invention, which includes the more specific preferred embodiment. Consequently, a more generic definition of the invention in the main claim must consequently be interpreted in a way that it also covers the more specific embodiments or the embodiments of its dependent claims. This hierarchy is an important aspect of the claim construction.[31]

3.2.2.4. *Indications of Purpose*

Indications of purposes, effects and functions mentioned in the patent claim usually do not restrict the scope of protection.[32] They illustrate for instance a possible field of application or an intended use of the claimed embodiment. If the particular effects and functions sought by the protected teaching are sufficiently achieved by the other physical features of the claim, such indications of purpose could be neglected when

25. Federal Supreme Court, X ZR 85/96, IIC 1999, 932 (in English), "Spannschraube."
26. Federal Supreme Court, X ZR 22/97, GRUR 99, 914, "Kontaktfederblock."
27. Federal Supreme Court, X ZR 255/01, IIC 2005, 971(in English) "Bodenseitige Vereinzelungseinrichtung."
28. Federal Supreme Court, decision of Feb. 12, 2008, X ZR 153/05, Mitt 08, 271, "Mehrgangnabe."
29. Federal Supreme Court, X ZR 17/02, GRUR 2006, 316, "Koksofentür."
30. Federal Supreme Court, X ZB 10/11, GRUR 2012, 1242, "Steckverbindung."
31. Federal Supreme Court, decision of Feb. 12, 2008, X ZR 153/05, Mitt 08, 271, "Mehrgangnabe."
32. Federal Supreme Court, X ZR 121/88, GRUR 1991, 436, "Befestigungsvorrichtung II."

determining the scope of protection. Nevertheless, where the indication makes demands on a particular spatial or physical attribute which is not yet reflected by the other features of the claim, but required to produce the effect or function sought be the protected teaching, it may have a limitative character. In such a situation they are thus treated like other features of the claim.[33]

3.2.2.5. Numerical Indications

A numerical indication (such as "an angle of less than 90°" or a parameter range between "5 to 20 Newton") in a patent claim may also be subject to interpretation. As a general rule, numerical limitations give more concrete boundaries than descriptive terms,[34] and so accused products falling outside the numerical limitations will generally not infringe.[35] Nonetheless, depending on the context of the patent, some variation may be tolerated.[36] It rather depends on how the skilled person in the art understands the meaning of the terms within the general context of the patented invention, taking into account the explanations in the description and the drawings. Numerical indications may differ within various contexts, so an accused embodiment that deviates slightly from a claimed numerical indication does not necessarily exclude infringement. Nevertheless, these are exceptions from the general rule that accused products falling outside numerical indications will not infringe.[37] Typically, a departure from a range or numerical value is acceptable if it stays within technical tolerances. For legal certainty reasons, the doctrine of equivalence generally does not help if the departure is more significant, even if the effects and advantages of the claimed teaching are still achieved by the accused embodiment. This is because numerical indications are deemed concretely selected by the patent applicant, and, in only very exceptional cases the skilled person would consider a solution outside the claimed range a still sufficient implementation of the teaching, for instance, if the specification of the patent provides evidence that the observation of the range are not critical for the teaching.

3.2.2.6. Reference to the Prior Art

If it is discussed in the body of the patent specification, the prior art (and its characterization in the patent disclosure) may represent a source for interpretation and

33. Federal Supreme Court, X ZR 105/04, GRUR 2006, 923, "Luftabschneider für Milchsammelanlage."
34. Federal Supreme Court X ZR 33/88, GRUR 1989, 903, "Batteriekastenschnur."
35. Federal Supreme Court, X ZR 43/01, GRUR 2002, 511, "Kunststoffrohrteil"; Federal Supreme Court, X ZR 73/01, GRUR 2002, 527, "Custodiol II"; Federal Supreme Court, X ZR 135/01, GRUR 2002, 519, "Schneidmesser II"; Federal Supreme Court, X ZR 12/00, GRUR 2002, 523, "Custodiol I."
36. Federal Supreme Court, X ZR 43/01, GRUR 2002, 511, "Kunststoffrohrteil"; Federal Supreme Court, X ZR 73/01, GRUR 2002, 527, "Custodiol II"; Federal Supreme Court, X ZR 135/01, GRUR 2002, 519, "Schneidmesser II"; Federal Supreme Court, X ZR 12/00, GRUR 2002, 523 "Custodiol I."
37. Federal Supreme Court, X ZR 135/01, GRUR 2002, 519, "Schneidmesser II"; see s. [...].

understanding of the claim.[38] In particular, if the patent describes the newly claimed invention in reference to the manner of the prior art, then this characterization will be useful for the proper understanding of the patent claims. The extent to which prior art documents mentioned in the description may be used for the claim construction is decided on a case-by-case basis. If prior art documents are not mentioned in the patent specification, then they are likely to be irrelevant for claim construction.[39] This is true even if this prior art was available at the date of the application or the priority date.[40] But such prior art may possibly help to identify and demonstrate the general expertise of the person skilled in the art (see section 2.2.3.1).

3.2.3. *Evidence Outside of the Patent Document*

3.2.3.1. General Expertise of the Skilled Person

The subject matter of the invention and the scope of protection have to be identified through the eyes of the person skilled in the art.[41] This fictitious person is tasked with giving the content of the patent a meaningful and consistent understanding.[42] He has the average skills of someone who is typically in charge of research and development in the technical field of the teaching of the patent. Although fictitious, he demonstrates the general expertise available in the concerned technical field, including the experiences and abilities of his professional peers,[43] at the time of the patent application, more precisely its priority date. The skilled person is not necessarily an expert with exceptional skills. For instance, he does not have an overview of the whole prior art. Rather, he is deemed to have a solid education with enough experience to properly perform his tasks within the technical field addressed by the patent. When determining the content of the patent disclosure, the court can refer to self-evident technical information which the skilled person reads in-between the lines when studying the patent. If the patent addresses several technical fields, the general expertise of all the fields involved must be taken into account.

3.2.3.2. Inadmissibility of Prosecution File Estoppel

A fundamental distinction between claim construction approaches in Germany and the U.S. concerns the role of the prosecution history. In the U.S., the prosecution history forms one of the core bodies of intrinsic evidence for construing patent claims, both in terms of ascertaining the ordinary meaning of claim terms, as well as for determining

38. Federal Supreme Court, X ZR 56/96, Mitt 1999, 365, “Sammelförderer.”
39. Federal Supreme Court, X ZR 45/85, GRUR 1987, 280, “Befestigungsvorrichtung.”
40. Federal Supreme Court, X ZR 124/88, GRUR 1991, 811, “Falzmaschine.”
41. Federal Supreme Court, X ZR 255/01, IIC 2005, 971 (in English), “Bodenseitige Vereinzelungseinrichtung.”
42. Appeal Court Düsseldorf, Mitt. 98, 179.
43. Federal Supreme Court, X ZR 255/01, GRUR 2004, 1023, IIC 2005, 971 (in English) “Bodenseitige Vereinzelungseinrichtung.”

if there has been a surrender of patent scope (i.e., prosecution history estoppel). By contrast, in Germany the prosecution history is basically irrelevant to the interpretation of the patent claims.[44] The claim construction process rests on an analysis of the patent claims, taken in view of the patent description and the drawings. These are the only interpretation sources listed in §14 of the German Patent Act and Article 69 EPC. Accordingly, prosecution files are not accorded the role they have in the U.S. for claim construction.[45] Even if statements made by the patentee are contained in the grant decision, they are generally irrelevant for the claim construction.[46] The patentee's statements may however present an indication of how the relevant skilled person in the art would understand the patent.[47] There is however an exception where the patentee has made statements during invalidation proceedings involving the particular opponent who is later party to the infringement proceedings (see below).

3.2.3.3. Effects of Invalidation Proceedings on the Claim Construction

As explained in prior chapters, invalidation proceedings (either nullity proceedings or oppositions) are separated from infringement proceedings. Invalidation proceedings may have an effect on the claim construction to be implemented by the infringement courts. When there are new limits imposed on the claims, either through nullity proceedings in the Federal Patent Court or in opposition proceedings, these limitations result in a retroactive and binding legal change to the wording of the claim. The relevant grounds of the decision dealing with the change to the wording of the claim are deemed to replace or stand alongside the patent description in the consideration of the claim construction.[48] However, the basis for the nullity or opposition ruling does not have binding effect on the infringement courts.[49] It does not bind the trial judge but may be regarded as persuasive as to how a skilled person would interpret the claim.

Even statements made by the patentee during nullity and opposition proceedings are mostly irrelevant for the claim construction. However, an exception may apply in the situation where the patentee declares, during nullity or opposition proceedings, that he does not claim patent protection for particular embodiments and this declaration causes the maintenance of the patent with a specific scope.[50] A third party may refer to that statement or declaration provided that the third party was involved in the invalidation proceedings. In that exceptional case the third party may assert that, according to the declaration, a narrower understanding of claim must be applied. Any other party, i.e., third parties which were not involved in these proceedings, cannot rely on such a declaration. Thus, statements of the patentee/proprietor can only be

44. Federal Supreme Court, X ZR 43/01, GRUR 2002, 511, 513, "Kunststoffrohrteil."
45. Federal Supreme Court, X ZR 43/01,GRUR 02, 511, 513, "Kunststoffrohrteil."
46. Federal Supreme Court, X ZR 73/95, NJW 1997, 3377, "Weichvorrichtung II"; Federal Supreme Court; X ZR 29/15, Decision of June 14, 2016, "Pemetrexed."
47. Federal Supreme Court, X ZR 57/96, GRUR 1998, 895, "Regenbecken."
48. Federal Supreme Court, X ZR 63/75, GRUR 1979, 308, 309, "Auspuffkanal für Schaltgase."
49. Federal Supreme Court, X ZR 72/05, GRUR 2007, 778, "Ziehmaschinenzugeinrichtung."
50. Federal Supreme Court, X ZR 6/91, GRUR 1993, 886, "Weichvorrichtung I"; Federal Supreme Court, X ZR 73/95, 1997 Mitt. 364, "Weichvorrichtung II."

used in German infringement proceedings if those statements have been made in parallel nullity or opposition proceedings between the same parties.[51] This is an exception to the rule that declarations made by the applicant in grant proceedings, or by the patentee in invalidation proceedings, are irrelevant to the claim construction. Nevertheless, such declarations, like statements made in the prosecution history, could potentially be useful to demonstrate how a person skilled in the art would understand the patent.[52]

4. IDENTICAL AND EQUIVALENT INFRINGEMENT

4.1. Identical Infringement

Once a claim has been interpreted, it remains to be determined if there has been infringement. An identical infringement is found if all features are reproduced in a literal or semantic manner by the accused embodiment. So-called sub-combinations, i.e., where the accused use does not reproduce all features of the claim, are not protected. The case law is unclear whether an exception to this rule can be made where the omitted feature is not substantial or decisive for the protected teaching.[53] However, it seems likely that even in those cases the principal of legal certainty prevails. That is, competitors should be in a position to identify the scope of protection with sufficient reliability, which might not be guaranteed in case of such partial infringements.

Account must thus be taken of all features, irrespective of whether they are contained in the preamble or the body of the claim. When determining whether there is infringement it is irrelevant whether individual features of the claim were known.[54] Likewise, in the case of dependent claims, they include all features of the claim to which reference is made.

In case of an identical use, there is no room for a "defense of the free state of the art." Thus, the accused infringer cannot argue that the attacked use or the accused embodiment was known or obvious in consideration of the state of the art. The infringement court is bound by the decision of the patent office granting the asserted patent.[55]

4.2. Doctrine of Equivalents

If one or several features of the claim are not reproduced identically, there may still be infringement under the doctrine of equivalents, as provided for in the EPC (see Figure 10.1), namely in the Protocol on the Interpretation of Article 69 EPC as provided in Article 2:

51. Federal Supreme Court, X ZR 6/91, GRUR 1993, 886, "Weichvorrichtung I"; Federal Supreme Court, X ZR 73/95, 1997 Mitt. 364, "Weichvorrichtung II."
52. Federal Supreme Court; X ZR 29/15, Decision of June 14, 2016, "Pemetrexed"
53. Federal Supreme Court, X ZR 55/89, GRUR 1991, 444, "Autowaschvorrichtung."
54. Federal Supreme Court, X ZR 102/91, GRUR 1994, 357, "Muffelofen."
55. Federal Supreme Court, X ZR 22/97, GRUR 99, 914, "Kontaktfederblock."

Equivalents
For the purpose of determining the extent of protection conferred by a European patent, due account shall be taken of any element which is equivalent to an element specified in the claims.

For assessing the question of an equivalent infringement, the following questions have been established by the German Federal Supreme Court.[56] In order to find infringement of the patent on the basis of the doctrine on equivalents, questions (1), (2) and (3) must each be answered in the affirmative and the accused infringer's "Formstein" defense (4) must fail.

(1) *Same Effect (Gleichwirkung)*: Does the accused embodiment solve the problem—underlying the claimed invention—with a feature which, although modified, has objectively the same effect? That is, to prove infringement by equivalents, the modified feature must achieve the same effect as the explicitly claimed feature, both in a feature-to-feature comparison,[57] and as viewed in the context of the overall invention.[58]

Figure 10.1. "Doctrine of Equivalents"

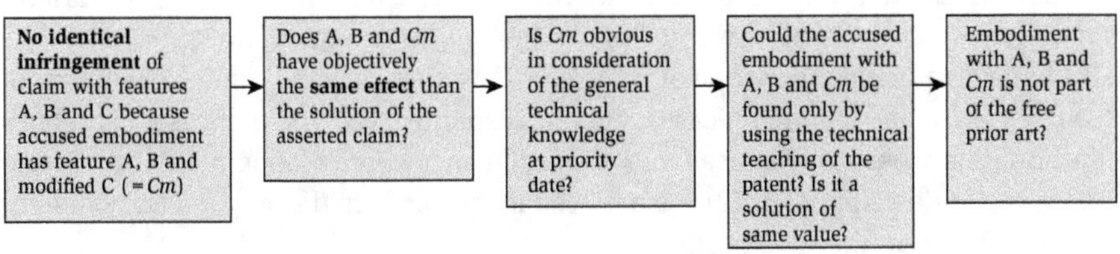

(2) *Obviousness of the Modified Feature (Auffindbarkeit)*: Would the general technical knowledge in the field (at the priority date) have taught a skilled person to practice the invention with the allegedly equivalent modification? The modified feature must be obvious for the skilled person after reading the patent specification. When determining if an accused technology is equivalent to the claimed invention, courts thus look to whether the feature that is not literally present in the claim is an obvious variant of what is claimed.[59] Infringement by equivalents is unavailable if the modified feature is inventive over the feature that is recited in the claim.[60] Infringement under the doctrine of equivalents is only available if the use of the modified feature would have been obvious in view of the literally claimed feature.

56. Federal Supreme Court, X ZR 135/01 GRUR 2002, 519, "Schneidmesser II."; Federal Supreme Court, X ZR 81/13, "Kochgefäß."
57. Federal Supreme Court, X ZR 1/05, GRUR 2007, 959, "Pumpeinrichtung"; and Federal Supreme Court, X ZR 128/98, GRUR 2000, 1005, "Bratgeschirr."
58. Federal Supreme Court, X ZR 128/98, GRUR 2000, 1005, "Bratgeschirr."
59. Federal Supreme Court, X ZR 16/93, GRUR 1994, 597, "Zerlegvorrichtung für Baumstämme."
60. Federal Supreme Court, X ZR 16/93, GRUR 1994, 597, "Zerlegvorrichtung für Baumstämme."

(3) *Same Value (Gleichwertigkeit)*: Is the modified feature so closely oriented towards and tied to the essence of the expressly claimed teaching that the accused embodiment has equal value as compared to the solution provided by the invention recited in the claims? The skilled person needs to identify the modified solution as an obvious variant and must additionally consider it to be of the same value in comparison to the claimed teaching.[61]

In practice, this question is challenging and resort to equivalents is likely to be denied on this basis, particularly if:

- the patent teaches away from the modification;[62]
- numerical limitations of the claims are not met, unless it is exceptionally possible to deduce from the patent description that the effect(s) of the claim can also be achieved with deviating values;[63] or
- the patent encourages particular materials to be used, and the accused embodiment does not make use of one of those.

More generally, the case law refers to the notion of a *"concrete selection"* taken by the applicant or patentee. This means, if it appears from the patent claim, that the applicant or patentee wanted to make a *"concrete selection"* for a particular variant, leaving the impression that he wanted to say *"for whatever reason I do it my way,"*[64] he might have disqualified the scope of protection for other variants. Under the notion of a *"concrete selection"* two main cases must be distinguished. The first case: (1) relates to the situation where the replaced means used in an accused embodiment is disclosed in the asserted description, or (2) the replaced means used in the accused embodiment is not mentioned in the specification:

> (1) For instance, if the patent description explicitly describes a plurality of specific embodiments suitable to achieve the effects of the invention, whereas only one of these embodiments has been included in the patent claim, it is generally considered to fall under the notion of a *"concrete selection"* made by the applicant or patentee. Therefore, an accused infringer, who uses an embodiment which is described in the description but not explicitly claimed, would not qualify as an infringer under the doctrine of equivalence.[65] The question of whether such *"concrete selection"* was made by the applicant or patentee must be responded from the perspective of the public audience faced by the patent. The notion of a *"concrete selection"* does not require a particular motivation on the part of the patentee. As it is explained by the Federal Supreme Court, such *"concrete selection"* can be made "for whatever reason."[66] The inclusion of the particular variant in the patent claims can thus even be unnecessary in the light of the patent's validity. Accordingly, if there is such *"concrete selection"* among different means or variants

61. Federal Supreme Court, X ZR 135/01, GRUR 2002, 519, "Schneidmesser II."
62. Federal Supreme Court, X ZR 55/89, GRUR 91, 443, 447, "Autowaschvorrichtung."
63. Federal Supreme Court, X ZR 135/01, GRUR 2002, 519, "Schneidmesser II."
64. Federal Supreme Court, X ZR 16/09, Decision of May 10, 2011, "Occluder."
65. Federal Supreme Court, X ZR 16/09, Decision of May 10, 2011, "Occluder"; Federal Supreme Court, X ZR 69/10, Decision of Sep. 13, 2011, " Diglycidverbindung."
66. Federal Supreme Court, X ZR 16/09, Decision of May 10, 2011, "Occluder."

disclosed in the patent description, the third question ("same value") must usually be denied and the use of means or variants, which are not claimed, would not fall within the scope of protection. An exception to this rule might be given if the equivalent means used by the accused embodiment is disclosed in the patent description but in a different context than in the context of the replaced claim feature.[67]

(2) With respect to the second case where the replaced means used by the accused embodiment is not disclosed in the patent description, the case law seems, at present, not yet settled. Even though not providing a complete picture, reference can be made to a set of guidelines determined by Federal Supreme Court. First, the Court clarified[68] that the patent description must not necessarily contain statements which lead the skilled person to the equivalent means. How this case law will impact particular cases has yet to be determined. Furthermore, the Court recently provided further guidelines in a case where the patent description generally referred to the use of a group of embodiments, such as a category of agents, but only one specific embodiment, i.e. one specific agent of that category was explicitly described and claimed by the patent. The Court remanded the case to the lower court and ruled that the situation would basically not mean that the applicant or patentee made a *"concrete selection"* and consciously excluded from the scope of protection all other undisclosed embodiments of that group or agents from the category.[69] The Court also indicated that the situation might be different and mitigate against patent infringement if the claimed embodiment(s) of the group is/are linked to specific characteristics which are necessary to achieve the effect(s) of the invention. Likewise, it would lean against a finding of infringement under the doctrine of equivalents if it becomes apparent from a comparison of the different claim versions submitted during the granting proceedings that the claims were narrowed down to particular embodiments in the granted patent in order to distinguish the prior art, not just for formal reasons such as to improve the clarity of the claim or to conform to written support. If the narrowing was to comply with such formalities, resort to the doctrine of equivalence would still be allowed.[70]
The scope of the doctrine of equivalence is thus still in flux in the case law. The case law is most unsettled when the patent description does not contain particular hints to the modified and replaced feature used by the accused embodiment. With two decisions rendered in 2016,[71] the Federal Supreme Court seems to direct the rather restrictive case law of the past towards a more patentee-friendly handling of the doctrine of equivalence.

(4) *Formstein Defense:* Does the allegedly equivalent solution belong to the prior art?
If questions one, two and three are answered affirmatively, the accused infringer may rely on a counter-defense called the *Formstein Defense*,[72] named after a landmark decision of the Federal Supreme Court rendered in 1986. This is, the accused infringer can defend himself by stating that the

67. Appeal Court Düsseldorf, I-2 U 29/12, Decision of Nov. 7, 2013, "WC – Sitzgelenk."
68. Federal Supreme Court, X ZR 36/13, GRUR 2014, 852 "Begrenzungsanschlag."
69. Federal Supreme Court, X ZR 29/15, "Pemetrexed."
70. Federal Supreme Court, X ZR 29/15, "Pemetrexed."
71. Federal Supreme Court, decision of Jun. 14, 2016, X ZR 29/15, "Pemetrexed"; Federal Supreme Court, decision of Aug. 23, 2016, X ZR 76/14, "V-förmige Führungsanordnung."
72. Federal Supreme Court, X ZR 28/85, GRUR 1987, 279, IIC 1987, 795 (in English), "Formstein."

accused embodiment is either identical to the prior art or it could have not been patented at the priority date of the asserted patent due to lack of inventive step. This defense has been exclusively developed for the doctrine of equivalents. It is inapplicable if the infringement is based on an identical infringement.[73] The reasoning behind this defense, which finds its counterpart in the U.S. in the *Wilson* case,[74] is derived from competition law, according to which the prior art should be free and available to the public. Under the German split system, the infringement courts are bound by the grant decision of the patent office. Accordingly, since infringement courts do not have jurisdiction to decide validity, the "Formstein defense" is not permitted in cases of identical infringement.

5. INFRINGING ACTS

The central provisions governing the consequences of infringing acts are contained in §§9, 10 of the German Patent Act. As soon as the UPCA comes into force,[75] a second set of provisions must be taken into account for European Patents with or without unitary effect, namely its Articles 25 and 26. Both sets of provisions are identically worded.

The pertinence of the German case law established under the German Patent Act will however not be imposed on these provisions of the UPCA. These provisions belong to an international treaty. Their interpretation primarily follows the interpretation concept of the Vienna Convention of the law of treaties. According to Article 31 of the Vienna Convention, *"a treaty shall be interpreted in good faith in accordance with ordinary meaning to be given to the terms of the treaty in their context and in the light of its object and purpose."* Article 32 of the Vienna Convention adds supplementary means of interpretation, namely *"the preparatory work of the treaty and the circumstances of its conclusion"* may be used in order to confirm the meaning resulting from the application of Article 31. The Vienna Convention only provides a basic set of interpretation rules. It does not exclude other aspects of interpretation, in particular the case law of the Member States. This seems to be particularly important as to those provisions of the UPCA which correspond to identical national provisions under which extensive case law has been established over decades. For this reason, it is incumbent upon the UPC to take into consideration the decisions and expressions of opinion of courts and industrial property offices in the Members States.

Accordingly, the interpretation of the UPCA starts from a different legal ground than the one of the German Patent Act. Even though the wording of the provisions is identical, the German case law established under that provision only serves as a guideline for the interpretation of Articles 25, 26 UPCA. A complete interpretation would thus require making a general synthesis of the different case laws of the Member

73. Federal Supreme Court, X ZR 22/97, GRUR 1999, 914, "Kontaktfederblock."
74. See *Wilson Sporting Goods Co. v. David Geoffrey & Assocs.*, 904 F.2d 677, 14 U.S.P.Q. 2d 1942 (Fed. Cir.).
75. Most likely the UPCA comes into force in 2018.

States. It is to be expected that in most of the cases, the main results of that analysis will likely show a consensus. Diverging positions in national laws to be balanced out by the case law of the UPC will thus represent the exception.

5.1. Direct Infringement

The infringement test requires a comparison of the claimed invention and the accused embodiment. The patent is infringed if the accused embodiment reproduces all features of the patent claim. Differences in efficiency, in particular in case of improved or inferior realizations, do not exclude patent infringement, as long as all features of the claim are fulfilled. If a feature of the asserted claim is neither met literally nor by equivalents in the accused embodiment, then there is no infringement (see previous sections).

An apparatus claim is infringed as long as the embodiment is objectively suitable to achieve the claimed properties and the effects as described in the description of the patent. It is sufficient if the infringing properties are the result of normal use made by the user, for instance if a particular wheel circumference of a tire (as claimed) is later achieved by the normal use of the tire.[76] It is irrelevant if the producer or supplier of the infringing devices explicitly proposes in the instruction manual another (presumably non-infringing) use of the apparatus, as long as the use of the teaching of the patent is possible. Accordingly, it is not necessary for the user of the product to necessarily use it in an infringing way. On the other hand, if the user of the accused embodiment needs to apply particular measures in view of achieving the claimed properties and the effects as described in the description of the patent, there is, as a general rule, no infringement.

The accused infringer may escape liability if he disables a particular functionality of the accused product that is sought in the patent. For example: The accused infringer sells a device with a multitude of software-based functionalities but one functionality (allegedly infringing) is disabled. The question whether there is still infringement depends on the "objective user" of the accused product and how easily the user could enable the disabled functionality. For instance, a device which does not make use of all features of the patented teaching when it is delivered, may thus exceptionally represent a direct infringement of the patent if it is self-evident and certain that the purchaser, i.e., "objective user" manipulates it in view of realizing the patented teaching. This could be the case if the accused infringer guides and controls that last act of manipulation committed by the "objective user." He then deliberately adopts the manipulation of the "objective user" with his delivery, which justifies treating him as if he had delivered an infringing device.[77] One decision of the Federal Supreme Court[78] stated:

76. Appeal Court Düsseldorf, decision of Jul. 29, 2010, 2 U 139/09, BeckRS 2010, 21759.
77. Appeal Court Düsseldorf, decision of Feb. 19, 2015, I-15 U 39/14.
78. Federal Supreme Court, X ZR 14/02, GRUR 2006, 399, "Rangierkatze"; District Court Düsseldorf, decision of Jan. 23, 2007 - 4a O 34/06, BeckRS 2009, 12319.

the patent is infringed provided the features of the patent claim are reproduced and the accused embodiment is objectively suitable to achieve the patented properties and effects. It does not preclude infringement if the device is usually applied in a different manner and if normally the user does not make use of [the infringing functionality]. Patent infringement is also given if the manufacturer explicitly recommends another use of the devices as long as the use of the patented teaching is possible.[79]

In this manner, German law is more accommodating to the patentee than U.S. law in establishing a case of direct infringement. The law in the U.S. would, by contrast, require proof of induced infringement in this circumstance, which entails a level of scienter absent from German law.

5.1.1. Products

Introduction: The central provision governing a direct infringement of a product claim is §9(1) N° 1 of the German Patent Act, which prescribes that a person not having the consent of the patentee shall be prohibited:

from making, offering, placing on the market or using a product which is the subject matter of the patent, or importing or storing the product for such purposes.

At least one of the indicated activities must be demonstrated and proven for the grant of an injunction against the infringement of a product claim. Usually, it is sufficient to demonstrate one case of offering for sale the accused product.

Territoriality: The concept of territoriality requires that the infringement occurs in Germany if a German patent or the German counterpart of European patent is subject to a lawsuit in front of a German infringement court.

Offer: The notion of an "offer" according to §9(1) N° 1 of the GPA broadly covers any holding out of the prospect of making available the product. A legally binding offer is thus not necessary (as opposed to the law in the U.S., which is more restrictive in requiring a formal offer). Also, it is not required that the offer is supposed to lead to any result or that the offered product be delivered.[80] The offer must however occur during the lifetime of the patent.[81] A promotional brochure showing the product is thus sufficient. In cases of an offer, the infringing act is not only committed where the offer has been made, but also where the offer is received or can be perceived by potential interested parties. An infringing offer can thus be expressed outside the territory of the court's jurisdiction if it is received inside that territory. Even the shipment of accused products to a company situated outside German territory was considered by the

79. Unofficial translation.
80. Federal Supreme Court GRUR 2003, 1031, "Kupplung für optische Geräte."
81. Federal Supreme Court GRUR 2007, 221, "Simvastatin": The entry of a generic drug in an announcement list represents an offer, even if it explicitly indicates that the generic is only available after the expiration of the patent. Nevertheless, a generic company can initiate the regulatory process in view of getting an approval for the generic drug prior to the expiration of the patent: Appeal Court Düsseldorf, Decision of Sep. 20, 2012 – I-2 U 44/12.

German Federal Supreme Court[82] to be an infringement of a German patent as long as it can be shown that it was known by the accused infringer that these products were supposed to be commercialized on the German market. This means the patentee is not limited to asserting patent rights against the importing company, but also against the originating company.

Offer through a Webpage: This basically applies to an offer published through a webpage on the Internet that could be received by an Internet user in Germany. Accordingly, it is irrelevant whether the server is located outside that territory, for instance in the U.S. or Asia. It is well-established case law that an English webpage is sufficient to constitute a potentially infringing "offer" under §9 of the German Patent Act. Thus a foreign company, even without any affiliates in Europe and without having shipped any products in the past onto the European Market, which presents its products on its website, could unknowingly infringe a European or German patent, provided that the webpage is objectively addressed to the European public. A diligent company could avoid these consequences by means of a disclaimer posted on the website clearly indicating that the concerned products are not available in Europe.[83] The disclaimer might however not be helpful as soon as the accused products are shipped into the jurisdiction of the German Court, an event which could potentially be triggered by a test purchase[84] initiated by a straw man associated with the patentee. Such test purchases are commonly accepted to justify the jurisdiction of German courts.[85]

Offer at Trade Shows: Even the first offer or advertisement of a product at a German trade show might meet the requirements of §9 of the German Patent Act.[86] However, the trade show must have the quality of a sales exhibition, which is supposed for trading goods. If the exhibition is simply for information purposes, without trading of goods, the demonstration of a product would not be considered to be an infringing act.[87]

Transit: Goods entering the EU are declared in transit if they are not intended to be put on the market in the country where the goods enter the borders. Either these goods are shipped to another EU Member State (so-called internal transit) or to a country outside of the EU (external transit). The Federal Supreme Court[88] recently repeated its case law that the placing of goods in transit proceedings at a German boarder does not infringe rights in Germany under § 9 German Patent Act.[89] Infringement of a German patent may only be found if the goods are subject to trading transactions taking place on the German territory or if the goods are imported for that

82. Federal Supreme Court, Jan. 30, 2007, X ZR 53/04, "Funkuhr II."
83. Federal Supreme Court, GRUR 2006, 513, "Arzneimittelwerbung im Internet."
84. Appeal Court Düsseldorf, decision of Jan. 28, 2010, 2 U 131/00, NJOZ 2010, 1781, "Testkauf patentverletzender DVDs."
85. Appeal Court Düsseldorf, decision of Jan. 28, 2010, 2 U 131/00, NJOZ 2010, 1781, "Testkauf patentverletzender DVDs."
86. Appeal Court Düsseldorf, decision of Mar. 27, 2014, Az. I-15 U 29/14 "Sterilcontainer."
87. Appeal Court Düsseldorf, decision of 27. March 2014, Az. I-15 U 29/14 "Sterilcontainer."
88. Federal Supreme Court, decision of Jun. 25, 2014, X ZR 72/13.
89. Federal Supreme Court, I ZR 246/02, GRUR 2007, 876, "Diesel II."

purpose. This view is in line with the case law of the ECJ[90] on "suspensive proceedings" under the Community Customs Code.[91] Accordingly, goods in transit do not infringe upon the exclusive rights resulting from a patent, unless the proprietor can demonstrate at least a concrete risk that the goods are intended to be put on the market in the country in question. This is, it must be shown that the suspected products may possibly not reach their destination and could thus enter into circulation on the German market.[92] A mere risk is not sufficient.[93] Rather there must be reliable indications to justify such suspicion. Those indications may include, *inter alia*, the fact that the destination of the goods is not declared, the lack of reliable information as to the identity or address of the manufacturer or consignor of the goods, or a lack of cooperation with the Customs Authorities. Although the ECJ puts the thresholds for the interception of goods in transit on the basis of the Customs Regulation relatively low, such indications might, as such, not be sufficient to establish infringement before the national courts.

The aforementioned "transit" case law will apparently not be affected by the UPCA and the UP Regulation. In particular, this counts for the situation if the goods are destined for a country outside of the EU (external transit). The transit would in that situation not constitute an infringement under Article 25 UPCA or - in case Article 25 UPCA is not applicable - an infringement of intellectual property rights applicable inside the EU. If goods are declared in transit because they are not intended to be put on the market in the EU entry state, but shipped to another EU Member State (so-called internal transit), the situation will be the following. In case of a European Patent with unitary effect, if the entry state and the destination state are both states in which the UPC has exclusive jurisdiction over that patent, the transit, as such, might not yet represent an infringing act under Article 25 UPCA. However, the fact that the goods shall be transported into a country, where the patent has unitary effect, with the apparent intention that it shall be brought there into circulation would likely represent a sufficient "threat" that the goods will be placed *"on the market"* in the sense of Article 25 UPCA justifying a claim for cease and desist. This does also apply in case of a traditional European Patent as long as the patent is in force and valid in the state of destination, where the goods shall be later brought into circulation. This would equally represent a sufficient "threat" that the goods will be placed*" on the market"* in the sense of Article 25 UPCA and justify a claim for cease and desist. As recently ruled by the Federal Supreme Court[94] the transit of goods—even though not representing an infringement of rights in the country of entry—could constitute an infringement of a patent which is in force in the country of destination. Whether this is the case needs to be decided case by case.

---

90. European Court of Justice, decision of Nov. 9, 2006; Case C-281/05, "*Montex Holdings Ltd v Diesel SpA*"; decisions of Dec. 1, 2011, Cases C-446/09, Philips, C-495/09 Nokia.
91. Chapter 14.
92. District Court Hamburg, decision of Apr. 30, 2009, 315 O 72/08, BeckRS 2009, 29649; see also decision of the European Court of Justice, C-281/05, GRUR 2007, 146 "Montex/Diesel."
93. Federal Supreme Court, decision of Apr. 25, 2012, I ZR 235/10 "Clinique happy."
94. Federal Supreme Court, decision of Apr. 25, 2012, I ZR 235/10 "Clinique happy."

Making: This act is fulfilled if it covers all steps of the manufacturing process up to the completion of the product.[95] Accordingly, it will not be sufficient if the activities are limited to preparatory acts unless the accused infringer controls the process from the beginning to the final step (extended workbench).[96]

Putting on the market: It broadly covers all acts where the power of disposal of the product is passed to a third party, without the necessity that its ownership is assigned. The delivery to the carried or shipper is thus sufficient.

5.1.2. Processes

Introduction: Process claims relate to a physical activity, such as a method, process or use.[97] The central provisions governing infringing acts of a process claim are contained in §9(1) N° 2 of the GPA and in Article 25 b) UPCA. Both provisions prescribe that a person not having the consent of the patentee shall be prohibited:

§9(1) N° 2 GPA	*Upcoming: Article 25 b) UPCA*
... from using a process which is the subject-matter of the patent or, where he knows or it is obvious from the circumstances that the use of the process is prohibited without the consent of the patentee, from offering the process for use within the territory to which this Law applies.[98]	... from using a process which is the subject-matter of the patent or, where the third party knows, or should have known, that the use of the process is prohibited without the consent of the patent proprietor, offering the process for use within the territory of the Contracting Member States in which that patent has effect.

The provision covers two case scenarios. The first scenario refers to the situation where the accused infringer uses himself the protected process ("*using a process*"), whereas the second scenario concerns an offer made by the accused infringer to a third party to perform the claimed process ("*offering a process*").

Process claims encompass all kind of methods, namely methods of working, manufacturing methods, and use methods. The main difference between both provisions relates to their territorial application. Article 25 b) UPCA will be applicable to traditional European patents and European patents with unitary effect. The latter type of patent has effect in all UPCA Contracting Member States. Accordingly the use of a process claim in any of these states would, in principle, fall under Article 25 b) UPC. As to traditional European patent, an infringement is basically given according to Article 25 b) UPCA in UPCA Contracting Member States where the patent has been validated and has thus effect. The traditional European patent might have been validated also in other EPC Member States, which do not belong to the group of UPCA Contracting

95. Federal Supreme Court, GRUR 1951, 452, "Mülltonne."
96. Federal Supreme Court, GRUR 1990, 997, "Ethofumesat."
97. Enlarged Board, G 2/88.
98. District Court Düsseldorf, GRUR RR 2001, 201, 204, InstGE 1, 26, 31g.

Member States. Due to the missing applicability of Article 25 b) UPCA in those states, the provisions of the national laws prevail.

A method is used if the essential steps of the method are performed by the accused infringer. Thus, preparatory acts alone are usually not sufficient. Nevertheless, it has been decided by the Appeal Court Düsseldorf that the infringer need not necessarily implement all the steps of the protected method to be liable for infringement. He would still infringe the patent if, for example, the final steps of the method are implemented by a third party, and can nonetheless be imputed to him.

As a consequence of territoriality, the use of the claimed method outside the territory addressed by §9(1) N° 2 GPA or Article 25 b) UPCA does not represent an infringement. However, an infringement might be found even if only a part of the method is implemented by the accused party within the territory, as long as the remaining method steps that are accomplished outside that territory are attributable to the accused party. The same approach can be mirrored to the inverse situation, namely if one part of the method steps is implemented outside the relevant territory by a third party and the remaining acts are accomplished by the accused infringer inside the relevant territory. In both scenarios the acts that were committed outside the territory addressed by §9(1) N° 2 GPA or Article 25 b) UPCA may be imputed to the accused infringer in order for infringement to be found.[99]

In client-server systems, where the server, database and user are situated in different countries, the approach described here for method claims may likely also be applicable to system claims. This would have the effect that all components of the system need not necessarily be located within the territory addressed by §9(1) N° 2 GPA or Article 25 b) UPCA

The second scenario ("*offering a process*") not only requires that the accused infringer makes an offer, but also that he knows or—at least—that he should have known that the use of the process is prohibited.[100] The principle of territoriality is explicitly reflected in that—according to §9(1) N° 2 GPA—the offer must be oriented to a use of the process in Germany. If the product is offered for a use which shall take place outside Germany, then there would be no patent infringement.

Product Directly Obtained by the Process: Furthermore, the patentee may exclude any third party—according to §9(3) GPA:

> *from offering, placing on the market, using or importing or storing for such purposes the product obtained directly by a process which is the subject-matter of the patent.*

This means in case of a process claim, similar rights as are known in the U.S. are conferred to the patentee. If the process is a manufacturing process, the patentee can also prohibit the commercialization of products directly generated by that method even though his patent does not contain any product claim. The product generated by the method must not necessarily possess a physical or corporal nature. The product could also represent an incorporeal sequence of electronic signals, as long as the signals are

99. Appeal Court Düsseldorf, Dec. 10, 2009, I-2 U 51/08, GRUR-RR 2010, 122, "Prepaid-Telefonkarte."
100. §9(1) N° 2 GPA reads "obvious from the circumstances".

reproducible by a reader.[101] However, the legal protection is limited to a "direct" generation of the product through the process. This is usually the case if the accused product was directly obtained by the patented process and was not subsequently subject to other manufacturing measures.

Moreover, for the application of §9(3) GPA or Article 25 b) UPCA it is irrelevant where the method has been implemented and where the product has been generated by the process. It would be sufficient for infringement if the method was implemented in the U.S. and the obtained product was later imported onto the German market or under the upcoming UPC a market of the UPCA Contracting Member States.

Shift of Burden of Proof: The position of the patentee asserting a process claims is strengthened by a shift of burden of proof:

§139(3) GPA	*Upcoming: Article 55 UPCA*
... if the subject matter of a patent is a process for obtaining a new product, the identical product when produced by any other party shall, in the absence of proof to the contrary, be deemed to have been obtained by the patented process. In the adduction of proof to the contrary, the legitimate interests of the defendant in protecting his manufacturing and business secrets shall be taken into account.[102]	(1) ... if the subject- matter of a patent is a process for obtaining a new product, the identical product when produced without the consent of the patent proprietor shall, in the absence of proof to the contrary, be deemed to have been obtained by the patented process. (2) The principle set out in paragraph 1 shall also apply where there is a substantial likelihood that the identical product was made by the patented process and the patent proprietor has been unable, despite reasonable efforts, to determine the process actually used for such identical product. (3) In the adduction of proof to the contrary, the legitimate interests of the defendant in protecting its manufacturing and trade secrets shall be taken into account.

§139(3) GPA provides a shift of the burden of proof in the case of process claims. The patentee must first prove that the product obtained by the patented process is new (i.e., shows at least one aspect that differentiates it over the prior art at the priority date of the patent-in-question). If the patentee can do so, he then he only needs to show that the product obtained by the accused infringer's process is identical with that product.

Sections 1 and 3 of Article 55 UPCA are identical with §139(3) GPA. However, Article 55 UPCA contains an additional section 2 which is unknown under the German

101. Federal Supreme Court, decision of Aug. 21, 2012, X ZR 33/10 "MPEG-2-Videosignalcodierung."
102. Appeal Court Munich, decision of Dec. 12, 2010, 6 U 4719/08.

law and will further strengthen the position of the patentee. Section 2 is based upon a "*substantial likelihood that the identical product was made by the patented process.*" It seems that section 2—in contrast to section 1—does not require a "new" product obtained by the patented process. This is, it is not required that product obtained by the patented process must show at least one aspect that differentiates it over the prior art at the priority date of the patent-in-question[103] which is a necessary determinant for the conclusion that the accused product is obtained by the patented process. Instead, section 2 does not require particular facts from which the assumption of a "*substantial likelihood*" can be drawn. However, the shift of the burden of proof according to section 2 additionally requires that proprietor "*has been unable, despite reasonable efforts, to determine the process actually used for such identical product.*"

5.1.3. *Product-by-Process Claims*

A product-by-process claim defines a product in terms of the method used in its manufacture. This type of claim typically provides a way for protecting products, like chemical compounds, that are difficult to describe by chemical make-up or structure, but can only be described by the way they are made. The patentability of such claims requires that the product can only be described in terms of how it can be made and, thus, cannot be described in terms of its composition, structure or other physical properties. The determination of the scope of protection conferred by such claims creates particular problems. According to a decision of the Federal Supreme Court,[104] the scope of protection shall not be limited to the manufacturing methods or processes recited in the claims. This is because the claims set forth the manufacturing method merely as an example of how the product is obtained (typical claim language: "is obtainable"). Thus, products which meet the particular properties conferred by the process, but are in fact obtained by another process, would thus also be covered by the claim. Nevertheless, the particular effects that the processes recited in the claims produce upon the final product shall be taken into account for the determination of the scope of protection.[105]

5.2. Contributory Infringement

The concept of contributory patent infringement is provided in §10 GPA. The provisions and its counterpart in the UPCA read:

103. EPO—T 238/98, EPO—T 748/98, EPO—T 620/99.
104. Federal Supreme Court, X ZB 13/90, GRUR 1993, 651, "Tetraploide Kamille."
105. Federal Supreme Court, X ZR 188/01, GRUR 2005, 749, "Aufzeichnungsträger."

§10 GPA	*Article 26 UPCA*
(1) A patent shall have the further effect that a third party not having the consent of the proprietor shall be prohibited from supplying or offering to supply, within the territory to which this Law applies, any person, other than a party entitled to exploit the patented invention, with means relating to an essential element of that invention for putting it into effect therein, when the third party knows or it is obvious from the circumstances that such means are suitable and intended for putting the invention into effect. (2) Paragraph 1 shall not apply when the means are staple commercial products, except where the third party induces the person supplied to perform any of the acts prohibited by the second sentence of Section 9. (3) Persons performing the acts referred to in Section 11.1 to 3, shall not be considered persons entitled to exploit the invention within the meaning of paragraph 1.[106]	(1) A patent shall confer on its proprietor the right to prevent any third party not having the proprietor's consent from supplying or offering to supply, within the territory of the Contracting Member States in which that patent has effect, any person other than a party entitled to exploit the patented invention, with means, relating to an essential element of that invention, for putting it into effect therein, when the third party knows, or should have known, that those means are suitable and intended for putting that invention into effect. (2) Paragraph 1 shall not apply when the means are staple commercial products, except where the third party induces the person supplied to perform any of the acts prohibited by Article 25. (3) Persons performing the acts referred to in Article 27(a) to (e) shall not be considered to be parties entitled to exploit the invention within the meaning of paragraph 1.

Neither §10(1) GPA nor Article 26 UPCA do require that the contributory infringement finally leads to a direct infringement. A threat of direct infringement is sufficient. Often contributory infringement is found in cases where the accused party sells a part which is supposed to be assembled by a third party into a patent-protected product or system. Other typical cases of contributory infringement concern the sale of a device with which a patented process can be implemented or a patented product can be produced.[107] In such cases, the patentee may proceed against the threat instead of suing the direct infringer.

Purpose-Oriented Offer or Supply: Without the requirement of an established direct infringement, the provision is intended to protect the patentee in advance of a threat of direct infringement. Nevertheless, the production or possession of a means is not yet a sufficient basis for a contributory infringement. The provision basically starts from the requirement that a "supply or offer" of a means takes place. Furthermore, the provision does not contain an absolute prohibition on provision of the means, with the understanding that the supplied or offered means may not make use of the patent claim and thus consequently further substantive aspects must be established in order to penalize the provider or supplier.[108]

106. Unofficial translation.
107. Federal Supreme Court; X ZR 113/04, decision of Jul. 27, 2007, "Rohrschweißverfahren."
108. Federal Supreme Court, May 4, 2004, X ZR 48/03, GRUR 2004, 758, "Flügelradzähler."

Thus, the offered or supplied means must not only be suitable for putting the claimed teaching into effect. The means must also be intended for that purpose. The contributory infringer must positively know that the supplied means is suitable for an infringing use and intended for that use by a third party (buyer), who himself must have the intention to use it in a patent infringing way. As such, knowledge or intention is typically difficult to prove, the patentee is only required to demonstrate that—in consideration of the circumstances—the supplied means are obviously suitable and intended for an infringing use. Indeed, according to § 10(1) GPA the knowledge and intention must be *"obvious from the circumstances."* The more it is obvious that the supplied means could be used for an infringement, the less problematic it is for the patentee to prove the existence of that knowledge on the side of the accused third party. Of course, if the supplied means can only be used in an infringing way and does not allow any non-infringing use, that knowledge can be assumed.[109] The assessment is problematic if the concerned means can be used in an infringing as well as in a non-infringing manner. It becomes even more complicated if the buyer must proactively manipulate the delivered product to render it suitable for a patent infringement. In such a situation, concrete hints showing that the buyer is indeed using the supplied product in an infringing manner must be proven.[110] Typically, recommendations or instructions contained in manuals or the product literature of the accused infringer represent useful sources for the indicated test. Even though Article 26(1) UPCA uses the terminology *"should have known,"* whereas § 10(1) GPA requires that the knowledge *"is obvious from the circumstances,"* there seem to be no difference between both provisions in that respect.

Supplied Means: The statement *"means relating to an essential element of the invention"* in the contributory infringement rule restricts the prohibition to the delivery of particular means. It requires the supply of means referring to an essential element of the invention that is capable of interacting functionally with one or more features of the patent claim to implement the protected invention. It generally does not matter which feature or features of the patent claim the means interacts with. It is thus irrelevant if the feature with which the means interacts is anticipated by the prior art or belongs to the "core" of the invention. It must represent a "(little) cog in the wheel"[111] to be considered as a *"means relating to an essential element of the invention."* This is for instance the case if its use is causal for realizing a step of the method set forth in the patent claim.[112] However, an element that is completely subordinate to the technical teaching of the invention would be a non-essential element of the invention, and thus not sufficient for a contributory infringement. For instance, means that merely relate to the subject matter or starting point of a protected method would not suffice to fulfill the requirement of the provision.[113] This represents the view of the Federal Supreme

109. Federal Supreme Court, X ZR 173/02, GRUR 2007, 679, "Haubenstretchautomat."
110. Federal Supreme Court, X ZR 173/02, GRUR 2007, 679, "Haubenstretchautomat."
111. Federal Supreme Court, Feb. 3, 2015, GRUR 2015, 467, "Audiosignalcodierung."
112. Federal Supreme Court, Feb. 3, 2015, GRUR 2015, 467, "Audiosignalcodierung."
113. Federal Supreme Court, Feb. 3, 2015, GRUR 2015, 467, "Audiosignalcodierung."

Court.[114] Nevertheless, according to the second subsection of the provision, even means that are staple commercial products (nails, screws etc.) can be means suitable for contributory infringement. But, this provision tightens the requirements for a contributory infringement made with these types of products. Accordingly, the supply of staple commercial products would only represent a contributory infringement if the supplier deliberately induces the purchaser to commit a direct infringement. The second subsection protects the supplier of objects that are generally traded. Suppliers of staple commercial products cannot be expected to monitor the intentions of their purchasers.

Contributory Infringement in an International Context: The "*offering for sale*" or the "*supplying*" of the means must occur on the German territory for there to be contributory infringement. Furthermore, the essential means must be aimed at putting the invention into effect on German territory (double domestic nexus) by the buyer.[115] A main difference to the UPCA consists in that Article 26(1) UPCA covers the territory of the Contracting Member States, whereas the provision of §10 GPA is limited to the German territory. This is, both supply of the essential means and the act of putting the invention into effect must occur in Germany under §10 GPA. For example, if an invention is protected by separate national patents in Germany and in France, a competitor offering to supply an essential component in Germany which is intended to be used in France would *not* be guilty of contributory infringement of the German patent. In an exceptional case the Federal Supreme Court decided, that a contributory patent infringement can even be committed under § 10 GPA by exporting means that relate to an essential element of a claimed invention, if such means contribute to the manufacture of an infringing product that is intended for being commercialized on the German market.[116] That ruling arose from a case in which the accused infringer manufactured wheelwork mechanisms for radio clocks. He supplied these wheelwork mechanisms from Germany to a company located in the UK, which used them to manufacture radio alarm clocks (according to the claimed invention). The foreign company subsequently imported the radio alarm clocks onto the German market. The accused company, namely the company that only manufactured the wheelwork mechanism, did not make a direct use of the patented teaching. It supplied only a component of the device, according to the claimed invention, to the foreign manufacturer. §10(1) Patent Act requires a "supply within the German territory" and this was critical in the *Funkuhr II* case as the supplied means was first exported to a company located in a foreign country. Nevertheless, the Federal Supreme Court ruled that it is sufficient for contributory infringement if the contributor knows or should know in consideration of the circumstances that the final product will ultimately find its way into German territory.

For a unitary patent or a traditional European patent, contributory infringement will be soon covered by Article 26 UPCA. This provision only requires that "*offering for*

114. Federal Supreme Court, May 4, 2004, X ZR 48/03, GRUR 2004, 758, "Flügelradzähler;" Federal Supreme Court, Feb. 3, 2015, GRUR 2015, 467, "Audiosignalcodierung."
115. Federal Supreme Court, GRUR 2005, 845, "Abgasreinigungsvorrichtung."
116. Federal Supreme Court, Jan. 30, 2007, X ZR 53/04, "Funkuhr II."

sale" or the "*supplying*" and intended use occurs in a Contracting Member State in which the patent has effect. Offer for delivery or supply of the essential means and the act of putting the invention into effect will not need to occur in the same country. It is sufficient that it occurs within the group of countries covered by the unitary patent, or where the European patent has effect. If it comes to contributory infringement, a European Patent will thus provide more protection than available in separate national patents.

Inducement: A person who actively and intentionally induces or aids a third party to willfully commit an infringement of a patent is also liable. This liability relies on the general rules of active and intentional inducement or aid (see §§26, 27 Criminal Code in conjunction with §830 of the Civil Code), which could be applicable in parallel to §10 GPA or Article 26 UPC. However, it requires that both the inducer and the induced party act willfully. Negligence is not sufficient.[117] In addition, the liability for inducement also requires that a direct infringement has effectively been committed by the third party.[118] For instance, a person who instructs a third party in how to use a staple commercial product or any other component to exercise the patented invention may be liable as an active inducer. In contrast hereto, several infringers who jointly and consciously act together in view of a patent infringement (such as distributor, producer or importer) are individually liable as direct infringers ("Nebentäter"). They must not necessarily act with intent. Negligence would be sufficient.

The following figure 10.2 contains an overview of the requirements of a contributory infringement according to §10(1) GPA.

Table 10.2. Overview: Contributory Infringement (§10(1) GAP)

Requirements		
Objective	*Subjective: Contributory infringer*	*Subjective: Third Party*
(1) Means must *"relate to an essential element of the claimed invention"*; (2) Offer or delivery of the means in Germany; (3) Suitability of the means for a patent infringing use in Germany; (4) Offer or delivery of the means to a third party, which is not authorized to use the claimed invention; (5) Offer or delivery of the means without the consent of the patent owner.	Knowledge of the objective suitability of the means for a patent infringing use and of its planed use by the third party **or** the latter is obvious from the circumstances	Intent to use the means in a patent infringing manner **or** the latter is obvious from the circumstances

117. Busse, Patentgesetz, §11, No. 30.
118. Busse, Patentgesetz, §11, No. 30.

6. EXHAUSTION

6.1. Putting onto the EU/EEA Market

Exhaustion of patent rights depends primarily on whether the protected product was placed onto the European market by the patentee or by a person who is authorized by the patentee (such as a licensee). According to European rules, patent rights are exhausted if this occurs anywhere within the EU or the European Economic Area (EEA).[119] In the event that the patented object is put into circulation by the patent-holder or by a third party with his consent in the EU or the EAA, the consequence of exhaustion follows from Article 34 of the Treaty on the Functioning of the European Union (TFEU)[120] (formerly Article 28 EC Treaty). According to this provision, all quantitative restrictions on imports and all measures having equivalent effect are prohibited between Member States. The right holder acquires, in return for his inventive activity, the exclusive right to manufacture and put into circulation commercial products, hence the right to exploit the invention either himself or by means of granting licenses to third parties. But if the product, according to the invention, is put into circulation by the holder himself, or with his consent, he loses this right. The right holder must accept the consequences of this choice as far as concerns trade within the Common Market. Indeed, if the product was first sold outside Europe, there may be an exhaustion of the patent rights in the particular market (e.g., Canada, China, etc.). Exhaustion of patent rights in a country outside the EU/EEA does not have any effect on European patent rights, so long as the patentee did not intend via agreement for ultimate delivery into the EU/EEA. The burden of proof for the existence of such an agreement would be on the defendant.[121]

6.2. Assertion of a Patent with Device Claim

As soon as the concerned product is put onto the EU/EEA market purposely by the patentee, the patent product claims are exhausted.[122] Thus, the exhaustion has a Europe-wide effect, which is also a consequence of the EU/EEA public law aimed at avoiding trade barriers. Thus, the buyer of the product is entitled not only to use, but also to sell the product. A device claim cannot be asserted against a third party buying the product. The patentee has received the benefits of his invention through the sale of the product. He has used up the patent rights with respect to the specific item covered by the patent and can no longer control its subsequent use in commerce.

119. Federal Supreme Court, Dec. 14, 1999, X ZR 61/98, GRUR 2000, 299, "Karate."
120. Article 34 TFEU reads "Quantitative restrictions on imports and all measures having equivalent effect shall be prohibited between Member States."
121. Federal Supreme Court, Dec. 14, 1999, X ZR 61/98, GRUR 2000, 299 "Karate."
122. Federal Supreme Court, X ZR 72/94, GRUR 1997, 116, "Prospekthalter" and Federal Supreme Court, X ZR 137/99, GRUR 2001, 223, "Bodenwaschanlage."

6.3. Assertion of a Patent with a Method Claim

According to the Supreme Court,[123] the situation is different with respect to method claims. If an apparatus, which is necessary for the implementation of a method/procedure, is put onto the market with the agreement of the patentee, the rights resulting from the patented method are not exhausted. Thus, method patents can implicitly or explicitly be licensed and the patentee is free to determine the scope of the use of the apparatus in the agreement with the buyer.[124] In case of method patents, the extent to which the buyer of the apparatus is entitled to implement the method must be determined by the contractual relationship between the patentee and the buyer. As there is no exhaustion of rights, the contractual liberty is not limited by antitrust law, and the parties are free to shape this relationship. If there is no written agreement, it would be necessary to establish the intention of the parties. In order to identify the implicit expression of intention, they usually refer to the interests of the parties at the specific moment of agreement, and the related specific factual circumstances.

6.4. Assertion of a Patent Containing Apparatus and Method Claims

According to a general opinion in the German case law,[125] the sale of an apparatus that is protected by a method claim and by an apparatus claim of the same patent leads to the exhaustion of the patent rights also with respect to the method claim (as opposed to patents having only method claims). Accordingly, the third party could use the method without the permission of the patentee. In this situation the patentee is considered to have obtained the benefits from the invention through his apparatus claim. This is not the case if only the method claim is used, but not the apparatus claim.

The existing case law deals mainly with situations where the apparatus claim is composed of features analogous to the method claims (i.e., the method claim describes the only use of the apparatus). This case law does not, however, give a clear answer as to cases where the method claim and the apparatus claim are focused on technically different aspects or teachings. There are good reasons to believe that the method claim is not covered by the exhaustion in such a situation.

6.5. Limits to the Concept of Exhaustion of Rights (Maintenance versus Rebuilding)

There are limits to the exhaustion doctrine that have been clarified in a decision by the Supreme Court.[126] It is a common view that the buyer of a patented apparatus is

123. Federal Supreme Court, X ZR 137/99, GRUR 2001, 2003, "Bodenwaschanlage"; cf. Commentary: Benkard/Scharen, §9 German Patent Act, Rn. 16 ff.
124. For instance District Court Düsseldorf 4 O 175/98.
125. Federal Supreme Court, X ZB 21/94, GRUR 1998, 130, "Handhabungsgerät"; District Court Düsseldorf, Mitt. 1999, 179, "Levitationsmaschine."
126. Federal Supreme Court, X ZR 48/03, GRUR 2004, 758 and IIC 2005, 963 (in English) "Flügelradzähler."

entitled to the "intended use" of the protected apparatus. This involves the repairing and maintenance of the apparatus during the normal lifetime of the product.[127] On the other hand, a "rebuilding" of the apparatus is considered a patent infringement. For instance, the concept of exhaustion would not apply to a case where spare parts belonging to patent exhausted products are reassembled in a new device.[128] The concept of exhaustion could not be extended to such a newly manufactured device even though only spare parts of patent exhausted products are used. There are cases where it is difficult to determine whether there has been an allowed "repairing" versus an illicit rebuilding of the apparatus. What is covered by an "intended use" is decided on a case-by-case basis. To assess whether the exchange of a part of the whole apparatus represents an infringement, the Federal Supreme Court requires a balancing of the patentee's interests in the economical exploitation of the invention against the interests of the buyer in an unhindered use of the inventive apparatus.[129] According to the Federal Supreme Court, the decisive question is whether the exchanged part plays a significant role for the technical effect of the claimed invention.[130] If yes, its replacement would not be covered anymore by the concept of exhaustion. Another issue being raised, and likely to be litigated, is the period of normal deterioration to be expected during the lifetime of the concerned product. Courts might find against an infringement, for example, if the accused activities do not artificially prolong the lifetime of the product.[131]

127. Federal Supreme Court, GRUR 2006, 837, "Laufkranz."
128. Federal Supreme Court, GRUR 1973, 518, "Spielautomat II."
129. Federal Supreme Court, GRUR 2004, 758, "Flügelradzähler."
130. Federal Supreme Court, GRUR 2004, 758, "Flügelradzähler"; Federal Supreme Court, GRUR 2006, 837, "Laufkranz"; Federal Supreme Court, GRUR 2007, 769, "Pipettensystem."
131. Federal Supreme Court, GRUR 1959, 232, "Förderrinne."

Figure 10.2. Simplified Overview Summarizing the Concept of Exhaustion

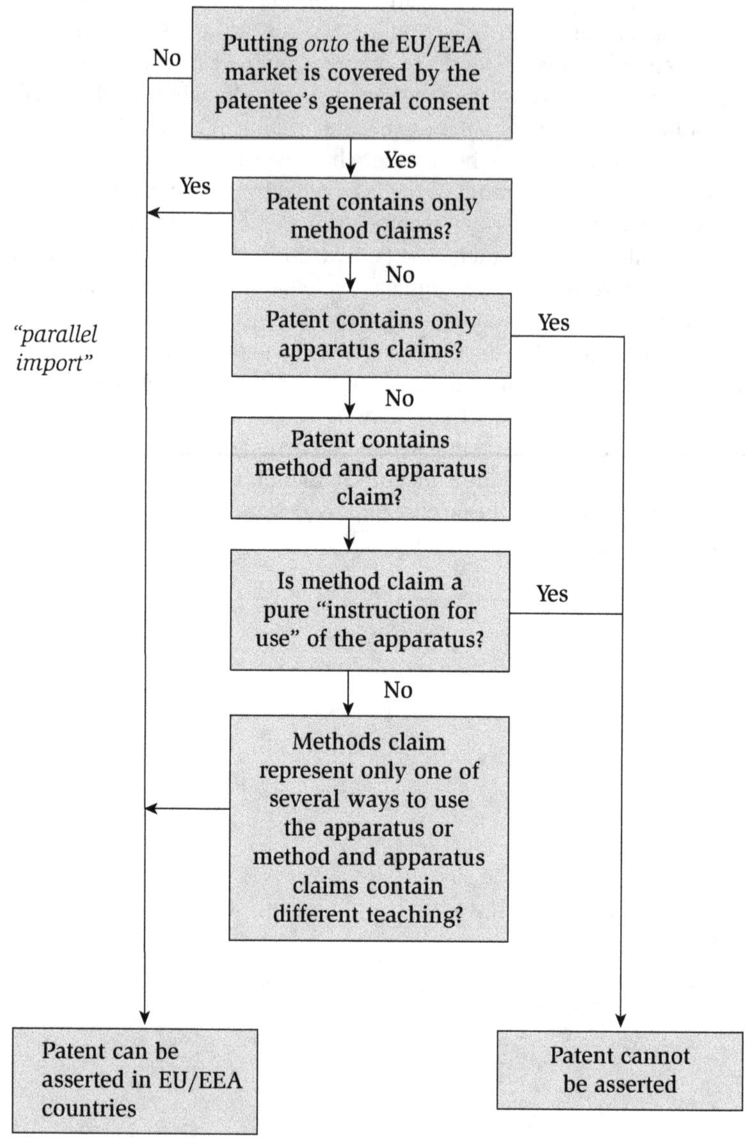

CHAPTER 11

Discovery and Evidence Taking

1. GENERAL FRAMEWORK

1.1. Introduction

Although in general, U.S.-style pre-trial discovery proceedings are unknown in German patent infringement proceedings, some discovery is available. The comparatively more limited form of discovery under German law usually requires patentees prior to commencing a court action to independently investigate and gather the relevant facts and evidence from the openly available sources, sometimes even by means of private investigators or through reverse engineering. However, discovery may be obtained through judicial measures if independent fact-finding is not successful. This is, the German procedural law provides judicial discovery means allowing the right holder to have access to evidentiary information that is otherwise inaccessible. Judicial measures can be applied *prior* to the filing of a lawsuit, as well as during main proceedings.[1] Most of the time, it is however recommended to start with discovery measures, preferably through swift interim measures, prior to lengthy main proceedings. Such interim measures provide a surprise effect. They minimize the risk that the evidence might be altered; in addition, obtaining this evidence before the main proceedings may allow the right holder to more properly structure the litigation. These advantages cannot be achieved if the introduction of discovery measures is combined with main proceedings.

The remainder of this chapter will explain the types of discovery available in German patent litigation, their rationale, historical development and procedural mechanics. This broad approach to the topic of discovery and evidence reflects the dynamic and evolving nature of the discovery process in Germany, where a wide range of outcomes is possible depending on the case.

1. Appeal Court of Düsseldorf, decision of Nov. 8, 2012, 2 U 108/10, "Fluidflusssimulation II."

Commonly, the facts relevant to the infringement proceedings are openly accessible to the patentee. For instance, the contested product may be freely available on the market and can be dismantled, reverse engineered and then analyzed. In many cases, extrajudicial investigation carried out by the patentee on his own initiative is sufficient to set out these relevant facts in the written pleadings during the proceedings. Note that many disputes common to U.S. litigation do not exist in German infringement proceedings, in particular due to the fact that invalidity is tried separately from infringement, and because the doctrine of inequitable conduct is inapplicable in Germany. This consequently reduces the need for discovery on those issues in German proceedings.

The patentee may use various means at his disposal to conduct this investigation and analysis. For example, he could hire a private investigator or a private expert. The private investigator could help identify further factual material concerning the contested embodiment. A private expert might be retained to carry out testing, or analyze the infringing quality of the product, such as the composition of a chemical substance.

Information on the contested method and documents that were discovered through proceedings before courts of other jurisdictions could also be used as evidence (for instance through a "*saisie contrefaçon*" in France or in Belgium). U.S. discovery may also form an important source of evidence, and could help point the way to independent investigation in Germany, unless applicable protective orders limit such use.[2] If the accused embodiments are not available on the German territory or if the patented method is implemented outside Germany, a diligent counsel needs to include in his assessment the possibility of applying legal tools available in foreign countries. With respect to the U.S., an important tool is a request under section 1782 of the U.S. Federal Rules of Civil Procedure which allows the conduct of discovery (testimony or document production) through a U.S. federal district court for use in a foreign court such as a German court. Section 1782 requests may be initiated either by a letter rogatory issued by the German court or directly by the party to the German proceedings, i.e., without any letter rogatory, addressed to the U.S. district court. Furthermore, customs actions may also be used to gather information relevant for later patent infringement proceedings. If infringing products are detected and detained by customs, the right holder is usually informed about the origin of the product and their distribution channels and he may take samples of the shipment to analyze, test and prove the infringing quality of the products.[3]

1.2. Burden of Proof and Duty of Presentation

The burden of proof normally rests with the plaintiff, although the duty of presentation may shift between the parties. The patentee's duty to gather information (fact

2. It needs to be taken into account that a German court is not bound by a protective order issued by a U.S. court. The protective order is addressed to the parties of the U.S. proceedings, for which reason it is likely that a German court would disregard U.S. protective orders, in case a party introduces material from U.S. proceedings into German proceedings and thus violates that order.
3. *See* Ch. 14, "Customs Actions."

presentation) prior to commencing the lawsuit parallels his burden of proof: He must normally prove each element of the asserted claims of action to prevail, and must substantiate every element of the claim.

At the beginning the plaintiff bears the burden of proof as well as the duty of presentation, but assuming the plaintiff has fulfilled his duty and sufficiently substantiated his claim by means of facts in the complaint, the duty then shifts to the defendant to present facts, and he is obliged to substantiate and give reasons why he believes that a factual assertion of the patentee is not true, incorrect or incomplete. This obligation results from §138 of the Code of Civil Procedure.[4] Unlike in the U.S., a bare denial is insufficient, with one exception: facts that were not subject to the party's own activities or personal perception and are beyond reasonable investigative efforts may be denied without giving reasons (§138(3) of the Code of Civil Procedure).[5]

The burden continues to shift as new facts are brought forth. Furthermore, facts must be truthfully and completely disclosed in response to allegations raised by the other party.[6] The burden of proof normally stays with the plaintiff. Nevertheless, if the defendant does not sufficiently comply with his duty of presentation in response of the plaintiff's factual submissions, these submissions could then be deemed as true. This could lead to a shift of the burden of proof from plaintiff to defendant. Through this method of allegation and response German courts attempt to spur efficient and effective fact disclosure.

2. HISTORICAL DEVELOPMENT

Historically, attempts to obtain discovery in Germany were not successful. And while the legal system did provide for mechanisms of compulsory discovery, its requirements were usually too difficult to overcome.[7] However, in a landmark decision in 2002[8] (the "*Faxkarte*" case), the Federal Supreme Court confronted the need for discovery and allowed for a broader application of inspection rights and compelled document production. At the center of this decision was source code that allegedly infringed a copyright. The source code was not accessible to the patentee/right holder. The patentee asserted that the defendant illegally copied the software and was now producing a practically identical user interface. The lower court found that the plaintiff/patentee failed to prove copyright infringement because he was not able to

4. *§138 Code of Civil Procedure*
   (1) Statements made by the parties concerning factual circumstances shall be complete and truthful.
   (2) Each party shall address facts alleged by the other side.
   (3) Facts which are not expressly denied shall be deemed as admitted, unless the intention to deny them is manifest from other statements of the party.
   (4) A declaration of lack of knowledge concerning facts is permissible only as to facts which were not subject to the party's own activities or personal perception. (unofficial translation)
5. Federal Supreme Court, BGHZ 100, 190, 196.
6. Federal Supreme Court, X ZR 114/00, GRUR 2004, 268, "blasenfreie Gummibahn II."
7. Federal Supreme Court, X ZR 18/84, GRUR 1985, 512, "Druckbalken."
8. Federal Supreme Court, I ZR 45/01, GRUR 2002, 1046 "Faxkarte."

demonstrate that the underlying source code was identical, and that the indirect allegations of illegal conduct were not sufficient. At the same time, and pursuant to standard German practice as described above, the accused infringer had not been required by the lower courts to disclose the source code, which would of course have clarified whether or not the code was identical and therefore infringing. The Federal Supreme Court overruled this decision and established that the law must grant the copyright-holder a right to preserve and demonstrate evidence of possible copyright infringement by suitable procedural measures (here: the disclosure of the defendant's source code). Even though the "*Faxkarte*" decision concerned a copyright matter, its reasoning has been extended by the infringement courts to all intellectual property rights, in particular to patents.[9]

The "*Faxkarte*" decision relies on provisions of the Civil Code.[10] Their procedural enforcement contained some legal uncertainties, which are today addressed by §140(c) of the German Patent Act, introduced in July 2008.[11] This new provision transposes the European Directive on the Enforcement of Intellectual Property rights of April 29, 2004[12] into German national law. Even though the provisions of the Civil Code[13] that were applicable in the "*Faxkarte*" decision are still in force and could still be applied in parallel,[14] §140c of the Patent Act provides the principal basis for obtaining discovery under German procedural law.

3. DISCOVERY BEFORE FILING A COMPLAINT

3.1. Requirements

3.1.1. "Sufficient Probability" of Patent Infringement

The first section of §140c of the German Patent Act provides:

> (1) Any person who, with sufficient probability, uses a patented invention in contravention of §§9 to 13 may be required by the right holder or another authorised person to present a document or to tolerate the inspection of an object that is within his power of disposal or of a method that is the subject matter of the patent if such is necessary to establish such party's claims. If there is a sufficient probability of an infringement to a commercial extent, the claim also extends to the submission of banking, financial or trading documents. If the alleged infringer claims that such information is confidential, the court shall adopt the necessary measures to ensure the protection required in the individual case.[15]

9. Appeal Court of Düsseldorf, decision of Aug. 13, 2015, 15 U 3/14, "Digitalwandler;" Federal Supreme Cour, GRUR 2013, 316, "Rohrmuffe"; Federal Supreme Cour, GRUR 2006, 962, "Restschadstoffentfernung."
10. Sections 809, 810 Civil Code.
11. The provision can be found in Ch. 17, s. 3.
12. 2004/48/EEC.
13. Sections 809, 810 Civil Code.
14. Federal Supreme Court, I ZR 63/06, GRUR 2009, 515, "Motorradreiniger."
15. Unofficial translation.

Accordingly, if the patentee is in a position to show a "sufficient probability" that his patent is infringed, he may seek production of documents and the inspection of the object in dispute, as set forth below. The existence of a sufficient probability is a substantive requirement that needs to be demonstrated in the request. Requests that are based on mere allegations, the proverbial "shot in the dark," will be dismissed. However, the requirement of sufficient probability of infringement is fulfilled where concrete indications pointing to an infringement could be deduced from a thorough examination of the defendant's commercial catalogues and advertising.[16] Difficulties as to whether there is in fact an infringing activity shall in principle, even due to the complexity of the underlying technology, not minimize the success of a request. For instance, a request may even be successful if it is foreseeable that the question of infringement will later require the involvement of a technical expert in the subsequent main proceedings. A request of inspection will however be unsuccessful if it can be clearly denied without the help of an expert that the contested product or method falls outside the scope of protection of the asserted patent.[17] Courts apply slightly different standards as to the existence of "sufficient probability," for which reason the selection of the right court is an important element for the success of the request.

Finally, the object or the document to be inspected must be in the possession or custody of the accused infringer. At least, he must be entitled to a claim of surrender in case the item to be inspected is in the possession of a third party.[18]

3.1.2. *Necessity and Principle of Proportionality*

The request must comply with the principle of proportionality. First of all, the patentee must show that he is unable to obtain the evidence in any other suitable way. The claim would thus be denied if there are other appropriate and accessible means to obtain the desired evidence. The plaintiff must demonstrate in detail that he tried all available avenues and each attempt failed.

Section of §140c of the Patent Act states that the claim seeking judicially enforced discovery "is excluded if its enforcement is disproportionate in the individual case."[19] Generally, the interests of the right holder predominate, but there might nevertheless be situations where the desired discovery intervention would be considered disproportionate to the infringing activity. The proportionality may however exceptionally be denied in a case where there are serious doubts as to the validity of the patent or its infringement. Different courts and chambers weigh such interests differently, but local counsel in Germany should be able to reasonably predict, on a case-by-case basis, the extent to which judicial discovery intervention is likely.

16. Appeal Court of Karlsruhe, decision of Oct. 16, 2012, W 6 72/12.
17. Appeal Court of Düsseldorf, InstGE 11, 298, "Weißmacher."
18. District Court of Nürnberg/Fürth, InstGE 5, 153, "Betriebsspionage."
19. Unofficial translation.

3.2. Procedural Implementation of the Request

3.2.1. General Outline

The discovery claim may be pursued through main action proceedings. Often it is desirable to pursue a discovery claim through preliminary injunction proceedings (§140c (3) Patent Act). Accordingly, at an early stage, before the infringement suit is filed, the right holder, usually the patentee or its licensee, may file for a preliminary injunction enabling the inspection of a device or a machine. Such a court order could be rendered ex parte, in view of surprising the accused infringer and to avoid any manipulations of the evidence by the accused infringer.

It should be noted that the scope of any order, ex parte or otherwise, would be limited to an object or document specified by the right holder in his request.[20] It is not a general search right and even in its broadest conception does not approach the scope of discovery proceedings known in the U.S.

If the discovery claim is enforced through preliminary injunction proceedings, it is questionable whether the applicant must file the request as soon as possible to satisfy a requirement of urgency. This requirement is normally applicable to preliminary injunction proceedings.[21] Some courts are of the opinion that a delay could be detrimental to the request,[22] other courts, such as the Appeal Court of Düsseldorf, do not apply a time requirement.[23]

Another instrument of obtaining discovery in the course or outside of patent infringement proceedings results from §485 Code of Civil Procedure. This instrument is called "independent evidentiary proceedings." Its admissibility follows its own rules and does not depend on the requirements of a substantive discovery claim, such as the claim resulting from § 140 c Patent Act. The request based on §485 Code of Civil Procedure is admissible if there is a *"concern that the evidence might be lost, or that it will become difficult to use it"*.[24] In addition, such request may be filed prior to legal proceedings to involve an expert preparation with a written report concerning the "*state or the value of an object*"[25] and other related aspects with an object to be discovered. This instrument may thus represent a helpful option in case the requirements of the substantive discovery claim are not fulfilled or difficult to prove. The measures of §485 Code of Civil Procedure may also be combined with a preliminary injunction based on § 140 c Patent Act.

---

20. Federal Supreme Court, I ZR 187/01, GRUR 2004, 420, "Kontrollbesuch."
21. *See* Ch. 9, s. 3.2.1 "Urgency."
22. Appeal Court of Cologne, OLG-Report 2009, 258; Appeal Court of Karlsruhe, decision of May 18, 2010—6 W 28/10, Appeal Court of Nürnberg, dec. of Aug. 17, 2015, "3 W 1412/15."
23. Appeal Court of Düsseldorf, InstGE 12, 108; Appeal Court of Frankfort/Main, decision of Jun. 10, 2010—15 U 192/09.
24. Section 485 (1) CCP.
25. Section 485 (2) CCP.

3.2.2. Protection of the Defendant's Secrecy Interests

Secrecy interests of the accused infringer will have to be sufficiently protected. This is independent upon which legal form of discovery is applied. §140c (3) of the Patent Act considers valid secrecy interests and states: "The court shall take necessary measures to ensure the protection of confidential information. This shall apply in particular in cases in which the injunction is imposed without prior hearing of the opposing party."[26] The text does not further specify how this should be implemented and leaves it to the courts to decide on a case-by-case basis. It has already been outlined by the Federal Supreme Court in the "*Faxkarte*" decision that the secrecy conflict should be solved flexibly by including in the inspection order a provision that takes into account both the right holder's interest in the inspection and the defendant's interest in secrecy. If discovery measures of §485 Code of Civil Procedure are combined with a summary measure based on § 140 c Patent Act involving the preparation of an expert opinion, secrecy interests may be protected through the application of the following steps:[27]

- First, the court appoints an independent expert (the right holder proposes a suitable person in the request).
- The expert carries out the investigation (e.g., the inspection of a machine that is located on the premises of the defendant). If the accused infringer refuses the investigation (for instance, he refuses access to the location), police power could be applied. The accused infringer is not required to actively support the inspection. His duty is mainly confined to positively tolerate the inspection.[28] Nevertheless, in case of a software-related infringement, the accused infringer might be obliged to provide passwords necessary to execute the inspection.[29]
- To efficiently protect the interests of the accused infringer, only the right holder's legal representatives, namely his attorney-at-law and/or patent attorney (and not the right holder himself) shall be admitted to attend the inspection. In addition, the right holder's representatives will be bound by court order not to disclose to his client (the right holder) the information he obtains during the inspection. This is an unusual situation for the right holder's legal representatives, who are not allowed to communicate to their client the results of the investigation. They must wait until the court lifts the secrecy obligation. The secrecy obligation under which attorneys may receive confidential information is considered to be sufficient for protecting the accused infringer's secrecy rights.[30] Attorneys-at-law and patent attorneys are

26. Unofficial translation.
27. District Court of Düsseldorf, InstGE 8, 103—Etikettiermaschine.
28. Federal Supreme Court, WuM 2007, 209.
29. Federal Supreme Court, WuM 2007, 209.
30. Federal Supreme Court, Nov. 16, 2009, X ZB 37/08, IIC 2010, 724 (in English), "Lichtbogen-schnürung."

considered "independent judicial bodies"[31] who are expected not to violate a court order of secrecy, all the more since such violation would represent a criminal offense.[32]

- The expert then establishes an expert report.
- The expert submits the report to the court.
- The court forwards the report to the representatives of both sides.[33] The report is not yet forwarded to the claimant (or right holder). The accused infringer (defendant) can then make statements regarding his secrecy interests.

The court then decides whether and to what extent the findings of the expert are to be disclosed to the right holder and to what extent the secrecy obligation of the right holder's representative may be lifted. This includes a weighing of the reciprocal interests.[34] The interests of the right holder typically prevail if a patent infringement can be deduced from the report. If the report indeed contains confidential information that should not be disclosed to the right holder, then there are different means that could be applied. For instance, the secrecy-relevant parts of the report could be redacted[35] before forwarding the document to the right holder. This is, in a first step, the accused infringer may be asked to redact those parts of the expert report which he claims contain protectable "secret information". The disclosure of the redacted report to the right holder poses no problem.[36] Which items in dispute that have been redacted, i.e., the allegedly secret information, are to be disclosed against the will of the accused infringer depends then on a court decision weighing the secrecy interests of the accused infringer the and patentee's interests. As indicated, the interests of the right holder typically prevail if the court is able to conclude that the report sufficiently supports the allegation of patent infringement.[37] If the court concludes that no prevailing secrecy interests of the accused infringer are concerned, the right holder's representative will be fully released from his secrecy obligation. This mechanism could also be combined with other available means for protecting the secrecy of confidential information, such as exclusion of the public from the hearing or from the pronouncement of the decision.

3.2.3. Scope and Aim of the Request

While the discovery request may target a discrete object for inspection, such as a machine on the defendant's premises, the accused infringer is not required to actively support the inspection. His duty is merely to render the inspection technically possible. In the above example he would have to provide access to the court-appointed

31. In German: "Organ der Rechtspflege" (§1 BRAO).
32. Federal Supreme Court, Nov. 16, 2009, X ZB 37/08, IIC 2010, 724 (in English), "Lichtbogenschnürung."
33. Federal Supreme Court, Nov. 16, 2009, X ZB 37/08, IIC 2010, 724 (in English), "Lichtbogenschnürung."
34. Appeal Court of Düsseldorf, InstGE 10, 198, "zeitversetztes Fernsehen."
35. District Court of Düsseldorf, InstGE 6, 189, "Walzen- Formgebungsmaschine."
36. Appeal Court of Düsseldorf, Aug. 20, 2012, I_2 W 13/12.
37. Appeal Court of Düsseldorf, InstGE 10, 198, "zeitversetztes Fernsehen."

inspector, including access to his property if that is where the machine is located. In the software context he may have to provide passwords when necessary to execute software. Often, a simple inspection of the object is not sufficient and a dismantling of the object—even when such dismantling amounts to destruction—is necessary to determine if it is infringing. The extent to which a destructive modification of the object is permitted requires a weighing of interests and might depend on whether and to what extent the patentee/right holder compensates for the cost of the modified or destroyed object. In some circumstances, the inspection could also include the seizure of samples.[38] The court's experience and common sense of course plays a role.

The discovery request could also cover the production of documents or the disclosure of the source code.[39] This includes documents that relate to the contested device or apparatus with which contested method is carried out, such as user manuals, operating guidelines, engineering drawings, etc. In case infringements being committed on a commercial scale, the claim may even be extended to the submission of banking, financial or trading documents (§140c (1) Patent Act). All this discovery would not lead to U.S. style discovery, however, because the request would still be limited to documents and objects that are sufficiently specified by the patentee/right holder. He may not simply ask for "all documents related to" or all "relevant documents" as might be claimed in American discovery proceedings. The right holder is rather required to sufficiently specify the focus of the discovery in the request. To some extent, his disadvantageous situation is taken into account, namely that his insight into the accused infringer's business is limited, but this does not release him from a basic duty to sufficiently specify the focus of the discovery.[40]

4. DISCOVERY AFTER FILING THE COMPLAINT

4.1. Discovery According to §140c Patent Act

The demand for discovery according to §140c Patent Act is considered a substantive and judicially enforceable claim of the patentee. It is typically a claim which is asserted and enforced in preparation for a lawsuit on the merits. Nevertheless, the claim may also be asserted as part of the general infringement-related proceedings resulting from the patent[41] (i.e., the right to prevent the accused infringer from using the patent, rendering of accounts, etc.). The parallel assertion of the discovery claim, together with the other patent infringement-related claims, by means of the same lawsuit on the merits, may prompt the court to rule on the different claims at different times. Indeed, if the court determines, after a hearing, that the submitted evidence is not completely sufficient to prove the infringement, a partial judgment (§301 Code of Civil Procedure)

38. Federal Supreme Court, GRUR 2013, 316, "Rohrmuffe."
39. Federal Supreme Court, GRUR 2013, 509, I ZR 90/09, "UniBasic IDOS."
40. Federal Supreme Court, I ZR 187/01, GRUR 2004, 420, "Kontrollbesuch."
41. District Court of Düsseldorf, decision of Aug. 10, 2010, 4b O 54/09 (not published); Appeal Court of Düsseldorf, decision of Nov. 8, 2012, 2 U 108/10, "Fluidflusssimulation II."

could be rendered concerning only the discovery claims, and a decision on the other asserted claims could come after the ordered discovery has been implemented.[42]

4.2. Procedural Means (§§142, 144 Code of Civil Procedure)

German procedural law provides additional mechanisms to allow patentees to gather evidence for proving infringement. However, in contrast to §140 c Patent Act these procedural means are not substantively and judicially enforceable claims.

According to §§142 and 144 Code of Civil Procedure, a court may order the disclosure of documents and the production of the contested device and product, provided that disclosure be proportionate and appropriate. The likely use of the protected subject matter may also be taken into account when rendering an order for disclosure. These provisions are as follows:

> §142 Code of Civil Procedure:
>
> The court can order that a party to the proceedings or a third party discloses a deed or other documents which are in its possession and which a party to the proceedings has referred to. To do so, the court may set a deadline and order that the disclosed documents are to remain, for a predetermined period, in the possession of the court. (...)[43]
>
> §144 Code of Civil Procedure:
>
> The court may order the inspection or an expert opinion. For that purpose the court may order, from a party to the proceedings or a third party, the production of an object which is in its possession and may set a deadline therefore. Is may also order the acquiescence of it provided a home is not concerned. (...)[44]

Accordingly, §§142 and 144 Code of Civil Procedure may help if it turns out during the proceedings that submitted evidence is not yet sufficient. A disclosure and inspection order requires that such disclosure be suitable and necessary to clarify the facts of the case, and that the request be proportionate and appropriate. When a court weighs the factors before rendering a disclosure order, the court will consider the protected nature of the rights of the party. A disclosure order may be made where there is a likelihood of patent infringement. Similar to § 140 a Patent Act, an order based on §§142 and 144 Code of Civil Procedure requires that the right holder show at least a sufficient probability that the patent is infringed.[45] Unless this minimum requirement is met, the court is not under duty to issue an order based on §§142 and 144 Code of Civil Procedure.[46] Where the documents requested contain commercially sensitive or confidential information, they may be protected by redaction and/or the different legal means available under the German procedural law:

42. District Court of Düsseldorf, decision of Aug. 10, 2010, 4b O 54/09 (not published).
43. Unofficial translation.
44. Unofficial translation.
45. Federal Supreme Court, GRUR 2013, 316, "Rohrmuffe."
46. Federal Supreme Court, GRUR 2013, 316, "Rohrmuffe."

In its decision of August 1, 2006, the Federal Supreme Court[47] advised:
"German law must be construed in such a way that it complies with the requirements of the TRIPS Agreement (Federal Supreme Court, GRUR 2002, 1046, "Faxkarte"...). Like the substantive provision of §809 Civil Code, the provision of §142 new Code of Civil Procedure is a means of overcoming a plaintiff's inability to produce evidence, as may particularly occur in the field of the especially vulnerable technical property rights. In the field of industrial property, a provision like that of §142 new Code of Civil Procedure also has the function of executing the measures that are required for the production of evidence pursuant to Article 6 Enforcement Directive, 2004/48/EC, to be implemented into national law by 26 April 2006, and which are known in French law in the form of the "saisie contrefaçon" or in the laws of the United Kingdom in the form of the search order ("Anton Piller Order").[48]

This decision demonstrates the effort of the Federal Supreme Court of recent years to effectively reach the international standards codified in the Agreement on Trade-Related Aspects of Intellectual Property Rights (TRIPS) and in the Enforcement Directive. This effort must be understood in light of the limited discovery that characterizes the history of German civil court procedures. The more flexible approach, which finds its basis in a recent case law starting with the *Faxkarte* decision in 2002 and the introduction of more discovery friendly provisions in the following years, is still evolving.

4.3. Reports of Court-Appointed Experts

Court experts may be appointed to clarify technical aspects of the case. Their function consists in providing the court with technical knowledge and expertise. They may be appointed, for instance, if the interpretation of a complex patent is problematic or if properties of the accused embodiment are in dispute and require a more complex technical examination. The court may appoint an expert if such an examination is required, or even if the court simply wants to be educated in an area of technical knowledge it does not already possess.

The expert may provide his understanding of technical terms used in the patent. His involvement may also be important to determine the scope of the relevant prior art and the common general knowledge at the priority date, in order to assess how the skilled person would understand the disclosures in the patent.[49] However, the court is not permitted to simply adopt the view of the expert, or to leave the construction of the patent claims entirely to an expert.[50]

In general, German courts are reluctant to appoint experts, and in the vast majority of cases, the court renders a decision without appointing an expert. The

47. Federal Supreme Court, Aug. 1, 2006, X ZR 114/03, IIC 2007, 97 (in English) "Restschadstoffentfernung."
48. Unofficial translation.
49. Federal Supreme Court, X ZR 176/99, GRUR 2001, 770, "Kabeldurchführung."
50. Federal Supreme Court, X ZR 76/04, GRUR 2006, 131, "Seitenspiegel."

probability of the involvement of a court-appointed expert differs from court to court[51] and depends on the subject matter of the case. Based on the authors' experience, the appointment of a court expert occurs in less than one quarter of all cases. The Federal Supreme Court[52] holds that courts with significant experience in patent matters may issue a decision on technical questions without the appointment of court experts, since usually the parties' submissions within the scope of the duties of presentation (see above)[53] suffice to make clear the technical aspects of the case and provide a sufficient basis for a decision.

If the court does order the appointment of an expert, the parties are usually asked to provide names of experts within the technical field concerned (such as professors). Parties should avoid identifying experts with whom they already have relationships. An expert that worked for, or still keeps a scientific or business relationship with either party, might be disqualified.[54] To avoid any disqualification of the expert, the parties should not directly contact him prior and during the proceedings.

4.4. Witnesses

Fact witnesses are rare in German patent infringement proceedings. Compared to the U.S., many grounds of dispute that would necessitate witnesses do not exist in German proceedings. There are no defenses of inequitable conduct. Facts outside the patent document are mainly irrelevant for the construction of the claim and, if they are relevant, they usually do not require testimony from a fact witness. Prosecution file estoppel is inapplicable.[55] All critical issues concerning damages are raised in separate proceedings.[56] These areas for potential disputes are thus taken away from the main infringement proceedings. Accordingly, there are only a few areas where a witness could be of use for evidence taking in German infringement proceedings. One exception might be the situation where the defendant asserts a right based on prior use (§12 Patent Act), for example if he claims that he independently invented the subject matter of the asserted patent. Another exception would be if the patent was fraudulently obtained by the plaintiff.[57]

5. ATTORNEY-CLIENT PRIVILEGES

In German court proceedings, it is unlikely that a court would order a party to disclose correspondence with its German attorneys. In U.S. court proceedings, the situation regarding a possible disclosure of correspondence of a party with its German or

51. *See* Ch. 8, s. 3.6.3: District Court of Düsseldorf: Low; District Court of Mannheim: Middle; District Court of Munich: Higher Probability.
52. Federal Supreme Court, X ZR 126/01, GRUR 2005, 569, 571, "Blasfolienherstellung." *See* Ch. 11, s. 1.2.
53. *See* Ch. 11, s. 1.2.
54. Federal Supreme Court, X ZR 126/01, GRUR 2008, 191, "Sachverständigenablehnung II."
55. *See* Ch. 10, s. 3.2.3.2 "Inadmissibility of Prosecution File Estoppel."
56. *See* Ch. 8, s. 5.4 "Rendering of Accounts and Lawsuit concerning the Amount of Damages."
57. *See* Ch. 8, s. 3.3.2 "Usurpation."

European attorneys is more complex. Unlike under U.S. law, general discovery proceedings are not recognized in German civil proceedings. Basically, no party is obliged to give the other side access to any document or other communication, such as e-mails, memos or letters. This is mainly the reason why "attorney-client privileges" have a different meaning in Germany than in U.S. litigation. The plaintiff has a limited right to request disclosure of documents from the defendant, which generally would not include attorney-client communications. To the extent such communications would exceptionally be relevant to the dispute, there are nonetheless mechanisms to secure these documents against production. This is, German attorneys-at-law and patent attorneys have a special right to refuse to give evidence, which sufficiently protects them from disclosing documents relating to their clients (§383(1) N° 6 Code of Civil Procedure: 6. "*Persons to whom facts are entrusted by virtue of their office, profession or status, the nature of which mandates their confidentiality, or the confidentiality of which is mandated by law, where their testimony would concern facts to which the confidentiality obligation refers.*). Indeed, German attorneys-at-law are bound by a professional secrecy obligation for both general advice and litigation (section 43a (2) Federal Attorney Regulation (BRAO). This duty relates to everything that has become known to the lawyer in connection with his professional relationship to a client. The duty thus covers any document or material that has become known to him in his professional relationship with the client, irrespective of its specific type or content.

For professional representatives at the EPO (European patent attorneys) the attorney-client privilege is explicitly enshrined in Rule 153 EPC:

(1) Where advice is sought from a professional representative in his capacity as such, all communications between the professional representative and his client or any other person, relating to that purpose and falling under Article 2 of the Regulation on discipline for professional representatives, are permanently privileged from disclosure in proceedings before the European Patent Office, unless such privilege is expressly waived by the client.

(2) Such privilege from disclosure shall apply, in particular, to any communication or document relating to:
   (a) the assessment of the patentability of an invention;
   (b) the preparation or prosecution of a European patent application;
   (c) any opinion relating to the validity, scope of protection or infringement of a European patent or a European patent application.

It is questionable whether the communication with in-house counsel is protected as well. An in-house counsel may act in his capacity as his employer's legal advisor. Being admitted to the bar, he observes a general duty of confidentiality[58] a breach of which represents a criminal offense under §203 Criminal Law. Such in-house counsel admitted as an attorney-at-law needs to have a lawyers' office separate from the offices

58. Section 2 BORA (Regulations concerning the Legal Profession).

of his employer. To best ensure the privilege, it is thus required that communications between in-house counsel and employees, officers or directors of the company be separately stored and kept in the counsel's single custody. Accordingly, communications containing legal advice, rather than business advice, are likely privileged even if they are made with in-house attorneys, although this is less certain than in the U.S. However, not every in-house lawyer in Germany is admitted to the bar. There are thus two requirements which need to be fulfilled to secure the data from production: First, that the in-house be admitted to practice as an attorney-at-law in Germany and, second, that the information be obtained in the course of providing legal advice and cannot be attributed to management, controlling, accounting or similar services.

6. UPCOMING: DISCOVERY AT THE UPC

Even though U.S.-style pre-trial discovery is not possible under the upcoming UPC system, at least some discovery comparable to the German national standards may be undertaken through judicial measures, in particular, if independent fact-finding is not successful. According to Article 59 UPCA, the court may order (at the request of one party, provided that reasonable evidence is produced in support of the claim) the "opposing party or a third party to present evidence" which is under their control. More stringent measures are possible according to Article 60(1) UPCA. Accordingly, if the patentee is in a position to show a "sufficient probability" that the patent is infringed, he may obtain evidence by means of a variety of measures. This may include that the court simply orders the production of evidence[59] or that the court orders measures such as the inspection of the premises where the object in dispute is preserved, and the physical seizure of the allegedly infringing goods including the materials and implements used in the production and/or distribution of these goods, as well as any related documents.

The existence of a sufficient probability of infringement needs to be demonstrated in the request. This criterion[60] is met where it was possible to deduce concrete indications pointing to an infringement from a thorough examination of the defendant's commercial catalogues and advertising. Requests based on mere allegations would be dismissed.

Measures to preserve evidence may even be ordered without hearing the other party, in particular if any delay is likely to cause irreparable harm to the applicant or where there is a demonstrable risk of evidence being destroyed or otherwise becoming unavailable.

The measure to preserve evidence will cease to have effect, at the defendant's request, if the applicant does not, within a period not exceeding 31 calendar days or 20 working days, whichever is the longer, bring action leading to a decision on the merits of the case before the court.[61]

59. Article 59 UPCA.
60. Rule 190 RoP.
61. Rule 198 RoP.

CHAPTER 12
Damages

1. GENERAL REMARKS

The patentee, or its exclusive licensee,[1] can obtain an award of monetary damages following a successful infringement ruling. As described in Chapter 8, section 5.4, after winning an infringement trial in first instance, the patentee must post a bond, and may demand the accused infringer to render an accounting. This accounting should enable the patentee to calculate the amount of damages. The patentee may then claim a particular amount to compensate for his injury. Often the parties will resolve the amount of damages out of court. If no agreement can be reached, the patentee must file a separate lawsuit seeking a court determination of the damages (so-called *Höheverfahren*). These proceedings, which are ancillary to the main infringement trial, are confined to the measuring of the amount. Like the infringement trial, there is no jury.

Unlike under U.S. law, there are no punitive damages in Germany for patent infringement. Nonetheless, it is recognized that infringement damages must be sufficiently high to provide a deterrent effect.[2]

There are three methods for measuring the actual damages:[3]

(1) reasonable royalty;
(2) patentee's lost profits; or
(3) infringer's profits.

This damages framework arises from the following statutory sections. Section 139(2) of the Patent Act provides that:

1. The non-exclusive licensee is principally not entitled to claim damages. He is not harmed by an unauthorized use of the patent as he would have anyway to accept other licensees of the patent besides him.
2. BGBl. I S. 1191.
3. Federal Supreme Court, X ZR 60/06, GRUR 2008, 94, "Zerkleinerungsvorrichtung."

> Any person who commits these acts intentionally or negligently shall be liable for compensation to the injured party for the damage suffered therefrom. For the assessment of the compensation account can be taken of the profits, which the infringer has made due to the infringement. The assessment of the damages can also be based on the amount which would have been due as a reasonable compensation if the infringer had requested authorization for the use.[4]

The "reasonable royalty" calculation method and the "patentee's lost profits" are explicitly mentioned in §139(2) of the Patent Act, whereas the "the infringer's lost profits" can be claimed according to general civil rules (§§249, 252 of the Civil Code).

It is up to the injured party to select the appropriate methodology, depending on the figures provided by the accused infringer. Even though the provisions of §139(2) Patent Act seem to leave this open, it is impermissible to mix or combine these various damages calculation methods.[5] The injured party can only select one of the three methods for calculating the damages. Following is an overview of the various damages methodologies recognized by German courts, and a summary of how these play out in practice.

2. REASONABLE ROYALTY

The award of a "reasonable royalty" provides a baseline measure of damages in those cases where the lost profits of the infringer or patentee do not justify a higher award. The royalty calculation is premised on the principle that an unauthorized user should not be better positioned than an authorized licensee.[6] The reasonable royalty is thus the price on which reasonable parties would have agreed if they had known the extent of the use of the patent when concluding a hypothetical agreement.[7] For this reason, this calculation method is also commonly called a "license analogy." Following is a framework for arriving at the appropriate royalty base and royalty rate:

2.1. Royalty Base (*Bezugsgröße*)

The royalty base for calculating royalty damages typically refers to the net revenues[8] achieved by the infringer with the sales of the product or assembly. The royalty-based calculation method relies on an abstract assessment of the infringing sales without investigating whether or to which extent the revenues are caused using the infringed patent or whether the accused product or assembly could have been sold at the same price even without using the accused features.[9]

4. Unofficial translation.
5. This results from the reasons of the legislator accompanying the Act when implementing §139 (2) Patent Act: BR-DR 64/07, 76.
6. Federal Supreme Court, X ZR 36/80, GRUR 1982, 286, "Fersenabstützvorrichtung."
7. Federal Supreme Court, X ZR 54/93, GRUR 1995, 578, 581, "Steuereinrichtung II;"
8. These are the revenues excluding sales tax: Federal Supreme Court, GRUR 2010, 239, "BTK"
9. Federal Supreme Court, GRUR 2010, 239, "BTK"

Where the defendant sells an assembly that is composed of many different components or features but the inventive aspects of the patent-in-suit are directed to only one or several components, parts or features of the assembly, the assessment additionally involves the question whether the royalty rate is to be applied against the revenue from the whole product or assembly or only of parts of it. This typically depends on what objective parties would have hypothetically considered as an appropriate reference in a license agreement. According to the case law of the Federal Supreme Court,[10] it has first to be determined which part(s) of the product or assembly is/are characterized by the invention. These are the parts of the assembly which considerably improve the device with respect to the asserted advantages of the invention of the patent-in-suit. If such parts can be identified within the concerned assembly, the next question is whether such parts represent marketable units and can be individually be bought on the market.[11] If this is the case, it is typically suggested to apply the royalty against the value of the marketable unit in which resides the invention and not of the entire assembly. The assessment thus leads to the smallest marketable unit of the entire assembly. This is similar to the "smallest salable patent practicing unit" (SSPPU) concept in U.S. patent law. For instance, if the invention concerns a part of the assembly (for instance: passenger car rear mirror), which can be bought as part of or together with the whole assembly (in the example the car), it can be assumed that the parties would have agreed on a royalty which is applied against the smallest salable part, namely here the car rear mirror. Of particular importance for that assessment are industry customs. In cases where the smaller part is not separately marketable, or the technical improvement is applicable to the entire assembly, then the royalty rate may be applied to the entire assembly. In addition, a strong interrelationship between the royalty rate and royalty base needs to be taken into account. That is, if it is not possible to refer to a small marketable unit and if consequently the entire assembly must be used as the royalty base, the applicable royalty rate will have to be reduced, thus providing a balancing effect.

For determining the base, all sales which are triggered by an offer made in Germany by the accused infringer are accounted for. This even includes sales to customers situated outside Germany. The base excludes accessory charges such as operational costs like sales taxes, freight costs, cash discounts and so on. Typically, the figures for determining the base will be obtained through the accounting ordered upon the successful conclusion of an infringement trial.[12] In case of an infringed process claim, it is commonly accepted to calculate the royalties on the net sales price of the sold products that were produced with the patented process.[13]

10. Federal Supreme Court, X ZR 54/93, GRUR 1995, 578, 581, "Steuereinrichtung II."
11. Federal Supreme Court, X ZR 8/90, GRUR 1992, 599, "Teleskopzylinder"; Appeal Court Düsseldorf, decision of Jul. 17, 2009, 2 U 38/08, BeckRS 2010, 21821 "Kappaggregat."
12. See Ch. 8, s. 5.4.
13. Appeal Court Düsseldorf, InstGE 4, 165, "Spulkopf."

2.2. Royalty Rate

2.2.1. General

The amount of the royalty is based on a hypothetical negotiation, namely what would have been due as a reasonable compensation if the infringer had requested authorization for the use on the basis of a non-exclusive license agreement.[14] All relevant facts need to be taken into account to achieve as appropriate a rate as possible. The assessment should start by determining the usual royalties in the concerned market. If there are pre-existing license agreements, those shall first and foremost be used as a benchmark for calculating the royalty rate. If such pre-existing license agreements can be used for determining the royalty fee, it is widely accepted to considerably increase the fee in order to compensate any benefits to the infringer who was not required during the time of the infringing use to satisfy any duties of a licensee, such as keeping records to establish the royalty reports necessary under standard license agreements. In particular, the infringer compared to a licensee does not bear the risk of paying royalty fees for an invalid patent.[15]

If such agreements are not available, the court will look to customary industry practice. In the pharmaceutical sector, we have seen royalty rates up to 10%. Within the chemical sector generally we have seen rates up to 8%. These are the known peak rates, and values can of course vary. The situation is more modest in the sectors of mechanical engineering, where royalties of 3%–5% are usual. In the telecommunication area these values might be even lower. Customary rates form a rough starting point for the determination of the rate.

2.2.2. Specific Factors

Other factors that may influence the royalty rate include the following considerations, which point to the value of the patented invention:

- Technological and economic importance of the invention:[16] The most critical fact consists in the determination of the technical improvement itself, as provided by the patented invention. Of importance are the advantages offered by the invention in view of the state of the prior art. In particular, the rate would be higher in a case where it is particularly difficult if not impossible to circumvent the patented invention and if reasonable and feasible alternatives to the invention do not exist.

14. Appeal Court Karlsruhe, GRUR RR 2014, 55, "Schadensberechnung."
15. Royalties paid prior to the revocation of the patent are not reimbursable. The argument behind this concept is that the licensee had an advantage over its competitors due to factual existence of the patent until its revocation. See also District Court Mannheim, InstGE 12, 160, "Orange Book License"; District Court Munich I, NJOZ 2011, 1318, "Gülleausbreitungseinrichtung": The District Court Munich found an increase of 66% reasonable.
16. Federal Supreme Court, X ZR 19/92, GRUR 1993, 897, "Mogul Anlage."

- Interaction between the royalty base and the amount of the rate: If an invention concerns an assembly that is composed of different parts, the base will be assessed either on the value of the entire device or on the part that most directly embodies the invention (see above). If a bigger base is identified, that will tend to lead to a lower royalty rate.
- Volume of sales: Mass-produced products usually justify lower rates, due to lower profits gained per item, whereas high value products sold in smaller quantities may confer higher rates. A further indicator which is taken into account is the infringer's profit attributable to the infringing product.
- An elevating factor for the rate is premised on the consideration that the infringer did not bear the typical risks of a normal licensee. The normal licensee bears the risk of paying a license for an invalid patent, and is usually bound to a no-contest clause.[17]
- A factor that tends to favor a lower rate may be that the product or part of the assembly against which the royalty is assessed embodies other inventions unrelated to the patented invention. And another factor that may be identified to reduce the royalty rate is if it can be shown that the revenue from the sales of infringing products are attributable to the marketing efforts or business connections of the accused infringer, moreso than the technical benefit of the patented invention.[18]

Back damages are typically augmented with pre-judgment interest. It is understood that the infringer shall not benefit from the fact that the payment for damages is claimed and paid a long time after the use of the patent started. By analogy, a licensee is under the duty to continuously pay royalties after the conclusion of the agreement. Typically, the licensee is obliged to report and pay royalties for the use of the licensed patent at the beginning of each year for the past calendar year. This amount is typically due on February 1st for the past calendar year. A licensee in default would have to pay this default interest starting from that date for the past calendar year. It is accepted case law that the infringer must pay this default interest for the respective time of the infringing use just like a licensee in default.[19] Accordingly, he would have to pay interest for each past calendar year starting from February 1st up to the present, compounded. Due to fact that the use of the patent by the infringer might have started many years back, that element of the damages could amount to a large sum of money. The interest rate is significant, presently set (since January 1, 2002)[20] at eight

17. Appeal Court Karlsruhe, GRUR RR 2014, 55, "Schadensberechnung"; District Court Düsseldorf, InstGE 1999, 83, GRUR 2000, 690, "Reaktanzschleife."
18. Appeal Court Düsseldorf, InstGE 4, 165, "Spulkopf II."
19. Appeal Court Karlsruhe, GRUR RR 2014, 55, "Schadensberechnung"; Federal Supreme Court, GRUR 2010, 239, "BTK."
20. Section 288 (2) of the German Civil Cod: The amount was set prior to Jan. 1, 2002 at 5% over the basic rate of interest, and prior to May 1, 2000, at 3.5% over the basic rate of interest.

percentage points above the basic rate of interest. Pursuant to section 247 (2) of the German Civil Code, the Deutsche Bundesbank announces the current basic rate of interest in the Federal Law Gazette.[21]

3. LOST PROFITS OF THE RIGHT HOLDER

Another measure of damages is based on the actual losses that the patentee (or licensee) incurred because of the infringement. The patentee has the burden to prove the extent of its lost profits. In practice, this means that the patentee will have to open its books for the infringer, which may be undesirable from a competitive perspective. Moreover, the burden is on the patentee to show that it did indeed lose profits due to the infringing acts—this is akin to the concept of "but for" infringement under U.S. law. The assessment thus requires that the injured party (patentee or exclusive licensee) demonstrate and prove that he uses the patent, and that there is at least a probability that he would have realized the lost profits.[22] For instance, he can show that particular business dealings were not possible due to the infringing activity.[23] This is a concrete, but challenging, way for demonstrating lost profits, and requires showing that the injured party would have indeed satisfied the needs of the market. It also is possible to show and prove the amount of lost profits hypothetically, by demonstrating that through the normal course of business a certain level of profits would have been made but for the infringement. The injured party must sufficiently substantiate this assumption based on facts to enable the court to estimate the amount. According to §287 of the Code of Civil Procedure, the Court may then decide on this at its discretion by taking into consideration all the circumstances. Nevertheless, it is difficult to show in a normal market situation that the right holder would have made the sales but for the infringement. This calculation methodology tends to be used most successfully in well-defined markets.

4. PROFITS MADE BY THE INFRINGER

The third method for calculating damages is based on the profits made by the infringer. Section 139(2) of the GPA explicitly states that *"when assessing the compensation, consideration may also be given to the profit which the infringer has obtained by infringing the right."* Most lawsuits seeking a court determination of damages are based on this framework. The court will apply some discretion in determining the amount (§287 of the Code of Civil Procedure) considering the factual circumstances as a whole.[24] The calculation method does not consider whether the harmed right holder

21. Previously and currently applicable basic rate of interest can be found on the website of the Deutsche Bundesbank: https://www.bundesbank.de.
22. Federal Supreme Court, I ZR 132/60, GRUR 1962, 509, "Dia-Rähmchen II."
23. Federal Supreme Court, VIII ZR 392/03, NJW 2006, 843, "Abstrakte Berechnung entgangenen Gewinns."
24. Appeal Court Düsseldorf, InstGE 5, 251, BeckRS 2005, 10332, "Lifter"; District Court Düsseldorf, decision of Jun. 30, 2009, 4a 146/08, "Rolladen II."

was in the position to make the profits on his own. Thus, it is not necessary that the right holder possesses its own operation enabling the production of products falling under the asserted patent. Unlike a compensation for actual damages suffered by the right holder, this method rather compensates for the unlawful acts committed by the infringer and the hypothetical possibility that this harmed right holder could have made the infringer profits.[25]

The following factors are relevant for the calculation method based on the infringer's profits:

4.1. Infringer's Revenue

The calculation method first requires the determination of the revenues broadly realized with the product infringing the patent. This information is typically provided by the infringer through a "rendering of accounts" proceeding.[26] Even if the patent covers only a part of an assembly, unit or composition, the revenues realized through the marketing of the whole product shall usually be taken into account.[27]

4.2. Deducible Costs

When assessing the infringer's profits, disputes often arise over what costs may, and may not, be deducted from the revenues to show profit. Generally, variable costs are deductible, whereas fixed costs are not. According to a decision of the Supreme Court,[28] overhead costs generally cannot be deducted from profits. It is assumed that these costs would have accrued anyway, even without the infringing activity. The allegation that overhead costs have been spent and are equally necessary for the production and distribution of the infringing product is usually not sufficient to render these costs deductible. In rare exceptions, if overhead costs are directly linked to the infringing device/product, they are deductible. This direct attribution must be demonstrated and proven by the accused infringer.[29] The same applies to the variable costs that are necessary for the production of the accused product. Typical variable costs are the material costs which by necessity must be spent to produce the infringing device.

By way of examples, following are costs that typically are **deductible**:

- the actual material costs necessary for the production and assembling of the infringing product;[30]

25. Federal Supreme Court, I ZR 132/60, GRUR 1962, 509, "Dia-Rähmchen II."
26. See Ch. 8, s. 5.4.
27. Appeal Court Düsseldorf, InstGE 7, 194, "Schwerlastregal."
28. Federal Supreme Court, I ZR 246/98, BGHZ 145, 366, "Gemeinkostenanteil:" This decision is based on a design patent infringement. It is commonly accepted that the guidelines given by the Federal Supreme Court in that decision are also applicable to patent infringements: Appeal Court Düsseldorf, decision from Jun. 3, 2015; I-15 U 34/14.
29. Appeal Court Düsseldorf, InstGE 5, 251, BeckRS 2005, 10332, "Lifter."
30. Federal Supreme Court, I ZR 6/04, GRUR 2007, 431, "Steckverbindergehäuse."

- costs for transportation of the infringing product, including packaging and freight costs;
- costs for employees being recruited especially and used for the manufacturing of the infringing device.[31] Thus, costs for employees, in particular their salaries are usually not deductible, even if the employee was involved in the production of the infringing products.[32] The accused infringer has to prove that he would have saved the costs for particular employees without the infringing activity. This might be possible if he is able to show that he has specially recruited the employee for the production of the infringing device;[33]
- costs for the acquisition of a machine that is exclusively used for the production of the infringing device. These costs are prorated according to the time of infringement and durability of the machine;[34]
- costs for the energy used in connection with the manufacturing of the infringing product;[35]
- Lease of the production facility and stockroom used exclusively for the infringing embodiment.

Following are examples of expenses that typically may not be deducted from revenue when determining the infringer's profits:

- costs of the management, salary of administrators, salary of employees dealing also with other products;[36]
- lease of the production facility and stockroom not exclusively connected with the infringing activity;[37]
- general marketing costs;[38]
- research and development costs;[39]
- costs for products that cannot be sold anymore because of an injunction;[40]
- costs in relation to liability claims of customers.[41]

31. Federal Supreme Court, I ZR 6/04, GRUR 2007, 431, "Steckverbindergehäuse."
32. District Court Düsseldorf, decision of Jun. 30, 2009, 4a 146/08, "Rolladen II;" this is however in dispute: Appeal Court Köln, GRUR-RR 2013, 398, "Bigfoot II."
33. Appeal Court Düsseldorf, InstGE 5, 251, BeckRS 2005, 10332, "Lifter"; District Court Düsseldorf, decision of Jun. 30, 2009, 4a 146/08, "Rolladen II."
34. Federal Supreme Court, I ZR 6/04, GRUR 2007, 431, "Steckverbindergehäuse"; District Court Düsseldorf, decision of Jun. 30, 2009, 4a 146/08, "Rolladen II."
35. Federal Supreme Court, I ZR 6/04, GRUR 2007, 431, "Steckverbindergehäuse."
36. Federal Supreme Court, I ZR 6/04, GRUR 2007, 431, "Steckverbindergehäuse."
37. Federal Supreme Court, I ZR 6/04, GRUR 2007, 431, "Steckverbindergehäuse;" the Appeal Court Köln seems to apply a more flexible approach as to employees which do not exclusively deal with the production of the patent infringing products: Appeal Court Köln, GRUR-RR 2013, 398, "Bigfoot II."
38. Federal Supreme Court, I ZR 6/04, GRUR 2007, 431, "Steckverbindergehäuse."
39. Federal Supreme Court, I ZR 6/04, GRUR 2007, 431, "Steckverbindergehäuse."
40. Federal Supreme Court, I ZR 6/04, GRUR 2007, 431, "Steckverbindergehäuse."
41. Federal Supreme Court, I ZR 6/04, GRUR 2007, 431, "Steckverbindergehäuse."

4.3. Share Factor (*Anteilsfaktor*)

The damage claim is focused on the profits that are specifically caused by the infringing activity.[42] That is, the accused infringer must only surrender the part of the profits that can be effectively attributed to the use of the invention.[43] Accordingly, it is important to identify the different factors that might have contributed to the profits. These factors need to be weighted and prorated. The "share factor" is the portion of the infringer's profits attributable to the patented invention, and thus subject to the damages claim.

In case of a device or an apparatus, the profits are tied to the purchase decision of the customer. This decision is usually triggered by factors beyond, or in addition to, the inventive aspects of the infringed patent. Many factors could potentially influence the purchase decision. For instance, the accused product makes use of a plurality of other intellectual property rights. These rights likely contribute to the achieved sales volume to some degree, or the accused product disposes of unique features which are unrelated to the inventive teaching but influential for the buyer's decision. Advertisement and sales efforts made by the infringer are typically disregarded.[44] However, a strong trademark, trade name or a predominant good will may positively influence the infringer's profits and thus influence the share factor, driving it down. The patentee shall not benefit from these attributes of the alleged infringer's product because they are not tied to the infringing activity.[45]

The determination of a share factor is particularly necessary if the inventive aspects of the infringed patent are only realized in particular parts or elements within an assembly. Another important aspect of this assessment is the question of whether there are alternative solutions available and the extent to which the accused infringer was in a position to design around the patent. The particular advantages resulting from the use of the patented invention and to which extent these advantages influence the decision to buy, shall be taken into account.[46]

Usually courts determine a share factor within a range of 20%–60% of the established profits. Thus the resulting compensation to be paid by the infringer will amount to 20%–60% of the actual profits that have been determined from the net revenue minus deducible costs as explained in the previous section. The court has some flexibility to determine the exact percentage, under its discretion, taking into account the circumstances (§287 German Code of Civil Proceedings). The totality (100%) of the profits may be considered in only one exceptional situation: if the misappropriated invention opens a new area of application. In other words, a situation where non-infringing alternative solutions are not available and, consequently, the

42. Federal Supreme Court, I ZR 6/04, GRUR 2007, 431, "Steckverbindergehäuse."
43. Federal Supreme Court, I ZR 322/02, GRUR 2006, 419, "Noblesse"; Federal Supreme Court, I ZR 107/90, GRUR 1993, 55, "Tchibo/Rolex II"; Appeal Court Düsseldorf, InstGE 5, 251, BeckRS 2005, 10332, "Lifter."
44. Appeal Court Düsseldorf, decision from Jun. 3, 2015; I-15 U 34/14.
45. Federal Supreme Court, I ZR 322/02, GRUR 2006, 419, "Noblesse"; Federal Supreme Court, I ZR 107/90, GRUR 1993, 55, "Tchibo/Rolex II"; Appeal Court Düsseldorf, InstGE 5, 251, BeckRS 2005, 10332, "Lifter."
46. Appeal Court Düsseldorf, decision from Jun. 3, 2015; I-15 U 34/14; Federal Supreme Court, GRUR 2012 1226, "Flaschenträger."

technical solution provided by the infringed patent represents the only factor that could trigger the customer's purchase decision. Such a situation might arise if the infringed patent concerns a medicament with a particular active agent against a particular disease for which no alternative solutions are available. Where the effect provided by the patented active agent cannot be obtained from any other drug it is assumed that the purchaser buys the infringing medicament for no other reason than curing the disease. In such a situation it could be justified to award the totality of the established profits without any reduction through a share factor.[47]

5. PERIOD FOR WHICH DAMAGES ARE TO BE PAID

A question often arises as to the time period over which damages must be paid.

5.1. Starting Time

5.1.1. General

The damages calculation time period basically runs from the commencement of the infringing activities until the end of the damages period as described in section 5.2. However, there is a requirement of fault on the part of the infringer. Unlike under United States law, German law presumes that anyone who participates in a commercial environment is required to sufficiently investigate and analyze opposing rights of third parties through publicly available means (e.g., patent registers). Thus under German law the infringer usually cannot escape liability by arguing that he did not know about the existence of the asserted patent or utility model. Accordingly, he must exercise reasonable care.[48] It is generally presumed that the infringer acted at least with negligence.[49] Furthermore, the award of damages does not require that the patentee mark the patented article as "patented,"[50] and failure to mark does not limit the damage claim. This is an advantage for patentees who do not exercise the invention, such as non-practicing companies and holding companies. It is presumed that the accused infringer knew about the patent or should have known about its existence.[51] Effective notice of the granted patent (and hence the availability of damages) is calculated starting one month from the publication of the grant of the patent or the publication of the registration of the utility model, unless the infringer was given earlier actual knowledge of the right (for instance by means of a special notice or communication from the right holder shortly after the publication). This one-month-from-publication period is considered to be sufficient for identifying and analyzing the granted right.[52]

47. District Court Düsseldorf, decision of Jun. 30, 2009, 4a 146/08, "Rolladen II."
48. This is a consequence of §276 (2) of the German Civil Code: "A person acts negligently if he fails to exercise reasonable care."
49. Federal Supreme Court, X ZR 79/90, GRUR 1993, 430, "Wandabstreifer."
50. Chapter 8, s. 3.2.1.2: Right to claim damages.
51. Federal Supreme Court, X ZR 79/90, GRUR 1993, 430, "Wandabstreifer."
52. Federal Supreme Court, X ZR 28/85, GRUR 1986, 803, "Formstein."

Ignorance of the right would be typically excusable only during that one-month period. Accordingly, it is recommended that potential defendant companies establish patent monitoring programs.[53]

5.1.2. *Published Patent Applications*

Damages claims result from the infringement of a granted patent or a registered utility model. Damages claims cannot be based on patent applications. Nevertheless, a European patent application may confer provisional protection from the date of its publication. According to Article 67 EPC,[54] it is left to the contracting states of the EPC to prescribe the content of this provisional protection. It could be less than what is conferred by a granted patent, but shall not be less than that which the laws of the state concerned attach to the compulsory publication of unexamined national patent applications. These are minimum conditions and hence there might be differences from country to country (see chart for key European countries following section 5.1.2.2). The German law provides this minimum protection by means of Article II, §1 IntPatÜG for European patent application corresponding to §33 of the Patent Act applicable to national applications:

> **§33** -
> (1) As from publication...the applicant may assert from any person who has used the subject matter of the application, although he knew or should have known that the invention used by him was the subject matter of the application, compensation appropriate to the circumstances. Further claims are excluded.
> (2) The claim to compensation cannot be asserted if the subject matter of the application is obviously unpatentable.[55]

5.1.2.1. *Requirements*

Use of the subject matter: Pursuant to §33 of the German Patent Act the patent applicant may demand compensation appropriate to the circumstance for the *"use of the subject matter"* of the patent application. The scope of protection of the claims contained in the application as published is key, provided the claims are supported by the application as originally filed. The demand for compensation is thus triggered by the use of these claims. The scope of protection is determined according to the general rules applicable to granted patents.[56] A later limitation, such as by adding an additional feature to the claim as published,[57] has a retroactive effect. However, compensation is

53. Chapter 6, s. 2.
54. The text of Art. 67 can be found in Ch. 17, s. 1.
55. This is an unofficial translation.
56. Chapter 10, Substantive Law of Claim Construction and Infringement.
57. Please note the claim may be modified after publication of the application. Such modifications may occur even after grant in opposition proceedings or later in national invalidation proceedings.

only due if the use still falls within the scope of the claim(s) as later narrowed.[58] Compensation that was paid earlier due to a broader claim contained in the published application, which was then narrowed to a scope that no longer covers the use, would have to be reimbursed.[59] Furthermore, any use of other (unclaimed) subject matter of the application which goes beyond the subject matter as claimed is not compensable.[60] Of course, such unclaimed and inventive subject matter could be detached from the application and explicitly claimed in a provisional application[61] from which publication a liability according to §33 Patent Act might exist.

Contributory use: As there is not yet a granted patent, the use of the invention described in the patent application is not deemed to be unlawful, and thus the applicant cannot prohibit that use. It is not sufficient if someone only contributes to a use of the subject matter or induces a third party[62] to use it. Someone who only furnishes means for such use would not be liable, but of course the user is liable.[63]

Level of knowledge of the user: The compensation claim requires that the person who has used the subject matter knew or should have known that the use falls within the subject matter of the invention claimed in the application. As with damages claims, usually a one-month-from-publication period is considered to represent a sufficient time window for the user to identify the published application[64] and to acquire that level of knowledge. If he is not doing this investigation, it is presumed that he acted at least with negligence and consequently he would be liable.

Translation of claims: Finally, §33 Patent Act necessarily requires, if the application is not in German, that a translation of the claims must be made available to the public by the GPTO or communicated to the user of the claimed invention.[65] An applicant who filed a European patent application in English or French could not assert any provisional rights during the time from publication until grant of the patent without such published or notified translation of the claims. Typically a translation is filed if the claimed invention in the application is already used by third parties or if there is a likelihood of such use. In any event a German version of the claims has to be submitted after grant of the patent (Rule 71 (3) EPC).

5.1.2.2. *"Compensation Appropriate to the Circumstance"*

According to the Federal Supreme Court, the amount of compensation attributable to published patent applications is limited to a "reasonable royalty"[66] calculated in compliance with the method as previously described in connection with damage claims

58. Federal Supreme Court, X ZR 22/73 GRUR 1977, 598, "Autoscooter-Halle."
59. Schäfers in Benkhard, Patentgesetz, 10th ed., §33, N° 4.
60. Schulte, Patentgesetz, 8th edn, §33, Kühnen, N° 6.
61. See Chapter 4, s. 1.3 "Divisional Application."
62. Federal Supreme Court, X ZR 79/04, GRUR 2006, 570, "extracoronales Geschiebe."
63. This is the opinion of the Federal Supreme Court (previous footnote) but still in dispute: see Schäfers in Benkhard, Patentgesetz, 10th ed., §33, N° 4.
64. Federal Supreme Court, X ZR 22/73 GRUR 1977, 598, "Autoscooter-Halle."
65. Article I, §1(2) of IntPatÜG.
66. Federal Supreme Court, X ZR 26/87, GRUR 1989, 41, "Offenend-Spinnmaschine."

(section 2). The calculation methods "own lost profits" or "the infringer's profits" are specific to the infringement of granted patents and are not applicable to §33 of the German Patent Act, which only covers the time period up until the grant of the patent. After the grant of the patent, the other damages claim methodologies can be asserted.

Table 12.1. Provisional Protection

	Germany	*France*	*Italy*	*U.K.*
Provisional right arises when?	When translation of the claims (in German) is made available to the public (GPTO) or communicated to the user	When translation of the claims (in French) is made available to the public (INPI) or communicated to the user	When translation of the claims (in Italian) is made available to the public (UIBM) or communicated to the user	When translation of the claims (in English) is made available to the public (IPO) or communicated to the user
Content of the right	Reasonable compensation only in case of direct use	Damages	Damages	Damages
Enforceability	Reasonable compensation can judicially be asserted against user, but court may stay the proceedings until grant	Seizure of products possible; court would stay the proceedings until grant	Seizure of products possible;	Seizure of products possible; court proceedings possible after grant

5.2. Statute of Limitation

According to §141 of the Patent Act, damage claims shall become time-barred by statute in compliance with the provisions of the fifth chapter of the 1st book of the Civil Code.[67] Damages claims thus become time-barred 10 years after they arose, provided the right holder did not know the circumstances giving rise to the damages, or at least if it cannot be proven that he negligently ignored these circumstances (§199(3) N° 1 Civil Code).[68] In contrast, a limitation period of only three years is applicable where the right holder obtained or could have obtained knowledge of the accused infringement. This period commences at the end of the year in which the right arose (§§195, 199 of

67. See also Ch. 8, s. 3.3.2, Legal and Procedural Defenses, subsection: "Statute of Limitation."
68. For the sake of completeness, it has to be noted that a thirty years limitation may exceptionally be applicable if the moment of the infringing act and the occurrence of the damage, i.e., the moment when the right arose, diverge in time (§199 (3) N° 2 Civil Code). In that particular case the right becomes statue barred latest 30 years from the infringing act. This limitation is usually irrelevant as the moment of the infringing act and occurrence of the damage do not diverge.

the German Civil Code). Accordingly, the relevant period for which damages have to be paid depends on the right holder's knowledge. If he was not aware of the infringing activity, he could claim damages for 10 years. In the case of established knowledge, a shorter time limit is applicable.

Nevertheless, for the time-barred period, the right holder could claim restitution for all the benefits the accused infringer has obtained without legal grounds at the right holder's expenses (claim to return of unjust enrichment according to §812 of Civil Code). This claim would be time-barred 10 years after it arises, or, irrespective of the date on which it arises, 30 years after the date on which the act causing the injury was committed. Accordingly, if the damages claim is already time-barred, at least a restitution claim under the provisions for the return of unjust enrichment would be applicable, calculated by analogy to a reasonable license.[69]

The right holder can avoid having his claims becoming time-barred by means of triggering a suspension of the limitation period. The period of time for which the limitation period is suspended is not included in the calculation of the limitation period. For instance, the limitation period is suspended during the time of pending negotiations up to a refusal to continue these negotiations. The right holder may also trigger a suspension by means of filing a lawsuit against the infringer or by means of other similar proceedings (see Section 204 (1) of the German Civil Code).

69. Federal Supreme Court, X ZR 81/72, GRUR 1977, 250, "Kunststoffhohlprofil"; Federal Supreme Court, X ZR 7/80, GRUR 1982, 301, "Kunststoffhohlprofil II."

CHAPTER 13

Inventorship and Ownership

Inventorship and ownership of patents in Germany is a complex topic. Of particular note is Germany's Act on Employees' Inventions (hereinafter "ArbEG"), which governs the extent to which employees' inventions are assigned to their employers. The requirements of ArbEG may be unknown to U.S.-based companies that employ workers in Germany. Companies that employ workers in Germany or acquire German entities must become familiar with the unique provisions of German law governing how companies acquire ownership of the inventions of German employees. Questions of whether employee inventions are, indeed, assigned to the employer can be quite challenging, and may be problematic when patents on these inventions are asserted in court. While in 2009 some of the most problematic provisions were amended to facilitate transfer of employees' inventions to their employers, pitfalls still remain, and the pre-2009 provisions continue to govern inventions reported by the employee to the employer prior to October 1, 2009.[1] Companies have successfully escaped liability from infringement by acquiring rights from a departed employee who was found to still own his invention. Following is an overview of the rules for inventorship and assignments, and in particular the requirements of the ArbEG for securing ownership by companies of inventions developed by their employees.

1. INVENTORSHIP

An invention arises from the mental acts of a human being. Consequently, under German law, an inventor cannot be a legal entity. When the invention is developed jointly by several people, they are co-inventors. Inventorship in Germany starts from the principle that each inventor must have made at least an independent and creative contribution to the inventive teaching. This contribution does not necessarily need to be inventive on its own.[2] This is analogous to the requirement under U.S. law that a

1. §43(3) ArbEG.
2. Federal Supreme Court, X ZR 142/01, GRUR 2004, 50, "Verkranzungsverfahren."

person must "contribute to the conception" of an invention in order to be deemed an inventor. As in both Germany and the U.S., the employee's contribution must be more than only insignificant in order to be inventive.[3] The simple provision of tools, as would be usually found in an employer/employee situation, is insufficient. It would also be insufficient if the contributor purely follows the instructions of the inventor.[4] The employee must enhance the intellectual underpinnings in order to qualify as an inventor.

The process of determining who is or is not an inventor on a patent may be difficult. For the reasons discussed below in the context of the ArbEG, there may be financial stakes for being included as an inventor on a patent, particularly for those inventions that become commercially successful for the company. Thus, the individual motivations for German employees to assert that they are inventors may be different than for U.S.-based inventors, and the challenge for legal departments is to resolve these inventorship claims in a manner consistent with the ArbEG.

In many respects, however, there are fewer strategic considerations at stake in making inventorship determinations in Germany. There is no best mode requirement, so the subjective understanding of each inventor's preferred way of carrying out the invention does not impose additional disclosure obligations. There is no inequitable conduct doctrine and an intentional withholding of material prior art to the EPO and GPTO would not lead to a finding of unenforceability. And there are no inventor depositions, so many of the headaches in the U.S. associated with long lists of inventors are inapplicable in Germany.

2. RIGHT TO THE INVENTION

When determining ownership, the starting principle is that the right to the invention belongs to the inventor (Article 60(1) EPC, §6 of the Patent Act):

> The right to a...patent shall belong to the inventor or his successor in title.

Inventorship establishes rights to the resulting patent. Inventorship confers "the right to the patent, the right to the grant of a patent and the rights deriving from a patent"[5] (§15(1) Patent Act). As long as it is not an employee's invention for which the special rules of the employee invention act are applicable,[6] the right to the invention can freely be assigned from the inventor to any third party. For instance, persons not considered "employees" by the Act on Employee's Invention (ArbEG) (*see* below), such as CEOs,[7] are basically free to transfer their rights to their inventions unless their contract with the company provides otherwise. An inventor who assigns his right to the invention remains an inventor. This is a personal right which is not transferable. But the assignment triggers a transfer of the proprietary rights connected to the invention,

3. Federal Supreme Court, X ZR 130/93, "Gummielastische Masse."
4. Federal Supreme Court, X ZR 142/01, GRUR 2004, 50, "Verkranzungsverfahren."
5. Unofficial translation.
6. *See* Ch. 13, s. 5.
7. Appeal Court Düsseldorf, 2 U 11/98, GRUR 2000, 49, "Geschäftsführer-Erfindung."

namely "the right to the patent, the right to the grant of a patent and the rights deriving from a patent"[8] to the assignee. The assignee can be a natural person or a legal entity.

The assignment of a patent or patent application can even be based on an implied agreement.[9] But this exceptional situation must be deduced from a special relationship between assignor and assignee, and the party that seeks to assert rights from an implied agreement must prove the existence of such a special relationship. Thus, even though a written assignment agreement is not legally mandatory, it is highly recommended.

Note that in the case of pending European patent applications, a written and signed agreement is mandatory to transfer ownership. This is based on Article 72 of the EPC, which supersedes the more flexible German law.[10] This is, an assignment of a European patent application shall be made in writing and shall require the signature of the parties to the contract. According to the case law[11] that strict formality exclusively relates to the assignment of the formal position resulting from the patent application.[12] Article 72 EPC does not apply to the right to the European patent (Article 60 EPC), for which the laws of the respective designated countries apply. Thus, the assignment of the German part of a European patent would not require a formal written assignment agreement, although it would nonetheless be highly advised.

3. CO-OWNERSHIP OF THE INVENTION

Where the invention is developed jointly by several people they are deemed co-owners of the invention (§6 of the Patent Act):

> If two or more persons have jointly made an invention, the right to a patent shall belong to them jointly.[13]

As noted above, to be a joint inventor it is necessary that each inventor has at least made an *independent and creative contribution* to the inventive teaching. The legal relationship between co-owners (including organization and administration of their co-ownership) may be governed by an agreement concluded by all of them. To avoid disputes about organization and administration of the co-owned invention, in particular, about the individual shares of the co-owners in the invention, the conclusion of a written agreement is recommended. Thus, as soon as a group of researchers

8. §15(1) Patent Act.
9. Federal Supreme Court, X ZR 42/67, decision of Apr. 28, 1970.
10. Federal Supreme Court, X ZR 98/90, GRUR 92, 692, "Magazinbildwerfer."
11. District Düsseldorf, 4a O 406/06; decision of Nov. 14, 2006.
12. There are three categories of rights which basically follow from an invention: The **first category** is called the ***right to the patent*** (see Art. 60 EPC) and englobes the sum of proprietary rights resulting from the invention. These rights emerge from the invention itself and do not require a patent application. The **second category** is the "***right to the grant of the patent***." This is the formal position which arises from the patent application vis-à-vis the patent office. Finally there is the **third category** which is called ***"rights out of the patent"*** and relates to the effects of the patent such as the rights resulting from an non-authorized use (§ 9, 10 Patent Act). The formalities of Article 72 EPC only apply to rights of the second category.
13. Unofficial translation.

intend to undertake a joint research and development project, they should agree on a written agreement, a so-called R&D Agreement, which sufficiently anticipates these matters.

In the absence of such an agreement the provisions of the German Civil Code dealing with the "community of co-owners" (§741 of the Civil Code)[14] will apply.[15] Such co-owners will have a share in the invention that corresponds to their creative contribution.[16] The determination of that share requires an evaluation of the performance of each contributor.[17] "In case of doubt it is to be assumed that the co-owners are entitled to equal shares" (§742 of the Civil Code).[18] Each co-owner is also entitled without the consent of the other co-owners to individually transfer his share in the community to a third party.[19]

In principle, each co-owner is allowed to individually assert patent claims[20] against infringers through court proceedings without the other co-owners necessarily joining these proceedings. This follows from an application by analogy of §1011 of the Civil Code according to the case law.[21] The co-owner is thus also litigating on behalf the other co-owners of the community. This follows from the external relationship of the community, which must not necessarily comply with the internal arrangements of the co-owners. Also, co-owners can principally use the invention for their own purposes to the extent that joint use by other co-owners is not impaired (§743(2) Civil Code).[22] A co-owner must usually not compensate the other co-owners for his individual use of the invention unless that use considerably exceeds his share in the invention and if such financial compensation in-between the co-owners is demanded for equity reasons.[23]

The administration of the co-owned invention is organized jointly by the community (§744(1) of the Civil Code). Administrative acts would cover the filing of patents or utility models and the granting of licenses. It is usually sufficient if the co-owners agree on proper administrative acts by a simple majority (§745(1) of the Civil Code). The vote need not be unanimous. But in the case of only two co-owners a simple majority would require that both co-owners agree on whether or not a particular administrative act shall be performed. Accordingly, one co-owner could principally block the other co-owner and in exceptional situation even hinder patent exploitation, as through licensing or enforcement against infringers[24] as a result of the internal

14. A translation of the German Civil Code can be found on webpage of the German Ministry of Justice: www.gesetze-im-internet.de/englisch_bgb/.
15. Federal Supreme Court, X ZR 152/03, GRUR 2005, 663, "Gummielastische Masse II", Appeal Court Düsseldorf, I-2 U 5/11, GRUR-RR 2012, 319, "Einstiegshilfe für Kanalöffnungen."
16. Federal Supreme Court, X ZR 152/03, GRUR 2005, 663, "Gummielastische Masse II."
17. Federal Supreme Court, X ZR 54/67, GRUR 1971, 210, "Wildverbissverhinderung."
18. Federal Supreme Court, X ZR 63/77, GRUR 1979, 540, "Biedermeiermanschette."
19. Federal Supreme Court, X ZR 223/98, GRUR 2001, 226, 227, "Rollenantriebseinheit."
20. The assertion may include the right to prevent the use of the patent, to claim damages and to be informed about the extent of use.
21. Federal Supreme Court, I ZR 168/97, GRUR 2000, 1028, "Ballermann," Appeal Court Düsseldorf, I-2 U 39/09.
22. Federal Supreme Court, X ZR 152/03, GRUR 2005, 663, "Gummielastische Masse II."
23. Federal Supreme Court, X ZR 152/03, GRUR 2005, 663, 664, "Gummielastische Masse II."
24. Busse, §6 N° 38, Federal Supreme Court, BGHZ 146, 341 (NJW 01, 1056).

relationship between the co-owners. The only way to overcome such a conflict is to compel consent from the denying co-owner through a court action. This action would, however, only be successful if the denial is considered abusive or clearly unreasonable (§745(2) Civil Code). Nevertheless, necessary acts of administration (§744(2) Civil Code) aimed at safeguarding the right to the invention can individually be carried out by each co-owner even without the consent of the other co-owners.

Despite these provisions, it is recommended that co-owners have a written agreement in place, in particular to avoid disputes about the administration of the co-owned invention. As soon as a group of researchers intends to undertake a joint research and development project, they should discuss these issues and agree them in writing.

4. LEGAL TITLE TO THE INVENTION

4.1. Legal Fiction in Favor of the Applicant

In the proceedings before the patent offices, the applicant is deemed to be entitled to exercise the rights to the patent (Article 60(3) EPC or §7(1) German Patent Act): "...the applicant...shall be deemed to be entitled to request the grant of the patent."[25] This legal fiction is aimed at avoiding a delay of the examination. Accordingly, an investigation about who is the right inventor or owner of the rights does not take place at the patent office. What counts is the name of the person or entity indicated in the documents filed and mentioned in the register.

If someone contends that he or she has been wrongly omitted from the right to the invention, it is left to the challenger to file a court action seeking an assignment of the application (§8 Patent Act, Article 60 EPC, Article II §5 IntPatÜG). By means of this action, for which the civil courts have jurisdiction, an examination of rights to the invention takes place. If a final decision determines that someone other than the applicant is entitled to the grant of the patent, the applicant can be replaced in the course of the granting proceedings by the entitled person, and if the patent is already granted the rights can be assigned to him.

The EPO will stay grant proceedings if a third party institutes proceedings against the applicant to establish that the third party is entitled to the grant of the European patent, instead of the original applicant. *See* Rule 14(1) EPC. The inventorship challenge is typically filed in national courts, such as the District Court in Munich. The patent will not be granted during the time of the stay. This stay of the grant proceedings can, of course, significantly delay the enforcement of the patent rights against infringers.[26] In exceptional cases, the EPO can order that the grant proceedings be resumed regardless of the pending national entitlement proceedings.[27] In order to determine whether the grant proceedings are to be resumed, all aspects relevant in

25. Unofficial translation.
26. EPO-J 0002/14 (Stay of proceedings) of Jun.15, 2015.
27. EPO-J 15/13 of May 9, 2014.

balancing the interests of the parties have to be taken into account. Relevant factors include, for example, if there are facts or evidence showing that the third party is not actively seeking a decision by the national court. Also, the length of the proceedings before the national court or national authority is also to be taken into consideration in a decision whether to resume the grant proceedings.[28]

4.2. Legal Function of the Register

Entries in the patent register have no "constitutive effect." That is, the acquisition of the patent right is not dependent on any entry on a national patent register. The true legal ownership of the patent may thus differ from what appears in the register. This divergence between the entries in the register and the actual legal situation may occur if the patent has been assigned by means of an agreement and so long as the new owner is not yet registered.

It has to be taken note, when filing a lawsuit, such as a nullity suit with the Federal Patent Court or an infringement action at one of the competent infringement courts, the person or entity that is mentioned in the register shall be the party to the proceedings (§30(3) Patent Act).[29] The entry in the register provides circumstantial evidence that the party is legally entitled to assert the rights resulting from the patent rights. This legal assumption is however refutable and could be challenged by the defendant by means of a substantiated submission.[30] In patent infringement proceedings, the registered owner has then to prove that he or she is the owner of the patent and entitled to the damages for the claimed period. If the patent has been assigned from the original applicant to a new entity and, eventually later to other entities, it may thus be required to submit in the infringement proceedings the different assignment contract(s) to prove a gapless chain from the original applicant to the entity named in the patent register. This may be a complicated task, in particular, in cases where a plurality of assignments occurred. In addition, it has to be taken into account that often the assignments fall under foreign law, which burdens the assessment by foreign law aspects. It is thus essential to assess the assignment situation prior to filing the patent infringement lawsuit.

If the legitimate owner is not mentioned in the register, it is necessary that the registered party explicitly authorize the new and legitimate owner to take action. Therefore, an assignment agreement should contain provisions dealing with the period until the new owner is finally named in the register after a requested change of the register (§30(3) Patent Act). Without any explicit authorization the new owner would be considered being an entitled party in the infringement proceedings until the patent office actually changed the registration.

28. For instance EPO- J 6/10 of Nov. 13, 2012.
29. Federal Supreme Court, X ZR 69/11, GRUR 2013, 713, "Fräsverfahren."
30. Federal Supreme Court, X ZR 69/11, GRUR 2013, 713, "Fräsverfahren."

5. EMPLOYEE INVENTIONS AND THE ACT ON EMPLOYEES' INVENTIONS (ARBEG)

The statute governing the assignment of employee inventions to an employer is the Act on Employee's Invention (ArbEG). The provisions of the ArbEG are mandatory on employers, which cannot simply require (as is common in the U.S.) that all inventions be assigned to the company. Rather, §22 of the ArbEG states that "the provisions of the Act cannot be modified by contract to the detriment of the employee."[31] For international entities acting within the German market, including through affiliates, it is crucial to know and apply these rules.

The law is based on the concept that inventions made by employees initially belong to them. Under the ArbEG, special mandatory proceedings have to be applied in order for the invention to become the property of the employer. The employer and employee may not agree upon an automatic transfer of rights as to inventions or technical improvements made by the employee during the employment. Such clause would be invalid according to §22 ArbEG.

An unofficial translation of the most important provisions of the ArbEG can be found in Chapter 17, section 5.

5.1. Scope of Application of the ArbEG

5.1.1. Material Scope of Application

The Act on Employees' Inventions covers technical inventions and makes a distinction between these and mere "technical improvements." Technical inventions could be subject to a patent or a utility model, whereas technical improvements are not eligible for protection under an industrial property right (§§3, 20 ArbEG).[32]

The Act on Employees' Inventions does not cover other achievements of employees made during the employment relationship. This means that artistic creations and designs do not fall under the binding rules of the Act and accordingly the parties are usually free to agree on these rights in advance.

5.1.2. Personal Scope of Application

The ArbEG defines "employee" as a person employed by the employer according to the German Labor Act.[33] This is a person who provides contractually owed labor tasks within an organization, in which he is under the direction of the contract partner

31. Unofficial translation.
32. Technical improvements, which are in practice of lower importance, are only eligible for compensation if they confer to the employer an advantage that is similar to a patent or utility model. This requires that the technical improvement be a useful achievement from the status quo with a commercial advantage, and not something obvious to the person skilled in the art or detectable without difficulty by any competitor: District Court Munich decision of Jan. 17, 2007, 21 O 1788/05, BeckRS 2008, 18310, "Keramikschneidwerkzeug."
33. Federal Supreme Court, X ZR 58/88, GRUR 1990, 193, "Autokindersitz."

(employer) with respect to content, way, time and location of implementing these tasks.[34] This applies to normal employees, also to executive employees.[35] The Act does not apply to the employer and to people holding positions in the company that are similar to the position of an employer (such as high officers[36]). Moreover, commercial agents and independent freelancers do not benefit from the provisions of the Act. Thus, in agreements concluded with such persons it is possible to agree that inventions made in the course of the contractual relationship are automatically assigned to the company. Without such an agreement a separate assignment would be necessary and additional compensation would be owed.

5.1.3. Territorial Application

The application of the ArbEG depends upon whether German law is applicable to the employment relationship. If the employment relationship falls under German law, the ArbEG would be applicable.[37]

A question often arises whether it is possible to evade the ArbEG by means of the choice of law agreed in the employment contract. Indeed, according to Article 8 of the Regulation EC 593/2008 (Rome II),[38] an employment contract is primarily governed by the law chosen by the parties. However, the same Regulation provides that the parties' choice of law may not have the effect of depriving the employee of the protection afforded to him by provisions that cannot be derogated. Article 8 of the Regulation EC No. 593/2008 requires that "such a choice of law may not, however, have the result of depriving the employee of the protection afforded to him by provisions that cannot be derogated from by agreement under the law that, in the absence of choice, would have been applicable pursuant to paragraphs 2, 3 and 4 of this Article." In the absence of a choice of law provision, the contract would generally be governed by the law of the country in which the employee habitually carries out his work in performance of the contract. This is called the "usual place of employment." It stays the usual place of employment even if the employee is temporarily employed in another country (Article 8(2) Regulation EC 593/2008).

Thus, the restrictive rules of the ArbEG are usually applicable irrespective of whether or not the parties have agreed on a choice of law when the employee's usual place of employment is in Germany. Of course, special considerations of each case

34. Federal Constitutional Court, decision of Feb. 18, 2000, 1 BvR 491, 562/93, NZA 2000, 653.
35. In German "Leitende Angestellte": Appeal Court Hamburg, 3 U 89/58, GRUR 1960, 488, "Geruchsbeseitigungsverfahren."
36. CEO of German Limited (GmbH): Federal Supreme Court, X ZR 165/04, GRUR 2006, 401, "Zylinderrohr."
37. Federal Supreme Court, decision of Nov. 27, 1975, X ZB 24/73, GRUR 1976, 385, "Rosenmuation"; Art. 60(1) EPC must be taken into account for European patents: "If the inventor is an employee, the right to a European patent shall be determined in accordance with the law of the State in which the employee is mainly employed; if the State in which the employee is mainly employed cannot be determined, the law to be applied shall be that of the State in which the employer has the place of business to which the employee is attached."
38. Regulation (EC) 593/2008 of the European Parliament and of the Council of Jun. 17, 2008 on the law applicable to contractual obligations (Rome I).

must be taken into account in making this determination. For exceptions to the general rule, particular attention should be paid to situations in which the employer or the employee does not reside in Germany or where the main tasks under the agreement shall be fulfilled partly in and partly outside the German territory.

5.2. Service Inventions and Free Inventions

The ArbEG is applicable to all inventions irrespective of where, when, in which technological area and why the invention has been made by the employee during the employment. But the Act distinguishes between two types of inventions, namely "service inventions" and "free inventions" (§4 ArbEG). (§4 (2) ArbEG) subdivides service inventions in two categories: They either result from the assigned duties under the employment contract or are "decisively based upon experiences or activities" of the company. Service inventions according to the first category are connected to duties actually assigned to the employee. This is mainly the case if the employee is instructed to perform research and development activities. The second category does not necessarily require the assignment of such duties. It rather requires that the employee gets to the teaching thanks to the employer's experiences or activities (i.e., any technological information, knowledge, know-how, practices, etc., *see* §4(2) ArbEG). An enhanced causal connection between the inventive act and the "experiences or activities" of the employer's company must be given. In the words of the law, the invention must "decisively" be based on such "experiences or activities." A main characteristic of both types of service inventions is that they are essentially based on the employer's own initiative or resources.[39]

By contrast, "free inventions" make up all other inventions made by the employee, which do not meet at least one of the two criteria of being "service inventions" (i.e., they do not result from duties under the employment contract or they are not decisively based on the company's know-how or developments). For example, an employee who is employed for improving software applications for aircraft invents a novel sports shoe. That invention would not fall within the category of a "service invention," provided that it is neither a result of the accomplishment of regular contractual duties nor decisively based on the know-how of the company.

In making the assessment between service inventions and free inventions, it does not matter when, for which reason, and where the inventor developed and completed the invention. The invention need not necessarily be developed at the usual working place of the employee. It is also irrelevant that third parties contributed to the invention.[40] All employee inventions made during the period of employment are governed by the ArbEG. It is irrelevant, for application of the Act, that the invention was made during working hours or while staying at home in the evening. Even inventions made during holidays are either service or free inventions (Table 13.1).

39. Federal Supreme Court, X ZR 155/03, GRUR 2006, 756, "Haftetikett."
40. Federal Supreme Court, X ZR 165/04, GRUR 2006, 401, "Zylinderrohr."

Table 13.1. Distinction Between Service and Free Inventions

Inventions made during the period of employment	
Service inventions =	**Free inventions** =
- Either result from obligatory duties of the employee (§4(2)(i) ArbEG) **or** - are decisively based on know-how or developments of the employer (§4(2)(ii) ArbEG)	- All other inventions which are not service inventions.
Employer is **entitled to acquire** a service invention	Free inventions are **basically at the free disposal of the employee,** but there is a duty to offer to employer a non-exclusive license under reasonable conditions if it falls within the range of the employer's actual or planned activities

5.3. Duty to Report

Service Inventions. Whenever an employee has made an invention he must fulfill particular obligations vis-à-vis his employer. A central obligation of the ArbEG is the duty to report all service inventions. This means that as soon as the employee has accomplished any service invention—including a creative improvement of a previously completed invention—he must prepare a report about that invention (§5 ArbEG). The aim of that report is to sufficiently inform the employer about the invention so that the employer can make a decision on whether to claim ownership or to release the invention.

The report need not necessarily be a signed document. The report can be submitted by fax or email so long as the report is sent in text form to the right addressee (employer or particular authorized people) and mentions the reporting party. Bigger companies usually contractually require employees to use forms with predetermined fields and questions. The use of such forms is commonly accepted[41] and is recommended for an accelerated treatment and to avoid oversights that could occur if the invention is only reported by email.[42]

A duly established report of a service invention needs to contain (§5(2) ArbEG):

- A detailed description of the technical problem (including disadvantages, drawbacks and unmet needs in the state of the art) and its solution. It should provide a clear and complete understanding of the invention including modes of application. The employee must also add any existing notes, to the extent

41. Federal Supreme Court, X ZR 26/03, GRUR 2006, 141, 142, "Ladungsträgergenerator."
42. Reports by Email are admissible since Oct. 1, 2009, Federal Gazette, BGBl. I S. 2521. Invention reports submitted by fax, telecopy and Email were not admitted prior to that date: Federal Supreme Court, X ZR 26/03, GRUR 2006, 141, 142, "Ladungsträgergenerator."

they are relevant to the understanding of the inventive solution. Preferably, he should make reference to drawings and photos.
- The employee shall describe how he arrived at the invention.
- He must mention the instructions, directions and technical aid received from the employer or supervisors.
- He must also mention the extent to which internal know-how and the developments of the company were important for solving the problem.
- The report shall also indicate eventual collaborators (they do not necessarily need to be co-inventors) as well as co-inventors, including the nature of their involvement and the scope of their contribution. However, co-inventors are entitled to submit a joint report and this is generally recommended to avoid contradictory descriptions.
- The employee should indicate—in the situation of co-inventors—the contribution he considers to have personally provided to the service invention (§5(2) ArbEG).

Free Inventions. If the employee believes the invention is free, he nevertheless has to sufficiently inform the employer about this invention as well (§18 ArbEG). The duty then shifts to the employer to object to this categorization of the invention. If the employer does not object to the categorization made by the employee within three months of the employee's notification, the invention can no longer be claimed as a service invention. §19 ArbEG sets forth the circumstances under which the employee needs to offer a non-exclusive license under reasonable conditions to his employer for any such free inventions, specifically, if the otherwise free invention falls within the range of the employer's actual or planned activities.

5.4. Acquisition of the Ownership of Service Inventions

The German system is based on the concept that the rights to an invention made by an employee initially belong to the employee and not the employer. Accordingly, an acquisition process must take place in order for the employer to become the owner of the invention. The acquisition process starts with the reception of the report. As soon as the employer has received a report in appropriate form, a four-month period commences during which the employer may claim ownership over the service invention by means of a declaration (§6(1) ArbEG). This four-month period may be extended in certain circumstances, such as if the report is incomplete (§5(3) ArbEG).

An important change in the law took place in 2009 regarding the mechanics of assigning inventions to the employer. Prior to 2009, a serious pitfall arose if the employer failed to act on the employee's report of a new invention. Under the previous ArbEG, the employer's claim had to be made "in a written statement, addressed to the employee, as soon as possible, and not later than four months from the receipt of a proper report"[43] (previous §6(2) ArbEG). The written statement had to be a signed, for

43. Unofficial translation.

instance emails were not sufficient, and the period started to run as soon as the invention was duly reported, or, in the absence of such a report, at the latest at the filing date of the patent application, which was usually filed in the name of the employer. The courts considered the filing of the application by the employer as the trigger for the four-month deadline.[44] Inadvertently, some employers failed to present adequate written statements to the employee-inventor. Often this was simply caused by lack of knowledge of the law or by a more or less unorganized handling of these issues by the employers. In such situations, the right to the invention stayed with the employee.

In many cases, such defects in the transfer of ownership went undetected for years. Many of those defects are still undetected. These oversights have caused and will continue to cause problems for companies trying to enforce or assign patents which suffer from improper compliance with the prior ArbEG. This is particularly critical for employers, if the employee meanwhile left the company and is consequently less inclined to help his ex-employer. In a worst-case scenario, he even could assign his rights to competitors.

The ArbEG was amended on October 1, 2009 to facilitate transfer of service inventions to employers. Now, after expiry of the four-month term following receipt of an invention report, an employer who stays passive automatically acquires rights to the service invention. This so-called automatism provision is provided in §6(2) ArbEG, [45]

which provides that the employer's "declaration is deemed to be executed, if the employer does not, within a four-month term starting from the receipt of a duly made report release the invention by means of a declaration executed in text form vis-à-vis the employee." Accordingly, the absence of an explicit claim no longer hinders the employer from acquiring the rights to the invention, because it is now presumed that the employer had made a claim to the service invention. This provision is not retroactive, and so the "automatism" provisions of the 2009 law do not cure any prior defects in earlier patents.

Also under the new law, the employer may explicitly claim a service invention by executing a declaration to the employee (§6(1) ArbEG). An explicit claiming of the service invention, instead of automatically acquiring the ownership by the indicated fiction of law (§6(2) ArbEG), might be best if the employer does not want to wait until the end of the four-month term, for instance in order to fulfill obligations towards business partners. An explicit declaration may also be useful to create a legal certainty between the parties. With either an explicit claim (§6(1) ArbEG) or an automatic claim (§6(2) ArbEG), all rights to the service invention pass to the employer. The employer becomes owner of the service invention and will be free to dispose of it, grant licenses or assign it to third parties (Table 13.2).

44. Federal Supreme Court, X ZR 155/03, GRUR 2006, 756, "Haftetikett."
45. Federal Gazette, BGBl. I S. 2521.

Table 13.2. Employer's Options with Respect to Service Inventions

Release communicated in text form to the employee: - Employee stays owner of the invention and is entitled to apply for an industrial property right.	**Explicit claiming** by means of a declaration to the employee before the end of the four-month term (§6(1) ArbEG): - Employer becomes owner of the invention upon receipt of the declaration.	**No reaction** of employer within time period of four months starting from receipt of duly made report (§6(2) ArbEG): - Employer becomes owner of the invention according to a fiction of law.

5.5. Obligations of Employer after Acquisition of the Service Invention

If the employer elects to acquire the service invention, the employee is entitled to compensation. The employer is the debtor of this claim, which stays with the employer even if the service invention is later assigned to a third party.[46] The compensation claim can be assigned by the employee and is inheritable.[47]

National Filing (§13 ArbEG): If the employer acquires the service invention, he is solely entitled, but also obliged to file a national patent application as early as possible after the acquisition.[48] This could be a German patent application, or a European patent application designating Germany, or an application under the Patent Cooperation Treaty, designating Germany, or, in case this appears to be more appropriate, a German Utility Model (§13(1) ArbEG: "domestic application"). The employer must keep the inventor informed about the progress of the prosecution of the patent. If the employer fails to file the application on time, the employee may start the application or registration proceedings on his own initiative in the name of the employer (§13(3) ArbEG).

International Filing (§14 ArbEG): The employer must inform the employee about those countries for which he does not intend to file a foreign application, and must so inform the employee sufficiently prior to the end of the term, until which priority rights can be claimed under international treaties.[49] The employee should have enough time to decide and to permit him to file applications in these States. However, the employee would have to bear the costs of these foreign applications filed in his own name. The employer may keep a non-exclusive right to use the invention in such States (§14(3) ArbEG).

If the employer intends to abandon a patent application or granted patent in particular countries, the employee may take over the application or the patent, but will

46. Federal Supreme Court, Jun. 2, 1987, X ZR 97/86, GRUR 1987,900, 901, "Entwässerungsanlage."
47. District Court Düsseldorf, decision of Sep. 17, 1991, "Reißverschluss."
48. A filing without delay is aimed at ensuring early priority rights.
49. In particular: Paris Convention.

then have to handle the prosecution in his or her name. The employer may retain a non-exclusive right of use as long as the employee does not show that this represents an undue burden on the employee.

The failure of the employer to sufficiently comply with the indicated duties aimed at the protection of service inventions may trigger damages claims which could be asserted by the employee against him.

Keeping the service invention as a trade secret: In case of legitimate interests, the employer could also decide to keep the invention as a trade secret (§17 ArbEG). However, this decision requires that the employer acknowledges that he would not question the patentability of the subject matter of the invention. If such an acknowledgement is made, this would result in compensation having to be paid to the employee in the same manner as with a patented invention. If the employer intends to keep the service invention secret, but believes that the employee's asserted invention is not patentable, the employer may ask for an opinion of the Arbitration Board for employees' inventions at the German Patent Office. If the Arbitration Boards concludes that the invention is not patentable, and the employee does not object to that opinion, the employer is entitled to keep the invention as a company secret with possibly very little or even no compensation for the employee.

Table 13.3. Protection of Service Inventions

Domestic Protection - Entitlement and duty to file for national protection right (PCT/EP designation DE, DE Patent, Utility Model). - Duty to inform the employee about status of prosecution. - Duty to assign related rights in case of intent to abandon an application/registration or granted right (but employer may reserve for himself right to use against reasonable compensation). **Foreign Protection** - Entitlement for protection abroad (outside Germany). - Duty to inform the employee about states in which no protection is sought, to release the service invention for these States and to enable employee to acquire and get protection in these states (but employer may reserve for himself non-exclusive right to use against reasonable compensation). - Duty to assign related rights in case of intent to abandon an application/registration or granted right (but employer may reserve for himself right to use against reasonable compensation).	**Trade Secret** (in case of legitimate interests): - Duty to acknowledge eligibility for protection or refer to Arbitration Board (§17 ArbEG).

5.6. Employee's Compensation

As soon as the employer has made a claim of a service invention, the employee is entitled to compensation (§9(1) ArbEG). The employer is obliged to compensate the employee even if the invention is later assigned to a third party.[50] The compensation claim can be assigned by the employee and is inheritable.[51] The amount of compensation should economically compensate the employee for the assignment of the rights to the employer.[52]

5.6.1. Individual Agreements on the Compensation

The provisions of the ArbEG are mandatory and the parties cannot, in most instances, contract around them. For example, it is impermissible for the parties to agree in advance on conditions that are objectively disadvantageous to the employee. A stipulation in an employment agreement which confers upon the employee a kind of all-inclusive flat rate for inventions made during the employment are, as a general rule, impermissible.[53] Nevertheless, the parties may reach agreements, in particular compensation agreements, concerning service inventions as soon as they have been reported to the employer (§22 ArbEG): "Agreements shall, however, be permissible concerning service inventions after they have been reported and concerning free inventions and proposals for technical improvement (Section 20(1)) after their notification."[54]

Nevertheless, the content of the individual agreements may be challenged in the following two events:

- significant inequity which can be asserted by both parties until six months after the termination of the agreement (§23(1) ArbEG)[55];
- both parties may claim from the other party an adaptation of the compensation in case of substantial changes being essential for the assessment (§12(6) ArbEG).

Even though the parties may waive the claim of adaptation of the compensation according to (§12(6) ArbEG), such agreements should be carefully reviewed with an eye toward later disputes. The agreement should clarify and describe the factors of the assessment that resulted in that particular compensation.

50. Federal Supreme Court, X ZR 97/86, GRUR 1987, 900, 901, "Entwässerungsanlage."
51. District Court Düsseldorf, 4 O 13/91, Mitt. 2000, 363, 368, "Reißverschluss."
52. Federal Constitutional Court, 1 BvR 587–588, NJW 1998, 3704.
53. Busse, Patentgesetz §22 ArbEG N° 5.
54. Unofficial translation.
55. Section 23(1) ArbEG reads: "Agreements concerning service inventions, free inventions, or proposals for technical improvement (§20(1)) permitted by this Act, shall be invalid and void to the extent that they are significantly inequitable.

The compensation is an important aspect of motivating employees. Typically, the compensation is paid as a lump sum,[56] but it can also be an ongoing payment. The agreement on a lump sum payment may have the advantage of removing insecurities due to future changes with respect to the scope of use of the invention and, more importantly, it eliminates administrative efforts on the side of the employer. A lump sum payment could be combined with a waiver of the claim of adaptation of the compensation according to (§12(6) ArbEG), but would require an additional payment to avoid an inequity according to (§23(1) ArbEG).[57]

Lump sum payments are usually used within incentive programs in view of motivating employees for better performances. To some extent, by means of an agreed lump sum the employer may additionally get a release from formal duties, such as the duty to protect the service invention or to release the invention for foreign countries.

5.6.2. Calculation Methods

The amount of the compensation is governed by a Directive issued by the Federal Minister of Labor,[58] which provides three methods for calculating the compensation paid to an employee for an invention, namely:

- License analogy (Directive, N° 6-11);
- Benefits to the employer (Directive, N° 12); and
- Estimation of the invention's value (Directive, N° 13)

All three methods decisively depend on the benefits that the employer receives from the service invention.[59] Thus, the compensation requires that the invention has an economical effect with determinable advantages for the employer.[60] A share of these benefits is allotted to the employee.[61] However, benefits relating to third parties, such as benefits of licensees or the assignee of the service invention, are irrelevant for the assessment.[62]

5.6.2.1. Contribution Factor (Directive, N° 30)

When assessing the amount of compensation a so-called contribution factor must be determined. The purpose of the contribution factor is to determine how much the employee as an individual contributed to the invention. For example, a scientist, whose duties of employment are mainly characterized by research and development, receives less compensation than someone who is not principally employed to perform research

56. Federal Supreme Court, Nov. 20, 1962, I ZR 40/61, GRUR 1963, 315, 317, "Pauschalabfindung."
57. Arbitration Board 2/05.
58. Directive dated Jul. 20, 1959, modified by Directive of Sep. 1, 1983 (Federal Labor Gazette, N° 169, BArbBl. 11/1983, 27).
59. Federal Supreme Court, X ZR 137/07, GRUR 2010, 223, 225, "Türrinnenverstärkung."
60. Federal Supreme Court, X ZR 137/07, GRUR 2010, 223, 225, "Türrinnenverstärkung."
61. Federal Supreme Court, X ZR 137/07, GRUR 2010, 223, 225, "Türrinnenverstärkung."
62. Arbitration Board, Decision 58/07.

and development. The "contribution factor" is based on three elements: the extent of the respective contributions of the employer and employee in defining the problem, which resulted in the invention, their respective contribution in finding the inventive solution and the position and duties of the employee within the company. Accordingly, if the calculation is based on the "License Analogy" method departing from a market oriented or reasonable royalty rate, the determined contribution factor would influence the royalty rate to be paid to the employee as compensation. In the case of an employee focused primarily on solving needs predetermined by the employer, the employee's compensation might be a low fraction of that reasonable royalty. The average contribution factor ranges between 15%–25%.

5.6.2.2. License Analogy

The "license analogy" is commonly applied by the courts[63] if the invention can be allocated to products manufactured by the employer. A number of factors are usually taken into account for a proper calculation of the employee's compensation. Comparable factors are also used for determining damages.[64]

- *Reference Base* (Directive N° 8): A reference base needs to be identified as the relevant basis for applying a reasonable royalty. (Directive N° 19). For instance, if the product (as protected by the patent) is composed of a plurality of components, German courts usually refer to those components of that product which are decisively influenced by the invention. The reference base for a patent that claims a car is not necessarily the value of the whole car. It rather depends on the influence of the invention on the car and which part or parts of the car are decisively characterized by the invention. On the other hand, if the decisive character of the invention influences the whole product (this could be the case with respect to pharmaceutical substances, where the inventive aspect is tied to an active agent) it is reasonable to refer to its whole value. If the invention influences only parts of the product, it is acceptable to take only a percentage of its value. To determine the reference value, German courts weigh the problem solved by the patented invention and its relevance for the product concerned.
- *Net Sales Revenues:*[65] These revenues do not contain costs for packaging, discounts, value added taxes VAT and agent's commissions.
- *Reasonable royalty rate*: For determining this rate, reference can be made to license agreements that have already been concluded by the employer with third parties. In absence of such license agreement(s), industry practices must be considered.[66]

63. Federal Supreme Court, X ZR 137/07, GRUR 2010, 223, 225, "Türrinnenverstärkung."
64. *See* Ch. 12, s. 2.
65. *See* Ch. 12, s. 2.1.
66. *See* Ch. 12, s. 2.2.

- *Scaling:* If the product is manufactured and sold in very high numbers, employers like to apply a sliding scale, which has a reducing effect on the compensation starting from a certain quantity. This must, however, be common practice in the relevant industry sector[67] or require that high numbers of sold products can be attributed to efforts and achievements of the employer. The success of a product is not necessarily triggered by the patent of which the product makes use. Also other factors such as the branding, advertisement, reputation of the company, *etc.*, might be decisive for the decision of the purchaser. Accordingly, the royalty rate is progressively reduced depending on the turnover achieved with the product. For instance, the Appeal Court Düsseldorf[68] applied in matter a scaling starting from a turnover which exceeded EUR 13 Million, i.e., for the turnover below EUR 13 Million, the full royalty, from EUR 13 Million to EUR 25 Million only ¾ of the royalty rate, from EUR 25 Million to EUR 50 Million only ½ of the royalty rate, above EUR 50 Million only ¼ of the royalty rate had to be paid. This is only an example. The case law gives examples where a scaling was applicable starting from even significantly lower turnovers (EUR 1.5 Million).
- *Plurality of Patents*: A further aspect which has decreasing effect on the royalty rate is the question whether other patents are used by the concerned product. If a plurality of patented inventions applies to a particular product, German courts consequently decrease the royalty of the different individual inventions.

5.6.2.3. Benefit to the Employer or the Invention's Value

Another rarely used method for the calculation of the employee's compensation is based on the benefit to the employer relating to the internal cost savings that the employer can achieve as a result of the invention. This method is most useful in cases where the invention consists of technical improvements that can only be realized within the company and therefore the license analogy method would not furnish a meaningful value.

The third (also rarely used) method is based on a free estimation of the value of the invention. This calculation method may be used where the value of the patent cannot be measured by a real royalty income (Table 13.4).

67. Federal Supreme Court, X ZR 71/86, GRUR 1994, 271, Vinylchlorid.
68. InstGE 4, 165, 181.

Table 13.4. Three Calculation Methods

License analogy:	Benefit to the employer:	Estimation of the invention's value:
Appropriate method, if the invention can be allocated to the manufacture and sale of products. This is the most commonly used calculation method.	Appropriate method for innovations and improvements which can only be realized within the company and have no direct effect on the turnover or sales of the company.	Useful in case of cross-licensing where the value of the concerned patent can often not be measured by a royalty income.

5.6.3. *Example (Licences Analogy Method)*

The compensation needs to be assessed on a case-by-case basis. However, the following simple formula can help with calculating the compensation (C) on the basis of the commonly used Licences Analogy method:

$$C = E \times A$$

C = Compensation of the employee: If there is more than one employee-inventor, C has to be shared according to their respective contributions.

E = Value of the invention: E makes reference to the quotient of the reference base (*see* above) and the reasonable royalty. If the reference base refers to the value of the whole product, the revenues of the net sales price have to be multiplied with reasonable royalty which price usually is paid for the invention on the market (turnover x reasonable royalty). The right royalty rate depends on many factors (*see* above). If the product is sold in high numbers, the employer may apply a slide scaling to the royalty rate, with decreasing effect.

A = Contribution factor: The contribution factor depends on the circumstances surrounding the tasks that led to the invention, how the problem was solved and the employee's role and position in the company. This factor is inherently open to dispute. Average factors range between 10 to 20 %. To determine the contribution factor, reference is made to the following point scale:

a + b + c =	3	4	5	6	7	8	9	10	11	12	13	14	15	16	17	18	19	(20)	(p)
A =	2	4	7	10	13	15	18	21	25	32	39	47	55	63	72	81	90	(100)	[%]

The following sub-factors of A (a + b + c) are used to assess the quantity of points (p). Each quantity of points corresponds to a percentage (such as 6 p = 10 %).

(a) **Contribution of the employee** (1-6 points): The employer sets the problem, but also gives the employee specific instructions as to the method he or she needs to employ to solve the problem (low number of points, *e.g.*, 1p). The invention lies outside or is far removed from the employee's usual area of responsibilities and he or she solved the problem independently (high number of points, *e.g.*, 6p).

(b) **Contribution of the company** (1 to 6 points): To what extent does the employee rely on company resources to solve the problem? The less the company contributes, the higher the number of points.

(c) **Position of the employee within the company** (1 to 8 points): The more the employee is involved in research and development, the lower the number of points.

Example:

- Inventor discovered the problem to be solved on his or her own: However, he knew of shortcomings in the company which led him to the problem:
  a = 2
- Inventor found solution using a combination of individual knowledge and company resources:
  b = 2
- Inventor holds a university degree and is a research assistant in the company:
  c = 4
  Result: a + b + c = 8 = Contribution Factor 15%. In total this would lead to compensation of 15 % of the reasonable royalty rate.

5.7. Resolution of Disputes

A particular system is provided by law to resolve disputes in the context of employees' inventions. The German Patent Office provides for an Arbitration Board (§29 ArbEG), consisting of a legal member who serves as chairman, and two technical members. The technical members are examiners from the German Patent Office selected according to the subject matter of the particular dispute (§30 ArbEG).

The main objective of the proceedings at the Arbitration Board is to find an amicable solution between the employer and employee. After introduction of the proceedings on petition of either the employee or the employer (§31 ArbEG), the Board makes a proposal, which becomes final if the parties do not object to the proposal within one month after its notification (§34(3) ArbEG). If at least one of the parties objects, the proposal is null and void and the parties can then introduce court proceedings (§37 ArbEG).

Even after termination of an employment agreement, the parties may still involve the Arbitration Board to solve existing disputes, but they can also directly file an action at a competent court.

CHAPTER 14
Customs Actions

1. INTRODUCTION

Customs actions have become an important strategic tool for combating IP infringement in cross-border trade. The EU first sought to use customs authorities to help combat product piracy in 1986 when it introduced a regulation to allow seizure of pirated goods upon importation into the European Market. Although originally limited to combating product piracy, the legislation is now applicable also against goods that infringe patents and utility patents, irrespective of piracy. Besides blocking the importation of suspect goods, customs actions can be a useful tool for acquiring information about the suspect good itself and its source, destination and distribution channels.

There are limited parallels between customs actions in Europe and proceedings before the U.S. International Trade Commission (ITC). Both sets of actions provide for seizures of infringing goods entering the borders. However, the U.S. ITC will not seize such goods until conducting its own hearing and determination into the validity and infringement of the patents. By contrast, the EU and national proceedings discussed herein provide a temporary wall against suspect imports, and it is left to the national courts to decide whether this wall shall be lifted or not (insofar as the importer contests the detention). Furthermore, to establish standing at the ITC, the right holder must show that an industry in the U.S. relating to articles protected by the patent exists or is in the process of being established. Such "domestic industry" requirement is inapplicable under the European or national customs actions rules.

In the European Union, customs authorities carry out the detention of suspect products without an in-depth assessment and analysis of validity and infringement of the intellectual property right. The customs authorities instead mainly rely on the submissions of the right holder. As soon as the authorities detect suspected goods (and usually after an initial consultation with the contact person named in the application), they order detention of the goods. The right holder even receives an opportunity to inspect the detained goods. Prior to court proceedings, customs actions are essentially formalities initiated by the filing of an application form. This application procedure is efficiently channeled through centralized offices in EU countries, such as the Zentralstelle Gewerblicher Rechtsschutz (ZGR) in Munich.

The right holder is able to stop the proceedings in all stages. The right holder can decide whether a further detention is necessary or an immediate release of the goods is preferred, and is thus in a position to minimize any further interference in the customs clearance. An importer that stays mute during the proceedings could be penalized, because silence may lead to the destruction of the products. If the importer does not explicitly object to the destruction of the seized goods, it is presumed that the importer has consented to the destruction. The number of cases where such presumed agreement leads to destruction of the products is significant. Most of these cases, however, concern clear counterfeits where the importer knows that an objection would obviously be without merit. If the owner of the seized goods objects to the detention, the right holder must initiate court proceedings. Then the case moves to the regular patent infringement courts.

The following graph illustrating the recent spike in the number of actions taken by the ZGR in Munich (*Zentralstelle Gewerblicher Rechtsschutz*), which is Germany's centralized customs authority. Decisions rendered by centralized customs authorities of other EU Member States are not considered in the graph of Figure 14.1.

Figure 14.1. Quantity of Decisions Rendered by the ZGR (Munich) from 1995 to 2014[1]

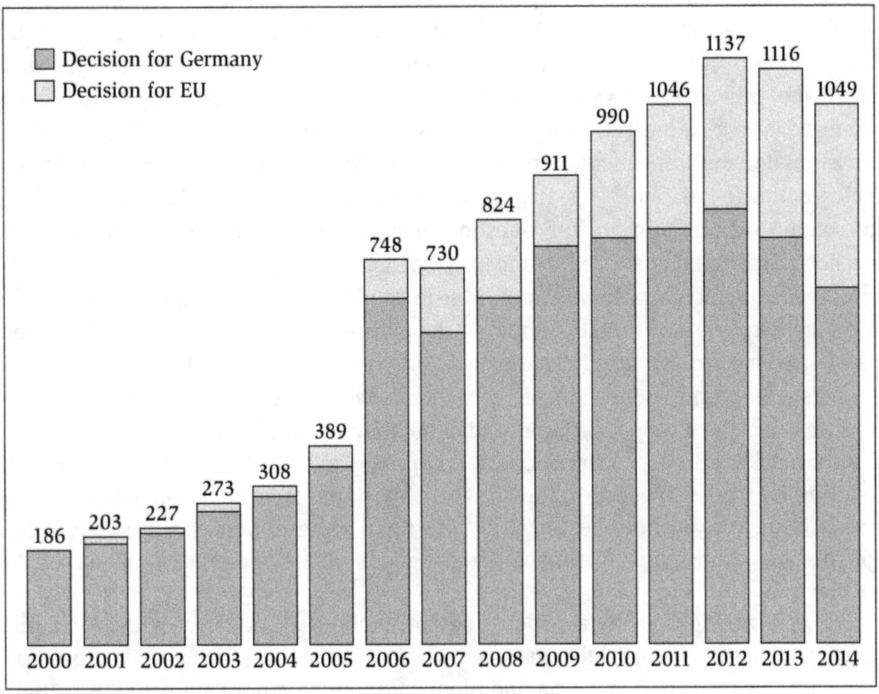

2. LEGAL FRAMEWORK

Customs actions can be based on both EU Community and German law. European law provides for such actions pursuant to Regulation (EU) No. 608/2013,[2] while the German law allows for seizures through section 142(a) of the German Patent Act. Both frameworks mainly differ in their territorial scope. National procedures are confined to the national boarders whereas customs actions based on EU rules refer to the protection of the borders of the European Union.

1. Bundesfinanzdirektion Südost, Zentralstelle Gewerblicher Rechtsschutz, Gewerblicher Rechtsschutz Statistik für das Jahr 2014: www.zoll.de; the Regulation is supplemented by Section 142(b) of the German Patent Act.
2. Regulation (EU) No. 608/2013 of the European Parliament and of the Council of Jun. 12, 2013 concerning customs enforcement of intellectual property rights and repealing Council Regulation (EC) No. 1383/2003(OJ L 181, Jun. 29, 2013, p. 15.).

2.1. EU Rules

European customs enforcement law aims to provide uniform measures throughout the European Union, as applied by national customs authorities. The primary EU rules are contained in the Regulation (EU) No. 608/2013 of the European Parliament and of the Council of June 12, 2013 concerning customs enforcement of intellectual property (hereinafter referred to as the Regulation).[3] The Regulation is completed by the Commission Regulation (EC) No. 1352/2013 of December 4, 2013, which sets forth provisions for the implementation of the Regulation (hereinafter referred to as the Implementing Regulation).[4] The Regulation is confined to procedural aspects and does not contain rules relating to the question of whether IP rights are infringing. This question needs to be answered by means of national law.

The Regulation is primarily applicable to goods which are leaving or entering the single market, i.e., from countries outside the European Union into the territory of the custom-free market (so-called customs territory of the Union, Article 1 of the Regulation). Its application is questionable as to goods which are shipped from third-party countries into the European Union and ultimately destined for another third-party country outside Europe. In the decision *Philips versus Nokia*[5] the European Court of Justice ruled that such goods in transit which are *prima facie* not intended for the EU market, principally cannot be seized by the right holder unless there is convincing evidence and a substantial likelihood that the goods will be rerouted for sale on the EU market.

The Regulation covers a wider range of intellectual property rights, including trademarks, designs, copyright, geographical indications, supplementary protection certificates for medicinal products and plants, Community and national plant variety rights, topography of semiconductor products, and tradenames.[6] It also covers utility models and national patents, including the national parts of conventional European patents. Furthermore, customs actions may also be based on the future European patents with unitary effect. Customs actions may only cover those European countries where an enforceable right is available. For instance, customs actions based on a European Patent that designates certain EU Member States are limited to those EU states where the European patent is valid and in force. European patents with unitary effect will be enforceable in those EU Member States participating in the enhanced cooperation (Article 2 of Regulation 1257/2012). A Community Design, even broader, would be enforceable in all EU Member States. Thus, an IP portfolio may cover the EU territory in different ways. In some territorial areas of the European Union, the protection may be strong and consist of multi-layer rights, whereas in other perhaps less commercially active parts of Europe, the protection may be weaker. European Patents with unitary effect will add a further protection layer to the right holder's toolbox. The text of the EC Regulation can be found in Chapter 17, section 6.

3. The full text of the Regulation is available in English at http://eur-lex.europa.eu/.
4. The full text of the Implementing Regulation is available in English at http://eur-lex.europa.eu/.
5. See EUCJ, 1 Dec. 1, 2011, C-446/09 and C-495/09.
6. Article 2 Regulation.

2.2. National Rules

Besides the pan-EU provisions, national law in any of the EU Member States may provide for additional protection. German law provides for additional protection under §142a of the Patent Act. Customs actions according to German national law are particularly useful in areas that are not covered by the Regulation (§142a (1) of the German Patent Act). The German national rules "complete" the Regulation in the following areas:

- **Movements of goods between EU countries:** The EU Regulation covers measures applicable at the external borders of the single market. These are mainly the customs at the border delimiting the territory of the European Union. The Regulation does not address transit of infringing goods across internal borders within Europe, such as that between Germany and France. For instance, infringing goods that have been produced in France or Spain and are later imported into German territory cannot be blocked based on the EU Regulation. Because these are goods that are already within the single market, the proper recourse is to national laws.
- **Illegal parallel imports of original goods (i.e., "grey market" goods):** The EU Regulation is limited in that it explicitly excludes coverage of original goods that have been produced with the consent of the right holder.[7] European patent rights are not necessarily exhausted even if original goods are concerned. This is particularly applicable to goods that the right holder or an authorized person has put into a market outside the European Union. Nevertheless, even if their re-importation into the European Market represents an infringement of patent rights, these goods cannot be seized pursuant to the Regulation. The new Regulation also does not apply to "goods manufactured by a person duly authorized by a right holder to manufacture a certain quantity of goods, in excess of the quantities agreed between that person and the right holder."[8] i.e., unauthorized overruns. However, measures according to §142a of the German Patent Act may help in such situations. It is commonly accepted case law[9] that illegal parallel imports (grey market products) or unauthorized overruns may be combatted pursuant to national law, such as §142a of the German Patent Act. For instance, the right holder may use German law to block a party who bought a patented good in a developing country at a low price from importing that product into Germany. It also is a very efficient tool to hinder the commercial activity of vendors using the internet to sell original goods bought in low-price countries for resale in European high-price countries.

7. Article 1(5) Regulation.
8. Article 1(5) Regulation.
9. Federal Financial Court, VII R 89/98, GRUR Int. 2000, 780, Jockey.

As set forth above, there are important areas that are left to national customs laws. If the right holder can rely upon a multitude of rights—for instance on a portfolio composed of community designs, European patents and German utility models—he will typically use both the European and the national track.

3. APPLICATION PROCEEDINGS

Regardless of whether the application is based on the Regulation or on §142a of the German Patent Act, it is principally the right holder that may apply for a customs action.[10] This is the person who is named in the register. As an exception, the right holder can also be the licensee, insofar as the licensee is formally authorized by the right holder to initiate customs proceedings.[11] Proof of ownership can be provided by means of an excerpt of the register. The application must be filed with the competent customs authorities. In Germany, the competent customs authority is the Zentralstelle Gewerblicher Rechtsschutz (Bundesfinanzdirektion Südost).

The Regulation provides for two different tracks: one is applicable to the Community rights with a Community-wide effect[12] (Article 4 of the Regulation), and the other is applicable to national rights, particularly European patents, national patents, utility models, SPCs and national trade marks.

Figure 14.2. Application Proceedings

3.1. Content of the Application

The application is made through standard forms[13] which are available on the customs authority's website. In Germany, the required data can be entered directly into an online form available on the ZGR website.[14] Later, if the application is granted, the ZGR forwards the data to the border authorities. That is, it is made available through the customs intranet, which is used by border personnel to detect suspected shipments. Accordingly, the success of the measure significantly depends upon the data and illustrations given by the right holder when completing the form.

10. Article 3 (1)(a) Regulation.
11. Article 3 (2)(a) and (3) Regulation.
12. Community trademark, Community design, a Community plant variety, or a designation of origin or geographical indication or a geographical designation protected by the Community.
13. See Annex I of the Implementing Regulation; a different form must be used if the right holder bases the application on the national regime, namely §142a of the German Patent Act.
14. www.ipr.zoll.de.

In addition to proof that the right holder is authorized to assert the patent rights,[15] the application should contain the following information:

- The name and address of a legal or technical person, usually the lawyer handling the filing procedure.[16] This person must be vested with a power of attorney. This is also the first contact person in the event that customs detects suspect goods.
- An accurate and detailed technical description of the goods—i.e., sufficient information to enable customs to distinguish authentic/original products from suspected goods. The right holder should add a list of those companies authorized to sell original goods.
- Available information on potential infringers and infringing goods. This information should be constantly updated.
- Information (if available) regarding the particularities of the packaging; schedule of arrival or departure; means of transportation; identity of the importers, exporters and holders of suspect goods; and details of the distribution channels used by potential infringers, including information concerning upcoming trade shows. Accordingly, a list of companies that potentially import suspect products into the European market, as well as those companies potentially receiving such products, should be added and constantly updated.

The effectiveness of an application for action by customs depends on the accuracy and thoroughness of the information that customs authorities receive regarding the goods and the potential infringer. The more information is available to customs, the greater the chance that infringing items will be detected.

3.2. Security

The relative ease of seizing good in Germany is counterbalanced by the potential payment of damages if it later turns out that the seizure was unjustified. The right holder must provide a guarantee. In case of customs actions based on the Regulation, it is sufficient to provide an assumption of liability for the case where the detained goods in question are subsequently found not to infringe the asserted IP rights, if the holder of the goods or declarant has suffered damage in that regard. The assumption of liability, which is contained as an undertaking in the application form (see Annex I of the Implementing Regulation), shall cover eventual damages resulting from an unjustified detention of goods. There is no rating of creditworthiness or other similar check; the signed undertaking is sufficient.

The situation is different in the case of customs actions based on German national rules. Here a security bond is necessary. According to §108(1) of the Code of Civil Procedure, this security bond shall be a written, irrevocable, unlimited in time, absolute, unconditional and directly liable bank guarantee to cover eventual damages

15. Article 6 (3)(a)(c) Regulation.
16. Article 6 (3)(k) Regulation.

resulting from an unjustified detention. For the time being, the ZGR requires a bond of EUR 10,000 from a bank that is officially accredited to operate and provide financial services within German territory. If it is too difficult to find a suitable bank, the right holder may also deposit the amount into a trust account with any deposit agency of a German Court.

4. GRANT OF THE APPLICATION

The application is processed ex parte. When the ZGR receives the application, it checks whether the requirements are met, specifically whether the application contains sufficient information to enable the detection of the goods in question, and whether a sufficient guarantee is provided. Following the filing of the application, the ZGR may informally contact the right holder if any information is missing. The ZGR does not, however, assess the validity of the rights. It is satisfied with an excerpt from the register showing that the rights are in force. The ZGR also does not check whether the applicant's statements are correct. Rather, the customs authorities rely on the written factual allegations and explanations of the right holder. Once the application is granted, the ZGR feeds the information contained in the application into the customs intranet, which is then available at the customs offices.

5. ONGOING UPDATES TO CUSTOMS

The order of the ZGR granting the application specifies a time period during which the customs authorities take action.[17] This period shall not exceed one year, but on expiration the ZGR may extend the period by request of the right holder.

During the time period of the validity of the customs order, the facts on the ground may change. For instance, the right holder may become aware of new potential infringers, or may obtain better information on the means of transportation and the commercial channels used for shipping the suspect goods. As new or more accurate information becomes available, the customs application should be updated. This can be done easily through the ZGR website.

According to Article 15 of the Regulation, the right holder is obliged to inform customs if the intellectual property right covered by the application ceases to have effect, if the right holder ceases for other reasons to be entitled to submit an application, or if any other modifications render the application on file inaccurate.

6. DETENTION PROCEDURE

A simplified picture of the detention procedure is provided in the following chart. Detention is carried out by the customs authorities without in-depth analysis of the

17. Article 11 (1) Regulation.

validity and infringement of the patent. But once goods are seized, proceedings then shift to the regular courts where the patent rights are analyzed (Figure 14.3).

Figure 14.3. Detention Procedure

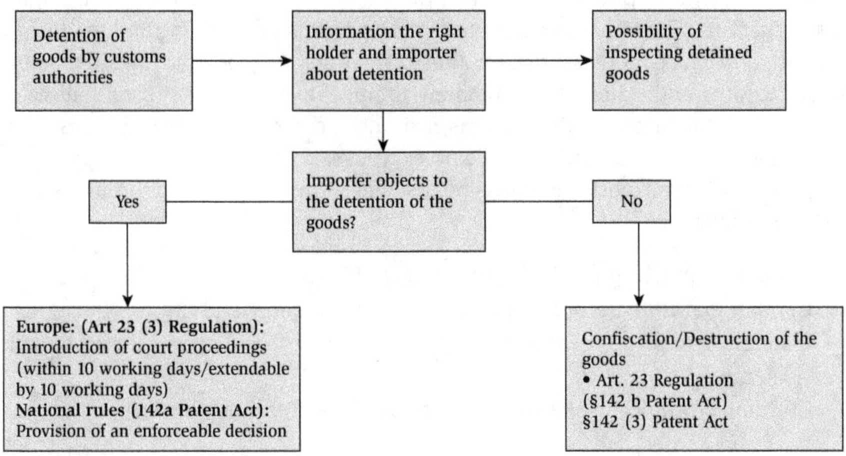

6.1. Customs' Detection and Assessment of Goods

If the customs authorities detect goods that they suspect infringe, according to the information found on the customs intranet, then they will detain these goods.[18] According to Article 2(7) of the Regulation, such goods are basically goods "with regard to which there are reasonable indications that they are prima facie subject of an act of infringement." Accordingly, the determination of the infringement of a right depends on a review of the factual information and documents provided by the right holder to the customs. The infringement must be more than a mere assumption.[19] Prior to detaining the goods, customs may ask the right holder to provide them with any other relevant information with respect to the goods. This possibility allows the customs authorities to broaden the basis for their review of the situation. Nevertheless, the Regulation stays silent as to what extent it is customs' duty to investigate the legal justification of the detention. The Regulation only stipulates that "where the customs authorities identify" suspected goods they shall suspend the release of the goods or detain them. This sets an even lower threshold for a legal review on the side of customs than was applicable in the previous Regulation of 2003,[20] which required that customs gained satisfaction "that goods [...] are suspected of infringing an intellectual property

18. Articles 17(1) Regulation.
19. Rogge/Grabinski, PatG, 10th ed., §142a R. 20; Cordes, GRUR 2007, 483 (485); Hermsen, Mitt. 2006, 261, (262).
20. EC No. 1383/2003.

right." In practice, however, the customs authorities do not have experts on intellectual property law and they primarily rely on the right holders' allegations.

A detention based on the national provisions even requires that "the infringement is obvious" (§142a(1) of the Patent Act). Even though the German framework seems to require a higher certainty as to whether the detained products indeed infringe the concerned patent, in practice, however, the customs authorities rely on the right holder's allegations. There has been some criticism of this practice in the literature[21] and by courts[22] because there is a risk for abuse. The trend may be thus toward greater review by customs authorities, but ultimately the likelihood of any substantial legal review, now or in the future, in the customs clearance process is low, because customs officers do not have any particular IP-related expertise.

Important German customs entry points where most suspected products are detected are as follows:

- German airports, in particular the airport of Frankfurt;
- German maritime harbors, in particular Bremen and Hamburg;
- Mail (close to 67 per cent of all suspected products are detected through mail clearance);
- Customs clearance at the special customs offices for tradeshows.

Other important entry points are harbors in France (Le Havre), Belgium (Antwerp) and The Netherlands, in particular the harbor of Rotterdam. These harbors are used for transit and have a high volume of important container traffic.

6.2. Notification of Detention

As soon as the customs authorities have detected suspected goods, they take action with regard to the detained goods. The customs authorities provide the following information to the right holder:

- Actual or estimated quantity, and the actual or presumed nature of the detained goods, including available images thereof, as appropriate;
- The names and addresses of the declarant or the holder of the goods; and
- The origin, provenance and destination of the suspected goods (Article 17(4) of the Regulation, §142a(2) of the Patent Act).

The right holder has an opportunity to inspect the detained goods.[23] In limited circumstances, the customs authorities may also send samples to the right holder to analyze the infringement; however, this is primarily limited to *"counterfeit and pirated*

21. See AIPPI, Question Q. 208, Answer of the German Group.
22. District Court Düsseldorf InstGE 9, 130, 137.
23. Article 19(1) of the Regulation.

goods" which, according to the legal definition provided in Art. 2 (5) and (6) of the Regulation, do not include items only protected by patents or utility models. Accordingly, the right holder typically must visit the customs office detaining the goods in order to inspect the detained goods.

The importer (usually the declarant) of the goods also will be informed about the detention. It may happen that innocent products are detained by customs. In such a situation, the right holder should clear the situation as soon as possible and take the necessary steps such that the detained goods are quickly released to minimize any further interference in the customs clearance and to avoid possible liabilities.

6.3. Measures after Notification of the Parties

6.3.1. EU Rules

6.3.1.1. Destruction

This procedure may result in the destruction of the detained products. It requires the following steps:

- The right holder confirms within 10 working days from the notification of detention in writing,[24] that, in its conviction, the suspected goods infringe the IP right. The right holder must confirm its agreement to the destruction of the goods. This obligation to confirm the infringement and authorize the goods' destruction shall challenge a careful consideration by the right holder, in view of the potential liabilities arising from an improper seizure.
- Where the owner, declarant or holder of the goods has not confirmed its agreement to the destruction of the goods, nor notified its opposition thereto, to the customs authorities within those deadlines, the customs authorities may deem the owner, declarant or holder of the goods to have confirmed its agreement to the destruction of those goods.[25] Accordingly, this agreement is presumed if the owner, declarant or holder of the goods has not explicitly objected to the destruction within the indicated 10-day period.[26]

Once the right holder informs the authorities that the detained goods infringe the patent, and provides an explicit or presumed agreement, the goods will be destroyed. In the case of clear counterfeits, the holder of the goods will commonly not object, and this leads to destruction of the goods without any further legal review.

24. Article 23 (1) Regulation: Within three working days in case of perishable goods. The 10-day period may be extended by a further 10 working days where circumstances warrant.
25. Article 23 (1) (c) Regulation.
26. See also §142b (4) Patent Act.

6.3.1.2. *Regular Proceedings*

Destruction proceedings are unavailable if the goods' owner, holder or declarant objects to the destruction in a timely manner. In that event, the right holder must initiate court proceedings within 10 working days[27] from the receipt of the notification of detention. This deadline can be extended further by 10 working days in appropriate cases, i.e., upon the duly justified request by the right holder. The Regulation, in particular Article 23, does not provide for a definition of the term "proceedings, to determine whether an intellectual property right has been infringed," but it is commonly understood that it is sufficient to file a regular lawsuit[28] with one of the competent patent infringement courts.[29] The requirement also is fulfilled by means of a request for a preliminary injunction, which may constitute a precautionary measure according to Article 24 (2) (b) of the Regulation, and would have the additional effect of defeating a subsequent request of the importer to release the detained products (see following section 6.3.1.3). Accordingly, the right holder has 10, at most 20, working days to prepare and file a complaint brief or to request a preliminary injunction with a competent German infringement court. The customs authorities do not provide a forum for adjudicating whether the patent is valid and infringed (as is the case with the U.S. ITC). Rather, the customs authorities form a temporary barrier against suspect imports, and it is principally left to the national courts to decide whether this barrier shall be removed.

6.3.1.3. *Possibility of Release*

If the right holder has initiated court proceedings and thus fulfilled the requirements of Article 23 of the Regulation, and absent action on the part of the declarant, owner, importer, holder or consignee, the goods will remain with the customs authorities. But the Regulation provides for relief to obtain an early release of the detained goods. This procedure is described in Article 24 of the Regulation. The early release can be requested by the owner, declarant or holder of the goods. The customs authorities then typically release the detained goods on provision of a guarantee, which shall be sufficient to protect the interests of the right holder. The amount of the guarantee shall basically be equal to the amount the importer of the goods would have to pay as damages for the infringement of the detained goods. The right holder's indications will be taken into account when determining the amount of the guarantee. However, if no agreement between right holder and importer can be reached on a reasonable amount, the customs authorities will determine it.

However, according to Article 24(2)(b) of the Regulation, the customs authorities will not release the detained products if the "authority empowered for this purpose has authorized precautionary measures." That is, customs would not release the detained goods even on the provision of a sufficient guarantee by the importer if the right holder

27. In case of perishable goods, the period shall be three working days, which is not extendable.
28. This can also be a request for a preliminary injunction.
29. Rundschreiben der Bundesfinanzdirektion Südost, Aug. 20, 2008.

can provide an executable court decision ordering the impounding of the detained goods. Accordingly, the maintenance of the detention requires not only that court proceedings have been initiated by the right holder, but also that a court reviews the situation and renders an executable decision. Without this decision ordering precautionary measures, the goods would be released against the guarantee. In view of the speed of the early release proceedings according to Article 24 of the Regulation, it seems to be necessary that the right holder requests precautionary measures through preliminary injunction proceedings.

Often the right holder is satisfied with the release because the short interruption in importation is enough to at least hinder exhibition at a trade show, and in the meantime the right holder can inspect the suspected good and obtain relevant information on parties and distribution channels.

6.3.1.4. *Proceedings for Small Consignments*[30]

The specific procedure for small consignments of counterfeit and pirated goods has been introduced in order to minimize the administrative burden and costs. It simplifies the standard proceedings and responds to the growing amount of infringing goods ordered through the internet and sent by postal services. The procedure allows for such goods to be destroyed without the explicit agreement of the applicant in each case. It only applies if the following are true:

- The suspected goods are counterfeit or pirated goods.[31]
- The goods are not perishable goods.
- The goods are covered by a decision granting an application.
- The right holder has specifically requested the use of the procedure. The form contains a box, which needs to be checked.
- The goods are transported in small consignments.[32]

Requesting the procedure entails the undertaking from the applicant to bear the costs related to the destruction of goods under this procedure, where requested by the customs authorities.

6.3.1.5. *Ex Officio Proceedings*

According to Article 18 of the Regulation, the customs authorities can also act without any underlying request of the right holder. If the customs authorities detain goods

30. Article 26 of Regulation (EU) No. 608/2013.
31. In particular infringements concerning signs which are identical to trade mark or cannot be distinguished in its essential aspects from it (Art. 2 (5)) and goods which infringe copy rights, related rights or designs (Art. 2).
32. These are postal or express courier consignments, which contain three units or less or have a gross weight of less than two kilograms.

suspected of infringing an IP right that are not covered by a valid application, they will try to locate the person or entity entitled to submit the application, which will have then four working days to file it.

6.3.2. German Rules (§142a of the German Patent Act)

The procedure based on the German national rules is comparable to European rules but not completely the same. Even under German law the absence of an objection and appropriate subsequent action may lead to the destruction of the detained products. Where no opposition to the detention is made by the importer, at the latest within two weeks of service of the notification of the detention, the customs authorities shall order confiscation of the detained products, which consequently results in the destruction of the detained products (§142a(3) of the Patent Act).

If the importer objects to the detention, the customs authorities inform the right holder, which must then indicate to the customs authorities whether it still seeks the maintenance of the detention. If the right holder withdraws its request, the customs authorities will release the detained products.

If the right holder intends to proceed, it must submit an executable court decision ordering the impounding of the detained goods. This is different from the European customs action proceedings, where it is sufficient to simply prove that regular proceedings on the merits have been initiated. The detention triggered by a German customs action requires not only that court proceedings have been initiated, but also that a court review the situation and render an executable court decision. As this decision must be provided within a short time frame, namely within two weeks, the right holder must initiate preliminary injunction proceedings to achieve this goal. Where the right holder can show that a court decision has been requested, but has not yet been received, the seizure shall be maintained for a further two weeks at most.

Figure 14.4. Procedure after Detention

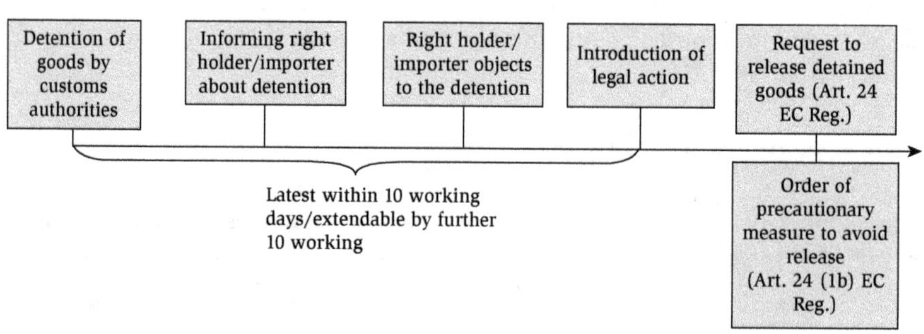

7. POSSIBLE LIABILITIES

Where the detention proves to have been unjustified from the beginning (for instance, where it is later found that there is no infringement of the asserted patent, or if the patent is invalidated), and the right holder did not timely withdraw the request to maintain the detention, the right holder shall be required to compensate the damages that the detention has caused to the person entitled to dispose of the goods.[33] The amount of damages may consist of the difference between the price the owner of the goods would have received when selling them earlier and the value of the goods after the detention. Because the detained products are released by customs in case of an unjustified detention, the calculation of damages is consequently linked to the temporary unavailability of the detained products. The claimant has the burden of proving the cause and amount of the damages. This is difficult to do in practice, and liabilities are usually kept within reasonable limits.

8. COSTS OF THE PROCEEDINGS

Except for the costs related to the storage, handling and destruction of detained goods, there are no fees to be paid to the customs authorities for the application procedure. The preparation of the application will involve some legal costs, as will the maintenance of the detention measures, depending on how many different seizures customs effectively makes and on how many follow-up court proceedings may be necessary.

33. Article 28 of the Regulation.

CHAPTER 15

Budgeting a Patent Enforcement Case

1. FINANCIAL ASPECTS OF GERMAN PATENT LITIGATION

When budgeting a patent enforcement case, the following financial aspects should be taken into account:

- *Fees of the party's own legal representatives*: The party's own legal representatives either bill on an hourly basis, depending on the workload, or they charge the statutory fees according to the Statutory Fees Act.[1] The Statutory Fees Act contains cost tables which set the statutory fees depending on the litigation value of the case.[2] Usually, the party's own legal representatives will bill on an hourly basis, or other alternative fee arrangement, the complexity of patent cases being such that statutory fees fall significantly short of the actual costs for handling them. Thus, the client and the law firm reach a written fee agreement (which may not undercut the levels set by the Statutory Fees Act).
- *Court Fees*: Court fees, which depend on the litigation value, have to be advanced by the plaintiff when filing the complaint. The court fees can be gathered from cost tables contained in the Court Fees Act.[3] The plaintiff makes a preliminary estimation of the litigation value in the complaint, which is usually decisive for the whole proceedings. Chapter 8, Section 7 explains how the litigation value is determined and what the court fees for first, second and third infringement proceedings are.

1. RVG (= Rechtsanwaltsvergütungsgesetz).
2. *See* Ch. 8, s. 7 "Litigation Value": Preliminary estimation of the litigation value is made by the plaintiff in the complaint. In most of the cases, the litigation value is not in dispute between the parties. Accordingly, the preliminary estimation of the plaintiff at the beginning of the proceedings is decisive for the calculation of the costs of the proceedings, including the overall risk assessment.
3. GKG (= Gerichtskostengesetz).

- *Eventual reimbursement*: The losing party is liable to pay the advanced court fees and must reimburse the statutory fees of the winning party. Since these fees depend only on the litigation value, the recoverable fees of the winning party do not depend on what the lawyers of the winning party have actually billed. Accordingly, the lawyers' billing on the basis of an agreed hourly rate is irrelevant. In case of a partial win, the costs are shared among the parties according to their prevailing parts.
- *Split patent litigation system*: The defendant in patent infringement proceedings usually challenges the validity of the asserted patent by filing a nullity complaint with the centralized Federal Patent Court in Munich or through opposition proceedings. Costs resulting from these proceedings are added to the overall costs.
- *Particularities for Non-European Companies*: Plaintiffs without a residence or principal place of business in a Member State of the European Community must, upon request of the defendant, provide a security, such as a bank guarantee, for the potential cost reimbursement claim in case the complaint is dismissed.[4]

2. INFRINGEMENT PROCEEDINGS

2.1. Costs of the Party's Own Legal Representative

As indicated above, the party's own legal representatives generally bill on an hourly basis. Accordingly, the fees depend upon the different tasks to be accomplished by the litigation team during the proceedings. The litigation team is usually composed of an attorney-at-law, a patent attorney and a junior associate, as well as secretaries and paralegals.[5] As the amount of the different tasks which have to be accomplished by the representatives in the course of the proceedings can often be anticipated, it is feasible to budget the costs of the proceedings. The right holder should ask the legal representatives at what stage of the proceedings the different costs will accrue. There might be starting costs accruing prior to the filing of the lawsuit. These costs comprise the evaluation of the patent, assessment of the infringing aspects of the contested embodiment, and then the preparation and filing of the complaint. Later, a few months after filing the complaint brief, a reply to the response to the complaint brief has to be drafted and finally (approximately twelve months after the introduction of the proceedings) the legal representatives will have to prepare for, and participate in, the hearing. Due to the reduced complexity of the proceedings relative to the U.S. (no general discovery, no depositions, no jury trial, no equitable conduct defenses), budgeting is more predictable in Germany than in the U.S. Empirically, the costs range from Euro (EUR) 60,000 for less complex cases to EUR 240,000 for more complex cases,

4. *See* Ch. 8, s. 7.3 "Security for Defendant's Legal Costs" (for infringement proceedings) and Ch. 7, s. 6.3 "Security for Defendant's Legal Costs" (for nullity actions).
5. Costs for secretaries, paralegals are usually included and are not additionally charged.

from filing the complaint until a first instance decision is taken. If special arrangements concerning an hourly rate are missing, the fees are calculated on the basis of the Statutory Fees Act.[6] These are the minimum fees which may not be undercut by particular agreements. Usually, the costs of second instance proceedings are approximately the same as those charged for the first instance, assuming they are calculated on an hourly basis. Third instance proceedings are rare. The court fees are increased by about 30 % relative to the second instance. As a rule, the costs of the third instance, if calculated on an hourly basis, are approximately the same as those of the previous instances. However, if they are calculated according to the Statutory Fees Act, the fees are then approximately 30 % higher.

2.2. Cost-Increasing Factors

- *Cost of private expert:* Depending on the complexity of the case, it may be advisable to retain a private expert. Costs of a private expert are highly variable and have to be added to the overall costs.
- *Costs due to appointment of court expert*: In less than approximately 20 % of all patent litigation cases, the Court of First Instance appoints an expert. This is even more unlikely in the second instance. According to our experience, the involvement of a court expert increases the costs of the proceedings (review of expert opinion, at least one additional brief). Furthermore, the proceedings become more expensive because the costs of the court expert (on average EUR 10,000–EUR 20,000) are borne by the losing party.

3. COSTS FOR NULLITY PROCEEDINGS

When budgeting a case, possible nullity or opposition proceedings need to be considered. The validity of the asserted patent may be challenged by filing a nullity complaint with the centralized Federal Patent Court in Munich or through EPO opposition proceedings (within the nine-month period after grant), and the costs resulting from such proceedings must be added to overall costs.

3.1. Average Costs for Legal Representatives

In validity proceedings, the parties' legal representatives generally bill on an hourly basis. Accordingly, the fees depend upon the different tasks which need to be performed by the litigation team during the proceedings, such as preparation of a reply to the complaint, preparation of at least one further brief prior to the hearing, preparation of the main hearing and participation in the main hearing, plus expenses such as translation costs and travel costs. Empirically, the costs range from EUR 50,000

6. RVG (= Rechtsanwaltsvergütungsgesetz).

for less complex cases to EUR 140,000 for more complex cases, from filing the complaint until a first instance decision is taken. If no special arrangement is reached between counsel and party, the fees are calculated on the basis of the Statutory Fees Act. In the second instance, these fees are slightly higher unless they are calculated on an hourly basis in which case they are roughly comparable to the first instance.

3.2. Cost-Increasing Factors

In nullity proceedings, a court expert may also be appointed. Nevertheless, the law has recently been modified in a way that may lead to fewer appointments of court experts. Instead, it seems that more private experts will be involved in these proceedings. The proceedings may thus become more expensive due to the involvement of private or court expert (on average EUR 10,000–EUR 20,000).

3.3. Opposition Proceedings before EPO

Besides a moderate opposition filing fee of less than EUR 1,000, no court fees have to be paid for opposition proceedings. Parties to opposition EPO proceedings do not regularly have a reimbursement claim even if they win. In the case of EPO opposition proceedings, national invalidation proceedings are not admissible. For this reason, the cost assessment should consider either the costs of the EPO proceedings or of the Federal Patent Court proceedings. The latter depend, however, upon the particular case.

4. REIMBURSEMENT

4.1. Proceedings before the Infringement Courts

The losing party is liable for the court fees paid by the winning party and has to reimburse an amount which corresponds to the statutory fees, including travel expenses and translation costs. If there is only a partial win, the costs are accordingly distributed among the parties (apportionment of costs). The winning party's attorney and patent attorney fees are reimbursed pursuant to the Statutory Fees Act. The reimbursable courts fees can be gathered from the table in Chapter 8, Section 7.2.

4.2. Invalidation Proceedings

4.2.1. EPO Opposition

Parties to opposition proceedings may normally not claim reimbursement of the costs. According to Article 104 EPC, each party to the opposition proceedings bears the costs it has incurred, unless the Opposition Division, for reasons of equity, orders a different apportionment. But such orders occur only in exceptional situations, such as when the opponent files a highly relevant document late, without any valid justification, and this renders both the oral proceedings and the patent proprietor's preparation useless.[7]

4.2.2. *German Invalidation Proceedings (First and Second Instance)*

The principles applicable to infringement courts are also applicable in invalidation proceedings. In other words, depending upon the litigation value, the winning party may claim reimbursement of the court fees and statutory fees plus expenses.

7. EPO – T 1306/05.

CHAPTER 16

Samples

This chapter contains samples of the most frequently encountered documents used in patent infringement proceedings. They represent schematic outlines, meant to illustrate the matters described in detail in the previous chapters.

1. WARNING LETTER

Explanations concerning the content of the warning letter can be found in Chapter 8, section 2.1

1.1. Body of the Warning Letter

Registered Mail[1]

Management

Company X

Address

Date

Ref.

Due to infringement of German Patent DE...

Dear Sirs,

1. The warning letter shall be addressed to the party who will be the prospective defendant. The letter is typically sent by registered mail to obtain a certificate of receipt to prove that the accused infringer received the warning letter.

This is to inform you that the patent attorneys and lawyers of our firm are representing the well known Company Y.[2] *We have been instructed by our client to inform you about the following:*

Our client is the owner of the German Patent DE...concerning a sport shoe. The mention of the grant of the patent has been published on October 20, 2009 and its application has been published on October 15, 2008. A copy of the German Patent is enclosed as

– Enclosure 1 –

The patent is in force.[3] *A nullity action filed against the asserted patent has recently been dismissed by the Federal Patent Court. The decision is final and confirms the validity of the patent as granted and is enclosed as*

– Enclosure 2 –

An excerpt of the register of the German Patent and Trademark Office is enclosed as

– Enclosure 3 –

Our client has taken note that on the present trade show ISPO Winter 2016 in Munich your company is exhibiting sport shoes having the features of at least claim 1 of German Patent DE....Our client became also aware that you are manufacturing the accused products in Germany.

These sport shoes, which infringe our client's patent, are named: "...." (hereinafter: "the Model)"[4] *A brochure of your company in which these sport shoes are shown and advertised is enclosed as*

– Enclosure 4 –

Brochures according to Enclosure 4 are distributed by employees of your company on the ongoing tradeshow. By producing and distributing the Model you are infringing our client's patent.

The claimed teaching of the patent of our client concerns a sports shoe, particularly, a running shoe which is provided with a rigid cover which covers the upper portion on the exterior surfaces thereof in the front region of the shoe. The main claim 1 reads:

A sport shoe comprising

1) *a sole;*

2) *an upper portion attached to the sole and*

3) *a rigid cover*
   - *made of resisting material;*
   - *angular in cross-section and*
   - *defining a securing band and a protective shield;*

2. It is advisable to add to the warning letter a power of attorney.
3. It is advisable to mention that no opposition or invalidation proceedings are pending.
4. The accused product should be concretely designated, such that the accused infringer understands to which products the accusations are addressed. This requires that the warning letter exactly identifies which products/infringing activities are concerned.

4) *the securing band is affixed between said sole and said upper portion,*

5) *the securing band extends from said sole, upwardly over the exterior of the upper portion in the area of the ball of the shoe.*

Further explanations of the patented subject matter can be taken from the description of the asserted patent (see Enclosure 1)[5]

A comparison of the features of main claim 1 with your Model exhibited by you on the ongoing ISPO Winter 2016 reveals that the accused sport shoes make use of all features of this claim of the patent and, thus, infringe our client's rights.[6]

Our client is thus entitled (§139 (1) German Patent Act) to ask you to refrain from the indicated activities. Furthermore, according to §§242 German Civil Code, 140 b German Patent Act, you are obligated to render full and true account about the indicated infringing activities in Germany in order to enable our client to calculate and determine the damages resulting therefrom. The damage claim results from §139(2) German Patent Act. Additionally, for the time after the publication of the patent application until the mention of the grant, our client claims a reasonable compensation according §33(1) German Patent Act.[7] *The duty to recall the accused shoes from customers and the duty to destroy them follows from §140 a German Patent Act.* [8]

Finally, according to law our client is also entitled to claim the reimbursement of the legal costs caused by the intervention of our firm which became necessary due to your unlawful conduct.

*In order to avoid otherwise inevitable commencement of legal actions against your company, we have to request you to sign and return the enclosed undertaking (**Enclosure 5**)*[9] *not later than*

Date[10]

at the latest.

According to law, only a binding and sufficiently penalized declaration of cease and desist as requested is considered as appropriate to avoid a law suit for infringement. A power of attorney is enclosed to the present letter.

Very truly yours,

5. A warning letter requires a sufficient description of the subject-matter and scope of protection. Nevertheless, reference can be made to the specification of the patent in case of simpler technologies. This applies to the example.
6. The accused technology should be well described in the warning letter, whereby the indicated claim chart can be used to show, feature by feature, that the accused embodiment uses the claimed invention. For this feature mapping, it is advisable to use available evidence (photos, advertisements, etc.).
7. See Ch. 12, s. 5.1.2.
8. The provisions can be found in Ch. 17, s. 3.
9. This undertaking can be found in the following section.
10. In patent Infringement cases, a time frame of two—three weeks is usually given to the accused infringer.

Patent- und Rechtsanwälte

(signature) *(signature)*

Rechtsanwalt *Patentanwalt*

Enclosures:

German Patent DE.... (Enclosure 1)

Decision of the Federal Patent Court (Enclosure 2)

Excerpt of the register of the German Patent and Trademark Office (Enclosure 3)

Brochure (Enclosure 4)

Undertaking (Enclosure 5)

Power of Attorney (Enclosure 6)

1.2. Undertaking of Cease and Desist

UNDERTAKING

Company X hereby undertakes towards Company Y

I. *in order to avoid the payment of a contractual penalty to Company Y for each case of non-compliance of € 25,000.00, to refrain from manufacturing, offering, putting on the market or using or possessing for the aforementioned purposes shoes of the following features:*

A sport shoe comprising

1) *a sole;*

2) *an upper portion attached to the sole and*

3) *a rigid cover*

- *made of resisting material;*
- *angular in cross-section and*
- *defining a securing band and a protective shield;*

4) *the securing band is affixed between said sole and said upper portion,*

5) *the securing band extends from said sole, upwardly over the exterior of the upper portion in the area of the ball of the shoe.*

II. to render to Company X account of the extent of the acts covered by section I and committed since November 20, 2009 [publication of the grant of the patent] *by establishing a list indicating:*

1) the names and addresses of the manufacturers, suppliers and other previous owners,

2) the names and addresses of commercial buyers and of the sales outlets for which the products were intended,

3) the quantity of products manufactured, supplied, received or ordered and the prices paid for the products concerned;

whereby as proof for the indicated details copies of the corresponding sales documents (e.g. invoices or alternatively delivery receipts) shall be provided, whereby those details that lie outside the investigation may be kept confidential by redaction;

II.b. to render account of the extent of the activities described under section I since November 15, 2008 [1 months after publication of the patent application] *by indicating*

1) the production quantities and times,

2) the individual supplies; broken down according to delivery quantities, delivery limes, delivery prices and type designations, and the names and addresses of commercial buyers,

3) the individual offers for sale, broken down according to quantities offered for sale, times of the sales, prices of goods offered for sale and type designations, and the names and addresses of commercial recipients of offers for sale,

4) the advertisement carried out, broken down according to advertising media, their circulation, the dissemination period and the dissemination territory,

5) production costs broken down according to individual cost factors, and profits made, whereby this information is only to be provided for infringing activities carried out in the period since November 20, 2009 [1 month after publication of the grant of the patent];

III. *to pay to Company Y*

1) *a reasonable compensation for all acts covered by section I and committed since November 15, 2008 until November 20, 2009;*

2) *all damages arisen and arising in the future by the acts covered by section I and committed since November 20, 2009;*

IV. *Company X shall recall delivered sport shoes according to section I from customers who are still in possession of these sport shoes, whereby these customers shall be informed by Company X about the infringing quality of these sport shoes and Company X shall seriously demand the back transfer of these sport shoes. Company X shall take a binding undertaking towards these customers to reimburse eventual payments and to bear eventual packaging and transport costs for the back transfer.*

V. *Company X shall—at its own cost—destroy or surrender to a bailiff, to be named by Company Y, all sport shoes according to section I, which are in its direct or indirect possession, for the purpose of destruction;*

VI. *to reimburse the costs attributable to the intervention of the patent attorneys and lawyers of the law firm...* [11]

11. The costs result from a litigation value. Assuming the litigation is based on EUR 0.5 million, the reimbursable fees (2 fees according to the Fees Statutory Act) are ca. EUR 6.550.

VII. *The District Court Düsseldorf is competent for all disputes in connection with the present undertaking.*

Date, Place Signature

2. INQUIRY LETTER[12]

Registered Mail

Management

Company X

Address

Ref.

Dear Sirs,

This is to inform you that the patent attorneys and lawyers of our firm are representing the well known Company Y. We have been instructed by our client to inform you about the following:

Our client is the owner of the German Patent DE...concerning a sport shoe. The mention of the grant of the patent has been published on October 20, 2009 and its application has been published on October 15, 2008. A copy of the German Patent is enclosed as

– *Enclosure 1* –

The patent is in force. A nullity action filled against the asserted patent has recently been dismissed by the Federal Patent Court. The decision is final and confirms the validity of the patent as granted. This decision is enclosed as

– *Enclosure 2* –

An excerpt of the register of the German Patent and Trademark Office is enclosed as

– *Enclosure 3* –

The teaching of the patent invention concerns a sports shoe, particularly, a running shoe which is provided with a protection cover which covers the upper portion on the exterior surfaces thereof in the front region of the shoe. Main claim 1 reads:

A sport shoe comprising

1) *a sole;*

2) *an upper portion attached to the sole and*

3) *a rigid cover*

- *made of resisting material;*
- *angular in cross-section and*
- *defining a securing band and a protective shield;*

12. See Ch. 8, s. 2.2.

4) *the securing band is affixed between said sole and said upper portion,*

5) *the securing band extends from said sole, upwardly over the exterior of the upper portion in the area of the ball of the shoe.*

Our client has taken note that on the ISPO Winter 2016 trade show in Munich your company is exhibiting sport shoes with such protection cover.

It appears that these sport shoes infringe our client's patent. The relevant sport shoes are named: "...." A brochure of your company in which these sport shoes are shown and advertised is enclosed as

– *Enclosure 4* –

Brochures according to Enclosure 4 are distributed by employees of your company on the ongoing tradeshow.

A comparison of the features of main claim 1 with your Model "..." exhibited by you on the ongoing ISPO Winter 2010 appears according to our opinion that the accused sport shoes make use of all features of at least claim 1 of the patent and, thus, infringe our clients rights.

The commercialization of the sport shoe with the type designation "..." constitutes in our view an unlawful use of our clients patent rights, and accordingly we demand that within...business days you indicate why you believe that you are entitled to continue selling your Model "...," in view of our client's patent rights.

A power of attorney is enclosed to the present letter.

Very truly yours,

Patent- und Rechtsanwälte

(signature)	*(signature)*
Rechtsanwalt	*Patentanwalt*

Enclosures:

German Patent DE...(Enclosure 1)

Decision of the Federal Patent Court...(Enclosure 2)

Excerpt of the register of the German Patent and Trademark Office (Enclosure 3)

Brochure (Enclosure 4)

Power of Attorney (Enclosure 5)

3. COMPLAINT BRIEF (INFRINGEMENT ACTION)

Explanations concerning the complaint in infringement proceedings can be found in Chapter 8, section 3.2.

District Court...

[Address]

Munich, date

Our Reference:

Complaint

Of

Company Y.,*[address], represented by its CEO...*

Litigation counsel: *Attorneys at law of the lawfirm...*

In cooperation with: *Patent attorneys of the lawfirm*[13]*...*

– plaintiff –

versus

Company X, [address]*legally represented by its chief executive director, at the same place,*

– defendant –

due to patent infringement.

Litigation value: € 1,000,000 (preliminary estimated).

The court fees in an amount of € 16.008 are paid by the enclosed cheque.

In the name and by authorization of plaintiff, we file suit against defendant at the District Court of Düsseldorf and ask to summon an early date for oral proceedings.

We will request,

I. *to sentence defendant*

1. *in order to avoid a penalty to be set by the court for each case of violation of up to € 250,000.00, as an alternative confinement, or confinement of up to 6 months, in case of repeated violations a confinement of up to a total of 2 years, to be imposed on defendant's managing director, to refrain from manufacturing, offering, putting on the market or using or possessing for the aforementioned purposes sport shoes comprising*

1) *a sole;*

2) *an upper portion attached to the sole and*

3) *a rigid cover*

- *made of resisting material;*

- *angular in cross-section and*

- *defining a securing band and a protective shield;*

4) *the securing band is affixed between said sole and said upper portion,*

5) *the securing band extends from said sole, upwardly over the exterior of the upper portion in the area of the ball of the shoe.*

---

13. The patent attorneys and litigation attorneys need not necessarily be from the same firm.

2. to render to plaintiff account of the extent of the acts covered by section 1 and committed since November 20, 2009 [publication of the grant of the patent] *by establishing a list indicating:*

a) the names and addresses of the manufacturers, suppliers and other previous owners,

b) the names and addresses of commercial buyers and of the sales outlets for which the products were intended,

c) the quantity of products manufactured, supplied, received or ordered and the prices paid for the products concerned;

- whereby as proof for the indicated details copies of the corresponding sales documents (e.g. invoices or alternatively delivery documents) shall be provided, whereby those details that lie outside the investigation may be kept confidential by redaction;

3. to render account of the extent of the activities described under section 1 since November 15, 2008 [1 months after publication of the patent application] *by indicating*

a) the production quantities and times,

b) the individual supplies; broken down according to delivery quantities, delivery limes, delivery prices and type designations, and the names and addresses of commercial buyers,

c) the individual offers for sale, broken down according to quantities offered for sale, times of the sales, prices of goods offered for sale and type designations, and the names and addresses of commercial recipients of offers for sale,

d) the advertisement carried out, broken down according to advertising media, their circulation, the dissemination period and the dissemination territory,

e) production costs broken down according to individual cost factors, and profits made, whereby this information is only to be provided for infringing activities carried out in the period since November 20, 2009 [1 month after publication of the grant of the patent],

- whereby the names and addresses of non-commercial recipients of offers shall not be disclosed to the plaintiff, but to a certified auditor domiciled in Germany and bound to confidentiality vis-à-vis the plaintiff, which shall be named by the defendant, provided the defendant bears the costs of the auditor and instructs and authorizes him to respond to concrete questions of plaintiff whether a particular recipient of an offer is named in the report.

II. *to find, that the defendant is obliged to*

a) *pay a reasonable compensation for all acts covered by section I.1. and committed since November 15, 2008 until November 20, 2009;*

b) *compensate Plaintiff for all damages invoked on plaintiff by the acts indicated under I.1, committed since November 20, 2009 and which will be invoked in future;*

III. *to have defendants bear the costs of the proceedings;*

IV. *to declare the decision to be provisionally enforceable—if need be, against a bond of security by a bank guarantee.*

REASONING

A. Introduction

Plaintiff is the proprietor of the German Patent (in the following "Patent-in-suit") on which the present complaint is based.

The Patent-in-suit is filed as

– Enclosures K 1 –

The grant of a Patent-in-suit was published on October 20, 2009. The corresponding patent application has been published on October 15, 2008. The Patent- in-suit is in force.

Evidence: *Extract of the register of the German Patent and Trademark Office.*

– Enclosure K 2 –

A nullity suit was filed on...against the German Part of the European Patent (Patent-in-suit), but was finally dismissed by the Federal Patent Court on....This decision is enclosed as

– Enclosure K 3 –

This decision has not been appealed and is thus final. With the present complaint, plaintiff asserts patent rights as to a shoe.

B. *The Parties*

The plaintiff is a renowned sports equipment manufacturer. It is an innovative enterprise, which invests several Millions of Euros in its Research & Development (R&D). The achievements of plaintiff's R&D are protected by intellectual property rights, such as patents. Among these patents is the presently asserted patent. The features of the claimed invention are reproduced in plaintiff's shoe models such as...of which photos are enclosed as

– Enclosures K 4 – [14]

The defendant operates in the same field. The parties are in direct competition. The defendant commercializes a sport shoe which is referenced as....(hereinafter: accused sport shoe) The accused sport shoe is illustrated on the second page of a flyer, provided as

– Enclosures K 5 –

B. Patent-in-suit

I. Subject-matter of the patent

The invention relates to a sports shoe. It relates, in particular, to a running shoe which is provided with a protective cover. It covers the upper on the exterior surfaces thereof in the region of the ball and extends from the sole.

---

14. It is not necessary for asserting claims from that patent that the right holder uses the invention. This information contained in the complaint is aimed at giving more background information and to illustrate the significance of the case to the court.

Not only the sole but also the upper on the exterior surfaces of the sport shoe in vicinity to the ball are subject to heavy stresses. In the case of running shoes the stress is particularly high. Therefore, the prior art proposes, as illustrated in the German Patent Application DE...provided as

– Enclosure K 6 –

to provide protecting supports which cover the critical areas. The document of Enclosure K 6 is cited in the description and is the closest prior art according to the decision of the Federal Patent Court (see page..., enclosure K 3). If these supports are subsequently fitted, for example by means of a lace, perfect fitting can usually not be obtained. If, however, the supports are formed on the sole and drawn up over the edge thereof a certain distance over the upper portion, the problem arises that, on the one hand, only soles with folds formed thereon can be used and, on the other hand, the fixing of the folds composed for instance of rubber on to the upper portion by gluing is not sufficiently durable.

II. Objective/Solution

The objective of the patent is to provide an improved sport shoe in view of the problem shown in the prior art. The invention overcomes this problem by providing a protecting cover of angular cross-section and permanent shape, one band of which serves for holding the cover in position and engages the underside of the shoe, preferably inserted between the upper portion and the sole. At the same time the holding band of the shoe cover is preferably located between the margin of the upper portion and the sole composed of one or several layers. It is preferably in the form of a thin tongue tapering towards its end. The advantage offered by the invention is that the normal components of the shoe, irrespectively of whether it is the upper portion or the sole, can be worked into the shape, and that no supplementary or securing means are required for fitting the protecting cover. This is realized by sport shoes with the following features, namely:

A sport shoe comprising

1) *a sole;*

2) *an upper portion attached to the sole and*

3) *a rigid cover*

- *made of resisting material;*

- *is angular in cross-section and*

- *definition a securing band and a protective shield;*

4) *the securing band is affixed between said sole and said upper portion,*

5) *the securing band extends from said sole, upwardly over the exterior of the upper portion in the area of the ball of the shoe.*

This feature chart is separately provided on a sheet as

– Enclosure K 7 –

C. Infringement of the patent-in suit

Defendant commercializes the infringing shoe via its website www.yyy.com. The accused sport shoe violates claim 1 of the patent-in-suit. The accused shoe is illustrated in a photo used in defendant's advertising, provided here as:

– Enclosure K 8 –

The photo contains the references of features 1)–5) of the asserted claim 1: It is a sport shoe with a sole (Feature 1) with an upper portion attached to the sole (Feature 2) and a protective (Feature 3) which is

- made of resisting material;

- is angular in cross-section and

- define a holding arm and a cover arm;

Furthermore, the holding band is secured between said sole and said upper portion (Feature 4) and the cover arm extends from said sole, upwardly over the exterior of the upper portion in the area of the ball of the shoe (Feature 5).

Accordingly, at least claim 1 of the Patent-in-suit is infringed.

D. Legal assessment

The jurisdiction of the District Court Düsseldorf follows from §32 Civil Procedural Code.[15] *Defendant is marketing the infringing products in the entire Federal Republic of Germany.*

The claims asserted in the present action are justified in view of the above stated submission. The defendant is obliged to cease and desist due to an illegal use of the subject matter of the patent-in-suit, §139 paragraphs 1 German Patent Act.

Furthermore, defendant must pay damages to the plaintiff according to §139 para. 2 German Patent Act. As a company which is specialized in this particular field, defendant could have recognized the patent infringement through ordinary diligence, §276 German Civil Code.

Since the plaintiff is not able to quantify damages caused by the infringing act of the defendant, because the extent of the infringing acts are not yet known, there is a legitimate interest of the plaintiff to be accepted with respect to the determination of the liability for damages according to §256 Civil Procedural Code.

In order to enable the plaintiff to quantify the damages, the defendant is obliged to render account, §§242, 259 German Civil Code. Plaintiff needs the required account to determine the amount of damages and the defendant is not unreasonably demanded

15. §32 of the Code of Civil Procedure reads: "Claims relating to unlawful acts are within the jurisdiction of the court in the district of which the act was committed" (unofficial translation), see also Ch. 8, s. 1.

with the provision of the required information. According to §140 b German Patent Law, the defendant is also obliged to provide information on the chain of distribution of the infringing products. [16]

(signature)

Rechtsanwalt

Enclosures K1–K 8

4. SETTLEMENT AGREEMENT

Sample 4 is based on a typical scenario: The patentee won the first instance trial. Accordingly, the patentee was able to enforce the decision. Even though the patentee still needs to provide security for the enforcement, it is a critical situation for the accused infringer. An appeal does not have suspending effect and thus the uninterrupted marketing of the contested products is endangered by the immediate enforcement of the first instance decision (see Chapter 8, section 5). Against this background, the accused infringer (defendant) might be interested (now more than at the beginning and during the first instance proceedings) in finding a solution and would try to settle the case with the patentee. This is the situation which led to the present settlement agreement:

Settlement Agreement

Between Company (right holder)

[Address]...duly represented by...

– in the following referred to as the Licensor –

and Company Licensee

[Address]...duly represented by...

– in the following referred to as Licensee –

Preamble

Licensor is the owner of the German counterpart of the European patent...relating to a sport shoe (hereinafter: the Patent).

Licensee has sold sport shoes. These sport shoes have been held in an infringement proceeding to infringe the patent of Licensor. The decision of first instance rendered by the District Court Düsseldorf on...[Docket number] has granted all requests of the complaint (hereinafter: the Decision). In order to terminate the litigation presently pending before the Court of Appeals of Düsseldorf...[Docket number] the parties enter into the following settlement agreement.

16. The sample does not include the destruction claim according to §140a(1) Patent Act. It does also not include a claim to recall the infringing products or to remove them definitively from the distribution channels §140a(1) Patent Act. Both claims require that the enforcement is not disproportionate in the individual case.

§1 Royalty for the past

(1) Licensee shall provide for the time until the execution of the present Agreement a written, complete and itemized listing comprising all offers, sales and deliveries of products as defined in section I of the Decision. This list shall contain individual deliveries, classified according to delivery amounts, times, prices.

(2) Licensee promises to pay a royalty of…€ per pair to Licensor for the sale of the sport shoes covered by the Decision, in particular those with the product name….

(3) The submission of the list according to §1 (1) as well as the payment of the resulting amounts shall be made within three weeks after the execution of this contract.

§2 License for the future

(1) Licensor grants to Licensee a non-exclusive license to produce and sell products that make use of the Patent (hereinafter Licensed Products).

(2) Licensee pays a royalty of €…per pair for sales of the Licensed Products after the execution of the present contract.

(3) The parties agree that the sport shoes produced by Licensee with product number…do not fall under the patent in litigation.

§3 Termination of litigation

(1) Licensee will withdraw the appeal filed with the Court of Appeals within two weeks after the execution of this agreement.

(2) Further, Licensee promises to pay all court fees, attorney fees and patent attorney fees in accordance with the Statutory Fee Act. The payment of these costs shall be made within two weeks after receipt of the respective invoice.

§4 Royalties and payment

(1) With respect to future sales Licensee shall report quarterly on the first day of the month with respect to the sales of the Licensed Product starting three months after execution of this agreement. The payment of the royalties is due with the report.

(2) If Licensee delays the report and/or the royalty payment more than two weeks, Licensor has the right to terminate this agreement for cause.

§5 Bookkeeping *and review*

(1) Licensee promises to keep a separate list on the deliveries of Licensed Products showing the precise number of the articles produced by Licensee under this agreement, the customers and the delivery dates, as well as other significant facts.

(2) Licensor will have the right to have an independent auditor, who is subject to confidentiality, review Licensee's bookkeeping and its compliance with Licensee's general bookkeeping. Patentee will bear the costs of reviewing the books.

(3) If errors are discovered Licensee will bear the auditing costs. In addition the royalties shall be doubled for the review period, if the deviation is more than 5 percent under the owed amount.

§6 No guarantees

(1) *Licensor does not guarantee the validity, technical utility or commercial exploitability of the patented invention.*

(2) *Licensor is not liable for the dependency of the patent on patents of third parties.*

(3) *Licensee holds Licensor harmless of any possible claims for product liability as far as these are based on the production of Licensee under the patent.*

(4) *If the patent should be declared invalid, then this contract shall end on the date of the final decision in the invalidation proceedings. Paid royalties shall not be refunded.*

§7 Assignment and sublicenses

This agreement cannot be assigned to third parties, and Licensee does not have the right to grant sublicenses.

§8 Obligation to defend and proceed against infringers

(1) *Licensor is not obligated to defend the Patent against attacks by third parties.*

(2) *In the case of infringement of the Patent, Licensor shall decide on bringing infringement action taking into account commercial aspects.*

§9 Duration of the contract

This contract is for the remaining duration of the Patent. The contract can be terminated by Licensee with a termination notice of six months to the first of January and the first of July of each year.

§10 Mutual release

With the performance of this agreement all mutual claims deriving from this litigation are settled.

§11 Jurisdiction and Applicable Law

German Law shall be applicable to the present Agreement. For all controversies under this agreement the District Court Düsseldorf shall have jurisdiction.

Place, Date Signatures

5. REQUEST FOR A PRELIMINARY INJUNCTION[17]

District Court....

Patent Chamber

(Address)

Munich,..., 2016

Our ref.:

17. Explanations concerning a request for preliminary injunction can be found in Ch. 9.

Request to grant a preliminary injunction

of

the Company Y...duly represented by the Executive Directors,

– plaintiff –

Authorized representatives: Attorneys-at-law and patent attorneys of the law firm...

versus

the Company X...duly represented by its legal representatives;

– defendants –

on grounds of alleged patent infringement.

Litigation value: Preliminarily estimated....

In the name and by authorization of plaintiff, we request, to sentence defendant, due to particular urgency without oral hearing,

I. *in order to avoid a penalty to be set by the court for each case of violation of up to € 250,000.00, as an alternative confinement, or confinement of up to 6 months, in case of repeated violations a confinement of up to a total of 2 years, to refrain within the territory of the Federal Republic of Germany from offering, putting on the market or using or possessing for the aforementioned purposes sport shoes comprising*

1) *a sole;*

2) *an upper portion attached to the sole and*

3) *a rigid cover*

- *made of resisting material;*

- *angular in cross-section and*

- *defining a securing band and a protective shield;*

4) *the securing band is affixed between said sole and said upper portion,*

5) *the securing band extends from said sole, upwardly over the exterior of the upper portion in the area of the ball of the shoe.*

II. *Defendant has to place in custody of a bailiff all sport shoes according to section I in view of their destruction;*

III. *Defendant has to give information as to the origin and distribution channels of the shoes according to section I by means of names and addresses of all commercial customers or orders and about quantities of the delivered shoes according to section I.*

IV. *to have defendants bear the costs of the proceedings;*

Reasoned statement:

A. The parties

The plaintiff is a renowned sport equipment manufacture. It is an innovative undertaking, which invests several Millions of Euros in its Research & Development (R&D).[18] *Main achievements of Plaintiff's R&D are protected by intellectual property rights, such as patents, including the patent at issue. The features of the claimed invention are reproduced in plaintiff's shoe models such as...of which photos are enclosed as*

– Enclosure AST 1 –

The defendant operates in the same field. The parties are in direct competition. At the ongoing tradeshow ISPO 2016, which takes place from February 6 to 11, 2016, plaintiff became aware that defendant exhibits and commercializes a sport shoe which is referenced as.... (hereinafter: accused sport shoe) The accused sport shoe is illustrated on the second page of a flyer, provided as

– Enclosure AST 2 –

which is distributed by employees of the defendant on the ongoing tradeshow. The flyer is also available at the defendant's booth which is in Hall B, and the booth can be found on position B134.

B. Patent

I. Background

The plaintiff is owner of the German Patent DE..., provided as

– Enclosure AST 2 –

concerning a sport shoe. The application date for the patent was.... The patent application was published on... The mention of the grant of the patent occurred on... The Patent (in the following: Patent) is in force, which can be taken from an excerpt of the patent registered, provided as

– Enclosure AST 3 –

A nullity suit was filed on...against the Patent, but was finally dismissed by the Federal Patent Court on.... This decision is enclosed as

– Enclosure AST 4 –

This decision has not been appealed and is thus final.

II. Subject-matter of the Patent

The invention of the Patent relates to a sports shoe. It relates, in particular, to a running shoe which is provided with a protective cover. It covers the upper on the exterior surfaces thereof in the region of the ball and extends from the sole.

18. The right holder does not need to be using the invention in order to assert the patent against the defendant. This section in the request serves to give more background information to illustrate the significance of the case to the court.

The sole and upper portion on the exterior surfaces of the sport shoe, in the vicinity of the ball of the foot, are subject to heavy stresses. In the case of running shoes the stress is particularly high. Therefore, the prior art proposes, as illustrated in the German Patent Application DE...provided as

– Enclosure AST 5 –

to provide protecting supports which cover the critical areas. If these supports are subsequently fitted, for example by means of a lace, perfect fitting can usually not be ensured. If, however, the supports are formed on the sole and drawn up over the edge thereof a certain distance over the upper, the problem arises that, on the one hand, only soles with folds formed thereon can be used and, on the other hand, the fixing of the folds composed for instance of rubber on to the upper by gluing is not sufficiently durable.

III. Objective/Solution

The objective of the patent is to provide an improved sport shoe in view of the problem shown in the prior art. The invention overcomes this problem by providing a protecting cover of angular cross-section and permanent shape, one band of which serves for holding the cover in position and engages the underside of the shoe, preferably inserted between the upper portion and the sole. At the same time the holding band of the shoe cover is preferably located between the margin of the upper portion and the sole composed of one or several layers. It is preferably in the form of a thin tongue tapering towards its end. The advantage offered by the invention is that the normal components of the shoe, irrespectively of whether it is the upper portion or the sole, can be worked into the shape, and that no supplementary or securing means are required for fitting the protecting cover. This is realized by sport shoes with the following features, namely

A sport shoe comprising

1) *a sole;*

2) *an upper portion attached to the sole and*

3) *a rigid cover*

- *made of resisting material;*

- *is angular in cross-section and*

- *defining a securing band and a protective shield;*

4) *the securing band is affixed between said sole and said upper portion,*

5) *the securing band extends from said sole, upwardly over the exterior of the upper portion in the area of the ball of the shoe.*

This feature chart is separately provided on a sheet as

– Enclosure AST 6 –

C. Infringement of the patent-in suit

The plaintiff became aware that the defendant is exhibiting at the present trade show ISPO 2016 a running shoe, namely the type...which makes use of claim 1 of the patent-in-suit. The accused shoe is illustrated on a photo which has been taken from the flyer of Enclosure AST 2, but separately provided as

– Enclosure AST 7 –

The photo contains the references of features 1)–5) of the asserted claim 1: It is a sport shoe with a plastic sole (Feature 1) and an upper portion which is attached to the sole (Feature 2) and a rigid cap (Feature 3) which is

- made of resisting material;

- is angular in cross-section; and

- defines a holding arm and a cover arm.

Furthermore, the holding arm is secured between said sole and said upper portion (Feature 4) and the cover arm extends from said sole, upwardly over the exterior of the upper portion in the area of the ball of the shoe (Feature 5).

D. Reason for the preliminary injunction/urgency

The plaintiff became aware of the accused shoe on.... The present matter is particularly urgent because the patent-in-suit concerns an invention of particular importance to the plaintiff. Its sport shoes...use the patented features and are one of its most successful products, also thanks to significant promotional investments. As already indicated, plaintiff invests Millions of Euros in its Research & Development (R&D) and main achievements of Plaintiff's R&D are protected by intellectual property rights, including the patent at issue.

The plaintiff also exhibits these products at the present tradeshow. It is indicated that the ongoing accused commercial activities of defendant with the accused shoe will negatively influence the sales of plaintiff and considerably harm plaintiff's business.

On...the plaintiff informed the defendant of the patent-in-suit with reference to the accused products. Nevertheless, the defendant indicated that it did not intend to stop the commercialization.

The validity of the patent-in-suit is sufficiently secured and confirmed by the final decision of the Federal Patent Court according to Annex AST 4.

The factual details described in the present request for a preliminary injunction are contained in an affidavit of the CEO of the plaintiff, who has knowledge of the circumstances. This affidavit is provided as

– Enclosure AST 8 –

E. Legal assessment

The jurisdiction of the District Court Munich follows from §32 Civil Procedural Code and from that the present case concerns a patent matter. Defendant is marketing the attacked products in the entire Federal Republic of Germany. The accused sport shoe is offered for sale at the present tradeshow and meanwhile advertised on defendant's website www.yyy.com and can thus be bought by any potential customer within the District of that Court.

The claims raised with the present action follow from the above made submission. The defendant is obliged to cease and desist due to an illegal use of the subject matter of the patent-in-suit, §139 para. 1 German Patent Act.

Furthermore, the claim to place in custody of a bailiff all sport shoes in view of the destruction follows from §1004 German Civil Code and 140 a Patent Act. The claim asserted by the request III to give information as to the origin and distribution channels of the shoes follows from §140 b Patent Act.

It is respectfully requested that the chamber indicate, if possible by phone, whether any further evidence is necessary to substantiate the claim.

(signature)

Rechtsanwalt

(Signature of the Counsel)

Enclosures AST 1–AST 8

6. PROTECTIVE BRIEF

In order to avoid an ex parte preliminary injunction, a prudent company that has reason to believe it will be accused of infringement should preemptively file a protective brief with all courts where preliminary injunctions might likely be filed. Details concerning protective briefs are contained in Chapter 9, section 6. The following sample presents an outline of the body of a protective brief.

District Court....

(Address)

Munich,..., 2016

Our ref.:

Protective brief

In presumed preliminary injunction proceedings of

Company Y...represented by the Executive Directors,

– presumed plaintiff –

versus

Company X...represented by its legal representatives;

– presumed defendant[19]***–***

19. It is recommendable to include all possible accused infringers: U.S. mother company; all affiliates provided they are commercially active on the German market.

Authorized representatives: Attorneys-at-law and patent attorneys of the law firm...

on grounds of alleged patent infringement.

We hereby declare to be authorized representatives in presumed proceedings against the presumed defendant in case that the presumed plaintiff should file a request for a preliminary injunction on grounds of the following facts of the case.

We request,

I. that a presumed request for order of a preliminary injunction be dismissed, or in the alternative that a decision about a presumed request for a preliminary injunction shall not be made without conducting previously an oral hearing;

II. that in case of a dismissal of the request for injunction or its withdrawal the costs for the injunction proceedings including the costs for the deposit of the protective letter be imposed upon the plaintiff.

In case the plaintiff should file a request for an order of preliminary injunction, we consent to providing the present protective letter to the plaintiff.

We agree to the determination of a date for an oral hearing on the terms of a shortened period of summons, to make the present protective letter accessible to the presumed plaintiff in case they should request a preliminary injunction.

Reasoned statement:

I. The parties

The presumed plaintiff supplies systems for the treatment of biological material. Also the defendants operate in this field. The parties are in direct competition with each other. The presumed defendant plans the introduction of a new product on the market (hereinafter: presumingly accused product)

This protective letter is primarily based on lack of validity and lack of infringement of the Patent. The presumed defendant reserves to extend the counter-statement in presumed preliminary injunction proceedings.

II. The patent-in-suit [20]

1. Background

The presumed plaintiff is owner of the European patent...(in the following: the Patent), provided as

– *Enclosure AG 1* –

concerning a method for isolating a portion of a layer of a biological material.

It is possible that a new product, i.e. the presumingly attacked product of the defendant, is challenged by the presumed plaintiff.

20. This part of the protective brief is similar to the complaint and request for a preliminary injunction (see above).

2. Subject-matter of the patent-in-suit

(...)

3. Objective/Solution

The objective of the patent is to provide (...)

III. Apparent lack of validity of the patent-in-suit

Initially, the Court's attention should be directed on the fact that the presumed plaintiff would proceed based on an invalid patent. (...) [21]

Conclusion: *All features of claim 1 are anticipated. A request for order of a preliminary injunction based on claim 1 is not justified due to lack of validity.*

IV. Lacking infringement of the patent-in-suit

The order of a preliminary injunction on basis of the patent cannot be considered under any aspect. The presumed defendant reserves to provide further facts for non-infringement. Nevertheless, as

– Enclosure AG...–

a chart is provided, which contains an overview showing that none of the independent and dependant claims are realized. [22]

V. Missing cause for a preliminary injunction

The present case is also not urgent.[23] ...

The factual details described in the present protective brief are contained in an affidavit of the CEO of the defendant, who has knowledge of the circumstances. This affidavit is provided as

– Enclosure AG...–

It is respectfully requested that the chamber indicate, if possible by phone, whether any evidence is missing. The defendant will see to it that it is provided as soon as possible.

Signature of the Counsel

Enclosures AG 1 – AG...

7. BANK GUARANTEE

BANK GUARANTEE (REF. NO.)

Issuing Bank: [a bank, which is officially accredited and entitled to operate in Germany]

21. This section contains all reasons why the possible defendant believes that the patent in suit is not valid.
22. It is advisable to include a non-infringement argument. Without a non-infringement argument there is a risk that the Court gets the impression that the accused infringer's activities are done in full awareness of the infringement.
23. This section of the protective brief shall contain all facts and arguments that may present obstacles to the grant of a preliminary injunction, such as missing "urgency."

Amount: Euro €[...]

Issue Date: [...]

Beneficiary: [Complete Address]

Applicant: [Complete Address]

Ladies/Gentlemen:

in the lawsuit at the District Court Düsseldorf with the court docket n°[...] between [...], (hereinafter: Plaintiff), and [...], (hereinafter: Defendant), the District Court Düsseldorf requested the Plaintiff by Court Decision of [...] to provide a security. This security can be provided by a written, irrevocable, unlimited in time, absolute, unconditional and directly liable bank guarantee in view of the provisional enforcement of item [...] of the aforementioned Decision

By order of the Plaintiff and for the account of Plaintiff in respect of eventual costs caused to the Defendant through the provisional enforcement of item [...] of the aforementioned Decision provided that the provisional enforcement turns out to be unjustified in case the Defendant finally prevails, we hereby establish our irrevocable, unlimited in time, absolute, unconditional and directly liable Bank Guarantee ("Bank Guarantee") to the amount of

[...€][24]

and waive the defense of rescission and set-off, including the plea of exhausted remedies according to §§770, 771 of the Civil Code.

The guarantee expires under §158 par. 2 of the Civil Code, if the guarantee is handed back to us by the defendant or with his consent by a third party.

Authorized Signatures(s)

24. Normally 110% of the litigation value.

CHAPTER 17

Legal Texts

This chapter contains English translations of most of the legal provisions referred to throughout this handbook. The quoted articles and rules of the EPC (sections 1 and 2) and the Council Regulation (EC) concerning custom actions (section 6) are official texts. The excerpts from the German Patent Act, Utility Model Act and Act on Employees' Inventions are unofficial translations, and in some instances represent the only available English translations. The complete text of the EPC can be found on the website of the EPO (< www.epo.org >).

(1) Excerpt of the (EPC).
(2) Chapter V of the Rules to the EPC - Biotechnological inventions.
(3) Excerpts of the German Patent Act.
(4) Excerpts of the Utility Model Act
(5) Excerpts of the Act on Employees' Inventions.
(6) Council Regulation (EC) concerning custom actions.

1. EXCERPTS OF THE EPC[1]

Article 52—Patentable inventions

(1) European patents shall be granted for any inventions which are susceptible of industrial application, which are new and which involve an inventive step.
(2) The following in particular shall not be regarded as inventions within the meaning of paragraph 1:
    (a) discoveries, scientific theories and mathematical methods;
    (b) aesthetic creations;

1. See website of the EPO: < www.epo.com > .

(c) schemes, rules and methods for performing mental acts, playing games or doing business, and programs for computers;
(d) presentations of information.

(3) The provisions of paragraph 2 shall exclude patentability of the subject matter or activities referred to in that provision only to the extent to which a European patent application or European patent relates to such subject matter or activities as such.

(4) Methods for treatment of the human or animal body by surgery or therapy and diagnostic methods practised on the human or animal body shall not be regarded as inventions which are susceptible of industrial application within the meaning of paragraph 1. This provision shall not apply to products, in particular substances or compositions, for use in any of these methods.

Article 53—Exceptions to patentability

European patents shall not be granted in respect of:

(a) inventions the publication or exploitation of which would be contrary to "order public" or morality, provided that the exploitation shall not be deemed to be so contrary merely because it is prohibited by law or regulation in some or all of the Contracting States;
(b) plant or animal varieties or essentially biological processes for the production of plants or animals; this provision does not apply to microbiological processes or the products thereof.

Article 54—Novelty

(1) An invention shall be considered to be new if it does not form part of the state of the art.
(2) The state of the art shall be held to comprise everything made available to the public by means of a written or oral description, by use, or in any other way, before the date of filing of the European patent application.
(3) Additionally, the content of European patent applications as filed, of which the dates of filing are prior to the date referred to in paragraph 2 and which were published under Article 93 on or after that date, shall be considered as comprised in the state of the art.
(4) Paragraph 3 shall be applied only in so far as a Contracting State designated in respect of the later application, was also designated in respect of the earlier application as published.
(5) The provisions of paragraphs 1 to 4 shall not exclude the patentability of any substance or composition, comprised in the state of the art, for use in a method referred to in Article 52, paragraph 4, provided that its use for any method referred to in that paragraph is not comprised in the state of the art.

Article 55—Non-prejudicial disclosures

(1) For the application of Article 54 a disclosure of the invention shall not be taken into consideration if it occurred no earlier than six months preceding the filing of the European patent application and if it was due to, or in consequence of:
  (a) 31 an evident abuse in relation to the applicant or his legal predecessor, or
  (b) the fact that the applicant or his legal predecessor has displayed the invention at an official, or officially recognized, international exhibition falling within the terms of the Convention on international exhibitions signed at Paris on November 22, 1928 and last revised on November 30, 1972.

(2) In the case of paragraph 1(b), paragraph 1 shall apply only if the applicant states, when filing the European patent application, that the invention has been so displayed and files a supporting certificate within the period and under the conditions laid down in the Implementing Regulations.

Article 56—Inventive step

An invention shall be considered as involving an inventive step if, having regard to the state of the art, it is not obvious to a person skilled in the art. If the state of the art also includes documents within the meaning of Article 54, paragraph 3, these documents are not to be considered in deciding whether there has been an inventive step.

Article 57—Industrial application

An invention shall be considered as susceptible of industrial application if it can be made or used in any kind of industry, including agriculture.

Article 58—Entitlement to file a European patent application

A European patent application may be filed by any natural or legal person, or anybody equivalent to a legal person by virtue of the law governing it.

Article 59—Multiple applicants

A European patent application may also be filed either by joint applicants or by two or more applicants designating different Contracting States.

Article 60—Right to a European patent

(1) The right to a European patent shall belong to the inventor or his successor in title. If the inventor is an employee, the right to a European patent shall be determined in accordance with the law of the State in which the employee is mainly employed; if the State in which the employee is mainly employed cannot be determined, the law to be applied shall be that of the State in which the employer has the place of business to which the employee is attached.

(2) If two or more persons have made an invention independently of each other, the right to a European patent therefore shall belong to the person whose European patent application has the earliest date of filing, provided that this first application has been published.
(3) In proceedings before the European Patent Office, the applicant shall be deemed to be entitled to exercise the right to a European patent.

Article 61—European patent applications filed by non-entitled persons

(1) If by a final decision it is adjudged that a person other than the applicant is entitled to the grant of the European patent, that person may, in accordance with the Implementing Regulations:
  (a) prosecute the European patent application as his own application in place of the applicant;
  (b) file a new European patent application in respect of the same invention; or
  (c) request that the European patent application be refused.
(2) Article 76, paragraph 1, shall apply mutatis mutandis to a new European patent application filed under paragraph 1(b).

Article 62—Right of the inventor to be mentioned

The inventor shall have the right, vis-à-vis the applicant for or proprietor of a European patent, to be mentioned as such before the European Patent Office.

Article 63—Term of the European patent

(1) The term of the European patent shall be 20 years as from the date of filing of the application.
(2) Nothing in the preceding paragraph shall limit the right of a Contracting State to extend the term of a European patent, or to grant corresponding protection which follows immediately on expiry of the term of the patent, under the same conditions as those applying to national patents:
  (a) in order to take account of a state of war or similar emergency conditions affecting that State;
  (b) if the subject matter of the European patent is a product or a process of manufacturing a product or a use of a product which has to undergo an administrative authorization procedure required by law before it can be put on the market in that State.
(3) Paragraph 2 shall apply mutatis mutandis to European patents granted jointly for a group of Contracting States in accordance with Article 142.
(4) A Contracting State which makes provision for extension of the term or corresponding protection under paragraph 2(b) may, in accordance with an agreement concluded with the Organization, entrust to the European Patent Office tasks associated with implementation of the relevant provisions.

Article 64—Rights conferred by a European patent

A European patent shall, subject to the provisions of paragraph 2, confer on its proprietor from the date of publication of the mention of its grant, in each Contracting State in respect of which it is granted, the same rights as would be conferred by a national patent granted in that State.

If the subject matter of the European patent is a process, the protection conferred by the patent shall extend to the products directly obtained by such process.

Any infringement of a European patent shall be dealt with by national law.

Article 65—Translation of the European patent

(1) Any Contracting State may prescribe that if the text, in which the European Patent Office intends to grant a European patent or maintain a European patent as amended for that State, is not drawn up in one of its official languages, the applicant for or proprietor of the patent shall supply to its central industrial property office a translation of this text in one of its official languages at his option or, where that State has prescribed the use of one specific official language, in that language. The period for supplying the translation shall end three months after the date on which the mention of the grant of the European patent or of the maintenance of the European patent as amended is published in the European Patent Bulletin, unless the State concerned prescribes a longer period.

(2) Any Contracting State which has adopted provisions pursuant to paragraph 1 may prescribe that the applicant for or proprietor of the patent must pay all or part of the costs of publication of such translation within a period laid down by that State.

(3) Any Contracting State may prescribe that in the event of failure to observe the provisions adopted in accordance with paragraphs 1 and 2, the European patent shall be deemed to be void *ab initio* in that State.

Article 67—Rights conferred by a European patent application after publication

(1) A European patent application shall, from the date of its publication under Article 93, provisionally confer upon the applicant such protection as is conferred by Article 64, in the Contracting States designated in the application as published.

(2) Any Contracting State may prescribe that a European patent application shall not confer such protection as is conferred by Article 64. However, the protection attached to the publication of the European patent application may not be less than that which the laws of the State concerned attach to the compulsory publication of unexamined national patent applications. In any event, every State shall ensure at least that, from the date of publication of a European patent application, the applicant can claim compensation reasonable in the circumstances from any person who has used the invention in the

said State in circumstances where that person would be liable under national law for infringement of a national patent.

(3) Any Contracting State which does not have as an official language the language of the proceedings, may prescribe that provisional protection in accordance with paragraphs 1 and 2 above shall not be effective until such time as a translation of the claims in one of its official languages at the option of the applicant or, where that State has prescribed the use of one specific official language, in that language:
   (a) has been made available to the public in the manner prescribed by national law, or
   (b) has been communicated to the person using the invention in the said State.

(4) The European patent application shall be deemed never to have had the effects set out in paragraphs 1 and 2 above when it has been withdrawn, deemed to be withdrawn or finally refused. The same shall apply in respect of the effects of the European patent application in a Contracting State the designation of which is withdrawn or deemed to be withdrawn.

Article 68—Effect of revocation or limitation of the European patent

The European patent application and the resulting patent shall be deemed not to have had, as from the outset, the effects specified in Articles 64 and 67, to the extent that the patent has been revoked in opposition proceedings.

Article 69[2]—Extent of protection

The extent of the protection conferred by a European patent or a European patent application shall be determined by the terms of the claims. Nevertheless, the description and drawings shall be used to interpret the claims.

For the period up to grant of the European patent, the extent of the protection conferred by the European patent application shall be determined by the latest filed claims contained in the publication under Article 93. However, the European patent as

2. *Protocol on the Interpretation of Article 69 EPC of 5 October 1973 as revised by the Act revising the EPC of 29 November 2000.*

Article 1 – General principles

Article 69 should not be interpreted as meaning that the extent of the protection conferred by a European patent is to be understood as that defined by the strict, literal meaning of the wording used in the claims, the description and drawings being employed only for the purpose of resolving an ambiguity found in the claims. Nor should it be taken to mean that the claims serve only as a guideline and that the actual protection conferred may extend to what, from a consideration of the description and drawings by a person skilled in the art, the patent proprietor has contemplated. On the contrary, it is to be interpreted as defining a position between these extremes which combines a fair protection for the patent proprietor with a reasonable degree of legal certainty for third parties.

Article 2 – Equivalents

For the purpose of determining the extent of protection conferred by a European patent, due account shall be taken of any element which is equivalent to an element specified in the claims.

granted or as amended in opposition proceedings shall determine retroactively the protection conferred by the European patent application, in so far as such protection is not thereby extended.

Article 70—Authentic text of a European patent application or European patent

(1) The text of a European patent application or a European patent in the language of the proceedings shall be the authentic text in any proceedings before the European Patent Office and in any Contracting State.
(2) However, in the case referred to in Article 14, paragraph 2, the original text shall, in proceedings before the European Patent Office, constitute the basis for determining whether the subject matter of the application or patent extends beyond the content of the application as filed.
(3) Any Contracting State may provide that a translation, as provided for in this Convention, in an official language of that State, shall in that State be regarded as authentic, except for revocation proceedings, in the event of the application or patent in the language of the translation conferring protection which is narrower than that conferred by it in the language of the proceedings.
(4) Any Contracting State which adopts a provision under paragraph 3:
  (a) must allow the applicant for or proprietor of the patent to file a corrected translation of the European patent application or European patent. Such corrected translation shall not have any legal effect until any conditions established by the Contracting State under Article 65, paragraph 2, and Article 67, paragraph 3, have been complied with mutatis mutandis;
  (b) may prescribe that any person who, in that State, in good faith is using or has made effective and serious preparations for using an invention the use of which would not constitute infringement of the application or patent in the original translation may, after the corrected translation takes effect, continue such use in the course of his business or for the needs thereof without payment.

Article 71—Transfer and constitution of rights

A European patent application may be transferred or give rise to rights for one or more of the designated Contracting States.

Article 72—Assignment

An assignment of a European patent application shall be made in writing and shall require the signature of the parties to the contract.

Article 73—Contractual licensing

A European patent application may be licensed in whole or in part for the whole or part of the territories of the designated Contracting States.

Article 74—Law applicable

Unless otherwise specified in this Convention, the European patent application as an object of property shall, in each designated Contracting State and with effect for such State, be subject to the law applicable in that State to national patent applications.

Article 75- Filing of a European patent application

(1) A European patent application may be filed:
  (a) with the European Patent Office, or
  (b) if the law of a Contracting State so permits, and subject to Article 76, paragraph 1, with the central industrial property office or other competent authority of that State. Any application filed in this way shall have the same effect as if it had been filed on the same date with the European Patent Office.

(2) Paragraph 1 shall not preclude the application of legislative or regulatory provisions which, in any Contracting State:
  (a) govern inventions which, owing to the nature of their subject-matter, may not be communicated abroad without the prior authorisation of the competent authorities of that State, or
  (b) prescribe that any application is to be filed initially with a national authority, or make direct filing with another authority subject to prior authorisation

Article 76—European divisional applications

(1) A European divisional application shall be filed directly with the European Patent Office in accordance with the Implementing Regulations.[3] It may be filed only in respect of subject matter which does not extend beyond the content of the earlier application as filed; in so far as this requirement is complied with, the divisional application shall be deemed to have been filed on the date of filing of the earlier application and shall enjoy any right of priority.

(2) All the Contracting States designated in the earlier application at the time of filing of a European divisional application shall be deemed to be designated in the divisional application.

(...)

---

3. *Rule 36 EPC*: European divisional applications: (1) The applicant may file a divisional application relating to any pending earlier European patent application, provided that: (a) the divisional application is filed before the expiry of a time limit of twenty-four months from the Examining Division's first communication under Article 94, paragraph 3, and Rule 71, paragraphs 1 and 2, or Rule 71, paragraph 3, in respect of the earliest application for which a communication has been issued, or (b) the divisional application is filed before the expiry of a time limit of twenty-four months from any communication in which the Examining Division has objected that the earlier application does not meet the requirements of Art. 82, provided it was raising that specific objection for the first time. (...)

Article 82—Unity of invention

The European patent application shall relate to one invention only or to a group of inventions so linked as to form a single general inventive concept.

Article 83—Disclosure of the invention

The European patent application shall disclose the invention in a manner sufficiently clear and complete for it to be carried out by a person skilled in the art.

Article 84—Claims

The claims shall define the matter for which protection is sought. They shall be clear and concise and be supported by the description.
(...)

Article 87—Priority right

(1) Any person who has duly filed, in or for
  (a) any State party to the Paris Convention for the Protection of Industrial Property or
  (b) any Member of the World Trade Organization,

(2) an application for a patent, a utility model or a utility certificate, or his successor in title, shall enjoy, for the purpose of filing a European patent application in respect of the same invention, a right of priority during a period of twelve months from the date of filing of the first application.

(3) Every filing that is equivalent to a regular national filing under the national law of the State where it was made or under bilateral or multilateral agreements, including this Convention, shall be recognized as giving rise to a right of priority.

(4) A regular national filing shall mean any filing that is sufficient to establish the date on which the application was filed, whatever the outcome of the application may be.

(5) A subsequent application in respect of the same subject matter as a previous first application and filed in or for the same State shall be considered as the first application for the purposes of determining priority, provided that, at the date of filing the subsequent application, the previous application has been withdrawn, abandoned or refused, without being open to public inspection and without leaving any rights outstanding, and has not served as a basis for claiming a right of priority. The previous application may not thereafter serve as a basis for claiming a right of priority.

(6) If the first filing has been made with an industrial property authority which is not subject to the Paris Convention for the Protection of Industrial Property or the Agreement Establishing the World Trade Organization, paragraphs 1 to 4 shall apply if that authority, according to a communication issued by the President of the European Patent Office, recognizes that a first filing made

with the European Patent Office gives rise to a right of priority under conditions and with effects equivalent to those laid down in the Paris Convention.

Article 88—Claiming priority

(1) An applicant desiring to take advantage of the priority of a previous application shall file a declaration of priority and any other document required, in accordance with the Implementing Regulations.
(2) Multiple priorities may be claimed in respect of a European patent application, notwithstanding the fact that they originated in different countries. Where appropriate, multiple priorities may be claimed for any one claim. Where multiple priorities are claimed, time limits which run from the date of priority shall run from the earliest date of priority.
(3) If one or more priorities are claimed in respect of a European patent application, the right of priority shall cover only those elements of the European patent application which are included in the application or applications whose priority is claimed.
(4) If certain elements of the invention for which priority is claimed do not appear among the claims formulated in the previous application, priority may nonetheless be granted, provided that the documents of the previous application as a whole specifically disclose such elements.
(...)

Article 90—Examination on filing and examination as to formal requirements

(1) The European Patent Office shall examine, in accordance with the Implementing Regulations, whether the application satisfies the requirements for the accordance of a date of filing.
(2) If a date of filing cannot be accorded following the examination under paragraph 1, the application shall not be dealt with as a European patent application.
(3) If the European patent application has been accorded a date of filing, the European Patent Office shall examine, in accordance with the Implementing Regulations, whether the requirements in Articles 14, 78 and 81, and, where applicable, Article 88, paragraph 1, and Article 133, paragraph 2, as well as any other requirement laid down in the Implementing Regulations, have been satisfied.
(4) Where the European Patent Office in carrying out the examination under paragraphs 1 or 3 notes that there are deficiencies which may be corrected, it shall give the applicant an opportunity to correct them.
(5) If any deficiency noted in the examination under paragraph 3 is not corrected, the European patent application shall be refused unless a different legal consequence is provided for by this Convention. Where the deficiency concerns the right of priority, this right shall be lost for the application.

Article 92—Drawing up of the European search report

The European Patent Office shall, in accordance with the Implementing Regulations, draw up and publish a European search report in respect of the European patent application on the basis of the claims, with due regard to the description and any drawings.

Article 93—Publication of the European patent application

(1) The European Patent Office shall publish the European patent application as soon as possible
  (a) after the expiry of a period of eighteen months from the date of filing or, if priority has been claimed, from the date of priority, or
  (b) at the request of the applicant, before the expiry of that period.

(2) The European patent application shall be published at the same time as the specification of the European patent when the decision to grant the patent becomes effective before the expiry of the period referred to in paragraph 1(a).

Article 94—Examination of the European patent application

- The European Patent Office shall, in accordance with the Implementing Regulations, examine on request whether the European patent application and the invention to which it relates meet the requirements of this Convention. The request shall not be deemed to be filed until the examination fee has been paid.
- If no request for examination has been made in due time, the application shall be deemed to be withdrawn.
- If the examination reveals that the application or the invention to which it relates does not meet the requirements of this Convention, the Examining Division shall invite the applicant, as often as necessary, to file his observations and, subject to Article 123, paragraph 1, to amend the application.
- If the applicant fails to reply in due time to any communication from the Examining Division, the application shall be deemed to be withdrawn.

  (...)

Article 97—Grant or refusal

- If the Examining Division is of the opinion that the European patent application and the invention to which it relates meet the requirements of this Convention, it shall decide to grant a European patent, provided that the conditions laid down in the Implementing Regulations are fulfilled.
- If the Examining Division is of the opinion that the European patent application or the invention to which it relates does not meet the requirements of this Convention, it shall refuse the application unless this Convention provides for a different legal consequence.

- The decision to grant a European patent shall take effect on the date on which the mention of the grant is published in the European Patent Bulletin.
(...)

Article 99—Opposition

Within nine months of the publication of the mention of the grant of the European patent in the European Patent Bulletin, any person may give notice to the European Patent Office of opposition to that patent, in accordance with the Implementing Regulations. Notice of opposition shall not be deemed to have been filed until the opposition fee has been paid.

The opposition shall apply to the European patent in all the Contracting States in which that patent has effect.

Opponents shall be parties to the opposition proceedings as well as the proprietor of the patent.

Where a person provides evidence that in a Contracting State, following a final decision, he has been entered in the patent register of such State instead of the previous proprietor, such person shall, at his request, replace the previous proprietor in respect of such State. Notwithstanding Article 118, the previous proprietor and the person making the request shall not be regarded as joint proprietors unless both so request.

Article 100—Grounds for opposition

Opposition may only be filed on the grounds that:

- the subject matter of the European patent is not patentable under Articles 52 to 57;
- the European patent does not disclose the invention in a manner sufficiently clear and complete for it to be carried out by a person skilled in the art;
- the subject matter of the European patent extends beyond the content of the application as filed, or, if the patent was granted on a divisional application or on a new application filed under Article 61, beyond the content of the earlier application as filed.
(...)

Article 105—Intervention of the assumed infringer

Any third party may, in accordance with the Implementing Regulations, intervene in opposition proceedings after the opposition period has expired, if the third party proves that proceedings for infringement of the same patent have been instituted against him, or following a request of the proprietor of the patent to cease alleged infringement, the third party has instituted proceedings for a ruling that he is not infringing the patent. An admissible intervention shall be treated as an opposition.

Article 105a—Request for limitation or revocation

- At the request of the proprietor, the European patent may be revoked or be limited by an amendment of the claims. The request shall be filed with the European Patent Office in accordance with the Implementing Regulations. It shall not be deemed to have been filed until the limitation or revocation fee has been paid.
- The request may not be filed while opposition proceedings in respect of the European patent are pending.

Article 105b—Limitation or revocation of the European patent

The European Patent Office shall examine whether the requirements laid down in the Implementing Regulations for limiting or revoking the European patent have been met.

If the European Patent Office considers that the request for limitation or revocation of the European patent meets these requirements, it shall decide to limit or revoke the European patent in accordance with the Implementing Regulations. Otherwise, it shall reject the request.

The decision to limit or revoke the European patent shall apply to the European patent in all the Contracting States in respect of which it has been granted. It shall take effect on the date on which the mention of the decision is published in the European Patent Bulletin.

(...)

Article 115—Observations by third parties

Following the publication of the European patent application, any person may present observations concerning the patentability of the invention in respect of which the application has been filed. Such observations must be filed in writing and must include a statement of the grounds on which they are based. That person shall not be a party to the proceedings before the European Patent Office.

The observations referred to in paragraph 1 shall be communicated to the applicant for or proprietor of the patent who may comment on them.

(...)

Article 123—Amendments

The conditions under which a European patent application or a European patent may be amended in proceedings before the European Patent Office are laid down in the Implementing Regulations. In any case, an applicant shall be allowed at least one opportunity of amending the description, claims and drawings of his own volition.

A European patent application or a European patent may not be amended in such a way that it contains subject matter which extends beyond the content of the application as filed.

The claims of the European patent may not be amended during opposition proceedings in such a way as to extend the protection conferred.

2. CHAPTER V—BIOTECHNOLOGICAL INVENTIONS[4]

Rule 26—General and definitions

For European patent applications and patents concerning biotechnological inventions, the relevant provisions of the Convention shall be applied and interpreted in accordance with the provisions of this Chapter. Directive 98/44/EC of 6 July 199819 on the legal protection of biotechnological inventions shall be used as a supplementary means of interpretation.

- "Biotechnological inventions" are inventions which concern a product consisting of or containing biological material or a process by means of which biological material is produced, processed or used.
- "Biological material" means any material containing genetic information and capable of reproducing itself or being reproduced in a biological system.
- "Plant variety" means any plant grouping within a single botanical taxon of the lowest known rank, which grouping, irrespective of whether the conditions for the grant of a plant variety right are fully met, can be:
- defined by the expression of the characteristics that results from a given genotype or combination of genotypes,
- distinguished from any other plant grouping by the expression of at least one of the said characteristics, and
- considered as a unit with regard to its suitability for being propagated unchanged.

A process for the production of plants or animals is essentially biological if it consists entirely of natural phenomena such as crossing or selection.

- "Microbiological process" means any process involving or performed upon or resulting in microbiological material.

Rule 27—Patentable biotechnological inventions

Biotechnological inventions shall also be patentable if they concern:

(a) biological material which is isolated from its natural environment or produced by means of a technical process even if it previously occurred in nature;
(b) plants or animals if the technical feasibility of the invention is not confined to a particular plant or animal variety;
(c) a microbiological or other technical process, or a product obtained by means of such a process other than a plant or animal variety.

4. This chapter is part of the Implementing Regulations to the EPC. The full text can be found on the website of the EPO: <www.epo.org>.

Rule 28—Exceptions to patentability

Under Article 53(a), European patents shall not be granted in respect of biotechnological inventions which, in particular, concern the following:

(a) processes for cloning human beings;
(b) processes for modifying the germ line genetic identity of human beings;
(c) uses of human embryos for industrial or commercial purposes;
(d) processes for modifying the genetic identity of animals which are likely to cause them suffering without any substantial medical benefit to man or animal, and also animals resulting from such processes.

Rule 29—The human body and its elements

(1) The human body, at the various stages of its formation and development, and the simple discovery of one of its elements, including the sequence or partial sequence of a gene, cannot constitute patentable inventions.
(2) An element isolated from the human body or otherwise produced by means of a technical process, including the sequence or partial sequence of a gene, may constitute a patentable invention, even if the structure of that element is identical to that of a natural element.
(3) The industrial application of a sequence or a partial sequence of a gene must be disclosed in the patent application.

3. GERMAN PATENT ACT

§1 Patentable Inventions

(1) Patents shall be granted for inventions in all technical areas that are new, involve an inventive step and are susceptible of industrial application.
(2) Patents shall also be granted on inventions within the meaning of subsection (1) if they concern a product consisting of or containing biological material, or if they concern a process by which biological material is produced or modified, or in which it is used. Biological material isolated from its natural environment or produced by means of a technical process may also constitute an object of an invention, even if it was already present in nature.
(3) The following shall not be regarded as inventions within the meaning of subsection (1):
   1. discoveries, scientific theories and mathematical methods;
   2. aesthetic creations;
   3. schemes, rules and methods for performing mental acts, playing games or doing business and programs for computers;
   4. presentations of information.

(4) The provisions of subsection (3) shall exclude patentability only to the extent to which protection is sought for the above-mentioned subject matter or activities as such.

§1a Human Body and its Elements

(1) The human body, at the various stages of its formation and development, including germ cells, and the simple discovery of one of its elements, including the sequence or partial sequence of a gene, cannot constitute patentable inventions.

(2) An element isolated from the human body or otherwise produced by means of a technical process, including the sequence or partial sequence of a gene, may constitute a patentable invention, even if the structure of that element is identical to that of a natural element.

(3) The industrial application of a sequence or a partial sequence of a gene must be disclosed in the patent application stating the function performed by the sequence or partial sequence.

(4) If the object of the invention concerns a sequence or partial sequence of a gene, the structure of which is identical to the structure of a natural sequence or partial sequence of a human gene, its use for which the industrial application is specifically described under subsection (3) must be included in the patent claim.

§2 Ordre Public and Morality

(1) Patents shall not be granted in respect of inventions the publication or exploitation of which would be contrary to ordre public or morality, provided that the exploitation shall not be deemed to be so contrary merely because it is prohibited by law or regulation.

(2) Patents shall not be granted in respect of:

1. processes for cloning human beings;
2. processes for modifying the genetic identity of the germline of human beings;
3. use of human embryos for industrial or commercial purposes;
4. processes for modifying the genetic identity of animals which are likely to cause them suffering without any substantial medical benefit to man or animal, and also animals resulting from such processes.

In the application of subsections 1 to 3, the relevant provisions of the Embryo Protection Act shall take precedence.

§2a Plant and Animal Varieties, Production of Plants and Animals, Microbiological Processes, Definitions

(1) Patents shall not be granted in respect of
   1. plant and animal varieties or essentially biological processes for the production of plants and animals.
   2. methods for the treatment of the human or animal body by surgery or therapy and diagnostic methods practised on the human or animal body. This shall not apply to products, in particular to substances or compositions, for use in one of these methods.

(2) Patents can be granted in respect of inventions which concern
   1. plants or animals, if the technical feasibility of the invention is not confined to a particular plant or animal variety;
   2. a microbiological or other technical process or a product obtained by means of such a process, where this is not a plant or animal variety....

§3 Novelty

(1) An invention shall be deemed to be new if it does not form part of the state of the art. The state of the art shall be held to comprise all knowledge made available to the public before the date governing the filing or priority date of the application by means of a written or oral description, by use or in any other way.

(2) The content of the following patent applications having an earlier filing or priority date which were made available to the public on or after the date governing the filing or priority date of the later application shall also be deemed to be comprised in the state of the art:
   1. national applications as filed with the German Patent and Trade Mark Office;
   2. European applications as filed with the competent authority if the application seeks protection in the Federal Republic of Germany and the designation fee has been paid in respect of the Federal Republic of Germany pursuant to Article 79 paragraph 2 of the European Patent Convention, and if, in the case of a Euro-PCT application (Article 153 paragraph 2 of the European Patent Convention), the requirements laid down in Article 153 paragraph 5 of the European Patent Convention are fulfilled;
   3. international applications under the Patent Cooperation Treaty as filed with the receiving Office, provided the German Patent and Trade Mark Office is the designated Office in respect of the application.

   If the earlier filing or priority date of an application is based on the claim to the priority of an earlier application, the first sentence shall apply only to the extent that the version of the application in question does not extend beyond the version of the earlier application. Patent applications pursuant to the first sentence, no. 1, in respect of which an order has been made in accordance with section 50 (1) or (4) shall be deemed to have been made available to the public after the expiry of a period of eighteen months following their filing.

(3) Subsections (1) and (2) shall not exclude the patentability of any substance or composition, comprised in the state of the art, for use in a method referred to in section 2a (1) no. 2, provided that its use for any such method is not comprised in the state of the art.

(4) Subsections (1) and (2) shall also not exclude the patentability of any substance or composition referred to in subsection (3) for any specific use in a method referred to in section 2a (1) no. 2, provided that such use is not comprised in the state of the art.

(5) For the application of subsections (1) and (2), a disclosure of the invention shall not be taken into consideration if it occurred no earlier than six months before the filing of the application and if it was due to, or in consequence of

1. an evident abuse in relation to the applicant or his legal predecessor, or
2. the fact that the applicant or his legal predecessor has displayed the invention at an official, or officially recognised, international exhibition falling within the terms of the Convention on international exhibitions signed at Paris on 22 November 1928.

The first sentence, no. 2, shall apply only if the applicant states, when filing the application, that the invention has been so displayed and files a certificate to that effect within four months of the filing. Exhibitions referred to in the first sentence, no. 2, shall be notified by the Federal Minister of Justice in the Federal Gazette (Bundesanzeiger).

§4 Inventive Step

An invention shall be considered to involve an inventive step if, having regard to the state of the art, it is not obvious to a person skilled in the art. If the state of the art also includes documents within the meaning of Section 3(2), these documents shall not be considered in deciding whether there has been an inventive step.

§5 Industrial Application

An invention shall be considered susceptible of industrial application if it can be made or used in any kind of industry, including agriculture.

§6 Right to the Invention

The right to a patent shall belong to the inventor or his successor in title. If two or more persons have jointly made an invention, the right to a patent shall belong to them jointly. If two or more persons have made an invention independently of each other, the right shall belong to the person who is the first to file an application with the Patent Office.

§7 Legal Fictions in favor of the Applicant and Applications by Non-entitled Persons

(1) To avoid the substantive examination of the patent application being delayed due to the need to determine the identity of the inventor, the applicant shall be deemed in the proceedings before the Patent Office to be entitled to request grant of a patent.

(2) If a patent is revoked by reason of opposition based on usurpation (Section 21(1).3) or if opposition results in the withdrawal of the patent, the opponent may himself file an application in respect of the invention, within one month after the official notification thereof, and claim the priority of the earlier patent.

§8 Assignment of the Patent in case of Deprivation

An entitled person whose invention has been applied for by a person not so entitled or the person infringed by the usurpation may require the patent applicant to surrender to him the right to the grant of a patent. If the application has already resulted in a patent, he may require the patentee to assign the patent to him. Such right may only be asserted by an action at law within two years after publication of the grant of the patent (Section 58(1)), subject to the fourth and fifth sentences. If the injured person has filed opposition on the grounds of usurpation (Section 21(1).3), he may bring an action within one year of the final conclusion of the opposition proceedings. The third and fourth sentences shall not apply if the patentee had not acted in good faith in obtaining the patent

§9 Prohibition of Direct use of the Patented Invention

A patent has the effect that the patentee alone is authorized to use the patented invention within the limits of valid law. A person not having the consent of the patentee shall be prohibited:

1. from manufacturing, offering, putting on the market or using a product which is the subject matter of the patent or importing or stocking the product for such purposes;
2. from using a method which is the subject matter of the patent or, if he knows or it is obvious from the circumstances that the use of the process is prohibited without the consent of the patentee, from offering the process for use within the territory to which this Act applies;
3. from offering, putting on the market, using or importing or stocking for such purposes the product obtained directly by a process which is the subject matter of the patent.

§9a Rights conferred by Biological Patents

(1) If the subject matter of the patent is biological material which has certain properties as a result of an invention, the provisions of Section 9 shall be applicable to every biological material which is obtained from this biological material by generative or vegetative reproduction in the same or a deviant form and which has the same properties.

(2) If the subject matter of the patent is a process which makes it possible to obtain biological material, which has certain properties as a result of an invention, the provisions of Section 9 shall be applicable to the biological material obtained directly by this process and every other biological material having the same properties which is obtained by generative or vegetative reproduction in the same or a deviant form from the material directly obtained.

(3) If the subject matter of the patent is a product which consists of or contains a genetic information as a result of an invention, the provisions of Section 9 shall be applicable to every material which includes this product and in which this genetic information is contained and performs its function. Section 1a, subsection 1 shall remain unaffected.

§9b Exhaustion in the case of Biological Material

If the patentee or with his approval a third party puts on the market biological material which has certain properties as a result of the invention within the territory of a Member State of the EU or another Contracting State to the Agreement on the European Economic Area, and if further biological material is obtained from this biological material by generative or vegetative reproduction, the provisions of Section 9 shall not be applicable if putting on the market was for the purpose of reproduction of the biological material. This shall not apply if the material obtained in this way is subsequently used for further generative or vegetative reproduction.

§9c Farmer's Privilege

(1) If reproductive plant material is put on the market by the patentee or with his approval by a third party to an agriculturist for the purpose of agricultural cultivation, the agriculturist may contrary to Sections 9, 9a and second sentence of 9b use his crop for generative or vegetative reproduction by himself in his own farm. Article 14 of Council Regulation (EC) No. 2100/94 as amended and the implementing regulations shall apply mutatis mutandis to the conditions and the extent of this authorization. Claims resulting for the patentee shall be asserted according to the implementing regulations enacted on the basis of Article 14, subsection 3 of Council Regulation (EC) No. 2100/94.

(2) If working animals or reproductive animal material are put on the market by the patentee or with his approval by a third party to an agriculturist, the agriculturist may contrary to Sections 9, 9a and second sentence of 9b use the

working animals or reproductive animal material for agricultural purposes. This authorization shall also extend to the provision of the agricultural working animals or other reproductive animal material for the continuation of his agricultural occupation, but not to the sale with the objective of or within the framework of reproduction as source of income.

(3) Section 9a, subsections 1 to 3 shall not apply to biological material which was obtained in the field of agriculture accidentally or was technically non-avoidable. An action shall therefore not lie against an agriculturist if he has not cultivated seeds or plants subject to this patent protection law.

§10 Prohibition of Indirect use of the Patented Invention

(1) A patent shall have the further effect that a person not having the consent of the patentee shall be prohibited from supplying or offering to supply within the territory to which this Act applies a person, other than a person entitled to exploit the patented invention with means relating to an essential element of such invention for exploiting the invention, where such person knows or it is obvious from the circumstances that such means are suitable and intended for exploiting the invention.

(2) Subsection (1) shall not apply when the means are staple commercial products, except where such person induces the person supplied to commit acts prohibited by the second sentence of Section 9.

(3) Persons performing the acts referred to in Section 11.1 to 3 shall not be considered persons entitled to exploit the invention within the meaning of subsection (1).

§11 Limitation of Effects of Patents

The effects of a patent shall not extend to:

1. acts done privately and for non-commercial purposes;
2. acts done for experimental purposes relating to the subject matter of the patented invention;
   - 2a. the use of biological material for the purpose of cultivation, discovery and development of a new plant variety;
   - 2b. studies and tests and practical requirements resulting therefrom which are necessary for obtaining an authorization according to the current medicinal product law regulations for putting on the market in the EU or for obtaining an authorization according to the current medicinal product law regulations in Member States of the EU or non-member States.
3. the extemporaneous preparation for individual cases in a pharmacy of a medicine in accordance with a medical prescription or acts concerning the medicine so prepared;

4. the use of the patented invention on board vessels of another State party to the Paris Convention for the Protection of Industrial Property, in the body of the vessel, in the machinery, tackle, gear and other accessories, where such vessels temporarily or accidentally enter the waters to which the territory of this Act extends on condition that such use serves exclusively the needs of the vessel;
5. the use of the patented invention in the construction or operation of aircraft or land vehicles of another State party to the Paris Convention for the Protection of Industrial Property or of accessories for such aircraft or land vehicles, where these temporarily or accidentally enter the territory to which this Act applies;
6. the acts specified in Article 27 of the Convention on International Civil Aviation of December 7, 1944, where such acts concern the aircraft of another State to which the provisions of that Article are applicable.

§12 Right based on Prior Use

(1) A patent has no effect against a person who, at the time of the filing of the application, had already begun to use the invention within the national borders, or had made the necessary arrangements for doing this. Such person shall be entitled to use the invention for the needs of his own business in his own plant or the plant of others. This right can only be inherited or transferred together with the business. If the applicant or his predecessor in title has, before applying for a patent, disclosed the invention to other persons and reserved his rights in the event of a patent being granted, a person learning of the invention as a result of such disclosure cannot, under the provisions under the first sentence, invoke measures which he has taken within six months after the disclosure.

(2) If the patentee is entitled to a right of priority, the date of the prior application shall be substituted for the date of the application referred to in subsection (1). However, this provision shall not apply to nationals of a foreign country which does not guarantee reciprocity in this respect, where they claim the priority of a foreign application.

§13 Right to Use in the Public Interest

(1) A patent shall have no effect where the Federal Government orders that the invention be exploited in the interest of public welfare. Nor shall the effect of a patent extend to any exploitation of the invention which is ordered in the interests of the security of the Federal Republic by the appropriate supreme federal authority or, on the latter's instructions, by a subordinate agency.

(2) Appeals against orders under subsection (1) shall be heard by the Federal Administrative Court where such orders have been made by the Federal Government or the appropriate supreme federal authority.

(3) In the cases mentioned in subsection (1), the patentee shall have a claim against the Federal Republic for reasonable compensation. In the event of dispute as to its amount, legal action may be brought before the ordinary civil courts. Any order by the Federal Government under the first sentence of subsection (1) shall be communicated to the person recorded as patentee in the Register (Section 30(1)) before the invention is exploited. If the supreme federal authority by which an order or an instruction under the second sentence of subsection (1) is issued learns that an entitlement to compensation has arisen under the first sentence, it shall give notice thereof to the person recorded in the Register as patentee.

§14 Scope of Protection

The extent of the protection conferred by a patent or a patent application shall be determined by the terms of the claims. Nevertheless, the description and drawings shall be used to interpret the claims.

§15 License, Assignment

(1) The right to a patent, the right to the grant of a patent and the rights deriving from a patent shall pass to the heirs. They may be assigned to others with or without restrictions.
(2) The rights under subsection (1) may be licensed in whole or in part, exclusively or non-exclusively, for the whole or part of the territory to which this Act applies. Where a licensee contravenes a restriction of his license covered by the first sentence, the right conferred by the patent may be invoked against him.
(3) The assignment of rights or the granting of a license shall not affect licenses previously granted to other persons.

§16 Term of the Patent

(1) The duration of a patent is 20 years, beginning on the day following the filing of the application in respect of the invention. If the purpose of an invention is the improvement or further development of another invention for which the applicant has already secured patent protection, he may apply, within 18 months from the date of filing of the application or, insofar as an earlier date is claimed as relevant for the application, from that date, for a patent of addition, which shall expire at the same time as the patent for the earlier invention.
(2) If the main patent lapses due to revocation, declaration of nullity, forfeiture or abandonment, the patent of addition shall become an independent patent; its duration shall be determined by the date of commencement of the main patent. Where there are several patents of addition, only the first shall become independent; the others shall be deemed patents of addition to that patent.

§16a Supplementary Protection Certificate

(1) Pursuant to Regulations of the EU concerning the creation of supplementary protection certificates, which shall be notified in the Federal Law Gazette, supplementary protection may be requested in respect of a patent that shall follow on immediately from the expiry of the term of the patent under Section 16. Annual fees shall be paid for supplementary protection in accordance with the schedule of fees.

(2) Unless otherwise provided by the law of the European Communities, the provisions of the Patent Act concerning entitlement of the applicant (§§6 to 8), effects of the patent and exceptions thereto (§§9 to 12), order to exploit the patent and compulsory license (Sections 13, 24), extent of protection (Section 14), licenses and their registration (Sections 15, 30), lapse of the patent (Section 20), nullity (Section 22), preparedness to grant licenses (Section 23), domestic representative (Section 25), the Patent Court and proceedings before the Patent Court (Sections 65 to 99), proceedings before the Federal Court of Justice (Sections 100 to 122a), reinstatement (Section 123), obligation of truth (Section 124), electronic document (Section 125a), official language, service of documents and legal aid (Sections 126 to 128), infringement (Sections 139 to 141a, 142a and 142b), joining of actions and advertising of patent (Sections 145 and 146) shall apply mutatis mutandis to supplementary protection.

(3) Licenses and declarations under Section 23 of the Patent Act that are effective for a patent shall also apply to supplementary protection.
(...)

§21 Grounds for Revocation

(1) A patent shall be revoked (§61) if it transpires that
1. the subject matter of the patent is not patentable under §§1 to 5,
2. the patent does not disclose the invention in a manner sufficiently clear and complete in order to be carried out by a person skilled in the art,
3. the essential elements of the patent have been taken from the descriptions, drawings, models, appliances or equipment of another person, or from a method used by another person, without his consent (unlawful deprivation),
4. the subject matter of the patent extends beyond the content of the application as originally filed with the competent authorities; the same shall apply if the patent was granted on a divisional application or on a new application filed in accordance with §7(2) and the subject matter of the patent extends beyond the content of the earlier application as originally filed with the competent authorities.

(2) If the grounds for revocation affect the patent in part only, the patent shall be maintained in the form of a corresponding limitation. The limitation may be implemented in the form of an amendment to the claims, the descriptions or the drawings.
(3) In the event of revocation, the effects of the patent and of the application shall be deemed not to have existed "ab initio." This provision shall apply mutatis mutandis to limited maintenance. (...)
(...)

§24 Compulsory License

(1) The non-exclusive authorization for the industrial use of an invention is granted by the Federal Patent Court in individual cases in compliance with the following provisions (compulsory license), if
   1. the applicant for a license has unsuccessfully endeavored during a reasonable time frame to obtain from the patentee an authorization to use the invention under reasonable and commercially usual conditions; and
   2. the public interest demands the grant of a compulsory license.
(2) If the applicant for a license is unable to exploit an invention for which he holds protection under a patent of later date without infringing a patent of earlier date, he shall be entitled to request the grant of a compulsory license with respect to the owner of the patent of earlier date if
   1. the conditions of item 1 of subsection (1) are fulfilled and
   2. if his own invention comprises, in comparison with that under the patent of earlier date, an important technical advance of considerable commercial significance.
   The patentee can require the applicant for a license to grant him a counter license under reasonable conditions for the exploitation of the patented invention of later date.
(3) Subsection 2 applies mutatis mutandis if a plant breeder cannot maintain or exploit a plant variety right without infringing a patent of earlier date.
(4) A compulsory license under subsection (1) may be granted for a patented invention in the field of semi-conductor technology only if such grant is necessary to remove an anti-competitive practice on the part of the patentee that has been established in judicial or administrative proceedings.
(5) If the patentee does not use the patented invention, or does not use it predominantly in Germany, compulsory licenses under subsection (1) may be granted to ensure an adequate supply of the patented product to the domestic market. Importing shall be deemed to constitute use of the patent in Germany in such case.
(6) The grant of a compulsory license in a patent shall be permissible only after the grant of the patent. It may be granted subject to restrictions and made dependent upon conditions. The scope and duration of use shall be restricted to the purpose for which they have been permitted. The patentee shall be entitled to remuneration from the holder of a compulsory license that shall be

commensurate with the circumstances and shall take into consideration the commercial value of the compulsory license. In the event of a significant change, with respect to the repeated remuneration that will become due in future, in the circumstances on which the determination of the amount of the remuneration was based, each party shall be entitled to require a corresponding adjustment. If the circumstances on which the grant of a compulsory license was based no longer apply and if it is unlikely that they will reoccur, the patentee may require the withdrawal of the compulsory license.

(7) A compulsory license in a patent may only be transferred together with the enterprise involved in the exploitation of the invention. A compulsory license in an invention that is the subject matter of a patent of earlier date may only be transferred together with the patent of later date.

(...)

§30 Register of the Patent Office

(1) The Patent Office shall maintain a Register in which shall be recorded the titles of patent applications, the files of which may be inspected by any person, and of granted patents, supplementary certificates of protection (Section 16a) and the names and addresses of applicants or of patentees and appointed representatives or persons authorized to accept service, if any (Section 25), it being sufficient to record one such representative or person authorized to accept service. The commencement, expiration, lapsing, order for limitation, revocation, declaration of nullity or supplementary certificates of protection (Section 16a), as well as the filing of opposition and of a nullity action shall also be recorded therein.

(2) The President of the Patent Office may determine that further particulars be entered in the Register.

(3) The Patent Office shall record in the Register any change in the identity of the person, of the name or of the address of the applicants or the patentees and of their representatives and persons authorized to accept service, if proof thereof is furnished to it. As long as the change has not been recorded, the former applicant, patentee or representative shall remain subject to the rights and obligations as provided in this Act.

(...)

§33 Reasonable Compensation

(1) As from publication of the notification pursuant to Section 32(5), the applicant may require from any person who has used the subject matter of the application although he knew or should have known that the invention used by him was the subject matter of the application, compensation appropriate to the circumstances. Further claims are excluded.

(2) The claim to compensation cannot be asserted if the subject matter of the application is obviously unpatentable.

(3) The provisions of Book 1, Division 5 of the German Civil Code (Bürgerliches Gesetzbuch) shall apply mutatis mutandis to limitation, with the proviso that the limitation shall become effective at the earliest one year after the grant of the patent. Where the person obliged obtains something as a consequence of the infringement at the expense of the person entitled, section 852 of the German Civil Code shall apply mutatis mutandis.
(...)

Section 59 – Opposition

(1) Within three months of publication of the grant of the patent any person may give notice of opposition to the patent, in the case of usurpation only the aggrieved party. Notice of opposition shall be given in a written reasoned statement. It may only be based on the claim that one of the grounds for revocation set out in section 21 exists. The facts justifying the opposition shall be detailed. The particulars shall, in so far as they have not already been included in the notice of opposition, be submitted in writing within the opposition period.

(2) Where a notice of opposition has been given to a patent, any third party who can prove that an action has been brought against him on account of an infringement of the patent may intervene in the opposition proceedings as an opponent after the expiry of the opposition period if he gives notice of intervention within three months of the date on which the action claiming the infringement was filed. The same shall apply to any third party who can prove that, following a demand by the proprietor of the patent that the third party refrain from the alleged infringement of the patent, he instituted proceedings for a ruling that he is not infringing the patent. The notice of intervention shall be declared in writing and reasoned within the time limit referred to in the first sentence. Subsection (1), third to fifth sentences, shall apply mutatis mutandis.

(3) A hearing shall be held in the opposition proceedings upon request of a party or if the Patent Division deems this to be expedient. When issuing the summons, the Patent Division shall draw attention to the points which in its opinion need to be discussed for the purposes of the decision to be taken. The hearing, including delivery of the decision, shall be public. Section 169, second sentence, as well as sections 171b to 175 of the Courts Constitution Act (Gerichtsverfassungsgesetz) shall apply mutatis mutandis, with the proviso that the public may also be excluded from the hearing at the request of one of the parties if there is concern that the interests of the applicant meriting protection are at risk.

(4) The chair of the Patent Division shall ensure that order is maintained during the hearing and shall thus exercise his domestic authority.

(5) In other respects, section 43 (3), second sentence, and sections 46 and 47 shall apply mutatis mutandis in the opposition proceedings.

§81 Nullity and Compulsory License Proceedings

(1) Proceedings for a declaration of nullity of a patent or a supplementary certificate of protection or for the grant or withdrawal of a compulsory license or for the adaptation of a compensation set by a judgment for a compulsory license shall be instituted by bringing legal action. The action shall be directed against the person recorded in the register as patentee or against the holder of the compulsory license. An action against a supplementary certificate of protection may be consolidated with an action against the basic patent and may also be based on the fact that one of the grounds for nullity exists in respect of the basic patent (§22).

(2) An action for a declaration of nullity of a patent shall not be brought as long as opposition may still be filed or opposition proceedings are pending. An action for a declaration of nullity of a supplementary certificate of protection shall not be brought as long as applications pursuant to Section 49a(4) can be made or proceedings for a decision regarding these applications are pending.

(3) In the case of an unlawful deprivation, only the injured party shall be entitled to bring an action.

(4) An action shall be filed with the Patent Court in written form. Copies of the complaint brief and of all written statements shall be attached for the opposing party. The action and all written statements are served ex officio on the opposing party.

(5) The complaint brief shall designate the plaintiff, the defendant and the matter at issue and shall contain a specific motion. The facts and documentary evidence relied on shall be stated. If the complaint brief does not fully comply with these requirements, the presiding judge shall invite the plaintiff to file the necessary additional materials within a specified period.

(6) If the plaintiff's general residence lies outside the EU or the member states of the Treaty on the European Economic Area, he shall furnish to the defendant, upon request, security for the costs of the proceedings. §110 (2) N° 1 to 3 of the Code of Civil Procedure shall apply mutatis mutandis. The Patent Court determines, at its equitable discretion, the amount of the security and shall fix a time limit within which that amount shall be furnished. If the time limit is not observed, the action shall be deemed to have been withdrawn.

82 Notice of Action and Objection

(1) The Patent Court shall serve notice of the action on the defendant and invite him to reply thereto within one month.

(2) If the defendant fails to reply in due time, a decision complying with the plaintiff's request may be rendered forthwith without a hearing and every factual allegation of the plaintiff assumed to be proved.

(3) If the defendant files an objection in good time, the patent court shall notify the plaintiff of the objection and shall set the date for the in-person hearing. With the parties' consent, an in-person hearing can be waived. Paragraph 2 shall remain unaffected.

§83 Timely Information by the Court

(1) In proceedings for a declaration that the patent or supplementary certificate is null and void, the patent court shall inform the parties as soon as possible about the aspects that it expects to be of particular importance for the decision or that are conducive to the concentration of the hearing on the questions that are of essence for the decision. There shall be no need for such an indication if the aspects to be discussed appear obvious in the light of the parties' submissions. §139 of the Code of Civil Procedure shall also apply.

(2) The patent court can set the parties a deadline within which they can comment on the indication pursuant to Paragraph 1 by means of pertinent petitions or additions to their submissions and otherwise submit a final comment. This deadline can be prolonged if the party concerned submits material reasons for such. Such reasons shall be substantiated.

(3) The powers pursuant to Paragraphs 1 and 2 can also be exercised by the presiding judge or a member of the court to be designated by the presiding judge.

(4) The patent court can reject a party's contestation or defense pleadings or an amendment of the action or a defense by the defendant on the basis of an amended version of the patent if such are not submitted until after expiry of the deadline set pursuant to Paragraph 2, and can decide the case without further investigations if

1. a postponement of an in-person hearing already set would be needed to take account of the new submission, and
2. the party concerned has failed to provide a sufficient excuse for the delay, and
3. the party concerned has been informed about the consequences of failing to comply with the deadline.

The exculpation shall be substantiated.

Infringement

§139 Right to Prevent the Use of the Patented Invention, Damages, Burden of Proof

(1) Any person who uses an invention contrary to Sections 9 to 13 may, if there is a risk of a recurrent infringement, be sued by the injured party to enjoin such use. This claim also applies in the event of the threat of a first infringement.

(2) Any person who commits these acts intentionally or negligently shall be liable for compensation to the injured party for the damage suffered therefrom. For the assessment of the compensation account can be taken of the profits which the infringer has made due to the infringement. The assessment of the damages can also be based on the amount which would have been due as a reasonable compensation if the infringer had requested authorization for the use.

(3) If the subject matter of a patent is a process for obtaining a new product, the same product when produced by any other party shall, in the absence of proof to the contrary, be deemed to have been obtained by the patented process. In the adduction of proof to the contrary, the legitimate interests of the defendant in protecting his manufacturing and business secrets shall be taken into account.

§140 Suspension in case of Reasonable Compensation

If, prior to the grant of a patent, rights based on an application, the files of which may be inspected by any person (Section 31(1), the second half of the second sentence and (2)), are claimed in court proceedings, and if the decision on the litigation depends on whether an action exists under Section 33(1), the Court may order that the proceedings be deferred until the decision is made on the grant of the patent. If a request for examination pursuant to Section 44 has not been filed, the Court may, at the request of the opposing party, set a time limit for filing the request for examination to the party claiming rights on the basis of the application. If the request for examination is not filed within that time limit, the rights deriving from the application involved in the litigation may not be claimed.

§140a Destruction and Recall

(1) Any person who uses a patented invention in contravention of Sections 9 to 13 may be required by the injured party to destroy the product that is the subject matter of the patent and that is in the possession of the infringer or is his property. The first sentence shall also apply in the case of a product that has been directly manufactured by means of a process that is the subject matter of the patent.

(2) The provisions of subsection 1 shall apply mutatis mutandis to materials and equipment that have served overwhelmingly for the manufacture of such products.

(3) Any person who uses a patented invention in contravention of Sections 9 to 13 can be required by the injured party to recall the products that are the subject matter of the patent or to remove them definitively from the distribution channels. The first sentence shall also apply in the case of a product that has been directly manufactured by means of a process that is the subject matter of the patent.

(4) The claims pursuant to subsections 1 to 3 are excluded if their enforcement is disproportionate in the individual case. The examination of proportionality shall also take account of the legitimate interests of third parties.

§140b Information about Distribution Channel and Origin of Goods

(1) Any person who uses a patented invention in contravention of Sections 9 to 13 may be required by the injured party to give information as to the origin and distribution channels of the products used, without delay.

(2) In cases where the infringement is obvious or in cases in which the injured party has filed an action against the infringer, the claim, notwithstanding subsection 1, also applies against a person who to a commercial extent
   1. had infringing products in his possession,
   2. made use of infringing services,
   3. provided services that were used for infringing activities, or
   4. according to information from a person specified in Numbers 1, 2 or 3, participated in the manufacture, production or distribution of such products or the provision of such services,

   unless the person would be entitled to refuse to testify in the proceedings against the infringer pursuant to Sections 383 to 385 of the Code of Civil Procedure. If the claim pursuant to the first sentence is asserted before the courts, the court can upon application suspend the litigation pending against the infringer until settlement of the litigation conducted on the claim to information. The party obliged to provide information can require the injured party to refund the expenditure necessary for the provision of the information.

(3) The person required to give information shall give particulars of
   1. the names and addresses of the manufacturers, the suppliers and other prior owners of the products, or of the users of the services, and the trade customers and points of sale for which they were intended, and
   2. the quantity of the products that have been manufactured, dispatched, received or ordered and the prices paid for the goods or services in question.

(4) The claims pursuant to subsections 1 and 2 shall be excluded if their enforcement is disproportionate in the individual case.

(5) If the party obliged to give information provides the information incorrectly or incompletely with intent or gross negligence, he shall be required to compensate the injured party for the resulting loss.

(6) Any person who has given true information without being required to do so pursuant to subsection 1 or subsection 2, shall only be liable to third parties if he knew that he was not required to give the information.

(7) In cases where infringement is obvious, the obligation to provide information may be imposed by injunction in compliance with Sections 935 to 945 of the Code of Civil Procedure.

(8) Such information may only be used in criminal proceedings or in proceedings under the Act on Minor Offences against the person required to give information or against a dependent person under Section 52(1) of the Code of Criminal Procedure, in respect of an act committed before the information was given, with the consent of the person required to give the information.

(9) If the information can only be given using traffic data (Section 3 No. 30 of the Telecommunications Act), the provision of the information shall be subject to a court order concerning the admissibility of the use of traffic data, application for which shall be filed by the injured party. For the issue of this order, the regional court in whose district the party obliged to provide information has his place of residence, his registered office or a business establishment shall have exclusive jurisdiction, without regard to the value in dispute. The decision shall be rendered by the civil chamber. The proceedings shall be subject mutatis mutandis to the provisions of the Act concerning Proceedings in Family Cases and in Matters of Voluntary Jurisdiction. The costs for the court order shall be borne by the injured party. An appeal can be filed against the decision of the regional court. The appeal shall be filed within a period of two weeks. The provisions concerning the protection of personal data shall for the rest remain unaffected.

(10) Subsection 2 in conjunction with subsection 9 limits the basic right to privacy of telecommunications (Article 10 of the Basic Act).

§140c Inspection of Infringing Object and Presentation of Documents

(1) Any person who with sufficient probability uses a patented invention in contravention of Sections 9 to 13 may be required by the right holder or another authorized person to present a document or to tolerate the inspection of an object that is within his power of disposal or of a method that is the subject matter of the patent, if such is necessary to establish such party's claims. If there is a sufficient probability of an infringement to a commercial extent, the claim also extends to the submission of banking, financial or trading documents. If the alleged infringer claims that such information is confidential, the court shall adopt the necessary measures to ensure the protection required in the individual case.

(2) The claim pursuant to subsection 1 is excluded if its enforcement is disproportionate in the individual case.

(3) The obligation to present a document or tolerate the inspection of an object can be imposed by an injunction pursuant to Sections 935 to 945 of the Code of Civil Procedure. The court shall take the necessary measures to ensure the protection of confidential information. This shall apply in particular in cases in which the injunction is imposed without prior hearing of the opposing party.

(4) Section 811 of the Civil Code and Section 140b subsection 8 shall apply mutatis mutandis.
(5) If there was no infringement or threat of an infringement, the alleged infringer can claim compensation for the loss incurred by him as a result of the application from the party who has applied for the presentation or inspection pursuant to subsection 1.

§140d Presentation of Banking, Financial or Trading Documents

(1) In the case of an infringement committed to a commercial extent, in the cases covered by Section 139(2), the injured party can also require the infringer to present banking, financial or trading documents or to provide suitable access to the corresponding documents that are in the infringer's power of disposal and that are necessary for the enforcement of the claim for damages if the satisfaction of the claim for damages is in doubt without such presentation. If the alleged infringer claims that such information is confidential, the court shall adopt the necessary measures to ensure the protection required in the individual case.
(2) The claim pursuant to subsection 1 is excluded if its enforcement is disproportionate in the individual case.
(3) The obligation to present the documents specified in subsection 1 can be imposed by an injunction in compliance with Sections 935 to 945 of the Code of Civil Procedure if the claim to damages is obvious. The court shall take the necessary measures to ensure the protection of confidential information. This shall apply in particular in cases in which the injunction is imposed without prior hearing of the opposing party.
(4) Section 811 of the Civil Code and Section 140b(8) shall apply mutatis mutandis.

Section 140e - Publication of the Judgement

Where an action has been brought under this Act, the successful party may be entitled in the judgment to make the judgment public at the expense of the unsuccessful party if the successful party demonstrates a legitimate interest. The nature and extent of the publication shall be laid down in the judgment. The entitlement shall lapse if it is not used within three months of the judgment becoming final. The pronouncement in accordance with the first sentence shall not be provisionally enforceable.

§141 Limitation

Rights based on the infringement of a patent shall become statute-barred in compliance with the provisions of the 5th Chapter of the 1st book of the Civil Code. If the infringer has obtained anything through the infringement at the expense of the claimant, section 852 of the Civil Code shall apply mutatis mutandis.

§142 Penalties

(1) Any person who, without the necessary consent of the patentee or the holder of the supplementary certificate of protection (Sections 16a and 49a)
   1. makes or offers, puts on the market, uses or imports or stocks for these purposes a product which is the subject matter of a patent or a supplementary certificate of protection (Section 9, second sentence, item 1) or
   2. uses or offers for use within the territory to which this Act applies a process which is the subject matter of a patent or a supplementary certificate of protection (Section 9, second sentence, item 2), shall be liable to imprisonment not exceeding three years or a fine.

   The first sentence, item 1, shall also apply if there is a product which has been directly produced by a process which is the subject matter of a patent or a supplementary certificate of protection (Section 9, second sentence, item 3).

(2) Where the offender acts by way of trade, he shall be liable to imprisonment of up to five years or a fine.

(3) The attempt to commit such an offense shall be punishable.

(4) Offenses under subsection (1) shall only be prosecuted on complaint unless the prosecuting authorities deem that ex officio prosecution is justified in view of the particular public interest.

(5) Objects implicated in an offense may be confiscated. Article 74a of the Penal Code shall apply. Where the claims referred to in Section 140a are upheld in proceedings under the provisions of the Code of Criminal Procedure with regard to compensation of the injured party (Sections 403 to 406c), the provisions on confiscation shall not be of application.

(6) If a penalty is pronounced, the Court shall, at the request of the injured party and if the latter can show a justified interest, order publication of the judgment. The nature of the publication shall be laid down in the judgment.

§142a Customs Action

(1) A product that infringes a patent protected under this Act shall be subject, at the request of the holder of the rights and against his security, to seizure by the customs authorities, on import or export, in those cases where the infringement is obvious and provided that Council Regulation (EC) N° 608/2013 dated June 12, 2013 concerning customs action against goods suspected of infringing certain intellectual property rights and the measures to be taken against goods found to have infringed such rights, is not applicable. This provision shall apply in trade with other Member States of the EU and Members of the Agreement on the EEC only insofar as controls are carried out by the customs authorities.

(2) Where the customs authorities order a seizure, they shall advise the person entitled to dispose and also the petitioner thereof without delay. The origin, quantity and place of storage of the product, together with the name and address of the person entitled to dispose, shall be communicated to the petitioner; the secrecy of correspondence and of mail (Section 10 of the Constitution) shall be restricted to that extent. The applicant shall be given the opportunity to inspect the product where such inspection does not constitute a breach of commercial or trade secrecy.

(3) Where no opposition to the seizure is made, at the latest within two weeks of service of the notification under the first sentence of subsection (2), the customs authorities shall order confiscation of the seized product.

(4) If the person entitled to dispose opposes the seizure, the customs authorities shall inform the applicant thereof without delay. The applicant shall be required to declare to the customs authorities, without delay, whether he maintains the request under subsection (1) in respect of the seized goods.

1. If the applicant withdraws his request, the customs authorities shall lift the seizure without delay.
2. If the applicant maintains his request and submits an executable court decision ordering the impounding of the seized copies or the limitation of the right to dispose, the customs authorities shall take the necessary measures.

   Where neither of the cases according to items 1 and 2 is applicable, the customs authorities shall lift the seizure after expiration of two weeks after service of the notification to the applicant under the first sentence; where the applicant can show that a court decision according to item 2 has been requested, but has not yet been received, the seizure shall be maintained for a further two weeks at most.

(5) Where the seizure proves to have been unjustified from the beginning and if the applicant has maintained the request under subsection (1) in respect of the seized product or has not made a declaration without delay (second sentence of subsection (4)), he shall be required to compensate the damages that the seizure has caused to the person entitled to dispose.

(6) The petition under subsection (1) is to be submitted to the Regional Finance Office and shall be effective for two years unless a shorter period of validity has been requested; the request may be repeated. The cost of official acts related to the request shall be charged to the petitioner in accordance with Section 178 of the Fiscal Code.

(7) Seizure and confiscation may be opposed by the legal remedies allowed by the fixed penalty procedure under the Act on Minor Offenses in respect of seizure and confiscation. The petitioner shall be heard in the review proceedings. An immediate appeal against the decision of the Local Court shall be admissible; it shall be heard by the Provincial High Court.

§142b Simplified destruction

For the procedure according to Council Regulation (EC) N° 608/2013, the provisions of §142a (5) and (6) shall apply mutatis mutandis, with the proviso that the Council Regulation does not contain provisions which contradicts this.

Part X

Procedure in Patent Litigation

§143 Patent Litigation

(1) For all actions whereby a claim arising out of one of the legal relationships regulated in this Act is asserted (patent litigation), the civil chambers of the regional courts shall have exclusive jurisdiction without regard to the value in dispute.
(2) The Governments of the Federal States shall have power to allot by statutory order patent litigation for the areas of several regional courts to one such court. The Governments of the Federal States may transfer those powers to the provincial administrations of justice. The Federal States may further by way of agreement assign tasks for which courts of one Federal State are responsible completely or partly to the competent court of another Federal State.
(3) Of the costs arising from the collaboration of a patent attorney in the case, fees according to Section 13 of the Federal Regulations on Fees for Attorneys-at-Law shall be refunded, as shall the necessary expenses of the patent attorney.

§144 Abatement of Costs

(1) If, in a patent case, a party satisfies the court that the awarding of the costs of the case against him according to the full value in dispute would considerably endanger his financial position, the Court may, at his request, order that party's liability to pay court costs to be adjusted in accordance with a portion of the value in dispute that shall be appropriate to his financial position. As a result of the order, the favored party shall likewise be required to pay the fees of his attorney-at-law only in accordance with that portion of the value in dispute. To the extent that the costs of the case are awarded against him or to the extent to which he assumes such costs, he shall be required to refund the court fees paid by the opposing party and the fees of the latter's attorney-at-law only in accordance with that portion of the value in dispute. To the extent that the extrajudicial costs are ordered to be paid by the opposing party or are assumed by that party, the attorney-at-law of the favored party may recover his fees from the opposing party in accordance with the value in dispute applying to the latter.
(2) The request under subsection (1) may be declared before and recorded at the registrar's office of the court. It shall be presented before the substance

of the case is heard. Thereafter, it shall only be admissible if the presumed or fixed value in dispute is subsequently increased by the court. Before the decision on the request is given, the opposing party shall be heard.

§145 Concentration of Action

Any person who has brought an action pursuant to Section 139 may bring a further action against the defendant on account of the same or a similar act on the basis of another patent only if, through no fault of his own, he was not in a position to assert that patent also in the earlier suit.
(...)

4. UTILITY MODEL ACT

§1 Admissible Subject Matter

(1) Utility model protection shall be afforded to inventions that are new, involve an inventive step and are susceptible of industrial application.
(2) The following, in particular, shall not be regarded as the subject matter of a utility model within the meaning of subsection (1):
   1. discoveries, scientific theories and mathematical methods;
   2. aesthetic creations;
   3. schemes, rules and methods for performing mental acts, playing games or doing business, and programs for computers;
   4. presentations of information.
   5. biotechnological inventions (Section 1(2) Patent Act).
(3) Subsection (2) shall oppose utility model protection only to the extent to which protection is sought for the above-mentioned subject matter or activities as such.

§2 Excluded Subject Matter

Utility model protection shall not be granted in respect of:

1. inventions the publication or exploitation of which would be contrary to public policy or morality, provided that the exploitation shall not be deemed to be so contrary merely because it is prohibited by law or regulation.
2. plant or animal varieties;
3. processes.

§3 Novelty and Industrial Application

(1) The subject matter of a utility model shall be considered to be new if it does not form part of the state of the art. The state of the art comprises any

knowledge made available to the public by means of a written description or by use within the territory to which this Act applies before the date relevant for the priority of the application. Description or use within the six months preceding the date relevant for the priority of the application shall not be taken into consideration if it is based on the conception of the applicant or his predecessor in title.

(2) The subject matter of a utility model shall be considered susceptible of industrial application if it can be made or used in any kind of industry, including agriculture.

§4 Application; Amendments, Divisional Applications

(1) Applications in respect of inventions for which utility model protection is sought shall be filed in writing with the Patent Office. A separate application shall be filed for each invention.

(2) The application may also be filed with a patent information center if this center was by announcement of the Federal Ministry of Justice in the Federal Law Gazette determined to receive utility model applications. An application which may contain a state secret (Section 93 Penal Code) may not be filed with a patent information center.

(3) Applications shall contain:
1. the name of the applicant;
2. a request for registration of the utility model, which must designate clearly and concisely the subject matter of the utility model;
3. one or more claims in which shall be specified what is to be protected by the utility model;
4. a description of the subject matter of the utility model;
5. the drawings to which the claims or the description refer.

(4) The Federal Ministry for Justice shall have power to issue by statutory order regulations concerning other requirements for the application. It may delegate such power by statutory order to the GPTO.

(5) Up to the time of the decision to register the utility model, alterations in the contents of the application shall be permissible insofar as they do not broaden the scope of the subject matter of the application. No rights may be derived from alterations which broaden the scope of the subject matter of the application.

(6) An applicant may at any time divide his application. The division shall be made by a statement in writing. The date of the original application and any priority that has been claimed shall continue to apply to each part of a divided application. For the period up to division the same fees which were payable for the original application shall be paid for the separated application.

(...)

§5 Branching Off

(1) Where an applicant has already sought, at an earlier date, a patent with effect in the Federal Republic of Germany for the same invention, he may file together with the utility model application a declaration claiming the date of filing relevant for the patent application. Any priority right claimed in respect of the patent application shall also apply to the utility model application. The priority right under the first sentence may be exercised up to the expiration of two months from the end of the month in which processing of the patent application or any opposition procedure is terminated, at the latest, however, by the end of the tenth year from the date of filing of the patent application.

(2) Where an applicant has filed a declaration under the first sentence of subsection (1), the Patent Office shall request him to communicate the serial number and the date of filing and to file a copy of the patent application, within two months of service of the request. Where the particulars are not provided in due time, the priority right under the first sentence of subsection (1) shall be forfeited.

§6 Priority

(1) Within a period of 12 months from the date of application for an earlier patent or utility model application filed with the Patent Office, the applicant shall enjoy a right of priority for the application for a utility model for the same invention, unless a domestic or foreign priority has already been claimed for the earlier application. Section 40(2) to (4) and (5), first sentence and (6) of the Patent Act shall apply mutatis mutandis, with the proviso in the case of Section 40(5), first sentence, that the earlier patent application shall not be deemed to have been withdrawn.

(2) The provisions of the Patent Act on foreign priority (Section 41) shall be applicable mutatis mutandis.

(...)

§7 Search

(1) The Patent Office shall upon request search for the prior art which is to be considered in assessing the registrability of the subject matter of the utility model application or the utility model.

(2) A request may be filed by the applicant or the registered proprietor or by any other party. Requests shall be filed in writing. Section 28 shall be applicable mutatis mutandis. Section 28 shall apply mutatis mutandis.

(3) (...)

§8 Registration

(1) Where an application complies with the requirements of Sections 4, 4a, 4b the Patent Office shall order registration in the Utility Model Register. No examination of the subject matter of the application as to novelty, inventive step or industrial applicability shall be carried out. Section 49(2) of the Patent Act shall apply mutatis mutandis.
(2) The registration shall contain the name and address of the applicant and of any duly appointed representative or person authorized to accept service (Section 28), together with the date of filing of the application.
(3) Summary lists of registrations shall be published in the Patent Gazette at regular intervals.
(4) The Patent Office shall record in the Register any change in the identity of the proprietor of the utility model or of his representative or the person authorized to accept service if proof thereof is furnished to it. Until such time as the change has been recorded, the former proprietor and his former representative or the person authorized to accept service shall continue to have the rights and obligations as provided under this Act.
(5) Anyone may inspect the Register and the files of registered utility models, including the files of cancellation proceedings. In addition, the Patent Office shall permit any person so requesting to inspect the files if and to the extent that a legitimate interest has been satisfactorily proved.
(...)

§11 Effect of the Registration

(1) Registration of a utility model shall have the effect that the proprietor alone is authorized to use the subject matter of the utility model. Any person not having his consent shall be prohibited from making, offering, putting on the market or using a product which is the subject matter of the utility model, or importing or stocking the product for these purposes.
(2) Registration shall have the further effect that any person not having the consent of the proprietor shall be prohibited from supplying or offering to supply within the territory to which this Act applies persons, other than those entitled to exploit the subject matter of the utility model, with means relating to an essential element of the subject matter of the utility model, for using it within the territory to which this Act applies, when such person knows, or it is obvious in the circumstances, that the means are suitable and intended for using the subject matter of the utility model. The first sentence shall not apply when the means are staple commercial products, except when such person induces those supplied to commit acts prohibited by the second sentence of subsection (1). Persons performing the acts referred to in items 1 and 2 of Section 12 shall not be considered to be persons entitled to exploit the subject matter of the utility model within the meaning of the first sentence.

§12 Limitation of Effects

The effects of the utility model shall not extend to

1. acts done privately for non-commercial purposes;
2. acts done for experimental purposes relating to the subject matter of the utility model;
3. acts of the kind specified in items 4 to 6 of Section 11 of the Patent Act.

§12a Scope of Protection

The scope of protection of the subject matter of the utility model shall be determined by the terms of the claims. When interpreting the claims, reference shall be made, however, to the description and the drawings.

§13 Inassertability

(1) Registration shall not afford utility model protection where a claim for cancellation of the utility model (Sections 15(1) and (3)), assertable by any person, exists against the person registered as the proprietor.

(2) If the essential elements of the registration have been taken from the descriptions, drawings, models, appliances or equipment of another person without that person's consent, protection under this Act may not be invoked against the injured party.

(3) The provisions of the Patent Act concerning the right to protection (Section 6), the right to the grant of protection (Section 7(1)), the right to assignment (Section 8), the right deriving from prior use (Section 12) and the official order of exploitation (Section 13) shall be applicable mutatis mutandis.

§14 Utility Model and Subsequently Filed Patent

If a subsequently filed patent infringes a right under Section 11, the right deriving from such patent may not be exercised without the consent of the proprietor of the utility model.

§15 Cancellation of the Utility Model

(1) Any person may assert a claim against the person registered as proprietor for cancellation of the utility model
   1. if the subject matter of the utility model is not registrable within the terms of Sections 1 to 3;
   2. if the subject matter of the utility model is already protected on the basis of an earlier patent or utility model application; or
   3. if the subject matter of the utility model extends beyond the content of the application as filed.

(2) In the case of Section 13(2), only the injured party may assert a claim for cancellation.

(3) Where the grounds for cancellation relate to a part only of the utility model, only that part shall be cancelled. The limitation may be effected in the form of an amendment to the claims.

§16 Cancellation Request

A request for cancellation of a utility model under Section 15 shall be filed with the Patent Office in writing. The request shall state the grounds on which it is based. The provisions of Sections 81(6) and 125 of the Patent Act shall apply mutatis mutandis.

§17 Cancellation Proceedings

(1) The Patent Office shall notify the proprietor of the utility model of the request and shall invite him to reply thereto within one month. If he fails to file a contesting reply in due time, cancellation shall be effected.
(2) In the contrary case, the Patent Office shall notify the person making the request of such reply and shall take all measures necessary for the investigation of the matter. It may order the examination of witnesses and experts. The provisions of the Code of Civil Procedure (Sections 373 to 401 as well as 402 to 414) shall apply mutatis mutandis to any such examination. A sworn minute-taker shall be called in for the proceedings relating to the taking of evidence.
(3) The decision on a request shall be taken on the basis of a hearing. The decision shall be pronounced at the session at which the hearing is closed or at a session to be fixed forthwith. The decision shall contain the grounds therefore, shall be in writing and shall be communicated ex officio to the parties. Section 47(2) of the Patent Act shall apply mutatis mutandis. Service of the decision is admissible instead of pronouncement.
(4) The Patent Office shall determine in what proportion the costs of the proceedings shall be borne by the parties. Section 62(2) and the second and third sentences of Section 84(2) of the Patent Act shall apply mutatis mutandis.

§18 Appeal

(1) Appeals against decisions of the Utility Model Section and the Utility Model Divisions shall be made to the Patent Court.
(2) In other respects, the provisions of the Patent Act governing proceedings on appeal shall be applicable mutatis mutandis. If an appeal is filed from a decision given in cancellation proceedings, Section 84(2) of the Patent Act shall apply mutatis mutandis in respect of the decision on the costs of the proceedings.
(3) Appeals against decisions of the Utility Model Section and against decisions of the Utility Model Divisions shall be heard by a Chamber of Appeal of the Patent Court. Appeals against rejection of an application for registration of a utility model shall be heard by a Chamber of Appeal composed of two

legal members and one technical member, and appeals against decisions of the Utility Model Divisions regarding cancellation requests by a Chamber of Appeal composed of one legal member and two technical members. For appeals against decisions about requests for legal aid sentence 2 shall apply mutatis mutandis. The presiding judge must be a legal member. Section 21g(1) and (2) of the Judiciary Act shall apply with regard to the allocation of business within the Chamber of Appeal. In the case of proceedings relating to appeals against decisions of the Utility Model Section, Section 69(1) of the Patent Act shall apply and, in the case of proceedings relating to appeals against decisions of the Utility Model Divisions, Section 69(2) of the Patent Act shall apply, mutatis mutandis.

(4) An appeal on a point of law against a decision of the Chamber of Appeal of the Patent Court in respect of an appeal under subsection (1) shall be filed with the Federal Court of Justice if the Chamber of Appeal, in its decision, has given leave to appeal on that point of law. Sections 100(2) and (3) and 101 to 109 of the Patent Act shall apply.

§19 Suspension of the Infringement Proceedings

If litigation is pending during cancellation proceedings and the decision on that litigation depends on the existence of utility model protection, the court may order that the hearing be postponed until the cancellation proceedings have been settled. It shall order such postponement if it considers the utility model registration to be invalid. If the cancellation request is refused, the court shall be bound by that decision only if it was taken in respect of the same parties.

§20 Compulsory License

The provisions of the Patent Act concerning the grant or withdrawal of compulsory licenses or with respect to the adaptation of the remuneration for a compulsory license stipulated by decision (Section 24) and the procedure for the grant of compulsory licenses (Sections 81 to 99 and 110 to 122a) shall apply mutatis mutandis in the case of registered utility models.

§21 Referral to the Patent Act

(1) The provisions of the Patent Act concerning the giving of opinions (Section 29(1) and (2)), reinstatement (Section 123), further processing of the application (Section 123a), obligation to observe the truth in proceedings (Section 124), electronic conduct of proceedings (Section 125a), official language (Section 126), service of documents (Section 127) and legal assistance from the courts (Section 128) and the reimbursement of witnesses and the remuneration of experts (128a) and relief for extensive judicial proceedings (128b shall also apply to utility model proceedings.

(2) The provisions of the Patent Act granting legal aid (Sections 129 to 138) shall apply mutatis mutandis in utility model proceedings and Section

135(3) shall apply with the proviso that the representative assigned under Section 133 shall have the right to appeal.

§22 Assignment and License

(1) The right to a utility model, the right to registration of a utility model and the right derived from such registration shall pass to the heirs. Such rights may be assigned to other parties, with or without restriction.

(2) The rights under subsection (1) may be licensed in whole or in part, exclusively or non-exclusively, for the whole or part of the territory to which this Act applies. Where a licensee contravenes a restriction of his license under the first sentence, the right afforded by the registration may be invoked against him.

(3) The transfer of rights or the grant of a license shall not affect licenses previously granted to third parties.

§23 Term, Maintenance and Cancellation

(1) Utility model protection shall start on the day of application and end ten years after the expiry of the month in which the application was filed.

(2) The term of protection may be renewed for the fourth until the sixth, seventh and eighth as well as the ninth and tenth year by payment of a renewal fee, calculated from the day of application. Such renewal shall be recorded in the Register.

(3) A utility model shall lapse if
   1. the registered proprietor abandons it by a written declaration made to the Patent Office or
   2. the renewal fee is not paid in time (Section 7(1), Section 13(3) or Section 14(2) and (5) Patent Cost Act).

§24 Right to Prohibit Use, Damages

(1) Any person who uses a utility model contrary to the provisions of Sections 11 to 14 may, if there is a risk of a recurrent infringement, be sued by the injured party to enjoin such use. This claim also applies in the event of the threat of a first infringement.

(2) Any person who undertakes such action intentionally or negligently shall be liable for compensation to the injured party for the damage suffered therefrom. For the assessment of the compensation account can be taken of the profits which the infringer has obtained through the infringement. The assessment of the damages can also be based on the amount which would have been due as a reasonable compensation if the infringer had requested authorization for the use.

§24a Destruction Claim

(1) Any person who uses a utility model in contravention of Sections 11 to 14 may be required by the injured party to destroy the product that is the subject matter of the utility model and that is in the possession of the infringer or is his property. The first sentence shall also apply to materials and equipment in possession of the infringing party that have served overwhelmingly for the manufacture of such products.
(2) Any person who uses a utility model in contravention of Sections 11 to 14 can be required by the injured party to recall the products that are the subject matter of the utility model or to remove them definitively from the distribution channels.
(3) The claims pursuant to subsections 1 and 2 are excluded if their enforcement is disproportionate in the individual case. The examination of proportionality shall also take account of the legitimate interests of third parties.

§24b Information about Distribution Channel and Origin of Goods

(1) Any person who uses a utility model contrary to the provisions of Sections 11 to 14 may be required by the injured party to give information as to the origin and distribution channels of the product used, without delay.
(2) In those cases where infringement is obvious or in cases in which the injured party has filed an action against the infringer, the claim, notwithstanding subsection 1, also applies against a person who to a commercial extent
   1. had infringing products in his possession,
   2. made use of infringing services,
   3. provided services that were used for infringing activities, or
   4. according to information from a person specified in Numbers 1, 2 or 3, participated in the manufacture, production or distribution of such products or the provision of such services,

   unless the person would be entitled to refuse to testify in the proceedings against the infringer pursuant to Sections 383 to 385 of the Code of Civil Procedure. If the claim pursuant to the first sentence is asserted before the courts, the court can upon application suspend the litigation pending against the infringer until settlement of the litigation conducted on the claim to information. The party obliged to provide information can require the injured party to refund the expenditure necessary for the provision of the information.
(3) The person required to give information shall give particulars of
   1. the names and addresses of the manufacturers, the suppliers and other prior owners of the products, or of the users of the services, and the trade customers and points of sale for which they were intended, and

2. the quantity of the products that have been manufactured, dispatched, received or ordered and about the prices paid for the goods or services in question.

(4) The claims pursuant to subsections 1 and 2 shall be excluded if their enforcement is disproportionate in the individual case.

(5) If the party obliged to give information provides the information incorrectly or incompletely with intent or gross negligence, he shall be required to compensate the injured party for the resulting loss.

(6) Any person who has given true information without being required to do so pursuant to subsection 1 or subsection 2, shall only be liable to third parties if he knew that he was not required to give the information.

(7) In cases where infringement is obvious, the obligation to provide information may be imposed by injunction in compliance with Sections 935 to 945 of the Code of Civil Procedure.

(8) Such information may only be used in criminal proceedings or in proceedings under the Act on Minor Offences against the person required to give information or against a dependent person under Section 52(1) of the Code of Criminal Procedure, in respect of an act committed before the information was given, with the consent of the person required to give the information.

(9) If the information can only be given using traffic data (Section 3 No. 30 of the Telecommunications Act), the provision of the information shall be subject to a court order concerning the admissibility of the use of traffic data, application for which shall be filed by the injured party. For the issue of this order, the regional court in whose district the party obliged to provide information has his place of residence, his registered office or a business establishment shall have exclusive jurisdiction, without regard to the value in dispute. The decision shall be rendered by the civil chamber. The proceedings shall be subject mutatis mutandis to the provisions concerning the Act concerning Proceedings in Family Cases and in Matters of Voluntary Jurisdiction. The costs for the court order shall be borne by the injured party. An appeal can be filed against the decision of the regional court. The appeal shall be filed within a period of two weeks. The provisions concerning the protection of personal data shall for the rest remain unaffected.

(10) Subsection 2 in conjunction with subsection 9 limits the basic right to privacy of telecommunications (Article 10 of the Basic Act).

§24c Limitation

(1) Any person who with sufficient probability uses a utility model in contravention of Sections 11 to 14 may be required by the right-holder or another authorized person to present a document or to tolerate the inspection of an object that is within his power of disposal, if such is necessary to establish such party's claims. If there is a sufficient probability of an infringement to

a commercial extent, the claim also extends to the submission of banking, financial or trading documents. If the alleged infringer claims that such information is confidential, the court shall adopt the necessary measures to ensure the protection required in the individual case.

(2) The claim pursuant to subsection 1 is excluded if its enforcement is disproportionate in the individual case.

(3) The obligation to present a document or tolerate the inspection of an object can be imposed by an injunction pursuant to Sections 935 to 945 of the Code of Civil Procedure. The court shall take the necessary measures to ensure the protection of confidential information. This shall apply in particular in cases in which the injunction is imposed without prior hearing of the opposing party.

(4) Section 811 of the Civil Code and Section 140b subsection 8 shall apply mutatis mutandis.

(5) If there was no infringement or threat of an infringement, the alleged infringer can claim compensation for the loss incurred by him as a result of the application from the party who has applied for the presentation or inspection pursuant to subsection 1.

(...)

§25 Penalties

(1) Any person who, without the necessary consent of the proprietor of the utility model
   1. makes, offers, puts on the market, uses or imports or stocks for these purposes a product which is the subject matter of a utility model (Section 11(1), second sentence) or
   2. exercises the right deriving from a patent contrary to Section 14 shall be liable to imprisonment of up to three years or a fine.

(2) Where the offender acts by way of trade, he shall be liable to imprisonment of up to five years or a fine.

(3) The attempt to commit such an offense shall be punishable.

(4) Offenses under subsection (1) shall only be prosecuted on complaint, unless the prosecuting authorities deem that ex officio prosecution is justified in view of the particular public interest.

(5) Objects implicated in an offense may be confiscated. Article 74a of the Penal Code shall apply. Where the claims referred to in Section 24a are upheld in proceedings under the provisions of the Code of Criminal Procedure with regard to compensation of the injured party (Sections 403 to 406c), the provisions on confiscation shall not be of application.

(6) If a penalty is pronounced, the Court shall, at the request of the injured party and if the latter can show a justified interest, order publication of the judgment. The nature of the publication shall be laid down in the judgment.

§25a Customs Action

(1) A product that infringes a utility model protected under this Act shall be subject, at the request of the holder of the rights and against his security, to seizure by the customs authorities, on import or export, in those cases where the infringement is obvious and provided that the Council Regulation 608/2013 [...] is not applicable. This provision shall apply in trade with other Member States of the EU and the EEC only insofar as controls are carried out by the customs authorities.

(2) Where the customs authorities order a seizure, they shall inform the person entitled to dispose and also the applicant thereof without delay. The applicant shall be informed about the origin, quantity and place of storage of the product, together with the name and address of the person entitled to dispose; the secrecy of correspondence and of mail (Section 10 of the Constitution) shall be restricted to that extent. The applicant shall be given the opportunity to inspect the product where such inspection does not constitute a breach of commercial or trade secrecy.

(3) Where no opposition to the seizure is made, at the latest within two weeks of service of the notification under the first sentence of subsection (2), the customs authorities shall order confiscation of the seized product.

(4) If the person entitled to dispose opposes seizure, the customs authorities shall inform the applicant thereof without delay. The applicant shall be required to declare to the customs authorities, without delay, whether he maintains the request under subsection (1) in respect of the seized copies.

1. If the applicant withdraws his request, the customs authorities shall lift the seizure without delay.
2. If the applicant maintains his request and produces an executable court decision ordering the custody of the seized copies or the limitation of the right to dispose, the customs authorities shall take the necessary measures.

   Where neither of the cases referred to in items 1 and 2 is applicable, the customs authorities shall lift the seizure on the expiry of two weeks after service of the notification to the petitioner under the first sentence; where the petitioner can show that a court decision according to item 2 has been requested but has not yet been received, the seizure shall be maintained for a further two weeks at most.

(5) Where the seizure proves to be unjustified from the beginning and if the applicant has maintained the request under subsection (1) in respect of the seized product or has not made a declaration without delay (second sentence of subsection (4)), he shall be required to compensate the damages that seizure has occasioned to the person entitled to dispose.

(6) An application under subsection (1) is to be submitted to the General Customs Office and shall be effective for one years unless a shorter period of validity has been requested; the request may be repeated. The cost of

official acts related to the request shall be charged to the applicant in accordance with Section 178 of the Fiscal Code.

(7) Seizure and confiscation may be opposed by the legal remedies allowed by the fixed penalty procedure under the Act on Minor Offenses in respect of seizure and confiscation. The petitioner shall be heard in the review proceedings. An immediate appeal can be filed against the decision of the Local Court; it shall be decided by the Higher Court.

§25b

For the procedure according to Council Regulation (EC) N° 608/2013, the provisions of §25a (5) and (6) shall apply mutatis mutandis, with the proviso that the Council Regulation does not contain provisions which contradicts this.

§26 Apportion of Litigation Value

(1) If a party to civil litigation in which an action is brought to assert a claim arising from one of the legal relationships regulated under this Act satisfies the court that the award of the costs of the case against him according to the full value in dispute would considerably endanger his financial position, the court may, at his request, order that party's liability to pay court costs to be adjusted in accordance with a portion of the value in dispute that shall be appropriate to his financial position. As a result of the order, the favored party shall likewise be required to pay the fees of his attorney-at-law only in accordance with that portion of the value in dispute. To the extent that the costs of the case are awarded against him or to the extent to which he assumes such costs, he shall be required to refund the court fees paid by the opposing party and the fees of the latter's attorney-at-law only in accordance with that portion of the value in dispute. To the extent that the extrajudicial costs are ordered to be paid by the opposing party or are assumed by that party, the attorney-at-law of the favored party may recover his fees from the opposing party in accordance with the value in dispute applying to the latter.

(2) A request under subsection (1) may be declared before and recorded at the registrar's office of the court. It shall be presented before the substance of the case is heard. Thereafter, it shall be admissible only if the presumed or fixed value in dispute is subsequently increased by the court. Before the decision is given on the request, the opposing party shall be heard.

§27 Utility Model Dispute

(1) For all actions whereby a claim arising out of one of the legal relationships regulated in this Act is asserted (utility model litigation), the civil chambers of the regional courts shall have exclusive jurisdiction without regard to the value in dispute.

(2) The Governments of the Federal States shall have power to allot by statutory order utility model litigation for the areas of several regional courts to one such court insofar as this is procedurally expedient. The Governments of the Federal States may transfer those powers to the provincial administrations of justice. The Federal States may further by way of agreement assign tasks, for which courts of one Federal State are responsible, completely or partly to the competent court of another Federal State.

(3) Of the costs arising from the collaboration of a patent attorney in the case, fees according to Section 13 of the Federal Regulations on Fees for Attorneys-at-Act shall be refunded, as shall the necessary expenses of the patent attorney.

(...)

5. ACT ON EMPLOYEE'S INVENTIONS

§1 Scope of Application

This Act applies to inventions and to proposals of technical improvement made by employees in private employment, by employees in public service, by civil servants, and by members of the army.

§2 Inventions

Inventions within the meaning of the Act are only those which may be the subject of a patent or of a utility model.

§3 Proposals for Technical Improvement

Technical improvement proposals within the meaning of this Act are proposals for other technical innovations that may not be the subject of a patent or of protection as a utility model.

§4 Service Inventions and Free Inventions

(1) Employee inventions within the meaning of this Act may be either bound or free.

(2) Bound inventions (service inventions) are those made during the employment relationship which:
   1. either resulted from the employee's duties in the private or public entity,
   2. or are decisively based on the experience or activities of the private or public entity.

(3) Other inventions of an employee are free inventions. They are however subject to the limitations contained in §§18 and 19.

(4) Subsections (1) to (3) apply mutatis mutandis to inventions made by civil servants and members of the army.

§5 Duty to Report

(1) An employee making a service invention is obliged to report the invention to his employer immediately in a separate notice in text form indicating that said notice represents the report of an invention. Where several employees have contributed to making the invention, a joint notice can be made. The employer shall inform the employee without delay and in text form of the date the report was received.
(2) In the report, the employee shall describe the technical problem, its solution and how the service invention was achieved. Existing notes shall be attached provided they are necessary for an understanding of the invention. The report shall indicate the service instructions and directions received by the employee, use made of the expertise and activities of the enterprise, the employee's collaborators and the nature and extent of their contribution, and the report should indicate the contribution which the reporting employee considers to have made personally.
(3) A report which does not meet the requirements of subsection (2) shall be deemed to be in order unless the employer states within a two months period that and to what extent the report needs to be supplemented. To the extent necessary, he must assist the employee in supplementing the report.

§6 Claim of a Service Invention

(1) An employer may claim a service invention by means of a declaration executed vis-à-vis the employee.
(2) The declaration is deemed to be executed if the employer does not, within a four months term starting from the receipt of a duly made report (sentences 1 and 3 of Section 5(2)), release the invention by means of a declaration executed in text form vis-à-vis the employee.

§7 Effect of the Claim

(1) With the claim all rights in the service invention shall pass to the employer.
(2) Dispositions made by an employee as to a service invention prior to the employer declaring a claim shall have no effect on his employer insofar as the employer's rights are concerned.

§8 Free Inventions

A service invention becomes free if the employer releases it by a statement in text form. The employee may dispose of a service invention that has become free without the restrictions stipulated in Sections 18 and 19.

§9 Compensation

(1) The employee shall have a right to reasonable compensation against his employer as soon as the employer has made a claim to a service invention.
(2) For assessing the compensation, account shall in particular be taken of the commercial applicability of the service invention, the duties and position of the employee in the entity, and the entity's contribution to the invention.

§11 Compensation Directives

After hearing the leading organizations of employers and employees (in accordance with Section 12 of the Act on Collective Labor Agreements), the Federal Minister of Labor shall issue guidelines for assessing the compensation.

§12 Assessment and Determination of the Compensation

(1) The nature and amount of the compensation shall be determined by agreement between the employer and the employee within a reasonable time after the claim to a service invention has been made.
(2) If several employees have contributed to a service invention, the compensation shall be determined separately for each of them. The employer must inform the employees of the total amount of compensation awarded and of the share assigned to each inventor.
(3) Where no compensation agreement is concluded within a reasonable time after a claim to a service invention was made, the employer shall fix the amount of compensation, giving his reasons in text form to the employee, and shall pay in accordance with his settlement. The compensation shall be determined at the latest three months from the grant of the property right.
(4) An employee who disagrees with the settlement may object to it in text form within two months. If he does not object, the settlement becomes binding for both parties.
(5) If several employees have contributed to the service invention, the settlement shall not bind any of them if one of them objects on the ground that his contribution to the service invention has been incorrectly determined. In this case, the employer may make a new compensation settlement for all parties.
(6) The employer and the employee may require the other to agree to a different compensation arrangement if a substantial change has occurred in the circumstances essential to the assessment or determination of the compensation. A refund of compensation payments already received may not be requested. Subsections (1) to (5) are not applicable.

§13 Domestic Application

(1) An employer is obliged and solely entitled to apply for the grant of domestic property rights for a reported service invention. Where the invention is capable of patent protection, he shall apply for a patent unless, on an assessment of the industrial applicability of the service invention, protection as a utility model seems to be more appropriate. The application shall be filed without delay.

(2) The employer's obligation to file such an application lapses:
   1. if the service invention has become free (Section 8);
   2. if the employee agrees that no application is to be filed;
   3. if the conditions stipulated in Section 17 are fulfilled.

(3) If, after making a claim to a service invention, an employer does not comply with his duty to apply for an industrial property right and also fails to do so within a further reasonable time period set by the employee, the employee may apply for an industrial property right for the service invention in the employer's name and at the employer's expense.

(4) If a service invention has become free, only the employee is entitled to apply for an industrial property protection therefore. Should his employer already have applied for industrial property protection for the service invention, his rights resulting from such application shall pass to the employee.

§14 Protection Abroad

(1) After making a claim to a service invention, an employer is also entitled to apply for industrial property protection abroad.

(2) For foreign countries in which the employer does not intend to obtain industrial property rights, he shall release the service invention to the employee and shall, upon request, enable the employee to acquire these rights. The release must be executed in sufficient time in order that the employee can take advantage of the priority dates under international treaties in the field of industrial property.

(3) When releasing a service invention under subsection (2), the employer may reserve for himself a non-exclusive right to use the service invention in the foreign countries concerned, based on a reasonable compensation, and may require the employee, also in return for reasonable compensation, to respect the employer's obligations arising from contracts existing at the time of the invention's release when exploiting the released service invention.

(...)

§16 Surrender of application and rights

(1) If an employer, before fully meeting the demand of the employee for reasonable compensation, intends to stop prosecuting an application for a service invention, or to surrender a grant or registration issued, he shall inform his employee accordingly and, at the employee's request and expense, must assign the rights to him and forward to him any documents necessary to maintain the rights.
(2) An employer shall be entitled to surrender a grant issued if his employee does not request assignment thereof within three months from receipt of the communication made to the employee.
(3) When making the communication as provided in subsection (1), the employer is entitled to reserve for himself, against payment of reasonable compensation, a non-exclusive right to use the service invention.

§17 Trade Secrets

(1) If legitimate interests of the entity require that a reported service invention should not be disclosed, the employer may refrain from applying for industrial property protection, provided that he acknowledges vis-à-vis the employee that the service invention is capable of protection.
(2) If an employer does not acknowledge that a service invention is capable of protection, he may refrain from applying for an industrial property protection if he involves the Arbitration Board (Section 29) in view of seeking an agreement on the service invention's eligibility for protection.
(3) When determining the compensation for an invention under subsection (1), due account must also be taken of the economic drawbacks that result for the employee in connection with the fact that industrial property protection will not be obtained for the service invention.

2. Free Inventions

§18 Duty to Notify

(1) An employee who has made a free invention during the term of an employment contract shall inform the employer in text form thereof without delay. He shall give the employer all the details as to the invention and, if necessary, concerning its accomplishment which the employer may need to assess whether it is indeed a free invention.
(2) If the employer does not contest that the invention is a free invention by means of a declaration in text form made to the employee within three months of the notification, the invention can no longer be claimed as a service invention (Section 6).

(3) There is no obligation to notify the employer of a free invention if the invention is obviously not capable of being used in the employer's enterprise.

§19 Duty to Offer

(1) Prior to exploiting otherwise a free invention during the employment, an employee must offer to the employer at least a non-exclusive right to use the invention on reasonable conditions if the invention falls within the range of the actual or planned activities of the employer's enterprise at the time the offer is made. Such offer may be submitted together with the notification required according to Section 18.

(2) If the employer does not accept the offer within three months, the prerogative lapses.

(3) If the employer declares within the time period provided by subsection (2) that he intends to acquire the rights offered to him, but claims that the terms offered to him are not reasonable, the court shall determine the terms on action by the employer or employee.

(4) The employer or the employee may request a new determination of the terms if the circumstances essential to the terms agreed or fixed have substantially changed.

§20 Proposals of Technical Improvement

(1) For proposals of technical improvement which afford the employer an advantaged position similar to that obtained from an industrial property right, an employee shall be entitled to reasonable compensation from his employer as soon as the latter exploits the technical improvement. Sections 9 and 12 shall apply mutatis mutandis.

(2) In all other cases, technical improvement proposals shall be regulated by collective or company agreements.

§22 Mandatory Applicability

The provisions of this Act cannot be modified by contract to the detriment of the employee. Agreements shall, however, be permissible concerning service inventions after they have been reported and concerning free inventions and proposals for technical improvement (Section 20(1)) after their notification.

§23 Inequitable Agreements

(1) Agreements concerning service inventions, free inventions, or proposals for technical improvement (Section 20(1)) permitted by this Act, shall be invalid and void to the extent that they are significantly inequitable. This provision applies also to compensation settlements (Section 12(4)).

(2) The employer and employee may invoke the inequity of an agreement or compensation settlement only if they do so, by means of a statement in text

form addressed to the other party, within six months following termination of the employment contract.
(...)

§26 Termination of Employment

The rights and duties arising from this Act are not affected by the termination of the employment relationship.
(...)

6. COUNCIL REGULATION (EC) NO. 608/2013 OF THE EUROPEAN PARLIAMENT AND OF THE COUNCIL OF 12 JUNE 2013 CONCERNING CUSTOMS ENFORCEMENT OF INTELLECTUAL PROPERTY RIGHTS AND REPEALING COUNCIL REGULATION (EC) NO. 1383/2003

[...]
Whereas:

(1) The Council requested, in its Resolution of 25 September 2008 on a comprehensive European anti-counterfeiting and anti-piracy plan, that Council Regulation (EC) No 1383/2003 of 22 July 2003 concerning customs action against goods suspected of infringing certain intellectual property rights and the measures to be taken against goods found to have infringed such rights, be reviewed.

(2) The marketing of goods infringing intellectual property rights does considerable damage to right-holders, users or groups of producers, and to law-abiding manufacturers and traders. Such marketing could also be deceiving consumers, and could in some cases be endangering their health and safety. Such goods should, in so far as is possible, be kept off the Union market and measures should be adopted to deal with such unlawful marketing without impeding legitimate trade.

(3) The review of Regulation (EC) No 1383/2003 showed that, in the light of economic, commercial and legal developments, certain improvements to the legal framework are necessary to strengthen the enforcement of intellectual property rights by customs authorities, as well as to ensure appropriate legal certainty.

(4) The customs authorities should be competent to enforce intellectual property rights with regard to goods, which, in accordance with Union customs legislation, are liable to customs supervision or customs control, and to carry out adequate controls on such goods with a view to preventing operations in breach of intellectual property rights laws. Enforcing intellectual property rights at the border, wherever the goods are, or should have been, under customs supervision or customs control is an efficient way to quickly and effectively provide legal protection to the right-holder as well as the users and groups of producers. Where the release of goods is

suspended or goods are detained by customs authorities at the border, only one legal proceeding should be required, whereas several separate proceedings should be required for the same level of enforcement for goods found on the market, which have been disaggregated and delivered to retailers. An exception should be made for goods released for free circulation under the end-use regime, as such goods remain under customs supervision, even though they have been released for free circulation. This Regulation should not apply to goods carried by passengers in their personal luggage provided that those goods are for their own personal use and there are no indications that commercial traffic is involved.

(5) Regulation (EC) No 1383/2003 does not cover certain intellectual property rights and certain infringements are excluded from its scope. In order to strengthen the enforcement of intellectual property rights, customs intervention should be extended to other types of infringements not covered by Regulation (EC) No 1383/2003. This Regulation should therefore, in addition to the rights already covered by Regulation (EC) No 1383/2003, also include trade names in so far as they are protected as exclusive property rights under national law, topographies of semiconductor products and utility models and devices which are primarily designed, produced or adapted for the purpose of enabling or facilitating the circumvention of technological measures.

(6) Infringements resulting from so-called illegal parallel trade and overruns are excluded from the scope of Regulation (EC) No 1383/2003. Goods subject to illegal parallel trade, namely goods that have been manufactured with the consent of the right-holder but placed on the market for the first time in the European Economic Area without his consent, and overruns, namely goods that are manufactured by a person duly authorised by a right-holder to manufacture a certain quantity of goods, in excess of the quantities agreed between that person and the right-holder, are manufactured as genuine goods and it is therefore not appropriate that customs authorities focus their efforts on such goods. Illegal parallel trade and overruns should therefore also be excluded from the scope of this Regulation.

(7) Member States should, in cooperation with the Commission, provide appropriate training for customs officials, in order to ensure the correct implementation of this Regulation.

(8) This Regulation, when fully implemented, will further contribute to an internal market which ensures right-holders a more effective protection, fuels creativity and innovation and provides consumers with reliable and high-quality products, which should in turn strengthen cross-border transactions between consumers, businesses and traders.

(9) Member States face increasingly limited resources in the field of customs. Therefore, the promotion of risk management technologies and strategies to maximise resources available to customs authorities should be supported.

(10) This Regulation solely contains procedural rules for customs authorities. Accordingly, this Regulation does not set out any criteria for ascertaining the existence of an infringement of an intellectual property right.

(11) Under the 'Declaration on the TRIPS Agreement and Public Health' adopted by the Doha WTO Ministerial Conference on 14 November 2001, the Agreement on Trade-Related Aspects of Intellectual Property Rights (TRIPS Agreement) can and should be interpreted and implemented in a manner supportive of WTO Members' right to protect public health and, in particular, to promote access to medicines for all. Consequently, in line with the Union's international commitments and its development cooperation policy, with regard to medicines, the passage of which across the customs territory of the Union, with or without transhipment, warehousing, breaking bulk, or changes in the mode or means of transport, is only a portion of a complete journey beginning and terminating beyond the territory of the Union, customs authorities should, when assessing a risk of infringement of intellectual property rights, take account of any substantial likelihood of diversion of such medicines onto the market of the Union.

(12) This Regulation should not affect the provisions on the competence of courts, in particular, those of Regulation (EU) No 1215/2012 of the European Parliament and of the Council of 12 December 2012 on jurisdiction and the recognition and enforcement of judgments in civil and commercial matters.

(13) Persons, users, bodies or groups of producers, who are in a position to initiate legal proceedings in their own name with respect to a possible infringement of an intellectual property right, should be entitled to submit an application.

(14) In order to ensure that intellectual property rights are enforced throughout the Union, it is appropriate to allow persons or entities seeking enforcement of Union-wide rights to apply to the customs authorities of a single Member State. Such applicants should be able to request that those authorities decide that action be taken to enforce the intellectual property right both in their own Member State and in any other Member State.

(15) In order to ensure the swift enforcement of intellectual property rights, it should be provided that, where the customs authorities suspect, on the basis of reasonable indications, that goods under their supervision infringe intellectual property rights, they may suspend the release of or detain the goods whether at their own initiative or upon application, in order to enable a person or entity entitled to submit an application to initiate proceedings for determining whether an intellectual property right has been infringed.

(16) Regulation (EC) No 1383/2003 allowed Member States to provide for a procedure allowing the destruction of certain goods without there being any obligation to initiate proceedings to establish whether an intellectual property right has been infringed. As recognised in the European Parliament Resolution of 18 December 2008 on the impact of counterfeiting on

international trade, such procedure has proved very successful in the Member States where it has been available. Therefore, the procedure should be made compulsory with regard to all infringements of intellectual property rights and should be applied, where the declarant or the holder of the goods agrees to destruction. Furthermore, the procedure should provide that customs authorities may deem that the declarant or the holder of the goods has agreed to the destruction of the goods where he has not explicitly opposed destruction within the prescribed period.

(17) In order to reduce the administrative burden and costs to a minimum, a specific procedure should be introduced for small consignments of counterfeit and pirated goods, which should allow for such goods to be destroyed without the explicit agreement of the applicant in each case. However, a general request made by the applicant in the application should be required in order for that procedure to be applied. Furthermore, customs authorities should have the possibility to require that the applicant covers the costs incurred by the application of that procedure.

(18) For further legal certainty, it is appropriate to modify the timelines for suspending the release of or detaining goods suspected of infringing an intellectual property right and the conditions in which information about detained goods is to be passed on to persons and entities concerned by customs authorities, as provided for in Regulation (EC) No 1383/2003.

(19) Taking into account the provisional and preventive character of the measures adopted by the customs authorities when applying this Regulation and the conflicting interests of the parties affected by the measures, some aspects of the procedures should be adapted to ensure the smooth application of this Regulation, whilst respecting the rights of the concerned parties. Thus, with respect to the various notifications envisaged by this Regulation, the customs authorities should notify the relevant person, on the basis of the documents concerning the customs treatment or of the situation in which the goods are placed. Furthermore, since the procedure for destruction of goods implies that both the declarant or the holder of the goods and the holder of the decision should communicate their possible objections to destruction in parallel, it should be ensured that the holder of the decision is given the possibility to react to a potential objection to destruction by the declarant or the holder of the goods. It should therefore be ensured that the declarant or the holder of the goods is notified of the suspension of the release of the goods or their detention before, or on the same day as, the holder of the decision.

(20) Customs authorities and the Commission are encouraged to cooperate with the European Observatory on Infringements of Intellectual Property Rights in the framework of their respective competences.

(21) With a view to eliminating international trade in goods infringing intellectual property rights, the TRIPS Agreement provides that WTO Members are to promote the exchange of information between customs authorities on such trade. Accordingly, it should be possible for the Commission and the

customs authorities of the Member States to share information on suspected breaches of intellectual property rights with the relevant authorities of third countries, including on goods which are in transit through the territory of the Union and originate in or are destined for those third countries.

(22) In the interest of efficiency, the provisions of Council Regulation (EC) No 515/97 of 13 March 1997 on mutual assistance between the administrative authorities of the Member States and cooperation between the latter and the Commission to ensure the correct application of the law on customs or agricultural matters, should apply.

(23) The liability of the customs authorities should be governed by the legislation of the Member States, though the granting by the customs authorities of an application should not entitle the holder of the decision to compensation in the event that goods suspected of infringing an intellectual property right are not detected by the customs authorities and are released or no action is taken to detain them.

(24) Given that customs authorities take action upon application, it is appropriate to provide that the holder of the decision should reimburse all the costs incurred by the customs authorities in taking action to enforce his intellectual property rights. Nevertheless, this should not preclude the holder of the decision from seeking compensation from the infringer or other persons that might be considered liable under the legislation of the Member State where the goods were found. Such persons might include intermediaries, where applicable. Costs and damages incurred by persons other than customs authorities as a result of a customs action, where the release of goods is suspended or the goods are detained on the basis of a claim of a third party based on intellectual property, should be governed by the specific legislation applicable in each particular case.

(25) This Regulation introduces the possibility for customs authorities to allow goods which are to be destroyed to be moved, under customs supervision, between different places within the customs territory of the Union. Customs authorities may furthermore decide to release such goods for free circulation with a view to further recycling or disposal outside commercial channels including for awareness-raising, training and educational purposes.

(26) Customs enforcement of intellectual property rights entails the exchange of data on decisions relating to applications. Such processing of data covers also personal data and should be carried out in accordance with Union law, as set out in Directive 95/46/EC of the European Parliament and of the Council of 24 October 1995 on the protection of individuals with regard to the processing of personal data and on the free movement of such data and Regulation (EC) No 45/2001 of the European Parliament and of the Council of 18 December 2000 on the protection of individuals with regard to the processing of personal data by Community institutions and bodies and on the free movement of such data.

(27) The exchange of information relating to decisions on applications and to customs actions should be made via a central electronic database. The entity which will control and manage that database and the entities in charge of ensuring the security of the processing of the data contained in the database should be defined. Introducing any type of possible interoperability or exchange should first and foremost comply with the purpose limitation principle, namely that data should be used for the purpose for which the database has been established, and no further exchange or interconnection should be allowed other than for that purpose.

(28) In order to ensure that the definition of small consignments can be adapted if it proves to be impractical, taking into account the need to ensure the effective operation of the procedure, or where necessary to avoid any circumvention of this procedure as regards the composition of consignments, the power to adopt acts in accordance with Article 290 of the Treaty on the Functioning of the European Union should be delegated to the Commission in respect of amending the non-essential elements of the definition of small consignments, namely the specific quantities set out in that definition. It is of particular importance that the Commission carry out appropriate consultations during its preparatory work, including at expert level. The Commission, when preparing and drawing up delegated acts, should ensure a simultaneous, timely and appropriate transmission of relevant documents to the European Parliament and to the Council.

(29) In order to ensure uniform conditions for the implementation of the provisions concerning defining the elements of the practical arrangements for the exchange of data with third countries and the provisions concerning the forms for the application and for requesting the extension of the period during which customs authorities are to take action, implementing powers should be conferred on the Commission, namely to define those elements of the practical arrangements and to establish standard forms. Those powers should be exercised in accordance with Regulation (EU) No 182/2011 of the European Parliament and of the Council of 16 February 2011 laying down the rules and general principles concerning mechanisms for control by Member States of the Commission's exercise of implementing powers. For establishing the standard forms, although the subject of the provisions of this Regulation to be implemented falls within the scope of the common commercial policy, given the nature and impacts of those implementing acts, the advisory procedure should be used for their adoption, because all details of what information to include in the forms follows directly from the text of this Regulation. Those implementing acts will therefore only establish the format and structure of the form and will have no further implications for the common commercial policy of the Union.

(30) Regulation (EC) No 1383/2003 should be repealed.

(31) The European Data Protection Supervisor was consulted in accordance with Article 28(2) of Regulation (EC) No 45/2001 and delivered an opinion on 12 October 2011,

HAVE ADOPTED THIS REGULATION:

CHAPTER I SUBJECT MATTER, SCOPE AND DEFINITIONS

Article 1 Subject matter and scope

1. This Regulation sets out the conditions and procedures for action by the customs authorities where goods suspected of infringing an intellectual property right are, or should have been, subject to customs supervision or customs control within the customs territory of the Union in accordance with Council Regulation (EEC) No 2913/92 of 12 October 1992 establishing the Community Customs Code, particularly goods in the following situations:
   (a) when declared for release for free circulation, export or re-export;
   (b) when entering or leaving the customs territory of the Union;
   (c) when placed under a suspensive procedure or in a free zone or free warehouse.
2. In respect of the goods subject to customs supervision or customs control, and without prejudice to Articles 17 and 18, the customs authorities shall carry out adequate customs controls and shall take proportionate identification measures as provided for in Article 13(1) and Article 72 of Regulation (EEC) No 2913/92 in accordance with risk analysis criteria with a view to preventing acts in breach of intellectual property laws applicable in the territory of the Union and in order to cooperate with third countries on the enforcement of intellectual property rights.
3. This Regulation shall not apply to goods that have been released for free circulation under the end-use regime.
4. This Regulation shall not apply to goods of a non-commercial nature contained in travellers' personal luggage.
5. This Regulation shall not apply to goods that have been manufactured with the consent of the right-holder or to goods manufactured, by a person duly authorised by a right-holder to manufacture a certain quantity of goods, in excess of the quantities agreed between that person and the right-holder.
6. This Regulation shall not affect national or Union law on intellectual property or the laws of the Member States in relation to criminal procedures.

Article 2 Definitions

For the purposes of this Regulation:

(1) 'intellectual property right' means:
   (a) a trade mark;
   (b) a design;
   (c) a copyright or any related right as provided for by national or Union law;
   (d) a geographical indication;
   (e) a patent as provided for by national or Union law;

(f) a supplementary protection certificate for medicinal products as provided for in Regulation (EC) No 469/2009 of the European Parliament and of the Council of 6 May 2009 concerning the supplementary protection certificate for medicinal products;

(g) a supplementary protection certificate for plant protection products as provided for in Regulation (EC) No 1610/96 of the European Parliament and of the Council of 23 July 1996 concerning the creation of a supplementary protection certificate for plant protection products;

(h) a Community plant variety right as provided for in Council Regulation (EC) No 2100/94 of 27 July 1994 on Community plant variety rights;

(i) a plant variety right as provided for by national law;

(j) a topography of semiconductor product as provided for by national or Union law;

(k) a utility model in so far as it is protected as an intellectual property right by national or Union law;

(l) a trade name in so far as it is protected as an exclusive intellectual property right by national or Union law;

(2) 'trade mark' means:

(a) a Community trade mark as provided for in Council Regulation (EC) No 207/2009 of 26 February 2009 on the Community trade mark;

(b) a trade mark registered in a Member State, or, in the case of Belgium, Luxembourg or the Netherlands, at the Benelux Office for Intellectual Property;

(c) a trade mark registered under international arrangements which has effect in a Member State or in the Union;

(3) 'design' means:

(a) a Community design as provided for in Council Regulation (EC) No 6/2002 of 12 December 2001 on Community designs;

(b) a design registered in a Member State, or, in the case of Belgium, Luxembourg or the Netherlands, at the Benelux Office for Intellectual Property;

(c) a design registered under international arrangements which has effect in a Member State or in the Union;

(4) 'geographical indication' means:

(a) a geographical indication or designation of origin protected for agricultural products and foodstuff as provided for in Regulation (EU) No 1151/2012 of the European Parliament and of the Council of 21 November 2012 on quality schemes for agricultural products and foodstuffs;

(b) a designation of origin or geographical indication for wine as provided for in Council Regulation (EC) No 1234/2007 of 22 October 2007 establishing a common organisation of agricultural markets and on specific provisions for certain agricultural products (Single CMO Regulation);

(c) a geographical designation for aromatised drinks based on wine products as provided for in Council Regulation (EEC) No 1601/91 of 10 June 1991 laying down general rules on the definition, description and presentation of aromatized wines, aromatized wine-based drinks and aromatized wine-product cocktails;

(d) a geographical indication of spirit drinks as provided for in Regulation (EC) No 110/2008 of the European Parliament and of the Council of 15 January 2008 on the definition, description, presentation, labelling and the protection of geographical indications of spirit drinks;

(e) a geographical indication for products not falling under points (a) to (d) in so far as it is established as an exclusive intellectual property right by national or Union law;

(f) a geographical indication as provided for in Agreements between the Union and third countries and as such listed in those Agreements;

(5) 'counterfeit goods' means:

(a) goods which are the subject of an act infringing a trade mark in the Member State where they are found and bear without authorisation a sign which is identical to the trade mark validly registered in respect of the same type of goods, or which cannot be distinguished in its essential aspects from such a trade mark;

(b) goods which are the subject of an act infringing a geographical indication in the Member State where they are found and, bear or are described by, a name or term protected in respect of that geographical indication;

(c) any packaging, label, sticker, brochure, operating instructions, warranty document or other similar item, even if presented separately, which is the subject of an act infringing a trade mark or a geographical indication, which includes a sign, name or term which is identical to a validly registered trade mark or protected geographical indication, or which cannot be distinguished in its essential aspects from such a trade mark or geographical indication, and which can be used for the same type of goods as that for which the trade mark or geographical indication has been registered;

(6) 'pirated goods' means goods which are the subject of an act infringing a copyright or related right or a design in the Member State where the goods are found and which are, or contain copies, made without the consent of the holder of a copyright or related right or a design, or of a person authorised by that holder in the country of production;

(7) 'goods suspected of infringing an intellectual property right' means goods with regard to which there are reasonable indications that, in the Member State where those goods are found, they are prima facie:

(a) goods which are the subject of an act infringing an intellectual property right in that Member State;

(b) devices, products or components which are primarily designed, produced or adapted for the purpose of enabling or facilitating the circumvention of any technology, device or component that, in the normal course of its operation, prevents or restricts acts in respect of works which are not authorised by the holder of any copyright or any right related to copyright and which relate to an act infringing those rights in that Member State;

(c) any mould or matrix which is specifically designed or adapted for the manufacture of goods infringing an intellectual property right, if such moulds or matrices relate to an act infringing an intellectual property right in that Member State;

(8) 'right-holder' means the holder of an intellectual property right;

(9) 'application' means a request made to the competent customs department for customs authorities to take action with respect to goods suspected of infringing an intellectual property right;

(10) 'national application' means an application requesting the customs authorities of a Member State to take action in that Member State;

(11) 'Union application' means an application submitted in one Member State and requesting the customs authorities of that Member State and of one or more other Member States to take action in their respective Member States;

(12) 'applicant' means the person or entity in whose name an application is submitted;

(13) 'holder of the decision' means the holder of a decision granting an application;

(14) 'holder of the goods' means the person who is the owner of the goods suspected of infringing an intellectual property right or who has a similar right of disposal, or physical control, over such goods;

(15) 'declarant' means the declarant as defined in point (18) of Article 4 of Regulation (EEC) No 2913/92;

(16) 'destruction' means the physical destruction, recycling or disposal of goods outside commercial channels, in such a way as to preclude damage to the holder of the decision;

(17) 'customs territory of the Union' means the customs territory of the Community as defined in Article 3 of Regulation (EEC) No 2913/92;

(18) 'release of the goods' means the release of the goods as defined in point (20) of Article 4 of Regulation (EEC) No 2913/92;

(19) 'small consignment' means a postal or express courier consignment, which:

(a) contains three units or less;

or

(b) has a gross weight of less than two kilograms.

For the purpose of point (a), 'units' means goods as classified under the Combined Nomenclature in accordance with Annex I to Council Regulation (EEC) No 2658/87 of 23 July 1987 on the tariff and statistical nomenclature and on the Common Customs Tariff if unpackaged, or the package of such goods intended for retail sale to the ultimate consumer.

For the purpose of this definition, separate goods falling in the same Combined Nomenclature code shall be considered as different units and goods presented as sets classified in one Combined Nomenclature code shall be considered as one unit;

(20) 'perishable goods' means goods considered by customs authorities to deteriorate by being kept for up to 20 days from the date of their suspension of release or detention;

(21) 'exclusive licence' means a licence (whether general or limited) authorising the licensee to the exclusion of all other persons, including the person granting the licence, to use an intellectual property right in the manner authorised by the licence.

CHAPTER II - APPLICATIONS

SECTION 1 Submission of applications

Article 3 **Entitlement to submit an application**

The following persons and entities shall, to the extent they are entitled to initiate proceedings, in order to determine whether an intellectual property right has been infringed, in the Member State or Member States where the customs authorities are requested to take action, be entitled to submit:

(1) a national or a Union application:
  (a) right-holders;
  (b) intellectual property collective rights management bodies as referred to in point (c) of Article 4(1) of Directive 2004/48/EC of the European Parliament and of the Council of 29 April 2004 on the enforcement of intellectual property rights ([21]);
  (c) professional defence bodies as referred to in point (d) of Article 4(1) of Directive 2004/48/EC;
  (d) groups within the meaning of point (2) of Article 3, and Article 49(1) of Regulation (EU) No 1151/2012, groups of producers within the meaning of Article 118e of Regulation (EC) No 1234/2007 or similar groups of producers provided for in Union law governing geographical indications representing producers of products with a geographical indication or representatives of such groups, in particular Regulations (EEC) No 1601/91 and (EC) No 110/2008 and operators entitled to use a geographical indication as well as inspection bodies or authorities competent for such a geographical indication;

(2) a national application:
  (a) persons or entities authorised to use intellectual property rights, which have been authorised formally by the right-holder to initiate proceedings in order to determine whether the intellectual property right has been infringed;
  (b) groups of producers provided for in the legislation of the Member States governing geographical indications representing producers of products with geographical indications or representatives of such

groups and operators entitled to use a geographical indication, as well as inspection bodies or authorities competent for such a geographical indication;

(3) a Union application: holders of exclusive licenses covering the entire territory of two or more Member States, where those licence holders have been authorised formally in those Member States by the right-holder to initiate proceedings in order to determine whether the intellectual property right has been infringed.

Article 4 **Intellectual property rights covered by Union applications**

A Union application may be submitted only with respect to intellectual property rights based on Union law producing effects throughout the Union.

Article 5 **Submission of applications**

1. Each Member State shall designate the customs department competent to receive and process applications ('competent customs department'). The Member State shall inform the Commission accordingly and the Commission shall make public a list of competent customs departments designated by the Member States.
2. Applications shall be submitted to the competent customs department. The applications shall be completed using the form referred to in Article 6 and shall contain the information required therein.
3. Where an application is submitted after notification by the customs authorities of the suspension of the release or detention of the goods in accordance with Article 18(3), that application shall comply with the following:
   (a) it is submitted to the competent customs department within four working days of the notification of the suspension of the release or detention of the goods;
   (b) it is a national application;
   (c) it contains the information referred to in Article 6(3). The applicant may, however, omit the information referred to in point (g), (h) or (i) of that paragraph.
4. Except in the circumstances referred to in point (3) of Article 3, only one national application and one Union application may be submitted per Member State for the same intellectual property right protected in that Member State. In the circumstances referred to in point (3) of Article 3, more than one Union application shall be allowed.
5. Where a Union application is granted for a Member State already covered by another Union application granted to the same applicant and for the same intellectual property right, the customs authorities of that Member State shall take action on the basis of the Union application first granted. They shall inform the competent customs department of the Member State

where any subsequent Union application was granted, which shall, amend or revoke the decision granting that subsequent Union application.

6. Where computerised systems are available for the purpose of receiving and processing applications, applications as well as attachments shall be submitted using electronic data-processing techniques. Member States and the Commission shall develop, maintain and employ such systems in accordance with the multi-annual strategic plan referred to in Article 8(2) of Decision No 70/2008/EC of the European Parliament and of the Council of 15 January 2008 on a paperless customs environment for customs and trade.

Article 6 **Application form**

1. The Commission shall establish an application form by means of implementing acts. Those implementing acts shall be adopted in accordance with the advisory procedure referred to in Article 34(2).
2. The application form shall specify the information that has to be provided to the data subject pursuant to Regulation (EC) No 45/2001 and national laws implementing Directive 95/46/EC.
3. The Commission shall ensure that the following information is required of the applicant in the application form:
   (a) details concerning the applicant;
   (b) the status, within the meaning of Article 3, of the applicant;
   (c) documents providing evidence to satisfy the competent customs department that the applicant is entitled to submit the application;
   (d) where the applicant submits the application by means of a representative, details of the person representing him and evidence of that person's powers to act as representative, in accordance with the legislation of the Member State in which the application is submitted;
   (e) the intellectual property right or rights to be enforced;
   (f) in the case of a Union application, the Member States in which customs action is requested;
   (g) specific and technical data on the authentic goods, including markings such as bar-coding and images where appropriate;
   (h) the information needed to enable the customs authorities to readily identify the goods in question;
   (i) information relevant to the customs authorities' analysis and assessment of the risk of infringement of the intellectual property right or the intellectual property rights concerned, such as the authorised distributors;
   (j) whether information provided in accordance with point (g), (h) or (i) of this paragraph is to be marked for restricted handling in accordance with Article 31(5);
   (k) the details of any representative designated by the applicant to take charge of legal and technical matters;

(l) an undertaking by the applicant to notify the competent customs department of any of the situations laid down in Article 15;
(m) an undertaking by the applicant to forward and update any information relevant to the customs authorities' analysis and assessment of the risk of infringement of the intellectual property right(s) concerned;
(n) an undertaking by the applicant to assume liability under the conditions laid down in Article 28;
(o) an undertaking by the applicant to bear the costs referred to in Article 29 under the conditions laid down in that Article;
(p) an agreement by the applicant that the data provided by him may be processed by the Commission and by the Member States;
(q) whether the applicant requests the use of the procedure referred to in Article 26 and, where requested by the customs authorities, agrees to cover the costs related to destruction of goods under that procedure.

SECTION 2 Decisions on applications

Article 7 Processing of incomplete applications

1. Where, on receipt of an application, the competent customs department considers that the application does not contain all the information required by Article 6(3), the competent customs department shall request the applicant to supply the missing information within 10 working days of notification of the request.
   In such cases, the time-limit referred to in Article 9(1) shall be suspended until the relevant information is received.
2. Where the applicant does not provide the missing information within the period referred to in the first subparagraph of paragraph 1, the competent customs department shall reject the application.

Article 8 Fees

The applicant shall not be charged a fee to cover the administrative costs resulting from the processing of the application.

Article 9 Notification of decisions granting or rejecting applications

1. The competent customs department shall notify the applicant of its decision granting or rejecting the application within 30 working days of the receipt of the application. In the event of rejection, the competent customs department shall provide reasons for its decision and include information on the appeal procedure.
2. If the applicant has been notified of the suspension of the release or the detention of the goods by the customs authorities before the submission of an application, the competent customs department shall notify the

applicant of its decision granting or rejecting the application within two working days of the receipt of the application.

Article 10 **Decisions concerning applications**

1. A decision granting a national application and any decision revoking or amending it shall take effect in the Member State in which the national application was submitted from the day following the date of adoption.

A decision extending the period during which customs authorities are to take action shall take effect in the Member State in which the national application was submitted on the day following the date of expiry of the period to be extended.

2. A decision granting a Union application and any decision revoking or amending it shall take effect as follows:
   (a) in the Member State in which the application was submitted, on the day following the date of adoption;
   (b) in all other Member States where action by the customs authorities is requested, on the day following the date on which the customs authorities are notified in accordance with Article 14(2), provided that the holder of the decision has fulfilled his obligations under Article 29(3) with regard to translation costs.

A decision extending the period during which customs authorities are to take action shall take effect in the Member State in which the Union application was submitted and in all other Member States where action by the customs authorities is requested the day following the date of expiry of the period to be extended.

Article 11 **Period during which the customs authorities are to take action**

1. When granting an application, the competent customs department shall specify the period during which the customs authorities are to take action. That period shall begin on the day the decision granting the application takes effect, pursuant to Article 10, and shall not exceed one year from the day following the date of adoption.
2. Where an application submitted after notification by the customs authorities of the suspension of the release or detention of the goods in accordance with Article 18(3) does not contain the information referred to in point (g), (h) or (i) of Article 6(3), it shall be granted only for the suspension of the release or detention of those goods, unless that information is provided within 10 working days after the notification of the suspension of the release or detention of the goods.
3. Where an intellectual property right ceases to have effect or where the applicant ceases for other reasons to be entitled to submit an application, no action shall be taken by the customs authorities. The decision granting

the application shall be revoked or amended accordingly by the competent customs department that granted the decision.

Article 12 **Extension of the period during which the customs authorities are to take action**

1. On expiry of the period during which the customs authorities are to take action, and subject to the prior discharge by the holder of the decision of any debt owed to the customs authorities under this Regulation, the competent customs department which adopted the initial decision may, at the request of the holder of the decision, extend that period.
2. Where the request for extension of the period during which the customs authorities are to take action is received by the competent customs department less than 30 working days before the expiry of the period to be extended, it may refuse that request.
3. The competent customs department shall notify its decision on the extension to the holder of the decision within 30 working days of the receipt of the request referred to in paragraph 1. The competent customs department shall specify the period during which the customs authorities are to take action.
4. The extended period during which the customs authorities are to take action shall run from the day following the date of expiry of the previous period and shall not exceed one year.
5. Where an intellectual property right ceases to have effect or where the applicant ceases for other reasons to be entitled to submit an application, no action shall be taken by the customs authorities. The decision granting the extension shall be revoked or amended accordingly by the competent customs department that granted the decision.
6. The holder of the decision shall not be charged a fee to cover the administrative costs resulting from the processing of the request for extension.
7. The Commission shall establish an extension request form by means of implementing acts. Those implementing acts shall be adopted in accordance with the advisory procedure referred to in Article 34(2).

Article 13 **Amending the decision with regard to intellectual property rights.**

The competent customs department that adopted the decision granting the application may, at the request of the holder of that decision, modify the list of intellectual property rights in that decision.

Where a new intellectual property right is added, the request shall contain the information referred to in points (c), (e), (g), (h) and (i) of Article 6(3).

In the case of a decision granting a Union application, any modification consisting of the addition of intellectual property rights shall be limited to intellectual property rights covered by Article 4.

Article 14 **Notification obligations of the competent customs department**

1. The competent customs department to which a national application has been submitted shall forward the following decisions to the customs offices of its Member State, immediately after their adoption:
   (a) decisions granting the application;
   (b) decisions revoking decisions granting the application;
   (c) decisions amending decisions granting the application;
   (d) decisions extending the period during which the customs authorities are to take action.
2. The competent customs department to which a Union application has been submitted shall forward the following decisions to the competent customs department of the Member State or Member States indicated in the Union application, immediately after their adoption:
   (a) decisions granting the application;
   (b) decisions revoking decisions granting the application;
   (c) decisions amending decisions granting the application;
   (d) decisions extending the period during which the customs authorities are to take action.

   The competent customs department of the Member State or Member States indicated in the Union application shall immediately after receiving those decisions forward them to their customs offices.
3. The competent customs department of the Member State or Member States indicated in the Union application may request the competent customs department that adopted the decision granting the application to provide them with additional information deemed necessary for the implementation of that decision.
4. The competent customs department shall forward its decision suspending the actions of the customs authorities under point (b) of Article 16(1) and Article 16(2) to the customs offices of its Member State, immediately after its adoption.

Article 15 **Notification obligations of the holder of the decision**

The holder of the decision shall immediately notify the competent customs department that granted the application of any of the following:

(a) an intellectual property right covered by the application ceases to have effect;
(b) the holder of the decision ceases for other reasons to be entitled to submit the application;
(c) modifications to the information referred to in Article 6(3).

Article 16 **Failure of the holder of the decision to fulfil his obligations**

1. Where the holder of the decision uses the information provided by the customs authorities for purposes other than those provided for in Article 21, the competent customs department of the Member State where the information was provided or misused may:
   (a) revoke any decision adopted by it granting a national application to that holder of the decision, and refuse to extend the period during which the customs authorities are to take action;
   (b) suspend in their territory, during the period during which the customs authorities are to take action, any decision granting a Union application to that holder of the decision.
2. The competent customs department may decide to suspend the actions of the customs authorities until the expiry of the period during which those authorities are to take action, where the holder of the decision:
   (a) does not fulfil the notification obligations set out in Article 15;
   (b) does not fulfil the obligation on returning samples set out in Article 19(3);
   (c) does not fulfil the obligations on costs and translation set out in Article 29(1) and (3);
   (d) without valid reason does not initiate proceedings as provided for in Article 23(3) or Article 26(9).

In the case of a Union application, the decision to suspend the actions of the customs authorities shall have effect only in the Member State where such decision is taken.

CHAPTER III ACTION BY THE CUSTOMS AUTHORITIES

SECTION 1 Suspension of the release or detention of goods suspected of infringing an intellectual property right

Article 17 **Suspension of the release or detention of the goods following the grant of an application**

1. Where the customs authorities identify goods suspected of infringing an intellectual property right covered by a decision granting an application, they shall suspend the release of the goods or detain them.
2. Before suspending the release of or detaining the goods, the customs authorities may ask the holder of the decision to provide them with any relevant information with respect to the goods. The customs authorities may also provide the holder of the decision with information about the actual or estimated quantity of goods, their actual or presumed nature and images thereof, as appropriate.
3. The customs authorities shall notify the declarant or the holder of the goods of the suspension of the release of the goods or the detention of the goods within one working day of that suspension or detention.

Where the customs authorities opt to notify the holder of the goods and two or more persons are considered to be the holder of the goods, the customs authorities shall not be obliged to notify more than one of those persons.
The customs authorities shall notify the holder of the decision of the suspension of the release of the goods or the detention on the same day as, or promptly after, the declarant or the holder of the goods is notified.
The notifications shall include information on the procedure set out in Article 23.

4. The customs authorities shall inform the holder of the decision and the declarant or the holder of the goods of the actual or estimated quantity and the actual or presumed nature of the goods, including available images thereof, as appropriate, whose release has been suspended or which have been detained. The customs authorities shall also, upon request and where available to them, inform the holder of the decision of the names and addresses of the consignee, the consignor and the declarant or the holder of the goods, of the customs procedure and of the origin, provenance and destination of the goods whose release has been suspended or which have been detained.

Article 18 **Suspension of the release or detention of the goods before the grant of an application**

1. Where the customs authorities identify goods suspected of infringing an intellectual property right, which are not covered by a decision granting an application, they may, except for in the case of perishable goods, suspend the release of those goods or detain them.
2. Before suspending the release of or detaining the goods suspected of infringing an intellectual property right, the customs authorities may, without disclosing any information other than the actual or estimated quantity of goods, their actual or presumed nature and images thereof, as appropriate, request any person or entity potentially entitled to submit an application concerning the alleged infringement of the intellectual property rights to provide them with any relevant information.
3. The customs authorities shall notify the declarant or the holder of the goods of the suspension of the release of the goods or their detention within one working day of that suspension or detention.
Where the customs authorities opt to notify the holder of the goods and two or more persons are considered to be the holder of the goods, the customs authorities shall not be obliged to notify more than one of those persons.
The customs authorities shall notify persons or entities entitled to submit an application concerning the alleged infringement of the intellectual property rights, of the suspension of the release of the goods or their detention on the same day as, or promptly after, the declarant or the holder of the goods is notified.

The customs authorities may consult the competent public authorities in order to identify the persons or entities entitled to submit an application. The notifications shall include information on the procedure set out in Article 23.

4. The customs authorities shall grant the release of the goods or put an end to their detention immediately after completion of all customs formalities in the following cases:
   (a) where they have not identified any person or entity entitled to submit an application concerning the alleged infringement of intellectual property rights within one working day from the suspension of the release or the detention of the goods;
   (b) where they have not received an application in accordance with Article 5(3), or where they have rejected such an application.
5. Where an application has been granted, the customs authorities shall, upon request and where available to them, inform the holder of the decision of the names and addresses of the consignee, the consignor and the declarant or the holder of the goods, of the customs procedure and of the origin, provenance and destination of the goods whose release has been suspended or which have been detained.

Article 19 **Inspection and sampling of goods whose release has been suspended or which have been detained**

1. The customs authorities shall give the holder of the decision and the declarant or the holder of the goods the opportunity to inspect the goods whose release has been suspended or which have been detained.
2. The customs authorities may take samples that are representative of the goods. They may provide or send such samples to the holder of the decision, at the holder's request and strictly for the purposes of analysis and to facilitate the subsequent procedure in relation to counterfeit and pirated goods. Any analysis of those samples shall be carried out under the sole responsibility of the holder of the decision.
3. The holder of the decision shall, unless circumstances do not allow, return the samples referred to in paragraph 2 to the customs authorities on completion of the analysis, at the latest before the goods are released or their detention is ended.

Article 20 **Conditions for storage**

The conditions of storage of goods during a period of suspension of release or detention shall be determined by the customs authorities.

Article 21 **Permitted use of certain information by the holder of the decision**

Where the holder of the decision has received the information referred to in Article 17(4), Article 18(5), Article 19 or Article 26(8), he may disclose or use that information only for the following purposes:

(a) to initiate proceedings to determine whether an intellectual property right has been infringed and in the course of such proceedings;
(b) in connection with criminal investigations related to the infringement of an intellectual property right and undertaken by public authorities in the Member State where the goods are found;
(c) to initiate criminal proceedings and in the course of such proceedings;
(d) to seek compensation from the infringer or other persons;
(e) to agree with the declarant or the holder of the goods that the goods be destroyed in accordance with Article 23(1);
(f) to agree with the declarant or the holder of the goods of the amount of the guarantee referred to in point (a) of Article 24(2).

Article 22 **Sharing of information and data between customs authorities**

1. Without prejudice to applicable provisions on data protection in the Union and for the purpose of contributing to eliminating international trade in goods infringing intellectual property rights, the Commission and the customs authorities of the Member States may share certain data and information available to them with the relevant authorities in third countries according to the practical arrangements referred to in paragraph 3.
2. The data and information referred to in paragraph 1 shall be exchanged to swiftly enable effective enforcement against shipments of goods infringing an intellectual property right. Such data and information may relate to seizures, trends and general risk information, including on goods which are in transit through the territory of the Union and which have originated in or are destined for the territory of third countries concerned. Such data and information may include, where appropriate, the following:
   (a) nature and quantity of goods;
   (b) suspected intellectual property right infringed;
   (c) origin, provenance and destination of the goods;
   (d) information on movements of means of transport, in particular:
      (i) name of vessel or registration of means of transport;
      (ii) reference numbers of freight bill or other transport document;
      (iii) number of containers;
      (iv) weight of load;
      (v) description and/or coding of goods;
      (vi) reservation number;
      (vii) seal number;
      (viii) place of first loading;

(ix) place of final unloading;
(x) places of transhipment;
(xi) expected date of arrival at place of final unloading;

(e) information on movements of containers, in particular:
(i) container number;
(ii) container loading status;
(iii) date of movement;
(iv) type of movement (loaded, unloaded, transhipped, entered, left, etc.);
(v) name of vessel or registration of means of transport;
(vi) number of voyage/journey;
(vii) place;
(viii) freight bill or other transport document.

3. The Commission shall adopt implementing acts defining the elements of the necessary practical arrangements concerning the exchange of data and information referred to in paragraphs 1 and 2 of this Article. Those implementing acts shall be adopted in accordance with the examination procedure referred to in Article 34(3).

SECTION 2 Destruction of goods, initiation of proceedings and early release of goods

Article 23 **Destruction of goods and initiation of proceedings**

1. Goods suspected of infringing an intellectual property right may be destroyed under customs control, without there being any need to determine whether an intellectual property right has been infringed under the law of the Member State where the goods are found, where all of the following conditions are fulfilled:
(a) the holder of the decision has confirmed in writing to the customs authorities, within 10 working days, or three working days in the case of perishable goods, of notification of the suspension of the release or the detention of the goods, that, in his conviction, an intellectual property right has been infringed;
(b) the holder of the decision has confirmed in writing to the customs authorities, within 10 working days, or three working days in the case of perishable goods, of notification of the suspension of the release or the detention of the goods, his agreement to the destruction of the goods;
(c) the declarant or the holder of the goods has confirmed in writing to the customs authorities, within 10 working days, or three working days in the case of perishable goods, of notification of the suspension of the release or the detention of the goods, his agreement to the destruction of the goods. Where the declarant or the holder of the goods has not confirmed his agreement to the destruction of the goods nor notified his opposition thereto to the customs authorities, within those deadlines, the customs

authorities may deem the declarant or the holder of the goods to have confirmed his agreement to the destruction of those goods.

The customs authorities shall grant the release of the goods or put an end to their detention, immediately after completion of all customs formalities, where within the periods referred to in points (a) and (b) of the first subparagraph, they have not received both the written confirmation from the holder of the decision that, in his conviction, an intellectual property right has been infringed and his agreement to destruction, unless those authorities have been duly informed about the initiation of proceedings to determine whether an intellectual property right has been infringed.

2. The destruction of the goods shall be carried out under customs control and under the responsibility of the holder of the decision, unless otherwise specified in the national law of the Member State where the goods are destroyed. Samples may be taken by competent authorities prior to the destruction of the goods. Samples taken prior to destruction may be used for educational purposes.
3. Where the declarant or the holder of the goods has not confirmed his agreement to the destruction in writing and where the declarant or the holder of the goods has not been deemed to have confirmed his agreement to the destruction, in accordance with point (c) of the first subparagraph of paragraph 1 within the periods referred to therein, the customs authorities shall immediately notify the holder of the decision thereof. The holder of the decision shall, within 10 working days, or three working days in the case of perishable goods, of notification of the suspension of the release or the detention of the goods, initiate proceedings to determine whether an intellectual property right has been infringed.
4. Except in the case of perishable goods the customs authorities may extend the period referred to in paragraph 3 by a maximum of 10 working days upon a duly justified request by the holder of the decision in appropriate cases.
5. The customs authorities shall grant the release of the goods or put an end to their detention, immediately after completion of all customs formalities, where, within the periods referred to in paragraphs 3 and 4, they have not been duly informed, in accordance with paragraph 3, on the initiation of proceedings to determine whether an intellectual property right has been infringed.

Article 24 **Early release of goods**

1. Where the customs authorities have been notified of the initiation of proceedings to determine whether a design, patent, utility model, topography of semiconductor product or plant variety has been infringed, the declarant or the holder of the goods may request the customs authorities to release the goods or put an end to their detention before the completion of those proceedings.
2. The customs authorities shall release the goods or put an end to their detention only where all the following conditions are fulfilled:

(a) the declarant or the holder of the goods has provided a guarantee that is of an amount sufficient to protect the interests of the holder of the decision;
(b) the authority competent to determine whether an intellectual property right has been infringed has not authorised precautionary measures;
(c) all customs formalities have been completed.

3. The provision of the guarantee referred to in point (a) of paragraph 2 shall not affect the other legal remedies available to the holder of the decision.

Article 25 **Goods for destruction**

1. Goods to be destroyed under Article 23 or 26 shall not be:
   (a) released for free circulation, unless customs authorities, with the agreement of the holder of the decision, decide that it is necessary in the event that the goods are to be recycled or disposed of outside commercial channels, including for awareness-raising, training and educational purposes. The conditions under which the goods can be released for free circulation shall be determined by the customs authorities;
   (b) brought out of the customs territory of the Union;
   (c) exported;
   (d) re-exported;
   (e) placed under a suspensive procedure;
   (f) placed in a free zone or free warehouse.
2. The customs authorities may allow the goods referred to in paragraph 1 to be moved under customs supervision between different places within the customs territory of the Union with a view to their destruction under customs control.

Article 26 **Procedure for the destruction of goods in small consignments**

1. This Article shall apply to goods where all of the following conditions are fulfilled:
   (a) the goods are suspected of being counterfeit or pirated goods;
   (b) the goods are not perishable goods;
   (c) the goods are covered by a decision granting an application;
   (d) the holder of the decision has requested the use of the procedure set out in this Article in the application;
   (e) the goods are transported in small consignments.
2. When the procedure set out in this Article is applied, Article 17(3) and (4) and Article 19(2) and (3) shall not apply.
3. The customs authorities shall notify the declarant or the holder of the goods of the suspension of the release of the goods or their detention within one working day of the suspension of the release or of the detention of the goods. The notification of the suspension of the release or the detention of the goods shall include the following information:

(a) that the customs authorities intend to destroy the goods;
(b) the rights of the declarant or the holder of the goods under paragraphs 4, 5 and 6.

4. The declarant or the holder of the goods shall be given the opportunity to express his point of view within 10 working days of notification of the suspension of the release or the detention of the goods.
5. The goods concerned may be destroyed where, within 10 working days of notification of the suspension of the release or the detention of the goods, the declarant or the holder of the goods has confirmed to the customs authorities his agreement to the destruction of the goods.
6. Where the declarant or the holder of the goods has not confirmed his agreement to the destruction of the goods nor notified his opposition thereto to the customs authorities, within the period referred to in paragraph 5, the customs authorities may deem the declarant or the holder of the goods to have confirmed his agreement to the destruction of the goods.
7. The destruction shall be carried out under customs control. The customs authorities shall, upon request and as appropriate, provide the holder of the decision with information about the actual or estimated quantity of destroyed goods and their nature.
8. Where the declarant or the holder of the goods has not confirmed his agreement to the destruction of the goods and where the declarant or the holder of the goods has not been deemed to have confirmed such agreement, in accordance with paragraph 6, the customs authorities shall immediately notify the holder of the decision thereof and of the quantity of goods and their nature, including images thereof, where appropriate. The customs authorities shall also, upon request and where available to them, inform the holder of the decision of the names and addresses of the consignee, the consignor and the declarant or the holder of the goods, of the customs procedure and of the origin, provenance and destination of the goods whose release has been suspended or which have been detained.
9. The customs authorities shall grant the release of the goods or put an end to their detention immediately after completion of all customs formalities where they have not received information from the holder of the decision on the initiation of proceedings to determine whether an intellectual property right has been infringed within 10 working days of the notification referred to in paragraph 8.
10. The Commission shall be empowered to adopt delegated acts in accordance with Article 35 concerning the amendment of quantities in the definition of small consignments in the event that the definition is found to be impractical in the light of the need to ensure the effective operation of the procedure set out in this Article, or where necessary in order to avoid any circumvention of this procedure as regards the composition of consignments.

CHAPTER IV LIABILITY, COSTS AND PENALTIES

Article 27 **Liability of the customs authorities**

Without prejudice to national law, the decision granting an application shall not entitle the holder of that decision to compensation in the event that goods suspected of infringing an intellectual property right are not detected by a customs office and are released, or no action is taken to detain them.

Article 28 **Liability of the holder of the decision**

Where a procedure duly initiated pursuant to this Regulation is discontinued owing to an act or omission on the part of the holder of the decision, where samples taken pursuant to Article 19(2) are either not returned or are damaged and beyond use owing to an act or omission on the part of the holder of the decision, or where the goods in question are subsequently found not to infringe an intellectual property right, the holder of the decision shall be liable towards any holder of the goods or declarant, who has suffered damage in that regard, in accordance with specific applicable legislation.

Article 29 **Costs**

1. Where requested by the customs authorities, the holder of the decision shall reimburse the costs incurred by the customs authorities, or other parties acting on behalf of customs authorities, from the moment of detention or suspension of the release of the goods, including storage and handling of the goods, in accordance with Article 17(1), Article 18(1) and Article 19(2) and (3), and when using corrective measures such as destruction of goods in accordance with Articles 23 and 26.
   The holder of a decision to whom the suspension of release or detention of goods has been notified shall, upon request, be given information by the customs authorities on where and how those goods are being stored and on the estimated costs of storage referred to in this paragraph. The information on estimated costs may be expressed in terms of time, products, volume, weight or service depending on the circumstances of storage and the nature of the goods.
2. This Article shall be without prejudice to the right of the holder of the decision to seek compensation from the infringer or other persons in accordance with the legislation applicable.
3. The holder of a decision granting a Union application shall provide and pay for any translation required by the competent customs department or customs authorities which are to take action concerning the goods suspected of infringing an intellectual property right.

Article 30 **Penalties**

The Member States shall ensure that the holders of decisions comply with the obligations set out in this Regulation, including, where appropriate, by laying down provisions establishing penalties. The penalties provided for shall be effective, proportionate and dissuasive.

The Member States shall notify those provisions and any subsequent amendment affecting them to the Commission without delay.

[...]

Index

C

S

T

U

V

W

Z

www.ingramcontent.com/pod-product-compliance
Lightning Source LLC
La Vergne TN
LVHW020002031026
849161LV00023B/832